# CALIFORNIA-NEVADA
# ROADS LESS TRAVELED

## A DISCOVERY GUIDE TO PLACES LESS CROWDED

**By Don W. Martin and Betty Woo Martin**
With special assistance from *Ickybod*

**Pine Cone Press**, *Inc.* ● Henderson, Nevada

## BOOKS BY DON AND BETTY MARTIN
*Adventure Cruising* ● 1996
*Arizona Discovery Guide* ● 1990, 1993, 1994, 1996, 1998
*Arizona in Your Future* ● 1991, 1993, 1998
*The Best of the Gold Country* ● 1987, 1990, 1992
*The Best of San Francisco* ● 1986, 1990, 1994, 1997
*The Best of the Wine Country* ● 1991, 1994, 1995
*California–Nevada Roads Less Traveled* ● 1999
*Inside San Francisco* ● 1991
*Las Vegas: The Best of Glitter City* ● 1998
*Nevada Discovery Guide* ● 1992, 1997
*New Mexico Discovery Guide* ● 1998
*Northern California Discovery Guide* ● 1993
*Oregon Discovery Guide* ● 1993, 1995, 1996, 1999
*San Diego: The Best of Sunshine City* ● 1999
*San Francisco's Ultimate Dining Guide* ● 1988
*The Toll-free Traveler* ● 1997
*The Ultimate Wine Book* ● 1993, 1999
*Utah Discovery Guide* ● 1995
*Washington Discovery Guide* ● 1994, 1997

**Library of Congress Cataloging-in-Publication Data**
Martin, Don and Betty —
California–Nevada Roads Less Traveled
Includes index.
1. California—description and travel
2. Nevada—description and travel

ISBN: 0-942053-28-1
Library of Congress catalog card number: 98-68454

COVER DESIGN ● **Dave Bonnot**, Columbine Type & Design, Sonora, California
CARTOGRAPHY ● **Vicky Biernacki**, Columbine Type & Design
ARTWORK ● **Judith Stoltenberg**, Blue J Graphics, Sonora
PHOTOGRAPHY ● **Betty** or **Don Martin**

**OUR COVER** ● *Although a major federal preserve, Lassen Volcanic National Park gets few visitors compared with most other parks. State Highway 89, shown here curving below Lake Helen, is definitely a "road less traveled."*

# WALK SOFTLY

It began decades ago with the simple, almost naive phrase: Take nothing but photographs; leave nothing but footprints. It has evolved into a new travel consciousness called eco-tourism. The message remains the same: As you tread this planet on your journeys of discovery, respect its fragility. Tourism by its very nature promotes crowding and intrusiveness. Crowds tend to litter, trample and tax an area's resources. Here's how you can help make the world a better place to visit and therefore a better place in which to live:

1. Walk softly wherever you travel. A million footprints have preceded yours and millions more will follow. Try to impact an environment as little as possible, whether it be a hiking trail or an old village street. If you can, avoid peak seasons when resources of popular tourist areas are heavily impacted; seek out places less visited.

2. As a hiker, don't leave established trails and never cut switchbacks; it creates ugliness and erosion. When you see others doing so, tactfully tell them why it's not a good idea.

3. Obviously, you shouldn't litter, but go a step beyond. Pick up what others have left behind. If you see someone littering, offer to carry it out. Perhaps they'll have second thoughts the next time. And remember, cigarette butts are litter—the ugliest kind. If you're on the water, never toss anything overboard.

4. Practice no-trace camping in the wilderness and even in established campgrounds. Don't leave a fire pit full of garbage for the next camper. Don't gather or cut firewood unless signs permit it. This strips vegetation and robs soil of important nutrients.

5. Protect all natural and manmade sites and resources. Avoid gathering "souvenirs" from the wild or from ghost towns or historic sites. A single bit of adobe or beach shell will be missed if thousands of people take one. If you discover a prehistoric artifact, leave it alone. If you move it, you may accidentally erase the story it has to tell.

6. Never put your initials, graffiti or any kind of mark on any structure, cave wall or cliff, tree or stone. And for heaven's sake, please don't deface ancient writings or structures.

7. Respect the traditions and privacy of others. Take time to learn their ways and learn what offends them. There's a difference between honest curiosity and boorish intrusiveness. Ask whose who live in a place if they mind having their picture taken.

8. Recycle and use recycled or recyclable materials whenever possible. When disposing of something, seek out and use recycling bins.

9. Support environmental groups with your actions and your donations, and patronize companies that practice eco-tourism.

10. Most importantly, teach your children these things by word and by example. They are the travelers of today and tomorrow.

*Take time to see the sky; find shapes in the clouds*
*Hear the murmur of the wind, and touch the cool water.*
*Walk softly; we are the intruders*
*Tolerated briefly in an infinite universe.*
    — Jean Henderer, National Park Service (retired)

# Contents

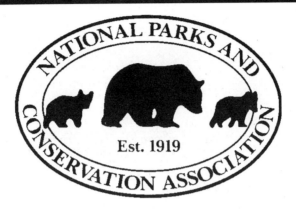

*The traveler sees what he sees; the tourist sees what he has come to see.*
— Gilbert K. Chesterson

## SEEKING PLACES LESS CROWDED

Have you ever traced a finger along a highway map, or glanced at a freeway offramp and pondered: "That road looks inviting; I wonder where it would take us?" Most of us have a little gypsy in our souls.

For many people, the best way to spend a vacation—or a retirement—is to load up the RV or family sedan and strike out on a voyage of discovery. Problem is, too many of us follow the same freeways and highways to the same places. We're drawn to our most popular parks, resort areas and historic sites; our voyages of discovery are disrupted by crowds and traffic.

This is the first in a series of guidebooks for gypsy spirits—those who want to follow roads less traveled to places less crowded. It's for folks with a sense of adventure, who prefer hideaway resorts to high rise hotels or woodsy campgrounds to asphalt RV parks.

We have toured, photographed and written about Western America for more than thirty years. Nearly everywhere we've gone, we've discovered fascinating and wonderful places that often are missed by the mainstream traveler. Many of these uncrowded areas offer as much appeal as the more popular vacation spots. In California and Nevada, for instance, we'll guide you to national parks that are both interesting and uncrowded, to wonderful beaches that even in summer aren't too heavily trodden, and to wineries whose tasting rooms aren't overwhelmed by visitors.

Traveling in *Ickybod*, our faithful Toyota-mount Winnebago, we've explored every corner of California and Nevada, following highways and byways—but very few freeways—to those special uncrowded places. After spending months on the road, we've stitched together a series of driving trips, with attendant maps to help keep you on course.

Along our less traveled roads, we suggest interesting places to dine and recline, seeking cafés and lodgings that may not be represented in regular travel guides. We're partial to quaint old hotels, bed & breakfast inns, country diners and hideaway resorts—places where you can relax, far from the madding crowds. Our selections range from budget accommodations to some of the West's most opulent resorts.

Our gypsy wanderings will appeal to RVers, particularly retired folks and others with lots of time to explore. Thus, the *Roads Less Traveled* series features "RV Advisories" that point out steep climbs, rough roads, hairpin turns and other conditions that might challenge large motorhomes or trailer rigs. And they help you find places to park in towns along the way. We also recommends interesting campgrounds along our routes.

The advisories are based on signs we've observed and on our own experiences with our twenty-one-foot *Ickybod*. Of course, our judgments are subjective and based on our driving ability, which may differ from yours.

**Don and Betty Martin**
On the road to somewhere

# THE WAY THINGS WORK

The routes outlined in this book aren't short scenic byways; most are long drives intended to consume a day or more. String a few together and you'll have a nice one or two-week vacation. These tours also can be used for weekend getaways.

Whenever possible, we've made our routes contiguous, so that you can blend easily from the end of one tour to the beginning of another. Since we take you into some pretty remote areas, we indicate refueling and provisioning stops along the way. However, don't push your luck or your fuel gauge too far. One-horse towns on some of our routes may have closed their only service station since we last checked.

Our maps are intended to give you a general overview of each driving route. However, they're rather simplistic, so we recommend that you use a marking pen to transfer the routes to more detailed highway maps.

### Helping you make it through the nights

It's pretty difficult to wander willy nilly about California and Nevada, enjoying the freedom of the road, if you have to book your lodgings or campsites in advance. In compiling this book, we've sought out interesting and often out-of-the-way places that usually don't require advance reservations, except possibly in peak summer. Of course, during major vacation periods, it couldn't hurt to call a day or two ahead.

Bear in mind that California contains twelve percent of the entire population of the United States. Add to this the millions who come from other areas to play every year, and even the most remote areas can be booked up during peak seasons. You can cut the crowd content by traveling in the spring and fall shoulder seasons, when the weather's still nice in most of California and Nevada. In fact, both states enjoy their finest weather from early September through late October. And winter's quite fine in the southern reaches of these states.

### Foraging for food

In our travels, we've sought out interesting and off-beat places to eat—everything from funky delis to nineteenth century hotel dining rooms. We seek places mostly for their character and good local reputations. We don't delve into the chef's culinary history nor do we try to rate specific dishes; this is a discovery guide, not a dining guide. Besides, if the chef is having a bad night or your waitress is recovering from one, your dining experience could be completely different from ours.

### Price guidelines

Since many establishments change their rates more often than gypsies change their addresses, we list price ranges indicated by dollar signs, instead of specific prices. We repeat this list at the beginning of each tour.

**DINING:** Dinner entrée with soup or salad, without drinks or dessert for under $10 = **$**; $10 to $14 = **$$**; $15 to $25 = **$$$**; over $25 = **$$$$**.

**RECLINING:** A two-person room for $35 or less = **$**; $36 to $50 = **$$**; $51 to $75 = **$$$**; $76 to $100 = **$$$$**; more than $100 = **$$$$$**.

**CAMPING:** Under $10 = **$**; $10 to $14 = **$$**; $15 to $19 = **$$$**; $20 or more = **$$$$**

# Getting camped

**State parks** ● Nearly a hundred of California's state parks with campgrounds accept peak season reservations through ParkNet, Inc. Simply dial (800) 444-PARK (7275) daily from 8 to 5 (Pacific Time) and have your VISA, MasterCard or Discover card handy. You can reserve sites up to seven months in advance, and as late as two days before your arrival, allowing you to be somewhat flexible in your travels. A processing fee is charged for each reservation.

You also can mail in a reservation—something a true gypsy would never do—by sending a check, money order or credit card number, to: ParkNet, P.O. Box 1510, Rancho Cordova, CA 95741-1510. And if you're really cool, you can use the internet. The state park department's website is **www.cal-parks.ca.gov.**

To learn all about this system, pick up the California State Parks *Camping Reservation Guide* by calling the State Department of Parks and Recreation at (916) 653-6995. You'll also find the brochure at state parks and at many visitor information centers. It lists all the state parks with reservable campsites and their facilities. Incidentally, state parks offer discounts for seniors 62 and over for day use and camping.

**Nevada:** Fourteen of Nevada's twenty-two state parks offer camping and some of these sites can be reserved in advance by calling (702) 687-4370. If you call weekdays 9 to 5 (Pacific time), you can talk with a *homo sapien*. At other times, leave your name and address and request a state parks brochure.

**National parks and such** ● We visit several relatively uncrowded national parks in this book, such as Lassen Volcanic, Sequoia-Kings Canyon and Joshua Tree, as well as many national monuments and recreation areas. For campsite reservations up to three months in advance, call (800) 365-PARK. (Not all parks and monuments are on the reservations system; check individual listings.)

Holders of Golden Age (62 and older) and Golden Access (disabled) passes get free admission to national parks and other federal preserves, and they can camp at half price in these places and in Forest Service and Bureau of Land Management campgrounds.

**U.S. Forest Service** ● Several national forest campgrounds in California and Nevada take reservations up to a year in advance. Call the National Recreation Reservation System at (800) 280-CAMP; sites can be reserved with a MasterCard or VISA. Forest Service campgrounds rarely have hookups, and many have chemical toilets. However, the price is right—from about $15 down to nothing, and many rival state and national park campgrounds in the beauty of their settings. Incidentally, except in a few very popular areas, reservations usually aren't needed.

---

This book is for those who've already been there and done that, and particularly for those who don't want to go there and do that.

# A BIT ABOUT THE AUTHORS

The Martins have written nearly twenty guidebooks, mostly under their *Pine Cone Press* banner. When not tending to their publishing company near Las Vegas, Nevada, they explore America and the world beyond, seeking new places and new experiences for their readers. Both are members of the Society of American Travel Writers.

Don, who provides most of the adjectives, has been a journalist since he was sixteen, when classmates elected him editor of his high school newspaper. (No one else wanted the job.) After school, he left his small family farm in Idaho and hitch-hiked about the country a bit. He then joined the Marine Corps and served as a correspondent in the Orient and as a public information specialist at bases in California. Back in civvies, he worked as a reporter, sports writer and editor for several West Coast daily newspapers, then he spent several years as associate editor of a San Francisco-based travel magazine. He now devotes his time to writing, travel, sipping fine Zinfandel and—for some odd reason—collecting squirrel and chipmunk artifacts.

Betty, a Chinese-American whose varied credentials have included a doctorate in pharmacy and a real estate broker's license, does much of the research, editing and photography for their books. She also has sold articles and photos to assorted newspapers and magazines. When she isn't helping Don run *Pine Cone Press, Inc.*, she wanders the globe—with or without him. Her travels have taken her from Cuba to Antarctica.

A third and most essential member of the team is *Ickybod*, a Toyota-chassis "Mini Winnie," the Martins' home on the road. Without *Ick*, they might be tempted to solicit free lodging and meals, and their guidebooks wouldn't be quite so candid.

# CLOSING INTRODUCTORY THOUGHTS:
## Keeping up with the changes

Nobody's perfect, but we try. This book contains thousands of facts and a few are probably wrong. If you catch an error, let us know. Also, drop us a note if you discover that a museum has become an auto repair shop or the other way around; or if a restaurant, resort or attraction we mentioned has closed.

All who provide significant information that we've not yet discovered will earn a free copy of one of our other publications. If you'd like to purchase a copy of this or other *Pine Cone Press* travel guides, ordering information is in the back of this book.

**Pine Cone Press, Inc.**
631 N. Stephanie St., #138
Henderson, NV 89014

# PART I

# CALIFORNIA NORTH

**N**orthern California is the most diverse region of the state and thus a fine place to begin exploring our *Roads Less Traveled*. The region contains some of California's highest mountains, its largest lakes, its most beautiful coastline and certainly its most famous wine country.

Our routes will take you to lofty redwood groves, funky old country towns, ice-crested alpine peaks and a lava wilderness. We'll take you to a place made famous because a bunch of birds developed an attitude, and we'll guide you to the best view of everyone's favorite city. If you get there at the right time, it isn't even crowded!

Most people think of northern California as San Francisco and its surrounding countryside. However, there's a lotta California north of the city. It's 360 road miles from San Francisco to the Oregon border, with plenty to explore along the way. Northern California isn't thinly populated, since it's home to twelve million people, and the San Francisco Bay Area is one of America's largest metropolitan regions. However, people thin out quickly as you drive away from population centers. For instance, you can be out of San Francisco—America's second most densely populated city—and into the open countryside in less than an hour.

We'll begin this section with a grand last look at San Francisco, and then we'll get outta town fast—as long as we don't attempt this during the rush hour.

## Tour One

# THE COAST NORTH
## THE GOLDEN GATE TO THE RUSSIAN RIVER

---

**W**e begin our initial tour with a *caveat*. The first portion of this route isn't less traveled. In fact, if you start out at the wrong time, you could get caught in one whopper of a traffic jam. That's because we're taking you across the famous Golden Gate Bridge, the main commute link between San Francisco and populated Marin County.

We'll take you to a high point for grand vistas of this great orange span, a place that most other travelers miss. Then we'll slip away from the crowds and head up the northern California coastline, past Point Reyes National Seashore and a string of quaint little towns both on the seacoast and inland. The tour ends at Jenner at the mouth of the Russian River.

Begin by picking a good time to get across the Golden Gate Bridge from San Francisco, which means just about any weekday between 10 and 2, or any weekend after Labor Day and before Memorial Day. If you're coming from the east, it may be faster to cross the Richmond-San Rafael Bridge and drive south on U.S. 101, since that's all freeway. If you cross the San Francisco-Oakland Bay Bridge on I-80, you'll have to travel over several miles of busy surface streets to reach the Golden Gate.

# TRIP PLANNER

**WHEN TO GO** ● Early fall through late spring are fine times to explore the coast north of San Francisco, since snow is virtually nonexistent. Expect to get wet in winter, although the rain merely dramatizes coastal views. Summer's nice, too, although the area can get crowded on weekends.

**DRIVING DISTANCE** ● The drive from San Francisco to the mouth of the Russian River covers about eighty miles.

**RV ADVISORY** ● A portion of the coastal highway above Stinson Beach is extremely narrow and twisting, with some cliff-edge exposure. Large RVs and trailers can make it, although they must be driven with great alertness. RVers will encounter no real challenges elsewhere on this route.

**WHAT YOU'LL SEE** ● An absolutely splendid view of San Francisco, grand coastal vistas, Point Reyes National Seashore, slender and scenic Tomales Bay, the two "Bodegas" made famous by Alfred Hitchcock, Sonoma Coast State Park and the charming old terraced town of Jenner.

**WHAT TO DO** ● Bask by the sea at Muir Beach (but don't go near the water); hike the trails of Point Reyes National Seashore and Bodega Head; pig out on an Italian feast in Occidental; cruise a canoe down the Russian River.

**TO BEGIN** ● From San Francisco, head for the Golden Gate Bridge.

## Useful contacts

**Bodega Bay Area Chamber of Commerce,** P.O. Box 146 (850 Coast Highway), Bodega Bay, CA 94923; (800) 905-9050 or (707) 875-3422.

**Point Reyes National Seashore,** Point Reyes, CA 94956; (415) 663-1092.

**Russian River Chamber of Commerce,** P.O. Box 331 (16200 First St.), Guerneville, CA 95446; (707) 869-9000.

**Russian River Region Visitors Bureau,** Box 255, Guerneville, CA 95446; (800) 253-8800. (WEB SITE: www.sonoma.com/rus-river; E-MAIL: rrrvb@netdex.com)

**Western Marin Chamber of Commerce,** P.O. Box 1045, Point Reyes Station, CA 94956; (415) 663-9232.

## Pricing guidelines

DINING: Dinner entrée with soup or salad, without drinks or dessert for under $10 = **$**; $10 to $14 = **$$**; $15 to $25 = **$$$**; over $25 = **$$$$**.

RECLINING: A two-person room for $35 or less = **$**; $36 to $50 = **$$**; $51 to $75 = **$$$**; $76 to $100 = **$$$$**; more than $100 = **$$$$$**.

CAMPING: Under $10 = **$**; $10 to $14 = **$$**; $15 to $19 = **$$$**; $20 or more = **$$$$**

Immediately after you've crossed the bridge, exit right to the **Vista Point** for a nice view across San Francisco Bay to the city skyline. However, this isn't the best view. For that, drive north from the parking area and exit almost immediately onto Alexander Avenue. Go left under the freeway and then left again, following **Marin Headlands** signs. As you head back toward the bridge, fork to the right and climb up this coastal bluff overlooking the Golden Gate. Stay alert for the Marin Headlands sign or you'll be swept right back onto the bridge. Then you'll have to pay a three dollar toll, find a place to turn around and re-cross the Golden Gate to get back where you started.

Incidentally, if you're approaching from the north on U.S. 101, pass through a large tunnel, then take the "Sausalito/Golden Gate National Recreation Area" exit just short of the bridge, without going to the Vista Point. Immediately after exiting the freeway, turn left at a stop sign to drive up Marin Headlands.

Several viewpoints on the headlands offer those incredible vistas you've seen in movies and TV commercials—the sparkling white skyline of San Francisco with the bay in the foreground, framed in the sweeping cables of the Golden Gate Bridge. These turnouts can be quite busy during the summer and on any sunny weekend, although you should be able to find parking space at other times.

For a different kind of viewpoint, park at the first turnout (Battery Spencer) and hike down a dirt road to Kirby Cove. Walk through a campground and you'll see that striking cityscape again, this time with the bridge suspended *over* it, and a nice little beach in the foreground.

---

*RV PARKING ADVISORY* ● Large motorhomes and trailer rigs will have a difficult time fitting into most of the Marin Headlands turnouts. Parking areas farther along the road have more room. Try to plan your visit on an off-season weekday.

---

A region often missed by travelers is the Rodeo Valley area behind Marin Headlands, where you'll find the remnants of two old army forts, more views of the bay, city and coast, and even an uncrowded swimming beach. (Considering the chilly waters of California's north coast, *most* swimming beaches are uncrowded.)

To discover this area, continue up Marin Headlands from Battery Spencer on Conzelman Road. You'll enjoy another mile or so of Golden Gate vistas, then pass the gated entrance to a radar installation and start downhill on a one-way road. You're now on the ocean side of the Marin Headlands, where the panoramic views spread from the Golden Gate Bridge to the open sea.

Heading downhill on this one-way cliff-edge road, you'll pass another old gun emplacement; pause and climb over the concrete abutments for a nice coastal view. At the base of the bluff, you'll blend onto the main Rodeo Valley road; continue straight ahead, following **Point Bonita** signs.

A short trail leads from a parking area to the old **Point Bonita Lighthouse,** perched on a narrow, rocky finger of the Marin Headlands.

The path to the light actually is a combination of a trail, a tunnel chopped through solid rock and a suspension footbridge. This is the southernmost point of Marin Headlands and the views seaward and bayward are predictably impressive. You can step inside the 1855 lighthouse building and view a few historic photos, although the lighthouse tower isn't open to visitors. Lighthouse hours are rather limited—Saturday through Monday 12:30 to 3:30. When it's closed, you can still walk most of the way out the rocky peninsula for those fine bay and ocean views.

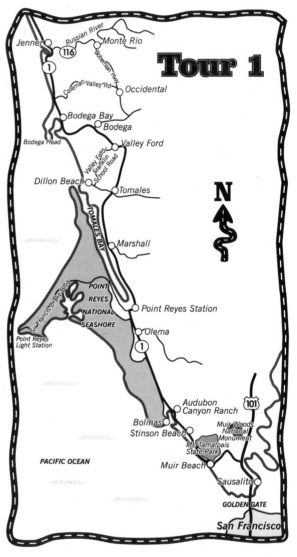

If you drive past the lighthouse parking area, you'll hit a rather complex coastal battery on a high plateau that provides views up and down the Pacific shoreline. Turn around at this point and head east toward the **Marin Headlands Visitor Center**. It's housed in the former Fort Barry Chapel, open 9:30 to 4:30 daily. You'll find exhibits on native people and Army life at old Fort Barry and displays concerning the flora and fauna of the Marin Headlands. Just beyond the visitor center, turn left onto Bunker Road and follow it past Rodeo Lagoon—a good birdwatching area—to Rodeo Beach and several surviving buildings of old Fort Cronkhite.

Now, reverse your route, follow Bunker Road back through Rodeo Valley, turn right onto McCullough and then left onto Conzelman. You can enjoy reverse-angle images of the Golden Gate and city skyline as you head back down from Marin Headlands. Instead of getting on the northbound freeway (a looping right turn), you might want to continue straight ahead on Alexander Avenue to the almost excessively charming Mediterranean style village of **Sausalito.** However, this can be a real traffic trap on weekends and during the commute hour. If you take this route, you'll end up on Bridgeway, which delivers you back to U.S. 101 after two or three miles. Once you hit the freeway, exit almost immediately, following State Highway 1 signs toward Mill Valley. (If you return to the freeway without driving through Sausalito, you'll pass through a rainbow-rimmed tunnel and follow a ridge above the town, then take the Highway 1 exit.)

After a mile or two, turn left at a stop light in the **Tamalpais Valley** to stay with Highway 1, called the Shoreline Highway in these parts. You'll travel through a few miles of busy, woodsy suburbia. The highway then begins a serious upward spiral through evergreen hills to get you over this section of the Coast Range and back to the Pacific Ocean, which you left at the Golden Gate Bridge. After cresting a ridge and twisting downhill again, watch on your left for a small sign to **Muir Beach.** This pretty little enclave is missed by most sunbathing crowds, who generally head farther north to the more popular Stinson Beach. Oddly enough, swimming isn't permitted here because of strong and unpredictable riptides. But what the heck, it's a great place for sunbathing and the water's usually too cold for swimming anyway.

In the farther reaches of the beach, you may find some sunbathers who really don't like tan lines. However, most of the nudies have moved farther north to **Red Rock Beach** just outside of Stinson Beach. Once a favored nude beach, Muir became *too* popular. The sunbathers grew tired of middle age voyeurs shedding their polyesters and waddling along the sand to leer at the pretty young girls. (As with most nude beaches, there is no shortage of pretty young men, either.) Red Rock Beach is much harder to find. Should you wish to let it all hang out, the easiest way to get there is to drive to Stinson Beach, then come back south to the first dirt turnout on your right. A steep, narrow trail leads down to the beach.

Meanwhile, back at Muir Beach, an attractive inn and restaurant are tucked among coastal trees near the entrance:

**Pelican Inn** ● *10 Pacific Way, Muir Beach, CA 94465-9729; (415) 383-6000. Seven rooms with private baths; full English style breakfast; $$$$$. Restaurant serves English and American fare; wine and beer. Lunch and dinner daily May through October and Tuesday-Sunday the rest of the year; $$$. MC/VISA.* □ What, you may ask, have pelicans got to do with an English style inn? That was the name of Sir Francis Drake's ship, and he supposedly made landfall north of here on the Point Reyes Peninsula in 1579. The great English navigator would have felt right at home in this charming little hideaway. He could have enjoyed a game of darts and a pint 'o stout in the Pelican's proper English pub, and dined on shepherd's pie or lamb. The rooms are snug and veddy Brit, with half-canopy beds and olde English furnishings. Built in 1978, the Pelican is a replica of a sixteenth century English inn.

Beyond Muir Beach, Highway 1 spirals steeply upward. Watch on your left for the **Muir Beach Overlook,** providing a nice glimpse of the tree-shrouded swatch of sand below. The highway then dips downward, swings away from the ocean and begins a steep upward spiral over another piece of the Coast Range. At the crest, the ocean reappears suddenly and dramatically. The highway becomes a cliff-hugger here, dipping and twisting downward, with frequent turnouts offering splendid visions of scalloped surf, curving bays, seastacks and steep headlands thatched with wind-bend cypress.

---

**RV ADVISORY** • Drivers of large motorhomes and trailer rigs will want to use extreme caution on this steep, downward spiral. And *all* drivers need to be very alert crossing the oncoming traffic lane to get to the coastside vista points.

---

## STINSON BEACH

**Population: 800**                    **Elevation: eighteen feet**

Six miles above Muir Beach, Stinson is one of the most popular strands on the north coast, so it's hardly a place less visited. On any sunny summer or fall day, you'll find it aswarm with beach boys, beach bunnies and families. However, coastal fog often shields the sun; you'll have Stinson pretty much to yourselves on overcast days and most any weekday from late fall through late spring.

Swimming is permitted at **Stinson Beach State Park**, since the strand is sheltered by Bolinas Bay, which calms the surf somewhat. However, only the bold are willing to stick their toes and other body parts into this chilly north coastal water. The beach is nearly three miles long, and you can lose most of the crowd by walking north toward the entrance to Bolinas Lagoon.

Although small, the town is a busy collection of cafés and motels. On a sunny weekend, it'll be a chore to find a place to park. Assuming you began this drive in the morning and hopefully on a weekday, you might want to take a lunch break here.

### DINING

**Parkside Café** • *43 Arenal Ave. (just off Calle del Mar); (415) 868-1272. American; wine and beer. Breakfast and lunch daily, dinner Monday-Thursday; hours may be shorter in the off-season. MC/VISA, AMEX; $$.* ◻ This is where the beach crowd congregates to fuel up on hefty omelettes and flapjack stacks before heading for the sand. Try one of the excellent hamburgers for lunch, along with a creative salad. Roast chicken, chops and a few pasta dishes are served in the evening. A brick patio is open when the weather is favorable.

**Stinson Beach Grill** • *3465 Shoreline Highway; (415) 868-2002. American; wine and beer. Late breakfast to dinner daily. MC/VISA; $$.* ◻ Occupying a weathered old cottage with a knotty pine interior, the grill is another favorite of locals and beach buffs. Its menu features Southwest fare, seafood and chicken entrées. Head for the outdoor deck if the weather cooperates. If it doesn't, find a place by the crackling stove inside. The café is on your left on the north side of town, a block from the beach.

## Stinson Beach to Bodega Bay

North of Stinson, the highway follows the level shoreline of **Bolinas Lagoon**, a nearly landlocked bay. For a pleasing view of the lagoon and the tiny town of Bolinas across the water, turn left onto Calle del Arroyo immediately beyond Stinson and follow it along a narrow sandspit.

Meanwhile, back on Highway 1, watch on your right for a sign to an interesting nature preserve, near the upper end of the lagoon:

**Audubon Canyon Ranch** ● *4900 Highway 1; (707) 868-9244. Weekends and holidays 10 to 4 mid-March through mid-July. Free; donations appreciated.* ◻ Bring your binoculars to observe a colony of great blue herons nesting in the tops of redwoods in this vee canyon. They also mate up there, which can't be a simple feat. Stop by the visitor center, which occupies a nineteenth century farmhouse, then follow a short trail to the heron nesting sites. Audubon Canyon and Bolinas Lagoon are fine places to observe dozens of other birds as well.

Just beyond Audubon Canyon Ranch, a sign should point to **Bolinas,** one of the worst-kept secrets on the north coast. Occupied by aging hippies and reclusive artists, this charming town on the southern tip of the Point Reyes Peninsula just wants to be left alone. So much so that locals keep taking down the directional signs out on Highway 1. To foil them, take the next left after the heron preserve, which will put you on Olema-Bolinas Road. Once you get to the village, you won't find any road barriers or tank traps, although you may be treated with studied indifference if you look too much like a tourist. Leave your camera in the car and act nonchalant.

If you didn't get lunch in Stinson, you can buy the ingredients at the **People's Store,** open daily 8:30 to 6:30; (415) 868-1433. It's at the end of a short gravel road past the Bolinas Bakery and Café. Left over from the Berkeley sixties, the store sells locally grown organic produce and other whole earth fare. The **Bolinas Bakery and Café** issues very tasty whole grain baked goods. Or you can sit down to a lunch of chicken potstickers, lasagna and other simple fare. Again, it's mostly organic. The bakery-café is open for breakfast through dinner daily, with wine and beer; (415) 868-0211; MC/VISA.

If you like tidepooling, go west on Terrace Avenue and follow signs to **Duxbury Reef Nature Preserve.** This onshore reef at Duxbury Point at the end of Maple Avenue is busy with tidepools which are busy with starfish, sea urchins and such.

From Duxbury Reef, work your way back through town on Overlook Drive, turn left (west) onto Mesa Road and follow it more than a mile to **Point Reyes Bird Observatory.** More than 400 species of birds have been observed and tagged at this ornithological study center. It's open during daylight hours and you can follow a nature trail to do some bird watching of your own. If you'd like to watch ornithologists catching and banding birds, call the observatory for the schedule; (415) 868-0655. It's generally done on fair weather Tuesday through Sunday mornings from May through October.

*Visitors have to walk down to Point Reyes light, since it sits below a coastal bluff. The hike back up is equivalent to climbing a 30-story building.*

Beyond the bird center, Mesa Road dead ends at the **Palomarin Trailhead,** where a three-mile trail leads into the southern end of Point Reyes National Seashore. This is a pleasant hike past inland lakes and meadows to Wildcat Beach.

North of Bolinas, Highway 1 veers away from the beach as it follows a crease of the villainous **San Andreas Fault,** the tectonic trigger for most of California's earthquakes. The 1906 San Francisco quake was born here, as was the 1989 Loma Prieta shaker, witnessed on TV by millions of World Series Fans. At this precise point, the North American and Pacific plates are in a slow motion collision, sending periodic shock waves throughout the state. The Point Reyes Peninsula moves northward about three inches a year.

The highway travels along the eastern edge of peninsula, most of which is occupied by **Point Reyes National Seashore.** It's a remote and hauntingly beautiful area of windy moors, grassy pasturelands, long and sandy beaches, tiny jewels of lakes and thick groves of cypress and eucalyptus. Although a major national preserve, Point Reyes is surprisingly uncrowded, except for sunny summer and fall weekends when Bay Areans head up this way.

If you brought your hiking shoes, your first incursion into Point Reyes can be at **Five Brooks Trailhead,** on your left about five miles from the Bolinas junction. Trails lead through pretty meadows, past small lakes and ultimately to the coast.

Continuing north on Highway 1, you'll encounter the rustic hamlet of **Olema,** where a left turn onto Bear Valley Road will take you to the national seashore's **Bear Valley Visitor Center**. It's open weekdays 9 to 5 and weekends 8 to 5; (415) 663-1092. Among attractions here are the

Earthquake Trail, where you can still see a fence offset sixteen feet by the 1906 'quake. You also can check out a mock-up Coast Miwok village, the Pierce Ranch with a barn knocked off its foundation by the '06 earthquake, and a working Morgan horse ranch.

Just north of the visitor center, Limantour Road will take you through the preserve's midsection to Limantour Beach. It's one of the few areas up here that's safe for swimming—if you can take the chill. En route, you'll pass **Point Reyes Hostel** which has the usual inexpensive hostel style lodging; P.O. Box 247, Point Reyes Station, CA 94956; (415) 663-8811.

From the visitor center, Bear Valley Road continues north briefly and then blends into Sir Francis Drake Boulevard. Hardly a boulevard, it's a two-lane road that meanders through the hilly Point Reyes heartland. It passes the woodsy little village of **Inverness** and skims the edge of long, fjord-like Tomales Bay, created by the seismic action of the San Andreas Fault. Then it swings inland, passing old dairy farms with their kelly green pasturelands, marshes rich in wildlife, and clumps of cypress tucked into the ravines of these rolling hills. Incidentally, these old dairies were responsible—indirectly, at least—for the preservation of this 65,000-acre sanctuary so close to the busy San Francisco Bay Area. Their presence prevented development of this region until Marin County Congressman Philip Burton pushed Congress into declaring it a national seashore in 1963.

Follow Sir Francis Drake to the end and you'll wind up at **Point Reyes Light Station,** open to visitors Thursday-Monday 10 to 5. Oddly, you need to walk *down* to the lighthouse, which occupies a coastal niche below a high bluff. Spur roads lead from Sir Francis Drake to several beaches—some long and sandy, others rocky and busy with tidepools.

Following Sir Francis Drake Boulevard out of the park, you'll wind up in **Point Reyes Station,** once a quiet little farming town and now a gentrified village busy with boutiques, galleries and restaurants. Its popularity has increased in recent decades since it's the major gateway to the national seashore.

If you're looking for dining, lodging or camping in the vicinity of Point Reyes National Seashore, the area offers several choices. However, the only camping within the park's boundaries are at four hike-in campgrounds, which must be reserved far in advance; call (415) 663-8054.

### DINING AND RECLINING

***Jenny's Farmhouse Restaurant*** ● *Highway 1, Olema; (415) 663-1264. American; wine and beer. Lunch and dinner daily. MC/VISA; $$.* ◻ This 1873 shingle-sided former stage stop has been fashioned into a cozy café. It features early American décor and a menu that ranges from fresh-caught fish and oysters to very good hamburgers.

***Point Reyes Seashore Lodge*** ● *P.O. Box 29 (10021 Highway 1), Olema, CA 94950; (800) 404-5634 or (415) 663-9000. Twenty-two units with TV and phones. Major credit cards; $$$$$.* ◻ Set among the trees near the Sir Francis Drake Boulevard and Highway 1 junction, this appealing lodge has rooms and suites with European décor. Some units have fireplaces and spa tubs.

**Manka's Inverness Lodge and Restaurant** • *P.O. Box 1110 (just off Sir Francis Drake), Inverness, CA 94937; (800) 585-6343 or (415) 669-1034. Twelve units; $$$$ to $$$$$. The restaurant serves American-continental fare, dinner Thursday-Monday; $$$. MC/VISA.* ☐ One of the coast's most romantic hideaways, Manka's appears to have emerged from a Bavarian wood. Built in 1917 as a hunting and fishing lodge, it's crafted of heavy log beams and dark woods, with old European accents. It has rooms in the main lodge and several outbuildings, including a two-bedroom "boathouse" built on a pier over Tomales Bay. The old world style dining room, true to its hunting lodge traditions, specializes in wild game.

**Station House Café** • *11180 Shoreline Hwy. (Main Street), Point Reyes Station; (415) 663-1515. American; full bar service. Breakfast through dinner daily. MC/VISA, DISC; $$.* ☐ This is the best of several restaurants in trendy Point Reyes Station, serving well prepared food at rather moderate prices. It's noted for its generous breakfasts served on a shaded patio when the weather's right. Dinners feature local seafood, steaks and chicken. Go for the fresh roasted oysters, for which Tomales Bay is famous.

**NOTE** • The Point Reyes region has many bed & breakfast inns. For a complete list, contact Inns of Point Reyes, P.O. Box 147, Inverness, CA 94937; (415) 485-2649 or (415) 663-1420.

## CAMPING

**Olema Ranch Campground** • *Highway 1, Olema, CA 94950; (415) 663-8001. RV and tent sites; full hookups $$$$.* ☐ This large campground adjacent to Point Reyes National Seashore offers grassy, shaded sites, with a coin laundry, mini-mart, rec hall, kids' playground, shuffleboard, badminton, volleyball and a sports field.

**Samuel P. Taylor State Park** • *At Lagunitas, four miles inland from Olema on Sir Francis Drake Boulevard; (415) 488-9897. RV and tent sites; $$$. For campsite reservations, call (800) 444-PARK; MC/VISA accepted.* ☐ This large park tucked among redwoods has shaded sites with barbecues, picnic tables, flush potties and showers. Hiking trails lead into nearby redwood groves.

Above Point Reyes Station, Highway 1 follows long, slender Tomales Bay for the next fifteen miles. This drive alongside the bay is one of the most pleasing in the north coast, with the calm blue waters on your left, the wooded headlands of Point Reyes Peninsula beyond, and a mix of pasturelands and woodlands on your right. This would be a great place to launch a boat, canoe or kayak and drift lazily along the shoreline or zigzag idly between the mainland and the peninsula. **Millerton Point** and **Tomasini Point,** both parts of Tomales Bay State Park, provide water access. Five miles north of Point Reyes Station, watch on your right for **Tomales Bay Oyster Company** at 15479 Shoreline Highway. This firm has been selling fresh and prepared oysters for nearly a century, and you can cook your own freshly-shucked shellfish at barbecue pits here. It's open daily 9 to 5; (415) 663-1242.

Just beyond Tomasini Point, you'll see **Marconi Conference Center State Historic Park** cresting a wooded hill on your right. There isn't much for the casual visitor here, although a museum is promised in the future, so you might inquire; (415) 663-9020. The center has an interesting background. Italian Guglielmo Marconi invented wireless transmission when he was only twenty-one. He eventually built a worldwide network of telegraph stations, opening this one in 1914. It became a U.S. Navy wireless station during World War I, then it was operated by RCA. Prior to becoming a conference center, is was headquarters for the Synanon drug and alcoholic rehabilitation center, which made headlines a couple of decades ago when its de-tox techniques came under fire.

The pleasantly shabby little town of **Marshall** appears next, crowded onto the Tomales Bay shoreline. In fact, the back feet of many buildings in this long, skinny village stand in the water. This used to be a popular hangout for escapees from the Bay Area, with several interesting restaurants. However, for reasons that escape us, cute old Marshall has fallen on hard times. A single restaurant survives. Dating back more than half a century, **Tony's Seafood** is noted for its fresh oysters, crabs and other aquatic fare. The oysters and crabs should be fresh; they're harvested right out back. The place looks a bit scruffy these days, but it's a worthy stop for shellfish fans, serving lunch and dinner Friday-Sunday, with beer and wine; no credit cards; (415) 663-1107.

As the Shoreline Highway swings away from Tomales Bay, you'll encounter **Tomales,** an old fashioned town even smaller than Marshall. It once was a thriving port but more than a century of erosion into Keyes Creek has moved it a mile inland. As you come into town, note the **Assumption of Mary** Catholic church on your left, with its squared Gothic belltower. A bit farther on, **Angel's Café and Deli** is a handy quick bite stop, offering sandwiches, salads and specialty coffees. For heartier fare, cross the street to an historic saloon:

**William Tell House** ● *Shoreline Highway; (415) 878-2403. American; full bar service. Lunch and dinner daily. MC/VISA; $$.* ☐ This brick and wood frame structure dates from 1877 when it was a popular drinking establishment. It still is, although it's better known these days for its old style restaurant. Decorative plates accent the walls and hurricane chandeliers hang from high ceilings. The menu leans toward seafood and pasta, with specials such as duck breast with fresh berry sauce.

Turn west in the middle of Tomales and head for a town rarely seen by passersby, stuffed into a narrow canyon between sea and sea cliffs. Started as a beach resort in 1886, **Dillon Beach** doesn't offer much for the casual visitor, although the drive out to the coast here is impressive. The short highway rises and dips through green pasturelands and occasional eucalyptus groves, providing—at its high points—glimpses of the Pacific, Tomales Bay and Point Reyes.

The town of Dillon Beach is a tightly packed collection of small wood frame homes, although a fancy new development called Oceana Marin occupies a bluff above. The entire commercial district is wrapped into **Lawson's Store and Gift Shop,** which has been here since the beginning.

Most folks come to Dillon to fish and dig for clams on a sand flat beyond town. People at the store can sell you the gear and tell you where to go. Behind Lawson's, the relatively new **Patio Café** serves breakfast through dinner Friday-Saturday and breakfast through late lunch Sunday. The fare is light, such as beer battered prawns, clam chips and fish and chips, with wine and beer; MC/VISA; (415) 878-2505.

If you drive beyond Lawson's, past an ugly mobile home park, you'll encounter a private beach with picnic tables (moderate day use fee) and beyond that, **Lawson's Landing,** an RV park where the fisherfolk and clamdiggers like to park their rigs. Sites are right on the beach and modestly priced, although they're rather close together.

---

*RV ADVISORY* ● There isn't much room on Dillon Beach's skinny streets for big rigs and trailers to maneuver, and few places to park. However, they can reach the beach and campground.

---

As you leave Dillon Beach, turn left onto Valley Ford-Franklin Road. It takes you through another six miles of bucolic countryside and back to Highway 1 at **Valley Ford.** This is a near twin to Tomales, with old false front stores and a handful of wood frame homes. Pressing northward, you'll encounter two towns made famous in 1962 when suspense master Alfred Hitchcock announced: "*The Birds* is coming!"

In filming this classic fright film about birds turning against humanity, Hitchcock used clever camera work to fuse the towns of **Bodega** and **Bodega Bay** into a single community. To reach Bodega, which is six miles inland from Bodega Bay, turn east off Highway 1 onto the Bodega Highway. A New England style town of weather-worn wood, this hamlet has changed little since the Hitchcock film. Note the white steepled 1862 **St. Teresa of Avila** Catholic church and the green-trimmed 1873 **Potter School** with a distinctive octagon belltower. Both played major roles in the film. The church is still active, although Potter School has functioned variously as an art gallery, restaurant and bed & breakfast inn; it's now a private home.

Return to highway 1 and continue toward Bodega Bay, where you'll first encounter **Lucas Wharf.** It's a weathered boat basin with a small commercial fleet and the nautically trimmed **Lucas Wharf Restaurant**, listed below. Just up the highway is the town Hitchcock made famous, sitting on a broad natural harbor. He wouldn't recognize the place today.

## BODEGA BAY

**Population: 950**                                    **Elevation: 45 feet**

The Tides wharf, which made such a great setting for *The Birds*, has been completely changed and modernized. The complex features a contemporary restaurant, fish market, gift shop and fish packing facility, with the upscale **Inn at the Tides** across the highway. It's still an appealing place to explore. Pick up a shrimp or crab cocktail at the Tides takeout and stroll along the small boat basin, where you can enjoy views across broad, nearly landlocked Bodega Bay to distant headlands.

*Fishing boats sit on their own reflections at Lucas Wharf in Bodega Bay.*

Before you do all this, you might want to stop at the **Sonoma Coast Visitor Center,** just across the highway, about midpoint between Lucas and the Tides. It's open daily 9 to 5 in summer, with shorter hours the rest of the year; (707) 875-3422.

Pushing northward from the Tides, you'll see a little pink and white striped saltwater taffy place, a few curio shops and small businesses and homes tucked tight against the twisting highway. After less than a mile, turn left at the "Westside Park/Bodega Head sign" and drive out the long, curved spit that enfolds the bay of Bodega. You'll pass **Tug Point Marina** with the usual boat launch facilities, several boat basins and **Westside Park,** which has a boat launch and campground, listed below.

Beyond Westside Park, you'll shed this rather commercial area and continue toward land's end at Bodega Head, passing the University of California at Davis' **Bodega Marine Laboratory.** The road travels through brushy, treeless moors, then splits at the base of Bodega Head. The right fork takes you to a Pacific overlook and **Bodega Head Trailhead.** From here, you can follow three short hiking trails up the coast for even more impressive overlooks. The left fork takes you to another parking area for a nice overview of Bodega Bay. That skinny arm you see to the right, jammed with RVs, is **Doran Beach County Park**; listed below. It occupies a slender peninsula that almost touches Bodega Head. If it did, you'd be looking at a coastal lake instead of a harbor.

## DINING

***Lucas Wharf Restaurant*** • *595 Highway 1; (707) 875-3522. American, mostly seafood; wine and beer. Lunch and dinner daily. MC/VISA; $$$.* ☐ This airy restaurant with views of the boat basin has a pleasing nautical look, with varnished plank floors and oak furnishings. Menu items include fisherman's stew, Cajun shrimp, assorted fresh catches of the day, plus chicken breast and New York Steak. At an adjacent deli, you can pick up an order of fish and chips, then sit and stare across the boat basin.

**The Tides Wharf** ● *800 Highway 1; (707) 875-3652. American, mostly seafood; full bar service. Breakfast through dinner Wednesday-Sunday. Major credit cards; $$$.* ☐ Sleeker and a bit pricier than Lucas, the Tides restaurant is part of a large complex that includes a fish market, curio shop and deli takeout. It, too, offers Bodega Bay views through large picture windows. The menu dances from fish and shellfish to a couple of steaks, fried chicken, pasta primavera and a vegetarian crepe dish.

## RECLINING

**Inn at The Tides** ● *P.O. Box 640, Bodega Bay, CA 94923; (800) 541-7788 or (707) 875-2751. (WEB SITE: www.innatthetides.com; E-MAIL: iatt@monitor.net) Eighty-six rooms and suites with phones, TV movies and refrigerators. Major credit cards; $$$$$. Rates include continental breakfast.* ☐ Across the highway from the Tides Wharf, this elegant shingle-sided complex has a pool, spa, sauna, gift shop and laundry. Some units have spa tubs and fireplaces and most feature Bodega Bay views.

**Bodega Bay Lodge** ● *103 Coast Highway, Bodega Bay, CA 94923; (800) 368-2468 or (707) 875-3525. Seventy-eight units with phones, TV/VCRs and honor bars; $$$$$. Duck Club Restaurant serves American fare, mostly seafood; breakfast and dinner; full bar service; $$$. Major credit cards.* ☐ Even more opulent than Inn at the Tides (and pricier), Bodega Bay Lodge is built on a downslope between the highway and the bay. Nearly all rooms have aquatic views and many have fireplaces and balconies. Resort amenities include a pool, spa and sauna, fitness center, complimentary evening wine and snacks, coin laundry and rental bicycles.

## CAMPING

**Bodega Bay RV Park** ● *2000 Coast Highway (1.2 miles north), Bodega Bay, CA 94923; (800) 201-6864 or (707) 875-3741. RVs only; full hookups $$$$.* ☐ This midsize park adjacent to the ocean has several pull-throughs, with showers, coin laundry, mini-mart and café, beach access, horseshoes, volleyball and hiking trails.

**Sonoma County regional parks** ● *For information, call (707) 527-2041. RV and tent sites; hookups $$.* ☐ The county's regional park system has two campgrounds in the area. **Doran Beach** just north of Bodega Bay has 138 rather crowded sites on a narrow peninsula, with showers. **Westside Park**, on the landspit that forms Bodega Bay, has forty-seven sites with showers and some pull-throughs. Neither accepts reservations, although there's usually space on summer weekdays and any time in the off-season.

**Sonoma Coast State Beach** ● *Coast Highway, north of Bodega Bay; (707) 875-3483. RV and tent sites; hookups $$$. For campsite reservations, call (800) 444-PARK; MC/VISA accepted.* ☐ Two elements of Sonoma Coast State Beach have camping—**Bodega Dunes** in a sand dunes area and **Wrights Beach**. Both have picnic tables, barbecue grills, flush potties and showers, with no hookups.

# Bodega Bay to Occidental and Jenner

North of Bodega Bay, the Coast Highway offers a splendid procession of seastacks, sea cliffs and crescent coves with sandy beaches. Don't expect it to be uncrowded in summer and on sunny fall weekends, although it's relatively free of folks the rest of the year. Much of this pretty coastal strip is part of **Sonoma Coast State Beach**, with lots of shoreline access, several vista points and picnic areas; campgrounds are listed above.

If you've seen enough beach, we're going to suggest an inland detour to the delightful little town of Occidental, which has an odd claim to fame. Two Italian restaurants have been drawing huge dining crowds for nearly a century, even though this hamlet is lost in the deep woods, miles from nowhere. Dining at Negri's or the Occidental Hotel has become periodic ritual for many northern California residents.

To get there, return to the Bodega junction and follow Bodega Highway five miles inland to the Bohemian Highway, near tiny **Freestone**, a fine little showplace of Victorian architecture. Take the twisting Bohemian Highway 3.5 miles through thick second growth redwoods and you'll arrive in **Occidental.** It occupies a beautiful setting, in a shallow basin rimmed on two sides by thickly wooded ridges. The town dates from 1876, established as a lumber camp to topple the giant redwoods in the area. It's a mini-outdoor museum of nineteenth century architecture—a mix of Western false front and Victorian.

People come here mostly for the peace and quiet of the surrounding redwoods, to browse in a few gift shops and galleries, and to eat. Here's where, and avoid them on weekends:

## DINING

**Negri's Italian Restaurant** ● *Main Street; (707) 823-5301. Italian-American; full bar service. Lunch and dinner daily. MC/VISA; $$.* ☐ The full name is "Negri's Original Occidental Family Style Italian Restaurant." It's all emblazoned in red neon across the old fashioned wood frame building, which dates from 1893. The large early American style dining room issues great quantities of pastas, chicken Parmesan and cacciatore, plus a couple of steaks.

**Union Hotel** ● *Main Street; (707) 874-3555. (WEB SITE: www.union-hotel.com) Italian-American; full bar service. Breakfast through dinner daily. MC/VISA; $$.* ☐ This more versatile complex has a main dining area with red checkered tablecloths, a very attractive garden patio, a bakery café where breakfast is served, a gift shop and a pizza parlor. Main dining room offerings include a range of Italian dishes, plus roast chicken, duck or steak. The building dates from 1879, although it didn't become a restaurant until early in the twentieth century,

**Howard's Café, Bakery and Juice Bar** ● *Light fare; wine and beer. Breakfast and lunch daily; $.* ☐ If you spend the night in Occidental—perhaps a necessity if you consume a hefty Italian dinner with wine—Howard's is a good place for breakfast. It features fresh squeezed juices, fruit smoothies, Belgian waffles, pancakes and—are you ready for huevos rancheros with tofu? Luncheon fare consists of 'burgers and assorted sandwiches, including a "cranberry gobbler." This is a tasty blend of sliced turkey, cranberry sauce, cream cheese and red onions. The café is housed in a neat old tree-shaded cottage, with a dining porch out front.

### RECLINING

You have three choices if you want to spend the night. Two are basic and quite inexpensive, both owned by the Italian restaurant people; one is considerably more charming and expensive.

**Negri's Occidental Lodge** • *P.O. Box 84, Occidental, CA 95465; (707) 874-3623. Twenty-six rooms with phones and TV. Major credit cards; $$$. Rates include continental breakfast.* ☐ This motel adjacent to Negri's restaurant has a swimming pool. Ask for a room on the balconied second floor, which offers a nice view across Main Street to the town and the redwood ridge above.

**Union Motel** • *P.O. Box 1, Occidental, CA 95465; (707) 874-3635. (WEB SITE: www.unionhotel.com). Rooms with TV and phones. MC/VISA; $$$.* ☐ Slightly less expensive than the Occidental, the Union Motel has similar features—without the forest view.

**The Inn at Occidental** • *P.O. Box 857 (3657 Church Street), Occidental, CA 95465; (800) 522-6324 or (707) 874-1047. Eight units with private baths; full breakfast. Major credit cards; $$$$$.* ☐ This 1887 Victorian mansion has been impeccably restored, dressed in wainscotting and print wallpaper, and furnished with antiques, original artwork and family heirlooms. It's surrounded by a walled English garden and some of the units overlook a fountain courtyard. AAA has given this elegant inn one of its rare four diamond awards.

From Occidental, you can cut back to the coast on winding, narrow Coleman Valley Road, striking Highway 1 a couple of miles north of Bodega Bay. Or you can continue on the equally twisting and winding but wider Bohemian Highway through lush second growth redwood and pine forests. After just over six miles (it will seem longer) you'll cross the Russian River at tiny **Monte Rio**. A turn to the west will take you to the final stop on this tour.

---

**RV ADVISORY** • Drivers of RVs and trailer rigs will be more comfortable taking the wider Bohemian Highway from Occidental. It get a little bumpy in spots, but so does Coleman Valley Road.

---

## JENNER

**Population: 300**                                   **Elevation: twelve feet**

This decidedly cute village is terraced into a steep, wooded headland above the mouth of the Russian River. There's not much to see here, although the scenery up and down the coast and along the Russian River estuary is quite pleasing. Also, you can drive down to the mouth of the Russian River to visit a resident harbor seal colony. Don't approach too closely, for the seals will either panic or bite, ruining their day and yours.

Otherwise, there's not much else to do, except lie on the beach. If you do arrive at mealtime or nap time, there are a couple of choices.

## DINING AND RECLINING

**River's End** • *1104 Coast Highway; (707) 865-2484. American; wine and beer. Lunch and dinner daily in summer; shorter hours the rest of the year. MC/VISA; $$$.* ☐ In a town this tiny, a creative restaurant is a surprise. River's End offers two good reasons to stop—fine ocean views from the dining room and a deck; plus properly done fresh fish and other creative entrées with *nouveau* accents.

**Jenner Inn** • *P.O. Box 69 (10400 Highway 1), Jenner, CA 95450; (707) 865-0829. (WEB SITE: www.jennerinn.com; E-MAIL: innkeeper@jennerinn.com. Thirteen units. MC/VISA, AMEX; $$$.* ☐ Another guidebook calls this "the cutest little place in Jenner," and we agree. Of course, it's also one of the *few* places in Jenner. Five units in this modest yet charming inn have kitchens, making it a nice hideaway if you'd like to hang out for a while. All lodgings are in a cluster of cottages with views of either the Pacific or the Russian River estuary.

Several serious coastal attractions are just above Jenner. Among them are **Fort Ross State Historic Park,** a replica of an early Russian fur trading post; **Stillwater Cove,** a beautiful beach wedged into a rocky enclave; and **Salt Point State Park,** a fine preserve rising through several ecological zones, from beach tidepools to a highlands area with an evergreen pygmy forest. Adjacent is **Kruse Rhododendron Preserve** which bursts into brilliant bloom in April and May.

The coast north of Jenner is as attractive as the area below, although it's usually more crowded. Busy State Route 116 brings 'em down the Russian River from Santa Rosa and other inland areas. If you head inland on this route, you'll enter the popular—and certainly not uncrowded—**Russian River resort area**. This was a favorite haunt of the rich and famous during its salad days between the two world wars, although it's now a more modest family destination. The Russian River is popular for tubing and canoeing and you can get details on all of this in **Guerneville,** the region's largest community, at the **Russian River Chamber of Commerce,** just north of Main Street at 16200 First St.; (707) 869-9009.

Incidentally, if you want to pass for a native, pronounce it *GURN-vill*.

☺  ☺  ☺

**Where do we go from here?** • Why, winetasting, of course! Take State Route 116 inland from Jenner, then continue straight through Guerneville on Main Street, which becomes River Road. Follow this east to the U.S. 101 freeway, head north to Healdsburg and you'll dovetail right into the next tour, the northern Sonoma wine country. Or you can go south on Highway 101 for a quick return to the San Francisco Bay Area.

Another option is to continue north from Jenner on Highway 1 to Mendocino—certainly an interesting drive—and pick up Tour Four. Or you could run Tour Three from Mendocino in reverse.

# TRIP PLANNER

**WHEN TO GO** • Any time of the year is fine for wine tasting. Spring is grand when brilliant carpets of wild mustard cover the vineyards, and fall is great because you can witness the "crush" or annual grape harvest. To avoid the crush of crowds, avoid summer weekends. However, northern Sonoma wineries aren't busy on summer weekdays and the tasting rooms are practically empty the rest of the year. Monday's not good, since that's closing day for several area restaurants.

**DRIVING DISTANCE** • This northern Sonoma winery tour covers about sixty miles.

**RV ADVISORY** • Most winery tasting room parking lots aren't very RV friendly. It would be a chore to get anything over twenty-one feet into many of them, so drivers of big rigs may need to look for parking places on the shoulder of the roads. However, some lots are large enough, so do a little advance scouting. Oddly, some of the smaller wineries are more accommodating since their "parking lots" might be patches of gravel in the front yard.

**WHAT YOU'LL SEE** • A pretty wine country that draws only a fraction of the winetasting crowds of the Napa and Sonoma valleys. You'll also enjoy splendid pastoral settings of vinelands, pasture-lands, meadows and ancient oaks bearded with Spanish moss.

**WHAT TO DO** • Sip wine; what else?

**TO BEGIN** • Take U.S. 101 to Healdsburg and Geyserville.

## Useful contacts

**Healdsburg Chamber of Commerce,** 217 Healdsburg Ave., Healdsburg, CA 95448; (800) 648-9922 or (707) 433-6935.

**Sonoma County Wine and Visitors Center,** 5000 Roberts Lake Rd., Rohnert Park, CA 94928; (707) 586-3795.

**Russian River Chamber of Commerce,** P.O. Box 331 (16200 First St.), Guerneville, CA 95446; (707) 869-9000.

**Russian River Region Visitors Bureau,** Box 255, Guerneville, CA 95446; (800) 253-8800. (WEB SITE: www.sonoma.com/rus-river; E-MAIL: rrrvb@netdex.com)

## Pricing guidelines

**DINING:** Dinner entrée with soup or salad, without drinks or dessert for under $10 = **$**; $10 to $14 = **$$**; $15 to $25 = **$$$**; over $25 = **$$$$**.

**RECLINING:** A two-person room for $35 or less = **$**; $36 to $50 = **$$**; $51 to $75 = **$$$**; $76 to $100 = **$$$$**; more than $100 = **$$$$$**.

**CAMPING:** Under $10 = **$**; $10 to $14 = **$$**; $15 to $19 = **$$$**; $20 or more = **$$$$**

# NORTHERN SONOMA
## CALIFORNIA'S OTHER WINE COUNTRY

Quick, where is California's largest premium wine producing area? No, it's not the famous Napa Valley. It's Sonoma County, just to the west. Although the Napa Valley has more wineries, Sonoma County has more vineyard acres and it produces more wine. Further, in a recent survey of wine competitions, Sonoma County won more medals and nearly *twice* as many award points as the Napa Valley.

Yet, most Sonoma County winery tasting rooms are surprisingly un-crowded, while some Napa wineries draw more than 350,000 visitors a year. A few popular wineries in the Sonoma Valley can get busy in sum-mer and during fall harvest time, although we're taking you to an area where only grapes—not people—are caught in a crush.

Our destination is northern Sonoma County, where 30,000 acres of vines share a hilly, bucolic landscape with pasturelands, tawny grasslands and groves of elderly oaks. This area is so pretty that even a prohibitionist would enjoy wandering through.

This has been a serious wine producing region only for less than thirty years, although some wine has been made here since pre-Prohibition days. Before it became a major wine producer, northern Sonoma produced an essential ingredient for another libation—hops for beer flavoring. It also was a large producer of plums, and the Healdsburg Chamber of Commerce once sponsored spring tours to view hundreds of acres of pretty pink and white blossoms. Nearly all of the plum acreage has shriveled and the hops are long gone, although a couple of the old hop kilns have been fashioned into wineries.

When wine became all the rage in the 1970s and particularly when it was determined to be good for you in the early 1990s, vintners began casting about for new lands. Most of the Napa and Sonoma valley areas already were planted with grapes. Further, vineyards in the southern San Francisco Bay area were shrinking instead of increasing. Old vines were being uprooted by expanding Silicon Valley. Vintners moved north and discovered what the local winemakers here had known for nearly a century: Northern Sonoma County has gravelly, loamy soil and sea breeze-tempered climate that's perfect for growing premium grapes.

Since the 1970s, more than a score of new wineries has joined a few old timers that date back to the early twentieth century. One of the latter-day entrants is the Gallo Wine Company of Modesto, the world's largest winemaker. Descendants of the founding Gallo brothers have bought so much acreage that they've become the area's largest grape growers. Their "Gallo of Sonoma" brands have gotten good reviews, although there are much more interesting wines from this region.

North Sonoma wineries are focused in three regions—the Dry Creek Valley west of Geyserville and Healdsburg, the upper Russian River Valley south of Healdsburg, and the Alexander Valley north and east. Our wine country drive will focus on the Dry Creek-Russian River area, portions of which local promoters call the Russian River Wine Road. (Tour Three from Calistoga to Mendocino hits some of the Alexander Valley wineries.)

If you're coming from the San Francisco Bay Area on U.S. 101, you can gain a quick introduction to area vinelands by stopping at the combined **California Welcome Center** and **Sonoma County Wine and Visitor Center** on the north side of Rohnert Park. To get there, take the Golf Course Drive exit and follow signs. The welcome center, which shares a large parking area (plenty of room for RVs) with a Doubletree Inn, has a wine oriented gift shop, tasting bar, wine sales and lots of free material on Sonoma County vineyards. Ask for a copy of the *Russian River Wine Road* map, a useful guide for this tour. The visitor center is open daily 9 to 5; tasting bar hours are 11 to 4; (707) 586-3795

Continuing northward, hop off the freeway again in **Healdsburg** to explore its attractively landscaped plaza rimmed by boutiques, cafés and a couple of wine tasting rooms. Take the second exit (central Healdsburg) and continue north for several blocks. Immediately after you bump over a set of railroad tracks, look to your left for the **Healdsburg Chamber of Commerce** in a skinny Spanish colonial style building at 217 Healdsburg Avenue. You can pick up pounds of information including that useful *Russian River Wine Road* map. It's open weekdays 9:30 to 5 and weekends 10 to 2; (707) 433-6935.

Continue north on Healdsburg Avenue and you'll soon see **Healdsburg Plaza** on your right. Find a place to park—RVs can fit at curbside unless you're here on a summer or fall weekend—and begin strolling.

The upscale **Oakdale Grocery** at the plaza's southeast corner is a good place for a light lunch. You can pick up sandwiches, salads and local wines at the deli and adjourn to a patio out front. The food here is fashionably overpriced and quite tasty. Oakdale Grocery is open Thursday-Saturday 9 to 8:30 and Sunday-Wednesday 9 to 7; (707) 433-3200.

If you walk north from here along the back side of the plaza, you'll encounter storefront tasting rooms for **Trentadue Winery** and **Windsor Vineyards,** two wineries that aren't on our tour.

From the plaza, you can either backtrack out of Healdsburg or continue north on Healdsburg Avenue, which rejoins the freeway after a couple of miles. Before you reach the freeway, watch on your left for **Simi Winery** tucked among huge shade trees. It's tasting room is open daily 10 to 4:30; (707) 433-6981. Continue north for about six miles to an old farm town that anchors the front end of our northern Sonoma County winery tour.

## GEYSERVILLE

**Population: about 1000**                    **Elevation: 150 feet**

Although it's virtually surrounded by vineyards, little Geyserville has assumed none of the gentrification of neighboring Healdsburg. However, it does offer some nice places to dine and recline.

Take the first exit, which puts you on Geyserville Avenue, parallel to the freeway. At midtown, a local legend of an Italian restaurant called Catelli's comes up on your left. If you prefer more contemporary dining, take the Independence Avenue exit south of Geyserville and follow signs to Château Souverain Winery, which has a stylish little café. Two grand places to sleep appear about half a mile beyond Catelli's, on opposite sides of Geyserville Avenue; another is a few miles down Canyon Road.

## DINING

**Catelli's the Rex** • *21047 Geyserville Ave.; (707) 433-6000. Italian-American; full bar service. Lunch Tuesday-Friday and dinner Tuesday-Sunday. MC/VISA; $$.* ☐ If you want to rub elbows with area winemakers, this is their hangout. Housed in an old brick building, "Catelli's the King" has been serving hefty Italian fare since 1938. You also can get a couple of American dishes here, but go for the chicken cacciatore, veal Parmesan or other classic Italian dishes, properly accompanied by good northern Sonoma County Zinfandel. The daily specials are inexpensive and tasty.

**Château Souverain Café** • *At Château Souverain Winery, 400 Souverain Rd.; (707) 433-3141. American; wine only. Lunch and dinner daily except Monday. MC/VISA, DISC; $$.* ☐ Château Souverain is one of the more imposing wineries in the area, capped with lofty squared towers simulating the hop drying kilns once common in this region. Tucked into its imposing interior is a stylish and cheerful little café with a frequently changing *nouveau* menu that focuses on local meats and veggies. (Sonoma County is noted for its farm chickens, ducks and seasonal produce.)

## RECLINING

In addition to the bed & breakfast inns below, you'll find a couple of modest motels in Geyserville, and more just to the south in Healdsburg and north in Cloverdale.

**Hope-Merrill and Hope-Bosworth houses** • *P.O. Box 42, Geyserville, CA 95441; (800) 825-4233 or (707) 857-3356. All units with private baths; full breakfast. MC/VISA, AMEX; $$$$* ☐ Geyserville has several splendid old Victorian homes and two—across the street from one another and jointly owned—have been fashioned into handsome bed & breakfast inns. The 1870 Eastlake style Hope-Merrill House has eight rooms and is furnished with European antiques. The slightly less expensive Queen Anne style Hope-Bosworth House has four units, with American décor, accented by arts and crafts. They're surrounded by elaborate gardens; guests at both inns can use a swimming pool at the Hope-Merrill.

**Campbell Ranch Inn** • *1475 Canyon Rd., Geyserville, CA 95441; (800) 959-3878 or (707) 857-3476. (WEB: www.campbellranchinn.com) Five units with private baths; full breakfast and evening dessert. MC/VISA, AMEX; $$$$.* ☐ This modern ranch style inn occupies a 35-acre knoll with views of surrounding vineyards and woodlands. Four rooms in the main house and a cottage have modern furnishings and king beds; the cottage has a fireplace and deck with a hot tub. Amenities include a tennis court, swimming pool, hot tub and bicycles.

Ancient vines and an old farm house create a pastoral scene on Westside Road in the Russian River Valley.

## Into the vineyards

**NOTE:** For more details on wineries here and elsewhere in California, pick up a copy of our *Best of the Wine Country*. It's available at book stores or you can order it directly from the publisher; see details in the back of this book.

A few northern Sonoma County wineries charge a tasting fee, although most do not. Generally, this fee is applied toward purchase, or you can keep the glass. (Fee tasting is common in the Napa Valley, resulting in a set of unmatched wine glasses for visitors.)

To get to the heart of the Dry Creek and Russian River winelands, continue north about a mile beyond the Hope-Bosworth and Hope-Merrill houses. At a stop sign, take Canyon Road left under the freeway and then make an immediate right for your first stop:

**Geyser Peak Winery** ● *22281 Chianti Rd., Geyserville, CA 95441; (800) 255-9463 or (707) 857-9400. Daily 10 to 5; no tasting fee. Gift items and picnic area. MC/VISA.* ❑ The large and attractive Geyser Peak complex, which sits at the gateway to the Dry Creek Valley, traces its heritage back to 1880. A new tasting room was opened in 1998.

From Geyser Peak, continue north on Chianti Road (essentially a freeway frontage road) two and a half miles to an elegant, iron gated winery:

**Silver Oak Cellars** • *24625 Chianti Rd., Geyserville, CA 95441; (707) 857-3562. Monday-Saturday 9 to 4; tasting fee. MC/VISA.* ☐ This elegant French Château style winery was opened by the Napa Valley's master of Cabernet Sauvignon, Justin Meyer, in 1992. He produces only cabernet—some of the finest and most expensive in California.

Retrace your steps down Chianti Road and turn right onto Canyon Road. You'll climb through an appealing hilly mix of vineyards and woodlands. The next sipping stop comes up within a mile, on your right:

**J. Pedroncelli Winery** • *1220 Canyon Rd., Geyserville, CA 95441; (800) 836-3894 or (707) 857-3531. Daily 10 to 5; no tasting fee. MC/VISA, AMEX.* ☐ John Pedroncelli was an optimist; he came to northern Sonoma County in the middle of Prohibition and bought winery property. The gamble paid off; Repeal came in 1933 and he was ready to produce wine for all of the county's thirsty Italians. His sons John and Jim and their families operate the enterprise today, which has some of the best wine buys in the county.

From casual Pedroncelli, we go to the most elaborate winery in the region, rivaling any of the imposing wine castles of the Napa Valley. Continue along Canyon Road until it ends at Dry Creek Road. Turn right and this grand château comes up shortly on your left:

**Ferrari-Carano Vineyards and Winery** • *8761 Dry Creek Rd., Healdsburg, CA 95448; (707) 433-6700. Daily 10 to 5; tasting fee. Gift shop. MC/VISA, AMEX.* ☐ Founded by the owners of El Dorado Hotel and Casino in Reno, Ferrari-Carano is a study in opulence, with five acres of formal gardens, and striking old world architecture. The winery and tasting room are in the imposing French château style *Villa Fiore*, the House of Flowers. From the tasting parlor, steps lead down to the wine cellar, basking regally beneath an arched colonnade.

Continue on Dry Creek Road for a couple of miles to a winery considerably more modest than Ferrari-Carano, although it the view is better from here. It's uphill to your right:

**Lake Sonoma Winery** • *9990 Dry Creek Rd., Geyserville, CA 95441; (800) 750-9463 or (707) 431-1550. Daily 10 to 5; no tasting fee. A few wine gift items, small deli and picnic areas. MC/VISA, AMEX.* ☐ Recently purchased by one of the owners of the imposing Korbel winery (our last stop), modest little Lake Sonoma Winery perches on a steep slope, offering a splendid view of Dry Creek Valley's vineyards and protective wooded hills. You can get fixin's at the deli, then dine on the porch and enjoy that grand view, or retreat to a nearby shaded picnic area.

If you plan to camp in this region, continue out Dry Creek Road to **Lake Sonoma Recreation Area,** a large reservoir backed up by Warm Springs Dam. Well-spaced sites, some shaded, are modestly priced; flush potties and showers are available. For information, call (707) 433-2200. If you aren't tenting or RVing, retrace your route on Dry Creek Road, then go right on Yoakim Bridge Road, which provides a short link to West Dry Creek Road. Turn right onto West Dry Creek and follow this narrow, winding lane a couple of miles to your next stop:

***Preston Vineyards and Winery*** • *9282 W. Dry Creek Rd., Healdsburg, CA 95448; (800) 305-9707 or (707) 433-3372. Daily 11 to 4:30; no tasting fee. Wine gift items and picnic area. MC/VISA.* □ "Drink Zin," says a neon sign over the winery. This small and informal facility, housed in a woodsy multi-gabled barn, specializes in that product. The place has a pleasant farmyard look, shaded by ancient trees.

Reverse your route on West Dry Creek Road and follow it four narrow, twisting miles through wooded hills to the next winery, on your left.

***Quivara Vineyards*** • *4900 W. Dry Creek Rd., Healdsburg, CA 95448; (800) 292-8339 or (707) 431-8333. Daily 10 to 4:30; no tasting fee. Wine gift items and picnic area. MC/VISA.* □ This modern winery presents a pleasantly bucolic picture, housed in an ivy entwined barn, with a wisteria draped arbor out front. The unusual name comes from Francisco Vásquez de Coronado's search for the golden cities of Cibola in the American southwest in 1540. He called the lands he explored "Quivara," and eventually returned to Mexico after finding no riches.

A quarter of a mile below Quivara, turn left onto Lambert Bridge Road and the next tasting room candidate soon arrives on your left:

***Pezzi King Vineyards*** • *3805 Lambert Bridge Rd., Healdsburg, CA 95448; (800) 411-4758 or (707) 431-9388. Daily 10 to 4:30. A few wine gift items; view deck and picnic area. MC/VISA.* □ This inviting winery complex of stone and dark woods perches on a slope above the vineyards; a deck provides a pleasing view of the vines. If you've passed this way before, you'll remember this as Robert Stemmler Winery.

Just down Lambert Bridge road on the right is your next stop:

***Dry Creek Vineyard*** • *3770 Lambert Bridge Rd. (P.O. Box T), Healdsburg, CA 95448; (800) 864-WINE or (707) 433-1000 (E-MAIL: dvc@drycreekvineyard.com) Daily 10:30 to 4:30; no tasting fee. Picnic area. MC/VISA.* □ Dry Creek is one of the oldest of northern Sonoma's new generation wineries, founded by David Stare in 1972. The tasting room is an appealing structure that suggests a small manor house, dressed in ivy and rimmed by old trees and new lawns.

Continue briefly on Lambert Bridge to Dry Creek Road and you'll see a neat place for an inexpensive lunch break—the weathered **Dry Creek General Store.** It comprises the entire town of Dry Creek, with a population of four. The venerable store has a deli, a good local wine selection and other essentials such as food, clothing and fishing worms. You can build lunch at the deli, buy a bottle of local wine and adjourn to picnic tables, where you can chat with local good old boys, sipping their Coors. To the left and uphill from the general store is another winery:

***F. Teldeschi Winery*** • *3555 Dry Creek Rd., Healdsburg, CA 95448; (707) 433-6626. Daily 10 to 5; no tasting fee.* □ This structure more resembles an oversized military barracks than a winery, but the wines— mostly Zinfandels—are fine. And you can discuss them knowledgeably with the host, Dan Teldeschi, since he's also the winemaker, owner and cleanup man. (F. Teldeschi is his father.)

Now, return to West Dry Creek via Lambert Bridge Road and turn left. After a short drive, you'll encounter:

**Lambert Bridge Winery** • *4085 W. Dry Creek Rd., Healdsburg, CA 95448; (800) 975-0555 or (707) 4331-9600. Daily 10:30 to 4:30; no tasting fee. Deli and a few wine gift items; picnic area. Major credit cards.* ⊓ Nestled into a wooded glen above scenic Dry Creek Valley, Lambert Bridge is one of the area's more inviting small wineries. The tasting room, with a distinctive counter made of barrel staves, is inside the redwood winery, within sight and aroma of aging wines.

Continue another 3.5 miles on winding, tree-cloaked West Dry Creek Road and watch for a small sign on the right, directing you up a narrow lane to:

**Everett Ridge Historic Vineyards and Winery** • *435 W. Dry Creek Rd., Healdsburg, CA 95448; (707) 433-1637. Daily 11 to 4:30. Picnic area. MC/VISA, DISC.* ⊓ Until recently, this was Bellerose, an earthy winery and tasting room in a wonderfully weather-worn barn dating from 1880. You'll see a couple of pieces of rusting farming equipment to complete the rustic rural scene. Not much has changed under the Everett Ridge name.

Shortly beyond Bellerose/Everett Ridge, you'll hit a stop sign and turn right onto Westside Road to enter the Russian River portion of this winery tour. This is one of the most scenic drives in the California wine country— a pleasing mix of hillside vineyards, forest glens and ancient oaks veiled with Spanish moss. Before heading down Westside Road, you may want to pause at Sonoma County's most elegant bed & breakfast inn and restaurant, just to the right:

**Madrona Manor** • *P.O. Box 818 (1001 Westside Rd.), Healdsburg, CA 95448; (800) 258-4003 or (707) 433-4231. (madronamanor.com; E-MAIL: madronamanor@aol.com) Twenty-one rooms with phones and private baths; full breakfast; $$$$$. Restaurant serves dinner nightly, American-continental fare; $$$. Major credit cards.* ⊓ An area newspaper called this French château style hideaway "the grand dame of Sonoma County country inns." It's nestled in eight acres of landscaped and wooded grounds, with rooms in the main house and a carriage house. They feature a mix of antique and modern furniture, including some of the original furnishings from the 1880s, when this was a country manor house. The elegantly coiffed Madrona Manor Restaurant serves multi-course *prix fixe* dinners or individual entrées. It has an extensive list of local wines.

Briefly down Westside Road, you'll shortly encounter the next two wineries, both on your right:

**Mill Creek Vineyards** • *1401 Westside Rd., Healdsburg, CA 95448; (707) 431-2121. Daily noon to 4:30; no tasting fee. Picnic deck. MC/VISA, AMEX.* ⊓ Rustic describes this winery, right down to the water wheel attached to the tasting room, although it has only ornamental value. This log structure is properly weathered although it was built in the 1970s.

**Armida Winery** • *2201 Westside Rd., Healdsburg, CA 95448; (707) 433-2222. Daily 11 to 5; no tasting fee. Picnic area. MC/VISA.* ⊓ Three geodesic domes on the brow of a wooded hill mark this relatively new winery. Production started in 1989 and the tasting room opened in 1994.

A mile and a half beyond Armida are two more close-together wineries, both on your right:

**Rabbit Ridge Vineyard** • *3291 Westside Rd., Healdsburg, CA 95448; (707) 431-7128. Daily 11 to 45:30; no tasting fee. MC/VISA.* ☐ Tucked into a slope above Westside Road, this winery's stylish tasting room offers several varieties not generally found in California, such as Sangiovese and Viognier.

**Belvedere Winery** • *4035 Westside Rd., Healdsburg, CA 95448; (707) 433-8236, ext. 40. Daily 10 to 4:30; no tasting fee. Picnic area and gift shop. Major credit cards.* ☐ A short driveway takes you to the Belvedere winery-tasting room, nestled amongst hillside vineyards. Lawns and blooming flowers give the grounds a park-like quality.

A couple of miles beyond are two more wineries, both on your left:

**Hop Kiln Winery** • *6050 Westside Rd., Healdsburg, CA 95488; (707) 433-6491. Daily 10 to 5; no tasting fee. Art exhibit in the tasting room; picnic area. MC/VISA, AMEX.* ☐ This is one of the most distinctive wineries in Sonoma County, housed in an ancient triple towered hop drying kiln. From the tasting room, suspended above the lower floor of the kiln, you can see some of the original hop drying equipment. However, we're here to taste wine, and most are quite good.

**Rochioli Vineyards and Winery** • *8075 Westside Rd., Healdsburg, CA 95448; (707) 433-2305. February-November 10 to 5 and December-January 11 to 4; no tasting fee. Art exhibit in the tasting room; picnic area. MC/VISA, AMEX.* ☐ Tucked behind an stone gateway and sheltered by grand old trees, Rochioli resembles a prosperous French countryside farm. Patio picnic tables provide views of the vineyards.

You'll next encounter the two final wineries on Westside Road, the first a mile beyond Rochioli and the second half a mile further, up a narrow lane. Both are on your right:

**Davis Bynum Winery** • *8075 Westside Rd., Healdsburg, CA 95448; (800) 826-1073 or (707) 433-2611. Daily 10 to 5; no tasting fee, except for some limited release wines. Picnic area. MC/VISA, AMEX.* ☐ Sitting a few hundred feet off the highway, Davis Bynum's masonry winery complex is dressed in attractive landscaping. The tasting room is cozy and simple, with current released written on a chalkboard.

**Porter Creek Vineyards** • *8735 Westside Rd., Healdsburg, CA 95448; (707) 433-6321. Daily 10:30 to 4:30 in summer, weekends only the rest of the year; no fee for tasting. MC/VISA.* ☐ This is the smallest of the area wineries; the tasting room is in a garage, with a plank laid across barrels for a counter. The small, hands-on production facility is a short distance away.

This wine tasting road now enters a lush canopy of second growth redwoods and other trees. A mile from Porter Creek, fork to the right, then Westside Road blends into busy River Road after three miles. The final winery stop arrives a couple of miles later, in a pretty valley flanked by vineyards and young redwoods:

**Korbel Champagne Cellars** • *13250 River Rd., Guerneville, CA 95446; (707) 887-2294. Daily 9 to 5 May-September and 9 to 4:30 October-April; periodic winery and garden tours; no tasting fee. Gift shop, deli, micro-brewery and picnic area. Major credit cards.* ☐ Korbel rivals Ferrari-Carano as the most elaborate winery in Sonoma County and it's considerably older. Founded in 1882, it has evolved into a baronial estate with great vine covered stone buildings, a tower right out of medieval Germany and formal gardens. It offers a tour that focuses on sparkling wine production, and it even has a micro-brewery.

Just east of the winery is a pleasant place to spend the night:

**Ridenhour Ranch House Inn** • *12850 River Rd., Guerneville, CA 95446; (888) 877-4466 or (707) 887-1033. (WEB SITE: www.ridenhour-ranchhouseinn.com; E-MAIL: frechberge@aol.com) Eight rooms with private baths, five with TV; full breakfast. MC/VISA, AMEX; $$$$.* ☐ This turn-of-the-century redwood ranch home is furnished with American and English antiques, accented with Oriental rugs. Six units are in the house and the other two occupy cottages. The inn has a hot tub for soaking away a long day in the wine country.

If you continue west into Guerneville, then turn left (south) across the Russian River on State Route 116, you'll encounter—on your left—one of the area's most inviting retreats:

**Applewood Inn & Restaurant** • *13555 Highway 116, Guerneville, CA 95446; (707) 869-9093. (WEB SITE: www.applewoodinn.com; E-MAIL: stay@applewoodinn.com) Eight units with private baths in the mansion; eight more in cottages; full breakfast; $$$$$. Applewood Restaurant services American-continental fare, dinner Tuesday-Saturday by reservation only; $$$. Major credit cards.* ☐ Surrounded by lush landscaping and young redwoods, this comely inn accomplishes that fine balance between opulence and comfort. The décor is a tasteful mix of American and European; many rooms have fireplaces and spa tubs. The complex has a pool, spa and landscaped grounds. This mission revival villa was built in 1922 during the heyday of Russian River resorts. The restaurant serves elaborate four-course dinners, with reservations for specific seatings.

☺ ☺ ☺

**Where do we go from here?** • If you reverse your route on River Road, you'll soon get back to the U.S. 101 freeway. Or you can continue into the busy and popular Russian River resort area, with **Guerneville** as its commercial center. To learn about the region, stop by the **Russian River Chamber of Commerce,** just north of Main Street at 16200 First St.; (707) 869-9000. A few miles north of Guerneville on Armstrong Woods Road is **Armstrong Redwoods State Reserve,** a lush grove of ancient big trees.

If you continue along the Russian River to **Jenner,** you can head north along the Pacific on State Route 1 and pick up Tour Four, the Redwood Coast. Our you can go south from Jenner and run Tour One, if you don't mind reading backward.

## Tour Three
# WINELANDS TO HEADLANDS
## CALISTOGA TO MENDOCINO ON HIGHWAY 128

This tour begins in a crowd and ends in one. In between, however, it follows a road that's usually less traveled and extremely versatile.

State Highway 128 rambles from tourist-busy Calistoga at the upper end of the Napa Valley, passes through two uncrowded winelands and a splendid redwood forest, and then bumps into the California coast just south of Mendocino, another popular tourist area.

Calistoga sits at the pretty end of the Napa Valley, where the Maya-camas and Sonoma mountains merge to form the region's northern border. The town, often busy with tourists and yet still charmingly old fashioned, sits at the base of brooding Mount St. Helena, the area's most prominent landmark. It dates from 1859 when Mormon entrepreneur Sam Brannan bought land from the local Indians and established a resort to take advantage of the region's hot mineral springs. The name is Brannan's distortion, a blend of California and Saratoga, the famed New York health spa. (It is rumored that, after drinking too many toasts to his new venture, he announced: *This will become the Calistoga of Sarifornia.*)

In 1880, an impoverished, tubercular Scottish writer spent his honeymoon in a mining shack on Mount St. Helena with his bride Fannie Osborne, her son and—good grief!—their dog. Giving the abandoned silver

# TRIP PLANNER

**WHEN TO GO** ● This is a year-around tour since the area isn't subject to weather extremes. Popular destinations on each end—Calistoga and Mendocino—can be quite crowded in summer so you might want to consider an off-season drive.

**DRIVING DISTANCE** ● About 115 miles, including a side trip to Robert Louis Stevenson State Park.

**RV ADVISORY** ● Nothing on this route will seriously challenge a large motorhome or trailer rig.

**WHAT YOU'LL SEE** ● Sharpsteen Museum, Sam Brannan cottage and Old Faithful Geyser in Calistoga; charming old Boonville; Navarro River Redwoods State Park in the Anderson Valley; New England style Mendocino and two state parks—Van Damme and Russian Gulch—which flank it; Ford House museum and visitor center in Mendocino.

**WHAT TO DO** ● Hike the trails of Robert Louis Stevenson State Park; try a mud bath at a Calistoga spa; take a glider or balloon ride over the Napa Valley; sip your way through the winelands of the Alexander and Anderson valleys; explore the tidepools and beaches around Mendocino.

**TO BEGIN** ● Get to Calistoga in the Napa Valley's upper end.

## Useful contacts

**Anderson Valley Chamber of Commerce,** P.O. Box 275, Boonville, CA 95415; (707) 895-2379.

**Anderson Valley Winegrowers Association,** P.O. Box 63, Philo, CA 95466. WEB SITE: www.avwines.com

**Calistoga Chamber of Commerce,** 1458 Lincoln Ave., #9, Calistoga, CA 94515; (707) 942-6333.

**Fort Bragg-Mendocino Coast Chamber of Commerce,** P.O. Box 1141, Fort Bragg, CA 95437; (800) 726-2780 or (707) 961-6300. (WEB SITE: www.mendocinocoast.com; E-MAIL: chamber @mcn.org)

**Mendocino County Vintner's Association,** P.O. Box 1409, Ukiah, CA 95482; (707) 468-1343.

## Pricing guidelines

**DINING:** Dinner entrée with soup or salad, without drinks or dessert for under $10 = **$**; $10 to $14 = **$$**; $15 to $25 = **$$$**; over $25 = **$$$$**.

**RECLINING:** A two-person room for $35 or less = **$**; $36 to $50 = **$$**; $51 to $75 = **$$$**; $76 to $100 = **$$$$**; more than $100 = **$$$$$**.

**CAMPING:** Under $10 = **$**; $10 to $14 = **$$**; $15 to $19 = **$$$**; $20 or more = **$$$$**

mine the fanciful name of Silverado, he published his first American work, *The Silverado Squatters,* then he left for the South Pacific. Robert Louis Stevenson often credited St. Helena's cool, dry air for restoring his health and inspiring his first major published work.

Thus doubly promoted, Calistoga has continued to thrive as a spa as well as the northern anchor to the famous Napa Valley wine country.

## CALISTOGA

**Population: 4,500**                                     **Elevation: 362 feet**

Since you must get to Calistoga to begin the tour, we'd suggest that you avoid the heavy traffic of Highway 29 through the Napa Valley and take the less crowded and more scenic Silverado Trail. It travels on the valley's eastern side, through the foothills of the Mayacamas Mountains. By following this route, you'll hit Highway 29 just north of town; it becomes Lincoln Avenue, Calistoga's main street.

Turn left and you'll quickly encounter two items of interest. At the **Calistoga Glider Port,** you can hitch a ride on the thermals to sail high above the winelands and the rugged ramparts of Mount St. Helena; see "Activities" below.

Just beyond the glider port is the **Calistoga Depot,** built in 1868; it's California's oldest surviving railroad station. However, it no longer hosts train passengers; it's a complex of shops and boutiques with a railway-theme restaurant called Smokehouse Café, listed below. Among its shops is a wine store housed in a vintage railway coach within the depot. Other shops line a balcony above and occupy other train cars outside.

The **Calistoga Chamber of Commerce** is behind Calistoga Depot, open weekdays 9 to 5, Saturday 10 to 4:30 and Sunday 11 to 4; (707) 942-6333.

Not far from here are the **Sharpsteen Museum** and **Sam Brannan Cottage.** The museum, at 1311 Washington Street, features local history displays, including a 32-foot diorama of Brannan's Victorian Hot Springs Resort. It's open daily 10 to 4 May to October and noon to 4 the rest of the year; (707) 942-5911. The next door Sam Brannan cottage is a typical resort cabin of the 1860s.

The heart of Calistoga is best explored on foot, particularly if you're in an RV, since parking is limited downtown. The handsome brick and masonry business district covers only a few blocks, and there's plenty of street parking on the fringes.

## ACTIVITIES

*Bicycle rentals* ● Palisades Mountain Sport, 1330-B Gerrard St., Calistoga, CA 94515; (707) 942-9687. Getaway Bike Shop, Foothill at Lincoln, Calistoga, CA 94515; (800) 859-BIKE or (707) 942-0332.

*Glider rides* ● Calistoga Gliders, 1546 Lincoln Ave., Calistoga, CA 94515; (707) 942-5000. Twenty to thirty-minute rides over the Napa Valley and the ramparts of Mount St. Helena. MC/VISA.

*Hot air balloon rides* ● American Balloon Adventures, P.O. Box 795, Calistoga, CA 94515; (707) 942-6546.

## DINING

**Brannan's Grill** • *1547 Lincoln Ave.; (707) 942-2233. American; full bar service. Lunch and dinner daily. MC/VISA; $$$.* ☐ The grill has an elegantly spartan clubby look with laminated woods, drop lamps and high backed booths. The menu has a *nouveau* tilt, offering rotisserie chicken with honey and lavender glaze, voodoo shrimp with rosemary and oregano and—for you vegans—grilled veggies with garlic mashed potatoes and red pepper jam.

**Café Sarafornia** • *1413 Lincoln Ave.; (707) 942-0555. American; wine and beer. Breakfast through dinner daily. MC/VISA; $$.* ☐ Taking its name from Brannan's garbled "Saratoga of California," this trendy-funky establishment serves pastas, creative sandwiches, pork chops and lively chilies. It has a Sixties Berkeley look with impressionistic art on the walls.

**Alex's** • *1437 Lincoln Ave.; (707) 942-6868. American-continental; full bar service. Dinner nightly, late lunch on weekends. Major credit cards; $$$.* ☐ Calistoga's longest established upper end restaurant, Alex has a pleasing bistro look with arched windows and ceiling fans; winery murals decorate the walls. Entrées such as calves liver, halibut, boneless breast of chicken and prime rib decorate the menu.

## RECLINING

Although regarded as a wine country destination, Calistoga is remains popular as spa retreat and several older resorts offer the classic mud baths, massages and mineral soaks. The town also is busy with bed and breakfast inns, many housed in its fine old Victorians. A brief sampler:

**Dr. Wilkinson's Hot Springs Resort** • *1507 Lincoln Ave., Calistoga, CA 94515; (707) 942-4102. Forty-two rooms and bungalows with TV and phones. Major credit cards; $$$$ to $$$$$.* ☐ This is one of Calistoga's oldest continually operating spas, founded in 1946 by young chiropractor "Doc" Wilkinson. It has the full range of mud baths, massages, facials and mineral baths. Dr. Wilkinson's has several outdoor mineral water pools.

**Golden Haven Hot Springs** • *1713 Lake St., Calistoga, CA 94515; (707) 942-6793. (WEB SITE: www.goldenhaven.com). Rooms and suites with TV and refrigerators. MC/VISA, AMEX; $$$ to $$$$$.* ☐ This is one of Calistoga's more affordable spas, with comfortable lodgings as well as the full range of mud baths, herbal mineral wraps, massages and such. Some of the units have kitchenettes; the complex has a mineral pool and a complete spa.

**The Pink Mansion** • *1415 Foothill Blvd., Calistoga, CA 94515; (800) 238-PINK or (707) 942-0558. Five rooms with private baths; full breakfast. MC/VISA, AMEX; $$$$ to $$$$$.* ☐ Pink, indeed! This multi-gabled Victorian with a witch's hat tower is pink with white trim, and that blushing color spreads to the interior as well. This 1875 mansion with Victorian and American antiques sits against a wooded slope of the Mayacamas Mountains, not far from the downtown area.

***Silver Rose Inn and Spa*** • *351 Rosedale Rd., Calistoga, CA 94515; (800) 995-9381 or (707) 942-9581. Twenty rooms with phones and private baths; extended continental breakfast. Major credit cards; $$$$$.* □ A combination B&B and spa, the Silver Rose consists of two facilities with lush landscaping and vineyard views—Inn on the Knoll and Inn the Vineyard. They're elegantly appointed and individually decorated, with stone fireplaces, spa tubs and a mix of early American, Asian and modern furnishings. The complex has a spa, a pool, tennis court and putting green.

## Side trip: Robert Louis Stevenson State Park

Before beginning our driving tour from Calistoga to Mendocino, we suggest a side trip to the old mine that inspired RLS to write "Silverado Squatters." And we can assure you that Robert Louis Stevenson State Memorial Park will be uncrowded when you arrive. This thatch of mountainside woodland is undeveloped, with only a hiking trail to the mine site.

To get there, head north from Calistoga on State Route 29, which twists through the foothills of Mount St. Helena. After about seven miles, as you approach the 2,960-foot highway crest, you'll see the state park sign. Casual parking areas are on both sides of the road just beyond. (RV parking is best on the right side.)

Near the left side parking area, you'll see foundation fragments of a former toll house, a few picnic tables and not much else. A one-mile trail leads through thick woodlands to a clearing where Robert, Fannie and her kid and dog spent a couple of months in an abandoned bunkhouse. A marble monument here, unfortunately chipped by vandals and difficult to read, quotes from an RLS poem that foretold his premature death a few years later in Samoa:

*Doomed to know not winter, only spring,*
*A being trod the flowery April blithely for a while,*
*Took his fill of music, joy of thought, and seeing,*
*Came and stayed and went, nor ever ceased to smile.*

If you'd like to explore the mine, little more than a narrow vertical slot in the mountain, you can clamber up a rough and rocky tailing dump to the left of the clearing.

For an impressive valley view, continue on the main trail which, after a tough scramble over a badly eroded area, emerges onto a forest service road. Follow it about 450 yards to a point where it makes a wide sweeping turn to the right. Go instead to the left, on a short, steep trail downward, which takes you to the top of the mine and grand vistas of the valley. (Got kids? Be careful of that slotted mine shaft!) From here, you can continue hiking up the road for more valley vistas until you reach St. Helena's summit, at 4,343 feet.

As you return from the mountain, instead of going all the way back to Calistoga, watch for a right turn onto Tubbs Lane. This will take you past two places of interest, both on the right:

***Château Montelena Winery*** • *1429 Tubbs Lane, Calistoga, CA 94515; (707) 942-5015. Daily 10 to 4.* □ This is one of the Napa Valley's most appealing wineries, a virtual mini-castle built in the 1880s by early

Calistogan Alfred L. Tubbs. The heavily wooded grounds includes a small lake with Oriental arched bridges, stone knights and Japanese maples.

### Old Faithful Geyser •

*1299 Tubbs Lane; (707) 942-6463. Daily 10 to 6; moderate fee.* ☐ One of the world's few geysers with a predictable timetable, Calistoga's Old Faithful hisses skyward about every fourteen minutes. It's similar to the more famous Yellowstone Old Faithful, although its volume is much smaller. This longtime attraction also has a gift shop in a cottage that's heated by thermal water.

Continue on Tubbs Lane to Highway 128 and turn right to begin this long and scenic drive through vineyards to the sea. First, however, if you'd like to see the area's other attraction, the **Petrified Forest,** turn left toward Calistoga for about a mile and then go right four miles. This small collection of stone trees is open daily 10 to 6 with a modest admission fee; (707) 942-6667.

## The Alexander Valley

Heading northwest on State Route 128, you'll pass through a forested area and then enter a pretty picture of vineyards and thickets with rugged hills on the horizon, some the shape and tawny color of bread loaves. Here and there, weathered old barns and occasional early American style homes accent the landscape. This is the Alexander Valley, one of the more pleasant yet lesser known of California's wine producing areas.

As we steer you through the valley, we'll list the wineries with

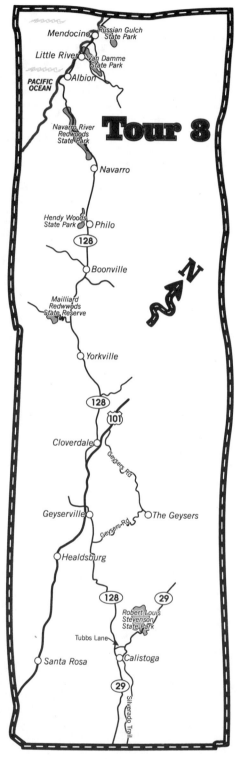

tasting rooms open to the public. The first, which appears on the left just after you pass a sign indicating Santa Rosa, is **Field Stone Winery**, bunkered into an oak shaded hill and open daily 10 to 5; (707) 433-7266. Just beyond on the right is the Spanish style **Hanna Winery**, reached by driving up a winding road through the vineyards, daily 10 to 4.

Another half mile takes you to **Alexander Valley Vineyards** on the right in a modern adobe brick building, daily 10 to 5; (707) 433-7209. Just beyond on the left is rather rustic **Johnson Winery** noted for a large pipe organ in its tasting room, daily 10 to 5; (707) 433-2319. A mile farther is **Sausel Winery** on the right, a nicely landscaped complex with a shaded picnic area; daily 10 to 4; (707) 433-2285.

After a couple of 90-degree turns, the highway takes you past the old **Alexander Valley Store and Bar**, where you can get provisions, local wines and a sip at the adjacent saloon. Just beyond, a short gravel road leads to the right to **Frommer Vineyards and Winery** with a tasting room above a landscaped lawn area, open 10 to 5; (707) 433-3054. Another 90-degree turn takes you past **Estancia Winery**, open by appointment only.

## Side trip: The Geysers

The Calistoga and Alexander Valley regions sit atop a burbling cauldron of thermal activity, as indicated by Old Faithful geyser and Calistoga's hot mineral springs.

Just beyond Estancia Winery, if you continue straight ahead instead of turning left to stay with Highway 128, you can drive sixteen miles on Geysers Road to an area simply called The Geysers. It's one of California's largest geothermal areas, where Pacific Gas and Electric and other firms are using the power of nature's steam to generate electricity.

There's not much to see up there and no scheduled tours, although it's an interesting drive through the rugged and tawny Mayacamus Mountains. If you like back roads that offer little more than curves and scenery, you can follow Geysers Road all the way to Highway 101 just above Cloverdale, through which our tour passes. The total distance is twenty-eight miles, compared with fifteen if you stay with State Route 128.

---

**RV ADVISORY** • Geysers Road is narrow and winding, although it's all paved and carefully-driven motorhomes and trailer rigs should be able to make it.

---

If you don't want to go all the way to The Geysers, you can get grand views of the Alexander Valley by driving six miles up to a crest in the hills, which are terraced by several vineyards. Watch for a gate identifying Hawkeye, Ridge and Geyser Peak ranches. This spot is a good turnaround point, ample enough for trailer rigs. You won't get any Alexander Valley views beyond this point.

Should you choose to continue toward The Geysers, you'll wind and twist through shallow vales and along ridges in the softly rounded Mayacamas foothills. About fourteen miles from your starting point, watch on your left for a California Civil Engineering Landmark, which identifies The Geysers as one of the first geothermal operations in America. From here, you can see buildings, pipes and puffs of steam across a narrow valley, and that's about the extent of The Geysers' visual offerings. You can drive across the small valley for a closer look, and then return to Geysers Road. From here, you can continue north and reach U.S. 101 after fourteen very twisting miles, or return to your starting point in the Alexander Valley.

Meanwhile, back on Highway 128, you'll encounter two more wineries before you emerge from this attractive valley of vineyards. **Murphy-Goode Estate Winery** occupies a good-looking red roofed oversized bungalow on your left, open daily 10:30 to 4:30; (707) 431-7644. Just beyond, also on the left, is **De Lorimier Vineyards and Winery** in a kind of rustic-modern barn style structure, open Thursday-Sunday 10 to 4:30; (707) 857-2000.

After passing De Lorimier, you'll cross the Russian River and then enter the side door of **Geyserville**, which we visited in the previous tour. Turn right onto the small town's main street, drive about a mile north and hop onto the U.S. 101 freeway for a quick seven miles to **Cloverdale**. Take the South Cloverdale Boulevard exit (business route 101) and cruise the Fifties style main street in this town of 5,400 residents.

Cloverdale has little of visitor interest, although this route will take you to the next link of Route 128 for its run through the Anderson Valley. You might pause at the **Cloverdale Historical Museum** near downtown at 215 N. Cloverdale Boulevard. Housed in a recently renovated nineteenth century brick home, it displays the usual pioneer paraphernalia, with a nice mockup of an early day Cloverdale general store. Call for hours; (707) 894-2067.

### DINING

On the north side of town, before Highway 128 separates from business route 101, you'll see two interesting lunch or early dinner stops:

**Quigley's** • *North Cloverdale Blvd.; (707) 894-1000. American; no alcohol. Lunch to early evening daily. No credit cards; $.* ☐ It's back to the Fifties in this nostalgic drive-in across from Cloverdale High School. Although Quigley's doesn't have car hops on rollerskates, it does have chrome-rimmed counter stools and black and white tile on an outdoor dining patio. There's seating inside as well. The menu is what it should be—hamburgers, hot dogs, corn dogs, shakes and such.

**Hamburger Ranch and Pasta Farm** • *31195 Redwood Highway (101/128 junction); (707) 894-5616. American; wine and beer. Breakfast through dinner daily. Major credit cards; $ to $$.* ☐ If Quigley's is nostalgic Fifties, Hamburger Ranch is nostalgic barnyard fifties. This cheerful café at the junction of highways 101 and 128 serves great hamburgers and immodestly calls itself world famous. In fact, it does post accolades from international clientele in its old fashioned red checkered dining room. In addition to those world famous hamburgers, the ranch serves elaborate dinners of chicken, babyback ribs, ribeye steak and assorted pastas. You can dine indoors or on a sunny patio with a view of the countryside.

## Heading for the Anderson Valley

Immediately beyond Hamburger Ranch, turn west onto Highway 128 and follow its twisting, undulating path through oak and madrone covered foothills that shelter the upper end of Anderson Valley. Before you reach the valley itself, you may want to take lodgings in an elegant new country inn, where you also can sip a bit of wine:

**Mountain House Winery and Lodge** ● *33710 Highway 128, Cloverdale, CA 95425; (707) 894-5683. (WEB SITE: www.mnthousewinery-lodge.com; E-MAIL: mountainhouse@sonic.net) Rooms and suites with private baths; expanded continental breakfast. MC/VISA, DISC; $$$$$.* ⊔ The original Mountain House was an old stage stop near the junction of Highway 128 and Mountain House Road, dating from 1859. The newest version, a few miles east, is a handsome fieldstone and wood frame New England style inn and winery, surrounded by elaborately landscaped grounds. It has rooms and suites with a mix of early American and modern furnishings in the inn and the winery building, plus cottages with fireplaces, decks and kitchen facilities. The inn has a picnic area and tasting room, plus wine tasting on the terrace when the weather cooperates.

Beyond the lodge, you'll pass the Mountain House Road junction and what's left of the original inn. You'll then whisk through tiny **Yorkville** and enter a rolling mix of oaks, pasturelands and vineyards called Yorkville Highlands. Two small wineries here offer tasting. **Yorkville Cellars** is just beyond town, with an oak-shaded tasting room, daily 11 to 6; (707) 894-9177. A couple of miles beyond, on the left with no vineyards in sight, is the modern barnboard tasting room of **Souzaô Cellars**, open weekends noon to 5; (707) 895-2733.

If you'd like to pause for a picnic or a hushed walk beneath giant *sequoia sempervirens*, turn left onto Fish Rock Road a few miles beyond Yorkville and take the short, twisting drive to **Mailliard Redwoods State Preserve.** Hiking trails wind through old growth redwoods and along the creek-sized Garcia River in this 200-acre refuge.

A few miles beyond the Mailliard Redwoods turnoff, you'll emerge into one of the prettiest rural vales in California. Similar to the Alexander Valley, 25-mile-long Anderson Valley is cradled by tawny, oak thatched hills. Vineyards and pasturelands form a green patchwork quilt on the valley floor and curve upward into the lowlands. Sheltered hollows in the hills harbor lush, silent redwood groves. One of California's most northern vineyard areas, the valley has a cool climate similar that of France's Champagne district, suitable for producing Chardonnay and other whites.

Anchoring the northern end of the Anderson Valley is a town once so sequestered that the people spoke their own language:

## BOONVILLE

**Population: About 1,000**                    **Elevation: 400 feet**

*Bright lighters* find this old country town charming, even though its *codgies* once resented outsiders. Settled in the late nineteenth century, this beautiful valley was a self sustaining farming, ranching and logging region, pretty much cut off from the rest of the world. The insular residents created their own language called *boontling*, generally based on the actions of their neighbors. For instance, Walter Levy was the first person in town to get a telephone so that's what the instrument was called. Lovemaking was called *burlappin'* because a clerk was caught in the act on a pile of burlap sacks in the back of his store.

Few people speak *boontling* today. The town's isolationist attitudes have changed, with the coming of a good highway, wineries, a successful microbrewery, a restored hotel, a few drop-out artists and of course—tourists. The tourists—*bright lighters*—have brought modest affluence to the town and they're no longer resented by the oldtimers—*codgies*—at least not openly. If you'd like a sample of *boontling* you can find dictionaries at curio shops. Or pick up a copy of the *Anderson Valley Advertiser,* an outspoken, off-the-wall publication, despite its innocuous name.

Some of Boonville's isolationist history is preserved in the **Anderson Valley Historical Museum**, northwest of town in an old one-room schoolhouse. Hours are irregular; if the flag is flying from the mast out front, someone's inside.

## RECLINING AND DINING

Two establishments—one old and renovated, one new and trendy—offer good causes to pause in Boonville:

**Boonville Hotel** • *Highway 128 (Box 326), Boonville, CA 95415; (707) 895-2210. Ten units with private baths; continental breakfast; $$$$ to $$$$$. Restaurant serves American regional fare; lunch Friday-Sunday in summer, dinner Wednesday-Monday all year; wine and beer; $$$. MC/VISA.* ☐ Instead of seeking the typically fussy Victorian look, restorers of this 1860 roadhouse created a clean, modern décor with lots of natural woods, wicker chairs and works of local artists on the walls. The art, usually for sale, changes periodically. So does the menu at the restaurant, which definitely has *bahl gorms*—good food. The fare, an American regional-rural mix with southwest accents, might include fettuccine with smoked salmon, grilled curried breast of chicken with chutney and jasmine rice, sliced pork tenderloin with cumin and cilantro, or creative pizza. The lodgings, like the restaurant and public areas, are simply attired. One can choose between cozy rooms in the hotel or a bungalow and studio near a creek.

**Buckhorn Saloon** • *14081 Highway 128, Boonville; (707) 895-BEER. American; beer and wine. Lunch and dinner daily. MC/VISA; $ to $$.* ☐ Look for the large stainless steel brewing tank out front, then step inside this Western-modern place with natural woods and leaded glass accents. Buckhorn is operated by the Anderson Valley Brewing Company, which recently was voted one of the best small breweries in the world. Try a pint of hearty High Rollers or one of the lighter beers, and accompany it with piroshki, teriyaki chicken, fish and chips or other brewpub fare.

The tour route, hilly until now, goes flat as you head into the heart of Anderson Valley, past vineyards and pasturelands. Bike lanes flank both sides of the asphalt; it's a fine place to pedal while enjoying this bucolic setting. Just short of the tiny town of **Philo** is **Indian Creek County Park,** perhaps the nicest campground in the valley. Its well-spaced sites are tucked beneath ancient redwoods. However, the park is a bit snug for large rigs and trailers. It has pit potties and no hookups; **$$**

Touring Anderson Valley wineries is a simple matter, since they're all alongside Highway 128. Beyond Philo, they start coming thick and fast. Start with **Scharffenberger Cellars** tasting room in a prim little cottage on the right, daily 11 to 5; (707) 895-2957. Just ahead is **Brutocao Cellars** in a barnwood style tasting room on the left, daily 10 to 5; (707) 744-1320. If you need picnic provisions to go with your wine—and most of these wineries have picnic areas—pause at **Gowan's Oak Tree**; it's a large country produce market on the left beyond Brutocao.

About half a mile beyond, a left turn will take you to **Hendy Woods State Park,** a mile off the highway. Its large campground has nearly a hundred sites which are shaded mostly with hardwoods and pines, not redwoods. Hiking trails lead from camping areas to a pair of old growth redwood groves. The campgrounds has flush potties and showers, no hookups; **$$$**. For reservations, call (800) 444-PARK; MC/VISA accepted.

Below the Hendy Woods turnoff, you'll arrive at "winery junction," where three vintners are clustered together, although **Edmeades Estate** on the left no longer offers tasting. Across the highway, nicely landscaped **Navarro Vineyards** has a cozy tasting room and an outside deck with views of vines and mountains. It's daily 10 to 6; (707) 895-3686. Just a few grapevines away, the **Greenwood Ridge** tasting room is in an interesting hexagonal structure, surrounded by a deck, picnic tables and ponds; open daily 10 to 6; (707) 895-2002.

The final three wineries appear in rather quick succession. On your left is **Husch Vineyards,** established in 1971 as Anderson Valley's first winery. It has tasting in a funky old "miner's cabin," daily 10 to 5; (707) 895-3216. Just beyond on the right is **Roederer Estate,** in a rustically elegant facility on a knoll above the vineyards, daily 9 to 6; (707) 895-2288. The valley's final facility, briefly down the road and also on the right is **Handley Cellars**. Its tasting room is decorated with African tribal artifacts, colored Mexican carvings and other items from the lady owner's international travels. It's open daily 11 to 6; (707) 895-3876.

Below Handley, you'll leave the wine valley, pass through tiny **Navarro** (sixty-seven people and an old store) and enter an appealing area of second growth redwoods. Many of these younger trees and some old growth groves are within large **Navarro River Redwoods State Park,** which flanks the roadside for the next several miles. Lofty trees form a thick canopy over the highway in this dramatic departure from the Anderson Valley's vinelands and pasturelands. The park flanks the Navarro River, which remains out of sight, although it can be reached by hiking trails. Midway through this elongated redwood preserve is **Paul M. Dimmick Campground,** a nice spot with sites tucked beneath old and new redwoods. It has flush potties, with no showers or hookups; **$$**.

Highway 128 dissolves into State Route 1 near the Navarro River Estuary. After a couple of miles, you'll climb high into the headlands of the Pacific, with seastacks, little cove beaches and crashing surf far below. Your road less traveled has become a highway much used, since this area draws hundreds of thousands of annual visitors.

*A mix of vineyards, rounded hills and an old fashioned split rail fence present a pretty picture in the Anderson Valley.*

Pressing northward toward the end of this tour, you'll encounter three coastal towns in quick succession—**Albion, Little River** and the popular art colony of **Mendocino.** If you want to explore some tidepools or let the surf tickle your toes, pause at the beachside parking area of **Van Damme State Park** between Little River and Mendocino. The park extends far back into a wooded canyon, with hiking trails and campsites; see "Camping" below.

**Photo op:** You may have seen those great photos of Mendocino's New England style buildings and a tall spired church, sitting on the headlands above Mendocino Bay. If you'd like to find a good vantage point for such a photo, make a sharp left turn opposite Comptche Road, just before you cross the highway bridge over Mendocino Bay. Drive a short distance to a shoulder parking area; big RVs and trailers will fit if the spaces aren't taken. Walk back about 150 yards, step through a small gate and follow a "Mendocino public access trail" across a treeless headland. It leads to a bluff and a clear view of that grand little town. Back in your vehicle, continue south and you'll soon return to the highway.

## MENDOCINO

**Population: 1,107**                    **Elevation: 90 feet**

Although it's aswarm with tourists in summer, Mendocino is quite uncrowded and therefore very appealing in the off season. Fall is grand since coastal weather is most stable then; winter's great if you like to storm watch. Even during slack seasons, it's best to avoid this popular destination on weekends.

This little coastal town was established in 1852 as a lumbering and shipping center. A century later, with most of the area mills closed and the shipping business gone, Mendocino went to sleep. In its depression, it had preserved its white clapboard and wood frame buildings and its quaint wooden water towers. Then in 1959, San Francisco art teacher Bill Zaca came for a visit, put money down on an aging Victorian home, quit his job and founded the Mendocino Art Center, which is still active.

The few artists already in town were joined by others. As word of this charming community spread, movie crews came to shoot scenes for *Johnny Belinda, East of Eden* and the *The Russians are Coming! The Russians are Coming!*

Tourists began coming, too, first by the handful and then by the herd. Entrepreneurs bought and spruced up aging Victorians and clapboard business buildings along Main Street. They turned old homes into bed & breakfast inns and storefronts into boutiques and they preserved and stabilized the old water cisterns. To the credit of town fathers and mothers, neon and fast food joints are forbidden. The result is a contrived although attractive Cape Cod look.

---

*RV PARKING ADVISORY* • As you approach town on Main Street, take the first curbside parking you see, for there's not much room in the downtown area. Or continue beyond the brief business district until you find more street parking. However, if you arrive on a summer weekend, plan a long walk back to town.

---

Most of Main Street's buildings are on the north side, providing the setting for those grand photos from across the bay. Two notable structures on the bay side are the tall steepled 1868 **Presbyterian Church,** the town's most famous landmark; and the 1854 Cape Cod saltbox **Ford House.** It contains a museum and a visitor center for **Mendocino Headlands State Park,** whose lands nearly surround the town's peninsular perch. The center exhibits historic photos and relics of Mendocino's days as a logging and shipping center. It's open daily 10 to 4 with a token admission fee; (707) 937-5804.

Another archive, just up from Main Street, is the **Kelley House Historical Museum** at 45007 Albion Street. Surrounded by gardens, this early American home contains more of the town's yesterday memories, open 1 to 4, daily in summer and Friday through Monday the rest of the year; (707) 937-5791. To visit the town's art colony beginnings, stop by the **Mendocino Art Center** at 45200 Little Lake Road between Williams and Kasten; (707) 937-5818. Most of Mendocino's galleries, boutiques and cafés occupy store fronts along Main and parallel Albion and Ukiah streets, one and two blocks north.

If you'd like to explore more of the chubby Mendocino peninsula, go west on Ukiah Street (a block inland and parallel to Main) and keep working seaward across the brushy, treeless moors. It's mostly within **Mendocino Headlands State Park,** a day use area with beach access, picnic areas, hiking trails and such. As you loop the headland and swing inland,

The Presbyterian Church is a noted Mendocino landmark, perched on a headland above gracefully curving Mendocino Bay.

turn left onto Lansing Street; it takes you to pretty little **Agate Cove**, with some nice seastacks and tidepools. This drive will deliver you back to Highway 1 at the north end of Mendocino and into the next chapter.

## DINING
### Mendocino and Albion

*Albion River Inn* ● *Highway 1, Albion; (707) 937-1919. (WEB SITE: www.albionriverinn.com) American; full bar service. Dinner nightly. Major credit cards; $$$* ☐ Perched at cliff's edge, the inn's simply attired dining room offers gorgeous views of the Pacific and the Albion River Estuary. Entrées include ginger-lime prawns, pasta with shittake mushrooms and roasted red peppers, grilled salmon, swordfish and steak.

*Bay View Café* ● *45040 Main St., Mendocino; (707) 937-4197. American-Southwest; full bar service. Breakfast through dinner daily. MC/VISA; $$.* ☐ Some will scoff at our inclusion of what's basically a tourist café. However, this restaurant provides nice views of Mendocino from its second floor dining room and outdoor deck, and it serves palatable food at reasonable prices. The menu tilts toward Southwestern fare, plus 'burgers, an Oriental stir fry and fresh catch of the day.

**Café Beaujolais** • *961 Ukiah Street (Evergreen), Mendocino; (707) 937-5614. (WEB SITE: www.cafebeaujolais.com) American nouveau; wine and beer. Dinner nightly. MC/VISA, DISC; $$$.* □ Mendocino's finest restaurant occupies a nineteenth century Cape Code house with a pleasing view of its own gardens. Once a modest breakfast and lunch café, it has evolved into a trendy dinners-only restaurant with a weekly changing menu of the *nouveau* school. You might find casoullete with duck, ham hocks, pork shoulder and pancetta; bouillabaisse with local fish and shellfish, or chicken with saffron-chanterelle sauce and garlic sautéed cabbage.

**Mendocino Hotel** • *45080 Main St., Mendocino; (707) 937-0511. American; full bar service. Breakfast or brunch through dinner daily. Major credit cards; $$ to $$$.* □ The impeccably restored Mendocino Hotel has two restaurants—one a study in Victorian elegance, the other contemporary and cheerful. The Victorian Room, where dinners are served, is dressed up in beveled glass, leaded glass ceiling inserts, wainscotting and such. The menu offers some creative touches—seafood plate with puff pastry, baked pork chops with apple and candied yam relish, plus prime rib and assorted pastas. The airy Garden Room Bar and Café, with white lattice, natural woods and several resident *ficus benjamima*, serves lighter fare for brunches and lunch.

**MacCallum House Restaurant** • *45020 Albion St., Mendocino; (707) 937-5763. American; full bar service. Dinner nightly and brunch weekends. Major credit cards; $$$.* □ Rivaling the Mendocino Hotel dining room's Victorian splendor, this B&B restaurant features a *nouveau* menu with fresh local organic ingredients. Recent offerings were roasted salmon, caramelized scallops, and duck breast in blackberry sauce. The less formal and less expensive Grey Whale Bar and Café serves lighter yet still creative fare such as salmon tacos and grilled Portobello mushrooms with cheddar cheese on sesame seed buns.

## RECLINING
### Mendocino, Albion and Little River

**Albion River Inn** • *P.O. Box 100 (3790 N. Highway 1), Albion, CA 95410; (800) 479-7944 or (707) 937-1919. (WEB SITE: www.albionriverinn.com) Twenty rooms and suites. Major credit cards; $$$$$.* □ This stylish inn perched on a bluff above the Pacific is dressed in early American elegance with modern touches. Rooms and suites are quite opulent—most with ocean views and many with spa tubs, fireplaces and private decks.

**Heritage House** • *5200 N. Highway 1, Little River, CA 95456; (800) 235-5885 or (707) 937-5885. (WEB SITE: www.innaccess.com/hhi/) Sixty-six rooms and cottages, all with private baths; continental breakfast. MC/VISA; $$$$$.* □ The Mendocino Coast's oldest hideaway resort, the Heritage House started humbly in 1949 with a few guest rooms in a farmhouse. The elaborate Victorian style facility now has intimate units in the main lodge and a scatter of cottages. Many have ocean views, fireplaces, spa tubs and other amenities; furnishings are a mix of antique and contemporary. This grand old resort occupies a 37-acre campus landscaped with lawns, gardens and huge eucalyptus trees.

**Little River Inn** • *7750 N. Highway 1, Little River, CA 95456; (888) 466-5683 or (707) 937-5942. Sixty-five room and cottages; $$$$ to $$$$$. Restaurant serves American fare; breakfast and dinner; full bar service; $$$. Major credit cards.* ☐ Got your clubs? The Little River Inn has a nine-hole golf course, putting and driving ranges, plus a couple of tennis courts. Although most of this 225-acre complex is across the highway from the ocean, many of its units have sea views. The main lodge and outbuildings are prim white Victorians with multi-gabled roofs and gingerbread eves.

**MacCallum House Inn** • *P.O. Box 206 (45020 Albion St.), Mendocino, CA 95460-0206; (800) 609-0492 or (707) 937-2089. (WEB: www.maccallumhouse.com; E-MAIL: machouse@mcn.org) Nineteen rooms and cottages with private baths and continental breakfast. Major credit cards; $$$$$. Restaurant listed above.* ☐ This restored 1882 Victorian estate is in the heart of downtown, yet it's an extensive complex with rooms and suites in the main house, several cottages and a refurbished old barn. Many units have spa tubs, wood stoves or fireplaces and decks. The public areas and rooms are elaborately decorated and furnished with Victorian and American antiques.

**Mendocino Hotel** • *P.O. Box 587 (45080 Main St.), Mendocino, CA 95460; (800) 548-0513 or (707) 937-0511. (WEB SITE: www.mendocino-hotel.com) Fifty-one rooms and suites with TV and phones; some private and some share baths. Restaurants listed above. MC/VISA, AMEX; $$$$ to $$$$$.* ☐ The 1878 Mendocino Hotel was restored beyond its original look a few decades ago, creating an almost overdone study in Victorian splendor. The lobby is particularly gorgeous, worth a peek whether you plan to stay or not. Step inside to admire its dark wood wainscotting, leaded glass, floral drapes and carpeting, and an unusual pewter fireplace. Rooms and suites also are elaborately coiffed.

**Stanford Inn by the Sea** • *P.O. Box 487 (Coast Highway at Comptche-Ukiah Road), Mendocino, CA 95460; (800) 331-8884 or (707) 937-5615. (WEB SITE: stanfordinn.com) Thirty-five rooms and suites with TV movies and refrigerators; full breakfast. Major credit cards; $$$$.* ☐ With elaborate grounds cascading down a coastal slope above the sea, the Stanford Inn is the north coast's most complete retreat. Facilities include beautifully furnished wood-paneled rooms with fireplaces, a year-around pool, sauna and spa and exercise facility. The extensive complex features a small working farm, organic gardens and greenhouses. Guest bicycles are available for exploring Mendocino.

## CAMPING

Two private campgrounds are tucked into the canyon-like estuary of the Albion River and two state park campgrounds occupy wooded canyons flanking Mendocino. Others are in next-door Fort Bragg; see Tour Four.

**Albion River Campground** ● *P.O. Box 217 (in the Albion River estuary), Albion, CA 95410; (707) 937-0606. RV and tent sites; full hookups $$$$. No credit cards.* ☐ Popular with fisherfolk, this campground has close-together unshaded sites on a sandbar of the Albion River. It has showers, fire rings, a mini-mart and access to fishing, boating, clamming and beach walking.

**Schooner's Landing** ● *P.O. Box 218 (in the Albion River estuary), Albion, CA 95410; (707) 937-5707. RV and tent sites; full hookups $$$$. No credit cards.* ☐ Just up the estuary from Albion River Campground, it has similar facilities, including a dock, boat launch and dive shop, plus showers and a nearby mini-mart.

**Russian Gulch State Park** ● *Just north of Mendocino off State Route 1; (707) 937-5804. RV and tent sites; $$$. For campsite reservations, call (800) 444-PARK; MC/VISA accepted.* ☐ Thirty well-spaced sites are tucked into a wooded canyon, with picnic tables and barbecue grills; flush potties and showers. See Tour Four, page 58, for details on other park amenities.

**Van Damme State Park** ● *Just south of Mendocino off State Route 1; (707). RV and tent sites; $$$. For campsite reservations, call (800) 444-PARK; MC/VISA accepted.* ☐ Seventy-two shaded and well-spaced sites occupy a lushly forested canyon just inland from the beach. Facilities include picnic tables, barbecue grills, flush potties and showers. See above for other park offerings.

☺  ☺  ☺

**Where do we go from here?** ● You have two obvious choices and both are pleasant. You can just keep reading and driving into the next chapter, following Highway 1 and then U.S. 101 into the redwoods. Or you can drive south over scenic coastal headlands to Jenner, where you can run Tour One in reverse.

# TRIP PLANNER

**WHEN TO GO** ● The northern end of State Route 1 is less crowded than other coastal routes, except for the Mendocino-Fort Bragg starting point. U.S. 101 freeway on the northern end of this tour can get busy, although we avoid it for the most part. On rare occasions, the twisting route over the Coast Range between Westport and Leggett can be dusted with winter snow, so check on road conditions.

**DRIVING DISTANCE** ● About 140 miles from Fort Bragg to Ferndale.

**RV ADVISORY** ● All of this route is negotiable by large rigs and trailers, although you'll encounter narrow, winding stretches along State Route 1 above Fort Bragg, and on a 22-mile section over the Coast Range to Leggett.

**WHAT YOU'LL SEE** ● Mendocino Botanical Gardens and the Guest House Museum in Fort Bragg; awesome coastal scenery followed by grand groves of coast redwoods; old fashioned tourist gimmicks on the Avenue of the Giants; Benbow Inn near Garberville; Scotia Inn and Scotia Museum; the charming "Victorian village" of Ferndale.

**WHAT TO DO** ● Explore old town in Fort Bragg; ride the "Skunk Trains" between Fort Bragg and Willits; squeeze your vehicle through a drive-through tree in the Redwood Empire; buy a redwood burl and bowl; take a cooling dip in the Eel River; tour the Pacific Lumber Company mill in Scotia; explore the nineteenth century outdoor architectural museum of Ferndale.

**TO BEGIN** ● Head north from Mendocino on State Route 1; see the end of Tour Three.

## Useful contacts

**Ferndale Chamber of Commerce,** P.O. Box 325, Ferndale, CA 95536; (707) 786-4477.

**Fort Bragg-Mendocino Coast Chamber of Commerce,** P.O. Box 1141 (332 N. Main St.), Fort Bragg, CA 95437; (800) 726-2780 or (707) 961-6300. (WEB SITE: www.mendocinocoast.com; E-MAIL: chamber@mcn.org)

**Garberville-Redway Chamber of Commerce,** P.O. Box 445 (773 Redwood Dr.), Garberville, CA 95542; (800) 923-2613 or (707) 923-2613.

## Pricing guidelines

**DINING:** Dinner entrée with soup or salad, without drinks or dessert for under $10 = **$**; $10 to $14 = **$$**; $15 to $25 = **$$$**; over $25 = **$$$$**.

**RECLINING:** A two-person room for $35 or less = **$**; $36 to $50 = **$$**; $51 to $75 = **$$$**; $76 to $100 = **$$$$**; more than $100 = **$$$$$**.

**CAMPING:** Under $10 = **$**; $10 to $14 = **$$**; $15 to $19 = **$$$**; $20 or more = **$$$$**

*Tour Four*

# THE REDWOOD COAST

## *MENDOCINO TO FERNDALE*

It would be more accurate to label this chapter "Redwoods and the Coast," since the two elements do not appear together on this drive. You'll skim along the coast on State Route 1 between Mendocino and Rockport, swing inland to pick up U.S. 101 at Leggett, and then drive through California's largest redwood forest.

Our tour begins where the previous one ended, between charming New England style Mendocino and bustling Fort Bragg. These are hardly places uncrowded. It's a chore to find a parking place in Mendocino on a busy summer weekend, and Fort Bragg is a thriving commercial center with the traffic to prove it. However, once you begin driving north, you'll enter one of the least traveled sections of the California coast. For more than forty scenic miles, you will encounter no community of size, so fuel up in Fort Bragg before you set forth.

Then, after an inland spiral through the Coast Range, you'll leave State Route 1 in Leggett and continue northward on U.S. 101. Again, this is a busily traveled route, although you can escape the freeway and freight trucks by following the legendary Avenue of the Giants through America's largest redwood forest. This was the original highway, then it was preserved as a scenic route after 101 was elevated to freeway status. Although California's redwood forests are popular destinations, the Avenue of the Giants is surprisingly uncrowded. We found little traffic, plenty of lodging vacancies and available campsites on a late summer weekend.

To begin, head briefly north from Mendocino on Highway 1, then go coastward toward **Russian Gulch State Park.** This 1,200 acre preserve stretches from seastacks to inland canyons, with tidepools, a wave-driven cauldron called Devil's Punch Bowl and several campsites; see "Camping" below. Take a loop hike into Russian Gulch Canyon by following the South Trail to a 36-foot waterfall, and then return on the North Trail.

Opposite the entrance to Russian Gulch, turn right onto Point Cabrillo Drive and follow it about two miles inland through a residential area. You'll then dip downward and arrive at **Caspar State Beach**, a tiny sheltered cove with offshore seastacks at the mouth of Caspar Creek. Just beyond, you'll return to Highway 1 and a short drive will take you to **Jughandle State Reserve**, a classic environmental slice of these coastal environs. Gradual

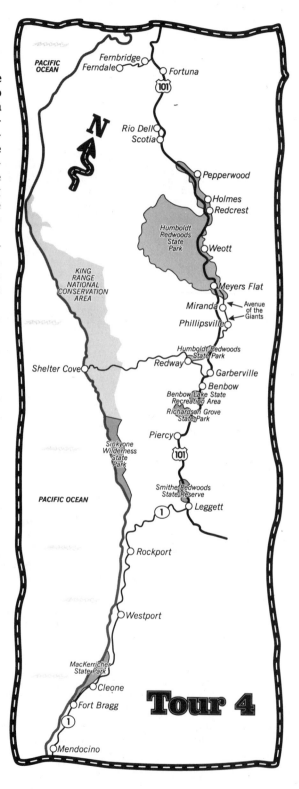

uplifting of the coast has created a series of "Ecological Staircases," each sheltering a different type of flora and fauna. These staircases, about 100 feet high, range from intertidal zones to spruce, pine, fir and redwood forests. This region's main commercial center is just beyond:

## FORT BRAGG

**Population: 6,275** **Elevation: sea level**

In contrast to compact Mendocino, Fort Bragg is rather a sprawl, with the typical suburban string of service stations, motels and strip malls. One's first impression is that of a moderately thriving working folks' town. It's an accurate one, since this has been a lumbering and fishing center for well over a century. Fort Bragg is the largest coastal city between San Francisco and Eureka. It was established in 1857 as an Army fort to herd native people onto the Mendocino Indian Reservation. No trace of the original fort remains.

Although it's primarily a commercial center, Fort Bragg has several elements of interest—a busy old boat basin at the Noyo River estuary, a fine downtown area of restored and often cheerily painted turn-of-the-century buildings, a botanic garden, a museum and the famous "Skunk Trains."

The first item of interest, about to be surrounded by the town's expanding suburbs, is a gathering of blooms and bushes on your left:

***Mendocino Coast Botanical Gardens*** • *18220 N. Highway 1, Fort Bragg, CA 95437; (707) 964-4352. Daily 9 to 5 March through October and 9 to 4 the rest of the year; modest admission charge. Garden-theme gift shop accepts MC/VISA. Gardens Grill Restaurant listed below.* □ This 47-acre island of botany extends from the highway to the sea. The non-profit facility is a complex of blooming plants and native trees, and something's a-bloom nearly every month. The gardens are especially lush from spring to early summer when rhododendrons and fuchsias come to life.

Continuing northward from the gardens, cross a lofty bridge over the estuary, turn right and loop down to **Noyo Harbor**. It's a working waterfront with a large fishing fleet and several fish processing centers. The harbor also has a couple of cafés and fish markets. You can catch deep sea fishing charters and whale watching trips from here; see "Activities" below. If you continue through the boat basin and under the highway bridge, you'll reach the beach at the mouth of the Noyo River, although you'll have to suffer five speed bumps en route.

The best smoked fish down here is sold by **Eureka Fisheries** on your left as you enter the waterfront area. It offers a tasty pepper-spiced smoked salmon, smoked albacore, shrimp and crab cocktails and a good selection fresh fish. You can enjoy your snacks at tables on the porch or on the nearby dock. It's open daily mid-morning to late afternoon; (707) 964-1600. A bit beyond Eureka Fisheries, on your left behind Anchor Lodge, is **The Wharf** a longtime locally popular seafood restaurant; see the "Dining" listing below.

Climb back out of the harbor and continue into the downtown area. The **Chamber of Commerce** is in a storefront on your right, at mid-block between Franklin and Laurel streets. It's open weekdays 9 to 5 and

Saturdays 9 to 3; (707) 961-6300. Across the street, in a large multi-gabled mansion, is the town's archive:

**Guest House Museum** • *343 N. Main Street. No phone; for info, call the chamber. Daily except Monday 10 to 2 in summer and Friday-Sunday 10:30 to 2 the rest of the year. Modest admission fee.* ◻ This imposing all-redwood Victorian mansion was built on the site of the old Fort Bragg Army hospital by lumber baron C.R. Johnson. Some of the rooms have period furnishings; others are busy with artifacts and photos tracing the history of the area.

To see the best of downtown's fine collection of late nineteenth century and early twentieth century buildings, park and then walk in a squared circle, making right turns from Main to Laurel to Franklin to Redwood and back to Main.

---

**RV PARKING ADVISORY** • Parking for long rigs is limited downtown, although you can find curb parking in nearby residential areas.

---

Continue through town for another block and check out the **Fort Bragg Depot Mall.** This large indoor mall has a couple of dozen shops and restaurants, plus several historical exhibits. Immediately beyond is the **North Coast Brewing Company,** with a store on the corner that will interest beer fans. Turn left at that corner and you can catch an excursion train that helped make Fort Bragg famous:

**California Western Railroad** • *100 Laurel Street (P.O. Box 907), Fort Bragg, CA 95437; (800) 77-SKUNK or (707) 964-6371. Round-trip and one way runs between Fort Bragg and Willits on three historic trains; varied schedules and prices.* ◻ In the early days, these log haulers were called the Skunk Trains because they burned a gasoline inefficiently and you could smell 'em a-comin'. Now one of the most popular attractions on the coast, the Cal Western Railroad operates a full-gauge steam train, diesel locomotives and several 1925 to 1935 diesel motor railcars. The trains run along the Noyo River through ancient redwood groves, offering one way or round trips to Willits and shorter round trips to a midpoint.

### ACTIVITIES

**Fishing and whale watching charters** • This is a partial list of charter boats operating out of Noyo Harbor: Anchor Charter Boats, (707) 964-4550; Tally Ho II, (707) 964-2079; and Telstar Charters, (707) 964-8770. Fort Bragg Marine at the harbor sells fishing gear and other things nautical, (707) 964-3310. Contact the chamber of commerce for others.

### DINING

**Egghead's Restaurant** • *326 N. Main St,; (707) 964-5005. American; no alcohol. Breakfast to midafternoon daily. MC/VISA.* ◻ This cute little diner's full name is Egghead Omelettes of Oz. It's worth a skip down the Yellow Brick Road to try one of forty omelette combinations, accompanied by excellent fried potatoes. Lunch fare includes very good 'burgers, quiche, sandwiches, soups and salads.

**Gardens Grill Restaurant** • *At Mendocino Botanical Gardens, 18220 N. Highway 1; (707) 964-7474. American; wine and beer. Lunch Monday-Saturday, dinner Thursday-Sunday, plus Sunday brunch. MC/VISA; $$.* ☐ This attractive dining room with a cheerful New England look serves a variety of American entrées with an emphasis on seafood. Offerings include blackened snapper, seafood pasta and grilled fish of the day. One can dine indoors or on an outside deck with a view of the gardens.

**North Coast Brewing Company** • *444 N. Main St.; (707) 964-3400. (WEB SITE: www.ncoast-brewing.com) American; wine and beer. Lunch and dinner daily except Monday. MC/VISA, DISC; $$.* ☐ The brewery across the street operates this lively beer bistro, with fare matched to its assorted beers, from mild to hearty. It has a good wine list as well. The café comes in two pieces: The Grill has chicken with wild mushrooms, roast pork loin Dijon, grilled salmon and such. Lighter fare issues from the Tap Room, such as quiche, hamburgers, chili and fish and chips. The two dining areas have a typical brewpub look, meaning they're decorated mostly with beer banners. The beers are worth bannering, winners of several international awards. Our favorite is Blue Star, light and a bit fruity and served with a wedge of lemon.

**The Wharf** • *Noyo Harbor at 780 N. Harbor Dr.; (707) 964-4283. American; mostly seafood; full bar service. Lunch and dinner daily. MC/VISA; $$.* ☐ Don't expect any culinary miracles down here, but do expect lots of fresh seafood in this long-established *fishhaus*. It offers a variety of catches of the day, a seafood platter plus a few steaks. Among specialties on the large menu are thick clam chowder, red snapper and petrale sole. The Wharf's floor to ceiling windows provide good views of the boat basin and mouth of the Noyo River.

## LODGING

Fort Bragg has a good assortment of motels; budget-minded Mendocino visitors make the short drive here to save on lodging costs. In addition to all those motels, the town has an interesting inn:

**Grey Whale Inn** • *615 N. Main St. (at First Street), Fort Bragg, CA 95437; (800) 382-7244 or (707) 964-0640. (WEB: greywhaleinn.com; E-MAIL: stay@greywhaleinn.com) Fourteen units with phones, TV and private baths; large continental breakfast. Major credit cards; $$$$ to $$$$$.* ☐ Built in 1914 as a small hospital, the Grey Whale is now a large inn. Its rooms and suites—nicely furnished with early American antiques, wicker and local art—have ocean or town views. Some units have fireplaces and one has a spa tub. Other amenities include a comfortable sitting area and a rec room with a pool table and TV.

## CAMPING

**Caspar Beach RV Park** • *14441 Point Cabrillo Dr., Mendocino, CA 95460; (707) 964-3306. RV and tent sites; full hookups $$$$. MC/VISA, DISC.* ☐ This well-maintained park has 115 sites just across the road from Caspar Beach. It has showers, a coin laundry and large convenience and souvenir mart. Tent sites have fire rings and tables; some are shaded.

**MacKerricher State Park** • *Three miles north of Fort Bragg, off State Route 1; (707) 937-5804. RV and tent sites; $$$. For campsite reservations, call (800) 444-PARK; MC/VISA accepted.* ◻ This large park has 143 sites in four camping areas, with picnic tables, barbecue grills, flush potties and showers. Most sites are well spaced and shaded by pines. See below for other park facilities.

**Russian Gulch State Park** • *Just north of Mendocino off State Route 1; (707) 937-5804. RV and tent sites; $$$. For campsite reservations, call (800) 444-PARK; MC/VISA accepted.* ◻ Thirty well-spaced sites are tucked into a wooded canyon, with picnic tables and barbecue grills; flush potties and showers. See above for other park amenities.

### Along the coast and into the trees

Heading north on Highway 1 from Fort Bragg, you'll soon see the turn-off to **MacKerricher State Park,** one of the larger and more interesting parks on the Mendocino Coast. Although it nudges the suburbs of Fort Bragg, the park itself is rather isolated from civilization—a blend of beaches, woodlands and brushy moors stretching for seven miles along the coast. It has a network of hiking trails including an interesting "interpretive boardwalk" that's well worth a stop. Just beyond Surfside Campground, this quarter-mile wooden sidewalk stretches over grassy moors. Several coastal overlooks have plaques discussing the flora, fauna and human history of the area. The final stop is Laguna Point, where you can watch harbor seals playing in the surf.

Pressing northward, you'll pass what's left of the old town of **Cleone,** once a busy lumber shipping port. (An exhibit on the MacKerricher park boardwalk discusses its earlier days.) The highway swings inland through woods and pasturelands for a few miles, then returns to the coast, where it's notched high into the headlands. Most of the traffic that was buzzing around Mendocino and Fort Bragg will have diminished at this point.

This is a beautiful drive, with vistas of seastacks, scalloped surf dancing into coastal coves and wind-bent pines and cypress crowning high, green headlands. **Westport,** with 238 folks, is a charming old collection of New England style clapboard homes. It's terraced into a headland above the Pacific, like a miniature Mendocino. The business district consists of a shingle-sided country store with a single gas pump. If you'd like to pause for a meal or for the night, you can do so at an 1890 retreat in the middle of town:

**Pelican Lodge and Inn** • *39921 North Highway 1, Westport, CA 95488; (707) 964-5588. Six rooms plus a honeymoon cottage. MC/VISA, DISC; $$$$.* ◻ This restored early American style inn with a false front offers comfortable, simply furnished rooms, a cocktail lounge and dining room. The cozy parlor is particularly appealing, with print wallpaper, wainscotting and a Franklin stove.

Just north of Westport, long and skinny **Westport-Union Landing State Beach** has RV and tent sites on a treeless bluff. The lower section is set back from the sea, although the northern end has a few sites with Pacific vistas. The park has pit potties and no hookups; **$$.**

If you're passing through here in an RV, a large vista point just beyond the state park offers a great lunch stop. You can sidle your rig up to a low railing and enjoy fine views of surf-scalloped coves and seastacks. Then just north of here, the coast suddenly disappears.

The highway swings inland above Westport-Union Landing State Beach and you'll not again see the sea on this route. What lies ahead is a rather wearying twenty-two mile stretch of almost continuous narrow, winding road through the thick forests of the Coast Range. Respite finally arrives in the form of the tiny town of **Leggett,** where State Route 1 disappears into U.S. 101.

---

**RV ADVISORY** ● This route is negotiable by large RVs and trailer rigs, although it has many corkscrew turns and narrow stretches, so drivers will have to stay alert.

---

## Meeting sequoia sempervirens

Although U.S. 101 is called the Redwood Highway the moment it leaves San Francisco, 188 miles south of here, this is the first area where you'll encounter the legendary big trees. These are *sequoia sempervirens,* the coast redwoods. This road was carved through their groves in 1922 with "pickaxes, yarders (small earth movers), shovels and whiskey."

Since their first discovery, redwoods have fascinated Californians, who initially regarded them as botanical novelties or simply a good supply of lumber, instead of the noblest of trees. Hardly had the early Redwood Highway been completed when tourist promoters began converting these grand trees into gimmicks. They built gift shops into their massive trunks and chopped tunnels through them to create "drive-through trees." One entrepreneur hollowed out a giant redwood log to build a "one log house," complete with furnishings. Every gift shop sold redwood burls, which are bark warts that sprout when placed into a bowl with water. Properly, it should be a polished *redwood* bowl.

Surprisingly, little has changed since that first skinny road was pushed between the big trees' trunks. Most of those curio shops are still there, selling their burls and other souvenirs made of redwood. The one log house still draws the curious and two drive-through trees survive. (Others have died from the trauma of being hollowed out.) While visitor attractions elsewhere have evolved into more advanced forms—from rubber monsters to sophisticated robots; from ferris wheels to multi-axis thrill rides—Redwood Highway tourist gimmicks have remained archaic and therefore kind of charming.

A grand hew and cry arose a few decades ago when Highway 101 through the redwoods was enlarged into a freeway. However, several miles of the original route north of Garberville were preserved and designated as the Avenue of the Giants. With trucks banished to the freeway and most other vehicles preferring this faster route, the original highway is even more peaceful now than it was before. Much of it passes through California's largest big tree preserve, Humboldt Redwoods State Park.

*"Ya gotta have a gimmick!" The Redwood Empire still has many old fashioned tourist attractions such as the Drive Thru Tree near Leggett.*

Having merged from Highway 1 to 101, you can start your redwoods exploration with a classic gimmick. Before continuing north, turn south toward Leggett and drive through town to **Drive Thru Tree Park.** Within a 200-acre redwood grove stands the Chandelier Tree, 315-feet high, twenty-one feet in diameter and with a six by six-foot hole chopped through it. The tree is older than Christ but presumably younger than God. After driving through it—don't try this in an RV—you can buy your burl at a large gift shop and wander about the grounds, which are quite pleasant. There's a small fee to enter the park, which was opened the year the highway was completed—1922.

Passing back through Leggett—which has a couple each of cafés, service stations and motels—press northward on Highway 101, which isn't yet a freeway. It follows the course of the South Fork Eel River, alternately dipping into shady redwood groves and then emerging into bright bankside sunshine. You'll encounter your first redwood state park immediately north of Leggett:

**Standish-Hickey State Recreation Area** ● *North Highway 101; (707) 925-6482. RV and tent sites; no hookups; $$$. For campsite reservations, call (800) 444-PARK; MC/VISA accepted.* ❑ This park has three camping areas among hardwoods, pines and some second growth redwoods alongside the Eel River. Campgrounds have flush potties, coin showers and no hookups. Short trails lead to the river, which is relatively tame and suitable for swimming.

Just above Standish-Hickey, don't fail to miss **Confusion Hill,** one of those early day tourist gimmicks that's still drawing 'em in. Not concerned with redwoods, this attraction focuses on an old shack that slid off its foundation in an area of apparently strong magnetic force. Inside the tilted shack, people appear to lean at funny angles. There are modest fees for visiting this "Gravity House" and for a 15-minute train ride through the redwoods. The most interesting things here are some nice redwood trunk carvings out front, including a three-tiered clown bear totem.

A bit farther along and on the right is the **Grandfather Tree**, yet another statistic-laden redwood. It's part of a nicely landscaped complex with a large gift shop and snack bar. There's more camping and an historic lodge in a state park just beyond:

**Richardson Grove State Park** ● *North Highway 101; (707) 247-3318 or (707) 946-2311. RV and tent sites, no hookups; $$$. For campsite reservations, call (800) 444-PARK; MC/VISA accepted.* ☐ Although it's unfortunately close to the busy highway, Richardson Grove has some nice sites under ancient redwoods, with flush potties and showers. The park also contains an historic redwood lodge, now a store and visitor center with a few interpretive exhibits, including a nice wildlife diorama. This grove of ancient trees is a pleasant place to picnic and you can get fixin's at the store. Sprouting between the store and visitor center is one of the tallest redwoods in California, reaching 344 feet.

North of Richardson, as Highway 101 becomes a full scale freeway, take the Benbow Drive exit and travel alongside the Eel River to three quite different places to stay and play. The first appears after about three miles and the others are a mile or so further:

**Benbow Lake State Recreation Area** ● *Benbow Drive; (707) 247-3318. RV and tent sites $$$; hookups $$$$. For campsite reservations, call (800) 444-PARK; MC/VISA accepted.* ☐ One of the few state parks with RV hookups, Benbow Lake SRA stretches along a calm section of the Eel, providing safe places for the kids to swim and splash. Some of the sites are near the stream; others are within rumbling distance of Highway 101, so be selective. An upper section of the recreation area, opposite Benbow Inn, has a grassy picnic area on a small lake.

**Benbow Valley RV Resort and Golf Course** ● *7000 Benbow Dr., Garberville, CA 95542; (707) 923-2777. (WEB SITE: www.campgrounds.com/benbow) RVs only; full hookups $$$$. MC/VISA.* ☐ If you want to rough it in style—particularly if you're a hacker—this well-groomed resort has a nine-hole golf course, swimming pool, rec room, showers, coin laundry and a playground. Grassy sites have young trees that promise future shade.

**Benbow Inn** ● *445 Lake Benbow Dr., Garberville, CA 95542; (800) 355-3301 or (707) 923-2124. (WEB SITE: www.benbowinn.com; E-MAIL: benbow@benbowinn.com) Fifty-five units with phones; some TV, VCRs and refrigerators; $$$$$. Restaurant serves American regional fare; breakfast and lunch Monday-Saturday plus Sunday brunch and dinner nightly; breakfast and dinner only in the off-season; $$$. Major credit cards.* ☐ Splendidly restored, this grand Tudor style inn surrounded by formal gardens is the most elegant lodging on the north coast. Even if you don't plan to dine or sleep, step into its opulent lobby to admire the heavy beam ceiling, half-timbered stucco walls and grand fireplace rimmed by overstuffed furniture. All rooms are nicely decorated; some have fireplaces, spa tubs and private patios. The elegant dining room provides views of the Eel River or of manicured gardens and you can sup amidst Elizabethan splendor or on an outside deck. The changing menu may offer fare such as grilled mahi mahi, salmon filet, farm trout *julienne* or braised lamb shank.

# GARBERVILLE

**Population: about 2,500**                    **Elevation: 533 feet**

At first glance, Garberville seems to consist mostly of low-rise businesses, service stations and motels. However, a Sixties counter-culture lurks harmlessly beneath the surface of this rather conservative appearing town. The surrounding forests once sheltered major marijuana farms. Some of this industry's alternative lifestyle attitudes are still reflected in the young people about town, with their ponytails, multiple earrings and tie-dyed T-shirts.

To learn more about the area (but not about the dope crop), stop at the **Garberville-Redway Chamber of Commerce**. It's in a small mall called Jacob Garber Square, on your right downtown. Hours are 9 to 5, daily in summer and weekdays only the rest of the year; (707) 923-2613.

## DINING

*Calico's* • *808 Redwood Dr. (adjacent to Sherwood Forest Motel); (707) 923-2253. American-Italian-Mexican; wine and beer. Lunch and dinner daily; $.* ☐ Where have all the Garberville flower children gone? You'll find many of them at Calico's, a spirited little Sixties style walk-up that features homemade pastas, 'burgers, assorted other sandwiches and a few Mexican dishes. You can sit inside this split-level diner or adjourn to sidewalk tables.

*Sicilito's* • *445 Conger Lane (a block east of Redwood Drive at Conger and Locust); (707) 923-2814. Italian and Mexican; wine and beer. Lunch and dinner daily. MC/VISA, DISC; $$.* ☐ Housed in a tin-roofed false front, this charming café is busily dressed in old advertising posters, license plates and other regalia. Its menu wanders from Parmesan chicken, pizzas and pastas to spicy steak ranchero.

*Woodrose Café* • *911 Redwood Dr., (707) 923-3191. American; wine and beer. Breakfast daily, lunch weekdays. No credit cards; $.* ☐ Like Calico's, Woodrose is a back to the Sixties hangout, with indoor and patio dining. The menu tilts toward Haight-Ashbury—organic fare such as granola, fruit smoothies and thick vegetarian soups. The sourdough garlic bread is excellent.

## Side trip: The Lost Coast

If you head west through Redway north of Garberville, you'll travel a twisting twenty-five miles to the small planned coastal community of **Shelter Cove**. It's in the heart of an area known as the **Lost Coast**, so-called because it's isolated by the inland detours of highways 1 and 101.

This is one of California's most remote regions—65,000 acres of rock-studded mountains, high grasslands, hidden redwood groves and forty miles of wilderness beach. The Bureau of Land Management's **King Range National Conservation Area** and **Sinkyone Wilderness State Park** occupy much of this wild region. If you'd like to learn more about it, contact the Bureau of Land Management, 555 Leslie St., Ukiah, CA 95482, (707) 462-3873; or Sinkyone Wilderness, P.O. Box 245, White-horn, CA 95989, (707) 986-7711.

The drive to Shelter Cove is interesting if not awesome, passing through a mix of rock studded grasslands and pine forests. The rockbound wilderness coast, which harbors seal and sea lion herds, tidepools and un-tracked beaches, *is* awesome. However, most of these areas can be reached by trail only. A narrow road, much of it rough and unpaved, will take you to coastal ramparts of the Sinkyone Wilderness.

If you'd like to stay the night in Shelter Cove, it offers a nice hideaway:

**Shelter Cove Ocean Inn** ● *148 Dolphin Dr., Shelter Cove, CA 95589; (707) 986-7161. Four units with private baths; full breakfast. Major credit cards; $$$$ to $$$$$.* ☐ Sitting just above the beach, this attractive Victorian style bed & breakfast has two rooms and two suites, all with ocean views. The beach, a golf course and a small landing strip are within walking distance. In addition to breakfast, guests can arrange for lunch and dinner for a fee.

---

**RV ADVISORY** ● The road to Shelter Cove, while troublesome with its tight twists and turns, is negotiable by large rigs. Most of the roads into the wilderness areas are dirt and mud, suitable to four-wheel drive vehicles only.

---

## The Avenue of the Giants

North of Garberville, you finally can escape busy U.S. 101 and enter the eternal twilight of thick redwood forests. The Avenue of the Giants winds lazily through the big trees for the next thirty-five miles. Early road builders removed as few redwoods as possible and the slender highway nearly brushes the trunks of many. Most of this route is contained within a huge state reserve:

**Humboldt Redwoods State Park** ● *P.O. Box 100, Weott, CA 95771; (707) 946-2409. Developed campsites at Albee Creek, Burlington and Hidden Springs campgrounds, all with flush potties and showers; no hookups; $$$. For campsite reservations, call (800) 444-PARK; MC/VISA accepted. In addition, there are several undeveloped camping areas include hike-in campgrounds.* ☐ Humboldt is the state's largest redwood preserve, covering 50,000 acres, of which 17,000 are old growth trees. The park contains several hiking trails and short nature walks, plus a fine visitor center about midway through the Avenue of the Giants.

To catch the scenic drive's lower end—and to enter Humboldt Redwoods State Park—take the Phillipsville exit. Immediately after leaving

*Filtered sunlight paints a classic scene in the Founders Grove at Humboldt Redwoods State Park.*

the freeway, pause at an informational sign that points out the highlights of this drive. You can pick up an *Avenue of the Giants Auto Tour* brochure from a pamphlet box here.

The next thirty-five lazily winding miles will carry you into redwood groves so thick that only occasional shards of sunlight can penetrate. You'll then emerge blinking into the sunlight, generally alongside the Eel River and often with that busy freeway on the opposite bank. A string of small towns through here provide the same things—curio shops, service stations, small motels and redwood gimmicks.

The **Living Chimney Tree** near Phillipsville is a burned-out redwood stump fused into a small shop and café. Farther along is the **Famous One Log House** in Miranda, built in 1946 as a tourist gimmick with a tiny kitchen, living room and two-bunk bedroom. The Redwood Empire's second surviving **Drive-Thru Tree** is near Meyers Flat, with a gift shop and café.

Lest you fear that the Avenue of the Giants is a constant parade of gimmicks, it isn't. Between these novelties are hushed redwood groves and sunny, inviting stretches of the Eel River. Between Myers Flat and Weott, pause at the **Humboldt State Park Visitor Center** where you can learn everything you ever wanted to know about *sequoia sempervirens.* The center is open daily from 9; closing hours vary with the seasons. Several hiking trails and a nature walk begin here.

To get the feel of the height and immensity of these trees, take a hike in one of the groves. A good one is the **Founders Grove,** just north of Weott. It was named for founders of the Save-the-Redwoods League, established in 1918 to help save these noble trees from woodsmen's axes.

Just beyond the Founders Grove turnoff, a left turn from Avenue of the Giants takes you under the freeway and through the **Rockefeller Forest,** the largest grove in the state park. After four miles, turn left into a parking area where short trails lead to various "personality trees." Star of the show is the Giant Tree, one of the tallest in America at 363 feet.

---

**RV ADVISORY** ● The route through the Rockefeller Forest is a bit of a squeeze for big rigs, although they can make it through. Drivers will have to pause occasionally to let oncoming vehicles slip past.

---

Back on the main route, Avenue of the Giants ends just beyond Pepperwood and you'll emerge—perhaps reluctantly—onto the freeway. Go north briefly and then take the Scotia/Rio Dell exit.

At a stop sign, turn left toward **Scotia,** the impeccably groomed company town of the Pacific Lumber Company. This is the world's largest chopper-downer of redwoods, although the original company owners actually preserved several old growth groves. A new management, which took over in 1985, seems less sensitive to preservation, which has brought cries of dismay from environmentalists. However, an agreement signed in late 1998 brought several thousand acres of the company's groves under government protection. Pacific Lumber established the town of Scotia in the 1880s, originally calling it Forestville. It's one of the few wholly-owned company towns left in America.

One reason Scotia has that neat-as-a-pin look is because much of it was destroyed by a 1992 fire and had to be rebuilt. Particularly appealing is a new all-redwood multi-gabled shopping complex. The town smells of fresh cut wood, since its huge sawmill is just beyond the small business district. Tours can be arranged at the museum-visitor center (below). Two Scotia attractions are definitely worth a look:

**Scotia Inn** ● *100 Main St., Scotia, CA 95565; (707) 764-5683. Fifteen rooms and suites with private baths phones; TVs available; continental breakfast; $$$$ to $$$$$. The dining room serves American fare; lunch weekdays and dinner Wednesday-Sunday; $$$. The less formal Bar and Grill serves lighter entrées; lunch and dinner daily; $$. MC/VISA, DISC.* ◻ This splendid redwood structure features a baronial lobby with laminated columns holding up a deeply coffered ceiling. The dining room is a study in nineteenth century finery with wood paneling, tulip chandeliers and maple furniture. Except for that maple, the inn is constructed entirely of redwood. Never actually restored, it has been flawlessly maintained since its completion in 1886 as a home for company officials. It was expanded into an inn two years later.

*Scotia Museum and Visitor Center* • *Main and B streets (just beyond Scotia Inn); (707) 764-2222. Open weekdays 8 to 4:30 Memorial Day to Labor Day only. Mill tours can be arranged here between 8 and 2 on weekdays.* ☐ Formerly a bank building, this structure has classic Greek lines, from massive columns to pediments—and they're all made of redwood. Inside, exhibits focus on the history of the Pacific Lumber Company, logging techniques and redwood products past and present. An old steam engine and steam donkeys (stationery engines used in logging) occupy the carefully groomed museum grounds.

There's nothing interesting in Rio Dell despite its pretty name, so return to the freeway from Scotia and head north past **Fortuna.** It also offers no tourist lures, although it's a good provisioning point, with several inexpensive motels. At the "Ferndale/Fernbridge" exit, head west to a place that's definitely alluring:

## FERNDALE

**Population: 1,430**                    **Elevation: 30 feet**

This Eel River Valley community was founded in 1852 by a pair of Vermonters, then Danish emigrants came to establish a prosperous dairy industry. Through the decades, the town was bypassed by progress while nearby Eureka and Scotia prospered as lumbering centers. Thus, little was changed in its downtown New England style stores and its neighborhood Victorian homes.

In recent years, tourists have discovered the place and preservation—not change—has become the keyword. The town attracts just enough visitors stop by to keep its few shops and cafés busy, but not enough to tempt the creation of tourist gimmicks.

As you enter Ferndale, note the spired 1881 **First Congregational Church** on your left at Main and Lewis Avenue, with a squared bell tower topped by a witch's hat spire. Continue on Main to Shaw, turn right and drive a block to the **Ferndale Museum** occupying an old false front building on your right. It has several rooms with period furnishings, plus the usual pioneer memorabilia and photos. It's open Tuesday-Saturday 11 to 4 and Sunday noon to 4 in summer, with shorter hours the rest of the year; (707) 786-4466.

Return to Main Street, drive another block and pause to check out the cute quarter-scale model of a Victorian home on display at Main and Washington. It was built by local resident Troy Lawn for an auction to raise funds for charity. Townfolk liked it so well that they bought it back from the winner. To see more of the town's historic treasures, pick up a souvenir edition of the *Ferndale Enterprise* available at shops and cafés.

### DINING

*Curley's Grill* • *460 Main St.; (707) 786-9696. American; wine and beer. Lunch and dinner daily. MC/VISA; $$.* ☐ Housed in a green false front once occupied by the phone company, this is a cozy little box of a café with walls adorned by local art. The creative dinner menu wanders from babyback ribs and roast pork loin with rosemary honey glaze to prawns in sherry and garlic.

*Hotel Ivanhoe* • *315 Main St.; (707) 786-9000. Italian; full bar service. Dinner nightly except Monday. MC/VISA; $$.* ⊓ This 1870 two-story board and batten balconied hotel houses the town's liveliest café. The dining room is nineteenth century casual while the bar is more elaborately decorated. Entrées are ample and typical—chicken Marsala and cacciatore, gnocchi, scampi and seafood fettuccini.

For quick bites, try the **Eureka Baking Company** at 543 Main, serving specialty coffees, baked goods, soups and sandwiches from breakfast through late afternoon. Another choice is the appealing little **Stage Door Café** in a wing of the old fashioned town theater at 451 Main, serving bagels, sandwiches, salads, soups and other light fare from breakfast through late afternoon.

## RECLINING

*The Gingerbread Mansion* • *P.O. Box 40 (400 Berding St.), Ferndale, CA 95536; (800) 952-4136 or (707) 786-4000. (WEB SITE: www.gingerbread-mansion.com; E-MAIL: kenn@humboldtl.com) Eleven rooms with private baths; full breakfast. MC/VISA, AMEX; $$$$$.* ⊓ Large and incredibly ornate, this three-story 1899 Queen Anne beauty is a study in Victorian filigree and finery. Its rooms and suites are busy with floral patterns, marble accents and other frills. Some have fireplaces and clawfoot tubs. Breakfast is served in a formal dining area overlooking a carefully groomed English garden. The inn is furnished with museum quality Victorian antiques.

*Hotel Ivanhoe* • *315 Main St., Ferndale, CA 95536; (707) 786-9000.* ⊓ When we last passed through, the hotel was preparing ten modestly priced guest rooms. It may be ready for occupancy by the time you arrive.

*Shaw House B&B Inn* • *P.O. Box 1125 (703 Main St.), Ferndale, CA 95536; (800) 557-SHAW or (707) 786-9958. (WEB: www.humboldt1.com/~shawhse; E-MAIL: shawhse@humboldt1.com) Seven units with private baths; full breakfast. MC/VISA, AMEX; $$$$$.* ⊓ Sitting primly behind elaborate gardens, this gorgeous filigreed Gothic home is the oldest in Ferndale, built by town founder Seth Louis Shaw in 1854. The interior décor is lavish—almost overdone—with wainscotting, lots of Victorian filigree and floral carpeting and wallpaper. Guest rooms and common areas are furnished with Victorian and early American antiques.

☺ ☺ ☺

*Where do we go from here?* • You can continue north on Highway 101 through Eureka and Arcata, then turn east on State Route 299 and run Tour Five in reverse. Or go east on 299 and then north from Willow Creek on State Route 96 for Tour Six.

To reach Interstate 5, head east on State Route 36, which branches from U.S. 101 between Fortuna and Rio Del. It offers no specific lures, although it's a pleasant if very twisting ramble through dairy valleys, mountain passes and high meadows, finally joining I-5 at Red Bluff. Drivers of large RVs and trailer rigs may find the many twists and turns to be a bother, although the route's all paved.

# TRIP PLANNER

**WHEN TO GO** ● Summer is the best time for this route because many of the museums and restaurants cut back on their hours or close the rest of the year. When we last checked, Shasta State Historic Park and some of the area restaurants were open only Wednesday through Sunday, so take that into account as well. Summer weekends can get busy around the Redding to Whiskeytown Lake area, although crowds thin out considerably beyond Whiskeytown.

**DRIVING DISTANCE** ● About 150 miles, including side trips to French Gulch, Lewiston and Trinity Lake.

**RV ADVISORY** ● The curves and slopes and relatively gentle on most of this drive. A couple of summit climbs get rather twisty, although they can be handled by any size rig.

**WHAT YOU'LL SEE** ● The historic mining towns of Shasta, French Gulch, Lewiston and Weaverville; Whiskeytown and Trinity lakes; striking Trinity River Gorge; and some fine wilderness views.

**WHAT TO DO** ● Play on the lakes; sip suds in the wildly decorated saloon in French Gulch; tour the Weaverville Joss House; go tubing, fishing or whitewater rafting on the Trinity River.

**TO BEGIN** ● Get to Redding and head west on Highway 299.

## Useful contacts

**Greater Redding Chamber of Commerce,** 777 Auditorium Dr., Redding, CA 96001; (800) 874-7562 or (530) 225-4100.

**Trinity County Chamber of Commerce,** P.O. Box 517, Weaverville, CA 96093; (800) 487-4648 or (530) 623-6101.

**Willow Creek Chamber of Commerce,** P.O. Box 704 (Highway 299-96 junction), Willow Creek, CA 95573; (530) 629-2693.

## Pricing guidelines

**DINING:** Dinner entrée with soup or salad, without drinks or dessert for under $10 = **$**; $10 to $14 = **$$**; $15 to $25 = **$$$**; over $25 = **$$$$**.

**RECLINING:** A two-person room for $35 or less = **$**; $36 to $50 = **$$**; $51 to $75 = **$$$**; $76 to $100 = **$$$$**; more than $100 = **$$$$$**.

**CAMPING:** Under $10 = **$**; $10 to $14 = **$$**; $15 to $19 = **$$$**; $20 or more = **$$$$**

FRENCH GULCH

← 3 MILES

HISTORICAL LANDMARK NO. 16

*Tour Five*

# THE TRINITY ROUTE
## *REDDING TO ARCATA ON HIGHWAY 299*

**N**o matter which direction you run it, you may wonder if the Trinity Highway between Redding and Arcata is a road less traveled, for it begins and ends as a freeway. However, within a mile or two, it tapers to two lanes, sheds local traffic and wanders blissfully through wooded hills, passing a major reservoir and two historic mining towns.

For much of route, it follows the Trinity River that has scoured its way through the Klamath Mountains and the Coast Range. It's a favorite stream for boating, tubing and fishing, and the route has been designated as a National Scenic Byway.

After you leave Redding, the freeway portion of Highway 299 ends within a mile to become a surface street. It does a right and left turn stutter-step through the downtown area, then it heads for the suburbs. If you take this drive on a summer weekend, you'll fall in step with lots of boat trailers. However, you'll lose most of them beyond the popular Whiskeytown Lake Recreation Area, about ten miles from Redding.

After you're freed from Redding's suburbs, you'll enter a dry region of brush and oaks, then a few conifers will appear as you begin a gradual climb toward the remnants of an old mining town.

**Shasta State Historic Park** • *P.O. Box 2430, Shasta, CA 96087;*
*(530) 243-8194. Visitor center open Wednesday-Sunday 10 to 5; modest ad-*
*mission fee. Litsch General Store open June through August only, Wednes-*
*day-Sunday 10 to 4.* ☐

*Oh! The bloom of the flowers I remember,*
*And the smiles I shall nevermore see;*
*For the cold chilly winds of December,*
*Stole my flowers, my companions, from me.*

Thus sang John Baker in 1874 as he stood on the scaffold behind the
Shasta County courthouse, hang noose around his neck. He sung as many
verses as he could remember—which was quite a few—trying to stall his
execution for murder.

Things have calmed considerably since Shasta was a large and rowdy
trading center for a gold producing area in the 1850s. That courthouse has
become a museum and the centerpiece for Shasta State Historic Park. It
offers an interesting mix of pioneer artifacts, old jail cells and a rebuilt
version of the gallows out back. Perhaps more interesting, a couple of
blocks down the road, is the 1893 Litsch General Store, one of the most
completely stocked such stores in America. Its shelves are laden with
canned goods, harnesses, hurricane lamps, syrup sold from kegs, and
Hosteter's Stomach Waters, in case you eat too many goodies from next-
door Blumb's Bakery. (Just kidding; nothing in the store is for sale. However, Blumb's is a regular bakery, open Friday-Monday 9 to 4.)

Between the museum and general store are the brick and masonry
shells of several other buildings. However, Shasta isn't a total ghost town;
about 750 people live in the area. Beyond Shasta, you'll climb into greener
hill country and shortly arrive at the place that takes away most of the
Trinity Highway's traffic:

**Whiskeytown National Recreation Area** • *P.O. Box 188, Whis-*
*keytown, CA 96095; (530) 246-1225. Moderate day use fee. Campsites for*
*RVs and tents are located at Oak Bottom, with showers, swimming beach*
*and a marina, and Brandy Creek, with flush potties and water; $$.* ☐
Named for an old mining camp, Whiskeytown is one of three large reser-
voirs of the Whiskeytown-Shasta-Trinity National Recreation Area, which
sprawls over much of north central California.

With its wooded shoreline, Whiskeytown could pass for a natural lake,
particularly after an *El Niño* year covers the reservoir's tell-tale bathtub
ring. The larger reservoir is popular for boating, fishing and swimming
and if you'd like to partake, you'll find the main visitor center on your left,
just off the highway. A short drive from here will take you along the lake-
shore and across the earth and rockfill dam, which of course spoils the il-
lusion of an alpine lake.

Back on The Trinity Highway, you'll skirt the north shore of the lake
and cross an arm of it on a low bridge. Just beyond that crossing, a right
turn will take you to **Whiskeytown,** although there's nothing left except
a post office and general store. There's a good reason for this; the rest of
Whiskeytown is beneath the reservoir.

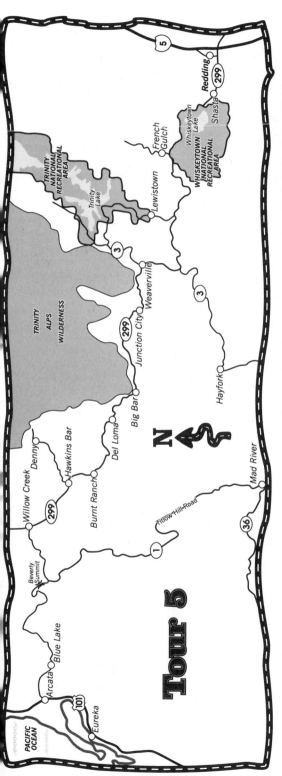

To explore an old mining town of considerably more substance, turn right onto Trinity Mountain Road five miles beyond Whiskeytown and follow it three miles to **French Gulch.** Bypassed by most travelers, this is a particularly appealing old mining camp—a gathering of wood frame and false front buildings dozing under the shade of ancient locust trees. This place is so enticing, you might want to stay awhile:

● ***French Gulch Hotel*** *P.O. Box 249 (14138 Main St.), French Gulch, CA 96033; (530) 359-2112. Eight units, private or share baths; full breakfast; $$$ to $$$$. Restaurant serves American fare, dinner Thursday-Saturday and Sunday brunch; $$. MC/VISA.* ☐ This weathered 1885 false front hotel is undergoing restoration by new owners, who operate it as a bed & breakfast. They've fixed up the rooms, which are simple but spotless. Most have wash basins, with down-the-hall-bath facilities, although the cozy bridal suite has its own bath. The appealing French Gulch Restaurant is decorated with old advertising posters, framed magazine covers and a early day artifacts. Among the menu items are chicken teriyaki, chicken fried steak, grilled pork chops and such.

If the French Gulch Hotel is early-American modest, **Bernice's Saloon** across the street is absolutely wild—not in patronage, but in décor. Housed in the 1854 E. Franck and Company Building, this classic Western style bar is jammed with pioneer relics, old posters, a large gun collection and—whazzis?—Playboy centerfolds. Check out a blow-up photo that appears to be Jackie Kennedy-Onassis, wearing no more than the Playboy bunnies. The ceiling is peppered with paper money and if you want to know how it all got up there, give the barkeep a dollar bill. There's a pool table here, usually occupied by good old boys in truckers hats who politely ignore the occasional tourist who walks in.

French Gulch was founded by French miners in 1849 and yielded $20 million in bullion. California's first stamp mills, used to crush the ore for processing, were operated near here.

Just beyond the French Gulch turnoff, Highway 299 begins a steep upward spiral to 3,213-foot Duckhorn Summit. After twisting down the other side, turn right onto Trinity Dam Boulevard at the "Trinity Lake and Dam" sign. Not a boulevard, it's an ordinary two-lane road that lazily winds through the woods, with no civilization in sight.

About the time you think you're safely lost in the wilderness, you'll encounter the old town of **Lewiston.** It's off to your left, with a fair collection of nineteenth century structures. Ignore the first turnoff, Texas Street, and continue another mile or so the "Lewiston Hotel" and "Historic district" signs. You'll shortly encounter the wonderfully cluttered—inside and out—**Country Peddler** antique and gift shop in a battered, corrugated roof cottage. It's more of an over-filled museum than an antique store; you'll enjoy it even if you aren't into collecting. Nearby is the turn-of-the-century steel **Lewiston Bridge,** recently restored to its original look.

The Country Peddler is at the intersection of Turnpike and Deadwood, and a right turn onto Deadwood will deliver you to places to eat and sleep and—a bit beyond—an RV park.

### RECLINING, DINING AND CAMPING

**Old Lewiston Inn Bed & Breakfast ●** *P.O. Box 688, Lewiston, CA 96052; (800) 286-4441 or (530) 778-3385. (WEB SITE: www.oldlewiston-inn.com; E-MAIL: nixons@snowcrest.com) Seven units; some private and some share baths; full breakfast. MC/VISA; $$$$.* ❑ This 1875 early American style inn sits contentedly behind a white picket fence, with rooms in an false front building and an adjoining cottage. If you'd like to sleep where a U.S. president once snoozed, ask for the Herbert Hoover Room. Units in the original inns have decks overlooking the Trinity River, and your hosts can give you a couple of fishing tips.

**Lewiston Hotel ●** *Deadwood Road; (530) 778-3823. American; full bar service. Dinner Thursday-Sunday. MC/VISA, DISC; $$.* ❑ The Lewiston Hotel's dining room appears to have been decorated by leftovers from the Country Peddler. You can pass the time studying the busily draped walls in this early American style restaurant while waiting for your steak, prime rib, fish of the day or pasta to arrive.

**River Oaks Resort ●** *Deadwood Road, Lewiston, CA 96052; (530) 778-3728. RV and tent sites; full hookups $$$.* ❑ This mobile home park,

*Yesterday gas pumps decorate the front of the Country Peddler in Lewiston. There's much more to see inside.*

alongside the Trinity River just beyond Lewiston's historic district, has thirty RV and tent sites. Facilities include showers, coin laundry, minimart, badminton, volleyball and horseshoes. The adjacent stream offers fishing, swimming and boating.

If you remain on Deadwood Road, you'll shortly blend back onto Trinity Dam Boulevard. It follows the Trinity River to the second major recreation area on this tour:

**Trinity National Recreation Area** • *C/o Weaverville Ranger District, P.O. Box 1190, Weaverville, CA 96093; (530) 623-2121. Campsites for RVs and tents are located at Mary Smith, Copper Gulch and Ackerman along this route; $$; plus the privately operated Lakeview Terrace listed below.* ☐ Like other elements of the NRA, the Trinity unit—which contains two lakes—appeals mostly to fisherfolks, boaters and waterskiers. Even if you're none of the above, this is still a very scenic drive.

You'll first encounter Lewiston Lake, a slender, deep aquamarine appendage below Trinity Lake. Rimmed by thick woods, it gets very little boat traffic and it's a nice place to drop in a canoe or kayak. A good place for camping and kayaking is tiny Copper Gulch Campground, which has sites down near the water.

Just beyond Copper Gulch is a pleasant pine and oak-shaded commercial resort with modest priced cabins and RV hookups:

**Lakeview Terrace** ● *HC01, Box 250, Lewiston, CA 96052; (800) 291-0308 or (530) 778-3803. (WEB: www.campgrounds.com/lakeview) Cabins $$$ to $$$$; RV sites with hookups $$$; no tents.* ⊡ Aptly named, this family resort is terraced into a wooded slope, across the road from Lewiston Lake. It has simple furnished cabins, several RV sites, a swimming pool, picnic tables and barbecue areas. (From mid-June through August, cabins are available only as weekly rentals.)

Continuing north into the recreation area, you'll pass through lakeside **Pine Cove Marina,** which has boat rentals, a launch ramp, fishing gear and such. It could be attractive except an ugly mobile home park disrupts any illusion of a pristine mountain lake. Just beyond, you'll see the imposing wedge of the earthfill **Trinity Dam.** The highway climbs the dam's left shoulder and travels alongside **Trinity Lake,** which is much larger, wider and busier than Lewiston Lake. The route curves through an armpit of this multi-tentacled reservoir and then heads south to connect with State Route 3.

If you want to get serious about playing in Trinity Lake, drive north on Highway 3 and you'll find more extensive facilities. Most are between here and **Trinity Center**, about fifteen miles north. Otherwise, go south through thick woodlands to a former mining town that once made national headlines over a stoplight.

## WEAVERVILLE

**Population: 3,500**                                    **Elevation: 2,045 feet**

Exceptionally appealing with its old brick and masonry storefronts lazing beneath huge trees, Weaverville seems smaller than its claimed population. The downtown area is only a couple of blocks long, and the town doesn't have much of a suburb.

Highway 3 ends at State Route 299 (Main Street) at a point that once generated considerable controversy. Traffic engineers wanted to install a signal at this intersection—the only one in Trinity County. Local folks kicked up such a fuss that the city abandoned the idea.

After you've passed through the stop*sign* at this intersection, turn right or left and look for a place to park, since you easily can cover the town on foot. RVs and trailers generally can find space along downtown curbs. The town's two attractions are just to the left of the main intersection:

**Weaverville Joss House State Historic Park** ● *P.O. Drawer 1217, Weaverville, CA 96093; (530) 623-5284. Visitor center open daily in summer 10 to 5; tours hourly from 10 to 4; hours may be shorter the rest of the year; small admission fee.* ⊡ Most early California mining camps had large Chinese communities and many erected temples, often called joss houses. The Weaverville temple, built in 1874, has survived intact because the last attendants, aware that the local Chinese population was dwindling, turned it over to the state. It has been impeccably restored, brilliant in its varnished red and black trim. The adjacent visitor center has a fine little museum tracing the Chinese migration to the California gold fields. Time your arrival for the beginning of a tour, since that's the only way you can get inside the joss house.

**Trinity County Museum** • *508 Main St.; (530) 623-5211. Daily 10 to 5 May-October; shorter hours the rest of the year. Free; donations appreciated.* ☐ This is one of the better small town museums you'll find in northern California. Its pioneer relics are nicely displayed, with interpretive signs telling you of Weaverville's past. Particularly clever is an exhibit called "You've come a long way, baby," with displays of a hand-crank wall phone with a modern flip phone, high button shoes with Reeboks and such. Next door is a reconstructed blacksmith shop.

Head back downtown from these two attractions to stroll past well-kept old storefronts. Note two outdoor spiral staircases on opposite sides of the street, erected more than a century ago because first and second floors of the adjacent buildings had different owners. Nearby is California's oldest continually operating pharmacy, **Weaverville Rexall Drug** at 219 Main. You'll find a few curio shops, galleries and even a natural foods store in this historic district, although the merchants don't seem to be too concerned about at attracting tourists. That venerable pharmacy and several other downtown stores were closed when we visited on a summer Saturday afternoon.

To learn more about this old mining town, which dates from 1848, stop by the **Trinity County Chamber of Commerce** at 210 North Main. It's open weekdays 9 to 5; (530) 623-6101.

## DINING

**Brewery Restaurant and Bar** • *401 Main St. (at Oregon Street); 623-3000. American; wine and beer. Breakfast through dinner daily. MC/VISA; $$.* ☐ Housed in a slender brick building across from the Joss House, the Brewery provides the town's best food and atmosphere. Its two small dining rooms are busy with Gay Nineties décor, including an entire surrey hung from the ceiling. The busy menu gallops from stuffed prawns and chicken sauté to various steaks. If you just need a beer, check out the old fashioned micro-brew bar in the rear. The place was for sale when we passed through; hopefully it will still be a restaurant when you arrive.

**La Casita** • *254 Main St. (at Highway 3 intersection); (530) 623-5797. Mexican; wine and beer. Lunch through early dinner Monday-Saturday, closed Sunday. MC/VISA; $.* ☐ It ain't gourmet but it's cute as heck. This tiny restaurant is trimmed in barnboard accented with bright serapes and such. It serves the usual range of smashed beans and rice dishes, with an emphasis on quesadillas. Prices are very low; it would be hard to spend $10 on dinner. During nice weather, you can dine at a patio out back.

**Noelle's Garden Café** • *252 Main St. (at Highway 3 intersection); (530) 623-2058. American; wine and beer. Lunch daily in summer and Tuesday-Saturday the rest of the year, dinner Friday-Saturday all year. No credit cards; $$.* ☐ Noelle shares a pitched-roof Victorian cottage with La Casita, with a deck out front and an old fashioned dining room within. It serves light fare such as baked goods, specialty coffees and stuffed pastries. Evening fare includes Oriental stir fry, chicken marsala and grilled catch of the day.

### RECLINING

**Weaverville Hotel** ● *P.O. Box 537 (201 Main St.); Weaverville, CA 96093; (530) 623-3121. Eight units with private baths, some with TV. MC/VISA; $$.* □ It's not fancy, but it's historic—dating from 1861—and it's right in the middle of downtown. The hotel's spartan rooms occupy the second floor above Brandy's Sport Shop and that's where you check in.

**Weaverville Victorian Inn** ● *P.O. Box 2400 (1709 Main St.); Weaverville, CA 96093-2400; (530) 623-4432. Rates include breakfast. Major credit cards; $$$.* □ Although the name suggests a B&B, this is a 65-unit inn with Victorian trim and modern furnishings. All rooms have TV/VCRs, movies, refrigerators and phones; some have spa tubs and wetbars. It's on the east side of town, a few blocks from the historic district.

### CAMPING

There are several campgrounds in surrounding Trinity National Forest and you can pick up information at the Weaverville Ranger station on the west side of town, on your left. It's open 8 to 4:30, daily in summer and weekdays only the rest of the year; (530) 623-2121.

**Sidney Gulch RV Park** ● *P.O. Box 677 (Highway 299, west of downtown), Weaverville, CA 96093; (800) 554-1626 or (530) 623-6621. RV and tent sites; full hookups $$$.* □ Located within walking distance of the historic district, this 40-site park offers showers, a coin laundry and picnic tables.

---

**FUELING ADVISORY** ● Service stations are rather scattered beyond Weaverville and fuel prices seem to increase with each mile.

---

Westward from Weaverville, Highway 299 crests 2,897-foot Oregon Mountain summit and then spirals quickly down the "main stem" the Trinity River. This inviting stream will be your roadside companion for most of the rest of the trip. This is a very pretty drive through a vee-shaped wooded valley. The highway hugs the river's edge, with several Forest Service campgrounds and river access areas along the route.

### Playing in the water

The Trinity River's temperament ranges from wild and lively to smooth and it's popular for rafting, canoeing, kayaking and tubing. The section between Helena and Burnt Ranch has some nice whitewater stretches, then it calms down in the Willow Creek area, suitable for tubing and canoeing. Three firms in the area market whitewater trips—Bigfoot Rafting Company, (800) 722-2223 or (530) 629-2263; Klamath River Outfitters, (800) 748-3735; and Aurora River Adventures, (800) 562-8475 or (530) 629-3843.

The first town of any size you'll encounter—and it isn't much—is **Helena,** where a couple of firms offer rafting rentals and kayak outings.

Pressing onward, you'll encounter **Big Bar**, with a Forest Service ranger station and a few small businesses, and then **Del Loma**, with an RV park and motel cabins.

West of Del Loma, the highway starts to climb while the river obviously stays in place, and this creates fine aerial views. The stream has cut its way through Trinity River Gorge, whose exposed rock walls are a mix of granite and old Pacific bedrock pushed up from the sea floor about 150 million years ago. If you have a geologist's eye, check the various rock textures as you drive through the gorge. As the highway climbs higher onto the canyon wall, several turnouts offer grand views down to the river, now little more than a twisted silken rope, accented by stretches of frothy white rapids.

You'll pass two more tiny hamlets as you make a long descent from the high canyon walls. **Burnt Ranch** has a post office, forest service campground and store, with no fuel. **Hawkins Bar** has a saloon, mini-mart and fuel, plus a museum about the size of a dog house. It was closed when we passed and no hours were posted. As you complete your descent from the canyon, you'll enter the only town of substance between Weaverville and Arcata.

## WILLOW CREEK

**Population: 1,576**                                    **Elevation: 590 feet**

"River fun and the mountain sun," says a sign as you enter town. Willow Creek is an orderly if ordinary string of service stations, small motels and cafés, made attractive by the surrounding tree-covered basin. It's a popular gathering grounds for folks coming from the foggy coast to swim, fish, boat and hike in that mountain sun.

The **Willow Creek Chamber of Commerce** is in a tiny quonset at the junction of highways 299 and 96. It's open weekdays 9 to 5 in summer and you can get brochures from a porch rack when it's closed; (530) 629-2693. Particularly useful is the *Willow Creek Visitor and Recreation Guide*, a brochure listing area outfitters, cafés, motels and RV parks.

Behind the chamber is the small **Willow Creek-China Flat Museum,** open Friday-Sunday 10 to 4. It has exhibits on the town's early days as a commercial center for area mines; logging, which thrived here after World War II; ranching and—Bigfoot.

### Oh Mah? Oh, my!

Standing before the chamber of commerce office is a large gorilla-like statue of *Oh Mah*, the legendary Bigfoot. Sightings of this eight-foot-tall hairy Neanderthal type creature are more common in the northern California wilds than Elvis sightings are elsewhere in the nation.

The Bigfoot legend was born in 1886 when people reported seeing a hairy, slump shouldered creature weighing as much as 800 pounds. These sightings were near Crescent City and between Willow Creek and Happy Camp on the Klamath River. Bigfoot apparently hibernated for several decades, then huge footprints were found in the snow in nearby mountains in 1935. These prints, larger than those of man or bear, inspired his name. In 1958, he allegedly invaded a construction camp, tossing equipment around and chasing terrified workmen into the brush, who reported that the critter was rather "foul smelling."

More than sixty other Bigfoot sightings have been reported since and even a few photos have been taken, although their authenticity has been questioned. Several other remote areas in western America claim Bigfoot sightings, and the elusive critter has made the cover of nearly every supermarket tabloid in the country, not to mention a few TV shows.

However, he, she or it first appeared in this wild region of California's far northland. Little Willow Creek proudly calls itself the gateway to Bigfoot Country.

### Side trips: Two wilderness drives

Willow Creek also is a gateway to the Trinity Alps, one of the wildest, most remote and untouched regions of America. Only hardy backpackers penetrate far into these wilds, marked with jagged peaks, high alpine lakes and glacial carved meadows. However, a narrow Forest Service road, paved as far as **Denny**, probes deeply into the flanks of the Trinity Wilderness Area. It's navigable by a family sedan in good weather. To get there, drive east a few miles on Highway 299 to **Hawkins Bar** and turn north onto Denny Road.

Another interesting backcountry drive is south on Forestry Road 1, which travels along Pilot Ridge, about thirty-five miles **Mad River** on State Route 36. At one point along this ridge—on a perfectly clear day— you can see the Pacific Ocean to the west and Mount Shasta to the east. To get there, continue a few miles west from Willow Creek on the Trinity Highway, climb toward Berry Summit and watch on your left for Titlow Hill Road. A sign will indicate the Horse Mountain ski area. If you crest Berry Summit, you've missed your turn.

Before attempting either of these drives, check on road conditions at the Lower Trinity District Ranger Station. You also can get detailed area maps there. The office is about a mile north of Willow Creek on Highway 96. Hours are Monday-Saturday 8 to 4:30; (530) 629-2118.

---

*RV ADVISORY* ● These two wilderness drives involve narrow, twisting roads that are unpaved and rough in areas; they aren't advised for RVs or trailers.

---

Continuing west from Willow Creek, Highway 299 leaves the Trinity River and does a rollercoaster number, crossing two mountain passes before beginning a long descent into Arcata at the coast. You'll first follow winding Willow Creek ten miles up to 2,859-foot Berry Summit at the crest of the Coast Range.

Just beyond the summit, a large vista point provides splendid views of the valley of the Mad River two thousand feet below, and its surrounding wooded mountains. Often, you may find the entire valley blanketed in clouds while you stand in bright sunshine, which should give you a lofty if not a heavenly feeling. This is a great place to pause for a late breakfast or lunch, for you may be able to watch that cottony cloud mass disintegrate to reveal the valley below.

A long, sweeping downhill spiral will take you into the valley, then you'll twist back up to 2,262-foot Lord Ellis Summit. From here, you'll begin a final descent to Arcata, the Pacific Ocean and civilization. The last part of this route is quick and monotonous, as Highway 299 becomes a freeway to whisk you through a coastal agricultural plain between Blue Lake and Arcata.

☺ ☺ ☺

*Where do we go from here?* • Right back to Willow Creek if you want to begin Tour Six by heading north on State Route 96. Or you could head south from Arcata on U.S. 101 to Ferndale and run Tour Four backward.

HOPE YOU ENJOYED
YOUR VISIT
PLEASE COME AGAIN

# TRIP PLANNER

**WHEN TO GO** ● The weather along the Klamath River is suitable from spring through fall, and summer is just fine because the area is never crowded. Although it doesn't get a lot of snow, these curving mountain highways can get icy in winter.

**DRIVING DISTANCE** ● About 190 miles if you begin in Arcata on the coast, and 150 miles if you peel off from Tour Five at Willow Creek. This is an easy day's drive, unless you plan to stop and do a lot of fishing, boating or otherwise playing along the Klamath River.

**RV ADVISORY** ● Sections of the highway through the Hoopa Valley Indian Reservation are very narrow, with the road squeezed between guard rails and steep banks. Large RVs and trailer rigs should be able to make it unless they're being operated by timid drivers.

**WHAT YOU'LL SEE** ● Mostly lots of scenery along the Trinity and Klamath rivers; the small museum on the Hoopa Indian Reservation; and Siskiyou County Museum and historic Siskiyou County Courthouse with its gold display, both in Yreka.

**WHAT TO DO** ● Raft, fish, swim or just dangle your toes in these two scenic rivers of California's far north; build lunch at Quigley's General Store and hang out down by the river; explore the historic district of Yreka; ride the Yreka Western Railroad steam train.

**TO BEGIN** ● Follow Highway 299 inland from Arcata and head north from Willow Creek on State route 96; see the end of the previous tour. If you're running this tour in reverse, take Interstate 5 to Yreka, then head north on Main Street (State Route 263) through dramatic Shasta River Canyon. The route soon connects with the Klamath River Highway.

## Useful contacts

**Siskiyou County Visitors Bureau,** 117 W. Miner St., Yreka, CA 96097; (800) 446-7475 or (530) 842-7857.

**Happy Camp Chamber of Commerce,** P.O. Box 1188, Happy Camp, CA 96039; (530) 493-2900.

**Northern Klamath River Chamber of Commerce,** P.O. Box 25, Klamath River, CA 96050.

## Pricing guidelines

**DINING:** Dinner entrée with soup or salad, without drinks or dessert for under $10 = $; $10 to $14 = $$; $15 to $25 = $$$; over $25 = $$$$.

**RECLINING:** A two-person room for $35 or less = $; $36 to $50 = $$; $51 to $75 = $$$; $76 to $100 = $$$$; more than $100 = $$$$$.

**CAMPING:** Under $10 = $; $10 to $14 = $$; $15 to $19 = $$$; $20 or more = $$$$

National Forest

Scenic Byway

State of Jefferson

*Tour Six*

# KLAMATH RIVER ROUTE

## *ARCATA TO YREKA ON HIGHWAY 96*

**M**ore than half a century ago, Mayor Gilbert Gable of Port Orford, Oregon, rekindled an old movement to form a new state. It was to be comprised of Josephine and Jackson counties in southern Oregon and Del Norte, Siskiyou and Modoc counties in northern California. Folks in the far northern town of Yreka quickly joined in, and the *Siskiyou Daily News* sponsored a "name the state" contest. Jefferson was selected to honor the author of our constitution.

Residents of these remote counties were irritated because they felt they weren't getting anything for their tax dollars. Roads were either nonexistent or in terrible shape, and these distant counties were so thinly populated that they received little attention from their elected legislators. The secession effort was half in jest, although residents certainly were serious about calling attention to their lousy roads and lack of governmental representation and services.

"Our roads are not passable; hardly jackassable," read signs along the area's muddied, rutted roadways.

Promoters of the State of Jefferson "officially" seceded from the union and named Yreka as its capital. Newsreel cameramen were invited to film the inauguration of Judge John L. Childs of Crescent City as governor of the new state. A major celebration was planned for the following weekend. Newsreel footage and photos of the inauguration would be released, providing national publicity for the "secession" and the creation of the State of Jefferson. Unfortunately, promotors had selected the weekend of December 6 and 7, 1941.

☹ ☹ ☹

Things haven't changed much in the northwesternmost reaches of northern California. It's still one of the least populated areas of the state. However, residents did finally get their roads. During the early 1940s, a bumpy and rutted dirt path alongside the Klamath River was paved in order to assist the transport of valuable chrome and copper deposits from area mines and timber for the war effort.

In honor of that early secessionist episode, the Klamath River portion of Route 86 was designated as the State of Jefferson Scenic Byway in 1992.

The Klamath River is a very popular playground for kayakers, whitewater rafters and seekers of trout and steelhead. Hundreds are drawn to the river each year for spring and fall steelhead runs. However, even if you don't fish, cut bait or run the rapids, the Klamath River Highway is a pleasant scenic drive. There are few towns of note along the way and this is definitely a road less traveled. At the end of this tour, we suggest spending some time in Yreka. Started as a mining camp and more than a century and a half old, it is one of the more appealing old towns in California's far north.

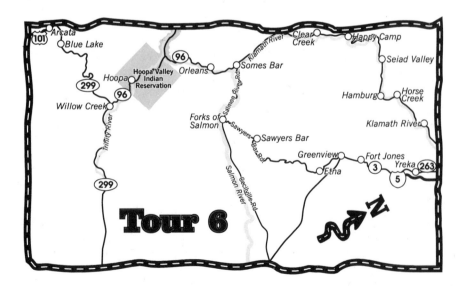

Highway 96 begins in downtown Willow Creek. About a mile north, you'll see the **Lower Trinity District Ranger Station** on your left, where you can load up on information concerning the region you're about to enter. It's open Monday-Saturday 8 to 4:30; (530) 629-2118.

You'll pass through a few miles of Willow Creek rural suburbia before climbing into the trees. Although this is the Klamath River Highway, your first streamside companion is the Trinity River, heading north to join the Klamath. The highway alternately skirts the stream's edge and then climbs thickly wooded canyon walls for tree-filtered aerial views.

You'll soon enter the **Hoopa Valley Indian Reservation** occupying a shallow, broad basin where the Trinity slows to a lazy meander. At the **Hoopa Valley Shopping Center** in the village of Hoopa, you can pause at a small museum, open weekdays 8 to 5 and Saturdays 10 to 4 (closed at noon for lunch). It has a nice display of reed basketry—for which the Hoopa are noted—plus beadwork, pottery and a few native artifacts. Next door is the small **Lucky Bear Casino**, offering a few slot and video poker machines; a bingo hall is adjacent.

Several miles beyond Hoopa, Highway 96 begins a steep climb from the valley and into the ramparts of a steep-walled canyon. Occasional turnouts provide splendid views of the river hundreds of feet below—emerald green with little white puffs of rapids.

---

*RV ADVISORY* • Sections of this route are extremely narrow, squeezed between a guardrail and the canyon wall. Drivers of big motorhomes and trailers will have to keep very alert.

---

**Weitchpec,** a tiny native hamlet of 150 people, occupies a dramatic perch above the confluence of the Trinity and Klamath rivers. The Hoopa Reservation follows both sides of Klamath from here northwest to the coast. Narrow but paved Martins Ferry Road (State Route 169) follows the river for nineteen scenic miles, then comes to a dead end.

Heading east from Weitchpec, you leave the reservation and enter Six Rivers National Forest. The route is busy with river access sites and Forest Service campgrounds. This region is popular with fisherfolk who vie for trout in the spring and summer and come for salmon and steelhead runs in the fall. The Klamath River Highway is relatively tame for the rest of the drive, reasonably wide and with gentle curves. The stream is part of the nation's wild and scenic river system, although it's not really a wilderness area. Stretches of very pretty and unpopulated river canyon are interrupted occasionally by little towns and small farming valleys.

Twenty-five miles beyond Weitchpec, **Orleans** comes and goes without much notice, with a market and service station. A few miles beyond, **Somes Bar** consists of a general store with two gas pumps. It's a major mecca for serious river runners. This is the point where the Salmon River—called the Cal Salmon to distinguish it from its more famous Idaho cousin—enters the Klamath. The Cal Salmon has some of the wildest whitewater in the American West, as my son Dan can attest; he's a licensed river guide. It is a river to be approached only by skilled boaters or

*Cloaked by a pretty wooded canyon, the Klamath River is a favorite destination for boaters and fisherpersons.*

as a member of a commercial run. (Several local river runners are listed at the end of this tour.)

## Side trip: Salmon River Country

A right turn from Somes Bar will take you on a twisting drive through the primitive Salmon River Country. The Salmon River Highway alternately hugs the shoreline and climbs canyon walls to follow the Cal Salmon's squiggly course through wilderness mountains. At tiny village of **Forks of Salmon,** you can pick up the north fork and follow Sawyers Bar Road forty-one crooked miles to **Etna.** Above you is the **Marble Mountain Wilderness,** one of America's most remote wild areas. No road leads into these alpine heights; it's the domain of backpackers only.

If you're a river kayaker or would like to become one, check into America's leading kayak school, on the river bank near Forks of Salmon:

**Otter Bar Lodge** ● *Box 210, Forks of Salmon, CA 96031; (530) 462-4772. (WEB SITE: otterbar.com) Seven lodge units with all meals and equipment; $$$$$.* ☐ This wilderness lodge offers one-week total immersion kayaking courses—no pun intended—for beginner, intermediate and advanced students. Facilities include comfy rooms, a hot tub and sauna.

At Etna, you can pick up State Route 3—a considerably improved high-. way—and follow it twelve miles through Scotts Valley to charming old **Fort Jones.** Stop by the stone walled **Fort Jones Museum** at the site of a former army outpost. Its displays include native basketry, firearms and early day room groups, and there's a carriage display. The museum is open Monday-Friday 10 to 4 Memorial Day through Labor Day, and by appointment only the rest of the year.

From Fort Jones, you can follow the **Scott River** north through the Scott Bar Mountains and rejoin the Klamath River Highway just west of Hamburg.

---

*RV ADVISORY* ● The drive along the Cal Salmon is *not* recommended for RVs, since sections of it are gravel roads, very narrow and notched into high river canyons. Any driver needs to approach this route with care.

---

Meanwhile, back on the Klamath River Highway, a forty-one mile drive will take you from Somes Bar to **Happy Camp** in a shallow valley. The town has lost its grin these days, looking a bit on the tattered side, although some of its old buildings are dressed up with historic murals. It's the largest town you'll hit on the Klamath River—about 1,100 folks—with a few cafés, service stations and motels. Logging cutbacks and recent reductions in steelhead runs have hurt the local economy. However, it's still an important staging area for rafting and fishing trips and locals can even tell you where to pan for a bit of gold. The Klamath River has been dredged heavily for gold during past decades, and you'll note gravel piles left by these dredges as you drive alongside the stream.

## Side trip: getting atop the world

If you want that top of the world feeling, watch on your left for a "Forest service auto tour" sign a few miles east of Happy Camp. This route, all paved but very narrow, climbs steeply and some might say precariously into the rugged mountains high above the Klamath River canyon. Views of the surrounding wilds are most impressive.

Five miles after you leave the highway, you'll see a graphic on your left discussing the 1987 Slater Fire that nearly engulfed Happy Camp—which would *really* have ruined its disposition. Another four miles of steep and narrow road takes you to a saddle with a large informal parking area; just beyond is Slater Butte Lookout. There's plenty of turnaround space, and it's a good place to do so, since you've already seen the most interesting part of the route. Beyond here, the road starts downhill, away from the Klamath River Canyon.

Views from here are awesome, with mountains galloping off in every direction—ridge upon ridge fading from deep green to soft blue to pale gray. You can see north to the Siskiyou Mountains in Oregon and south, west and east to the Salmon and Marble mountains of California's far north. At points along the drive, the Klamath River appears below as a tiny silken thread.

*DRIVING ADVISORY* ● Small RVs and family sedans can make this grade to the Slater Butte vista point, since it's all paved with only a couple of hairpin turns. *Ickybod*, our 21-foot Winnebago, experienced no serious problems. However it's almost all one lane with occasional turn-outs for passing, so it should *not* be attempted with a big motorhome or trailer. Also, you'll encounter frequent cliff-edge exposure with no guard rails; those with vertigo problems should not attempt it. (Even those who don't suffer that malady may experience a little dry mouth.)

Continuing eastward on Highway 96, you'll whisk through **Seiad Valley** and **Hamburg.** If it's time for a break, **Hawk's Roost** in Seiad has modest priced RV and tent sites, with a coin laundry; (530) 496-3400. **Steelhead Lodge and RV Park** in Hamburg offers modest priced housekeeping units, grassy RV sites right on the river with hookups, a café, tavern and coin laundry; (530) 496-3256. **Rainbow Resort** in Hamburg has housekeeping cabins, a mini-mart and fuel; (530) 496-3242.

The final town in this slow stroll along the State of Jefferson Scenic Byway is named for the stream. When you first encounter **Klamath River,** population 150, you'll see a thin scatter of buildings in a shallow farming valley. However the *real* Klamath River is a couple of miles beyond, wrapped up in an historic general store.

**Quigley's,** occupying an wood frame, tin roofed building, has been serving folks along the river since 1911. It retains the flavor of an old general store, although a deli has been added, where you can grab a bite or build a picnic lunch. You also can pick up Klamath River information from a brochure rack. An adjacent RV park has rec vehicle and tent sites right over the river, with horseshoe pits, showers and a coin laundry; full hookups **$$.** For generations, Quigley's has been a friend of river-runners. White water enthusiasts are invited to take out or put in at the beach behind the store. The store's hours vary but you can count on it being open during the daylight; (530) 465-2224.

You're now about fifteen miles from the end of the drive, and the Klamath River Canyon makes a dramatic geological change. The forested ravine gives way to steep, rumpled canyon walls hundreds of feet high and marked with jagged dikes. These are some of the oldest rocks in northern California—volcanic and sedimentary rock pushed up from a primeval ocean floor during the Paleozoic era, hundreds of millions of years ago.

One of our favorite campgrounds, the Forest Service's **Tree of Heaven** is on your right, about ten miles from Quigley's. The highway climbs high up the canyon wall, and a side road spirals down to the campground. It's right alongside the river, with grassy sites and huge shade trees. Tree of Heaven (named for a species of locust imported by Chinese miners) has a launching area for river-runners, since the ten-mile stretch between here and Quigley's is very popular. You'll even find a small fishing pier and a short trail that leads west along the river through lush blackberry vines. (They're generally ripe in August.) There are no hookups and only pit potties (don't camp too near one); **$$.**

A few miles beyond Tree of Heaven, take a hard right onto a curving concrete bridge and follow the Shasta River through an even more dramatically narrow, steep-walled canyon. This was the original highway before Interstate 5—visible from here—was built. The highway hugs the canyon wall hundreds of feet above the stream, then it levels out in a high meadowland and rounds a turn to suddenly reveal the great conical mass of Mount Shasta.

After several miles, the highway becomes Main Street for our favorite little city in northern California.

## YREKA

**Population: 7,000**                                    **Elevation: 2,625 feet**

There's a wonderful story about how Yreka got its start, which is probably campfire talk. Supposedly, a muleskinner named Abraham Thompson stopped to make camp here in March of 1851. He noticed that grass clumps pulled up by his grazing mules had gold flakes tangled in their roots. Word got out and folks came by the swarm—two thousand within six weeks. Yreka soon was the largest, liveliest and wickedest mining town in northern California. It had two dozen saloons before anyone got around to building a church. Incidentally, the town's odd name may be a Shasta Indian word meaning "north mountain."

You'll notice a dramatic change in the terrain as you approach Yreka. It occupies the northern edge of a broad, flat ranching valley that stretches nearly thirty miles south to the town of Weed. Surrounding mountains create a rain shield, making the Shasta Valley one of the driest areas north of San Francisco. Towering above the valley, almost always in view, is that grand vision of Mount Shasta, the most imposing landmark of California's far north.

Coming into town from Shasta River Canyon, you'll first pass through a residential area of mature old homes and trees and then you'll hit downtown Yreka. Turn right onto Miner Street and you'll be in an outdoor architectural museum of nineteenth century brick, masonry and iron front buildings. Find a place to park and start walking. Downtown Yreka is compact and fun to explore.

---

*RV PARKING ADVISORY* • Yreka is very RV friendly. A special lot has been set aside for big rigs and trailers at North and Third streets. To reach it, turn right from Main onto North, which is a block short of Miner Street; the parking area is a block away.

---

Begin your visit at the **Siskiyou County Visitors Bureau** which is cleverly combined with Sue's Coffee and Cones at the corner of Miner and Broadway. Ask for a walking tour map that will point out historic buildings along Miner Street and dozens of fine old homes nearby. Even when the bureau isn't manned, the kids at Sue's can provide brochures and give directions. Hours are Monday-Saturday 8 to 10 and Sunday 11 to 9. While you're there, you can get a light breakfast, lunch or evening snack. The place has a pleasing old fashioned soda fountain look. Phone numbers are

(530) 842-0808 for Sue's and (530) 842-7857 for the visitors bureau. If you're interested in fishing or river play in the area, the old fashioned and cluttered **Don's Sporting Goods** at 321 Miner can provide all the equipment and some good advice. To learn about Yreka's yesterdays, check out its fine museum, reached by heading south on Main Street; it's on the left, just beyond Siskiyou County Hospital:

**Siskiyou County Museum** • *910 S. Main St.; (530) 842-3836. Tuesday-Saturday 9 to 5; small admission fee.* ⊡ Yreka's yesterdays are displayed indoors and out at this archive within walking distance of the historic district. Exhibits also cover area geology and native people. Several historic buildings have been moved here to create a pioneer village, including a stocked general store.

Need to stretch your legs? The **Greenway Hiking Trail** takes several interesting wraps along the banks of Yreka Creek. You can pick it up behind the museum.

All that glitters may not be gold, although you'll see the real thing in a display in the foyer of the old fashioned **Siskiyou County Courthouse**. It's at 311 Fourth Street, between Butte and Lane. This is said to be the largest public gold display between Alaska and San Francisco. The local **Forest Service ranger station** has a nice interpretive display in its office at 1312 Fairlane Road in Yreka, with exhibits on resource management, mining and the flora and fauna of the surrounding national forest; open weekdays 9 to 4:30; (530) 842-6131.

If you'd like to take a ride into yesterday, catch the **Yreka Western Railroad's** Blue Goose steam train. This 1915 Baldwin locomotive makes spring through fall excursion and dinner runs from the old fashioned Yreka railway depot, chugging across the broad Shasta Valley to Montague, six miles east. For information: Yreka Western Railroad, P.O. Box 660, Yreka, CA 96097; (800) YREKA-RR or (530) 842-4146.

## DINING

Several restaurants are in Miner Street's vintage storefronts although none feature old fashioned décor. For that, you need to head briefly south on I-5 and take the next exit west to The Old Boston Shaft. That restaurant has an old style interior look, although the exterior resembles one of those fat-roofed 1960s family cafés.

**Lalo's** • *219 W. Miner St.; (530) 842-2695. Mexican; wine and beer. Lunch and dinner daily. Major credit cards; $$.* ⊡ Tucked between old brick walls, Lalo's features a south of the border look with Mexican arches and bright *Latino* accents. The menu lists the usual fajitas, chimichangas, tacos and other tortilla wrapped things.

**Ming's Restaurant & Lounge** • *210 W. Miner St.; (530) 842-3888. Chinese-American; full bar service. Lunch and dinner daily. MC/VISA; $$.* ⊡ Talk about an architectural identity crisis! Ming's is a Chinese restaurant in an old western brick building with a tropical theme. Which means you can get a maitai with your *mu shu* pork or Navy grog with your noodles. Ming also features several American dishes. Coziest seating is in the cocktail lounge, with dim lighting, high backed booths an lots of woven rattan. You almost expect Sydney Greenstreet to push through the beaded curtain, except there isn't one.

**Old Boston Shaft** • *1801 Fort Jones Rd.; (530) 842-5768. American-continental; full bar service. Lunch weekdays, dinner Monday-Saturday, closed Sunday. Major credit cards; $$$.* ☐ The Shaft is Yreka's best restaurant, serving a variety of well prepared gringo and European dishes. The building, whose shape suggests a Fifties style diner, has been covered with angular barnboard to give it that proper mining camp look. The theme carries inside, with distressed wood walls, ceiling beams and other Western touches. The name comes from a former mine in the area. To get here, take the Etna/Fort Jones exit from the freeway just south of town and you'll see it almost immediately, across from a traffic signal.

For quick bites, try **Miner Street Bakery** at 328 W. Miner, (530) 842-6770; or **Miner Street Deli** at 319 W. Miner, (530) 842-1854. Both are in the historic district.

## GOING NEAR THE WATER

We mentioned earlier that the Klamath is one of California's most popular whitewater rafting and kayaking streams. Here's a list of operators who can help you get all wet:

**Access to Adventure**, 92520 Highway 96, Somes Bar, CA 95563, (800) KLAMATH or (530) 469-3322; whitewater trips on the Klamath, Cal Salmon, Scott and Trinity rivers, plus hiking and mountain biking. The firm also operates Marble Mountain Ranch, a wilderness retreat.

**Cutting Edge Adventures**, P.O. Box 1334, Mount Shasta, CA 96067, (800) 594-8435 or (530) 926-4646. (E-MAIL: ctngedga@snow-crest.net); whitewater trips on the Klamath, Cal Salmon, Scott and upper Sacramento, plus a kayaking school.

**Klamath River Outfitters**, 3 Sandy Bar Rd., Somes Bar, CA 95563; (800) RIVER-35 or (530) 469-3349; a variety of whitewater rafting, steelhead and salmon fishing outings on the Klamath.

**Orange Torpedo Trips**, P.O. Box 1111-D, Grants Pass, OR 97528, (800) 635-2925 or (541) 479-5061; several multi-day trips on the Klamath in paddle-it-yourself inflatable kayaks.

**River Trips Canoeing**, 808 W. Lennox St., Yreka, CA 96097, (800) 446-7475 or (530) 842-7857; gentle whitewater and calm water canoe trips on the Klamath, plus canoeing classes.

☺ ☺ ☺

*Where do we go from here?* • The end of this drive dovetails nicely into Tour Seven to Lava Beds National Monument and Alturas. You also can take I-5 forty miles south to Mount Shasta city and pick up Tour Nine, the Mount Lassen route. Also, since Yreka sits beside I-5, you can go anywhere from here. Of course, it's hardly a road less traveled.

# TRIP PLANNER

**WHEN TO GO** ● Fall through early winter is best because you can see large concentrations of migrating waterfowl and bald eagles at the Klamath Basin National Wildlife Refuge. Facilities of the area's other major attraction, Lava Beds National Monument, are open then as well, although there will be fewer ranger programs. It can get bitter cold in this area in winter, particularly as you travel farther east to Alturas.

**DRIVING DISTANCE** ● It's about 150 miles from either Yreka or Weed to Alturas.

**RV ADVISORY** ● Nothing on this route is particularly challenging for any size rec vehicles.

**WHAT YOU'LL SEE** ● Living Memorial Sculpture Gardens on Highway 97; lots of views of Mount Shasta; droves of birds at Klamath Basin National Wildlife Refuge, the volcanic wildness of Lava Beds National Monument, and Modoc County Historical Museum in Alturas.

**WHAT TO DO** ● Take your binoculars and get close to the Klamath Basin birds; crawl through the lava tubes of Lava Beds; clear your sinus at Mezzetta's Tulelake Horseradish Company; explore remote Cedarville in the Surprise Valley.

**TO BEGIN** ● Head northeast on U.S. 97 from Weed, or cut over to Highway 97 from Yreka, via Montague and Granada.

## Useful contacts

**Alturas Chamber of Commerce**, 522 S. Main St., Alturas, CA 96101; (530) 233-2819.

**Siskiyou County Visitors Bureau**, 117 W. Miner St., Yreka, CA 96097; (800) 446-7475 or (530) 842-7857.

**Tulelake Chamber of Commerce**, P.O. Box 592, Tulelake, CA 96134; (530) 667-5178.

### Across the border

**Klamath County Tourism**, P.O. Box 1867 (1451 Main St.), Klamath Falls, OR 97601; (800) 445-6728 or (541) 884-0666. (WEB: www.klamathcountytourism.com; E-MAIL: tourklco@cdsnet.net)

**Lake County Chamber of Commerce**, 126 N. E St., Lakeview, OR 97630-1577; 947-6040.

## Pricing guidelines

**DINING:** Dinner entrée with soup or salad, without drinks or dessert for under $10 = **$**; $10 to $14 = **$$**; $15 to $25 = **$$$**; over $25 = **$$$$**.

**RECLINING:** A two-person room for $35 or less = **$**; $36 to $50 = **$$**; $51 to $75 = **$$$**; $76 to $100 = **$$$$**; more than $100 = **$$$$$**.

**CAMPING:** Under $10 = **$**; $10 to $14 = **$$**; $15 to $19 = **$$$**; $20 or more = **$$$$**

# THE SHASTA ROUTE

## *ACROSS THE TOP TO LAVA BEDS & ALTURAS*

If you're a longtime California resident, you'll remember Shasta Bottling Company's slogan for its line of soft drinks: "It hasta be Shasta." That could be said for the first half of this tour as well.

Mount Shasta, one of the world's most isolated promontories, dominates the horizon on much of this trek across the top of the state. Although five California peaks are higher, none is more dramatically poised than 14,162-foot Shasta and its Siamese twin Shastina. They rise together like a double scoop of vanilla ripple, 10,000 feet above the floor of the Shasta Valley. From the time you start northeast on U.S. 97 until you leave Lava Beds National Monument, you'll have the sense that this great peak is watching you.

Mount Shasta marks the dividing line between the Cascade and Klamath mountains. Although these ranges were formed by faulting, Shasta obviously is a volcano, which has spread lava flows throughout the region for more than a million years. This great mountain, with a mass of eighty cubic miles, is sleeping although not necessarily dormant. It last erupted in 1786 and seismologists say it will awaken every 250 to 350 years.

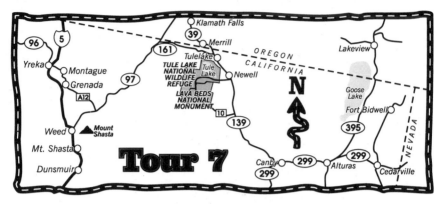

From some angles, Shasta is a nearly symmetrical cone with a Mount Fuji grace. However, from this vantage point, 12,330-foot Shastina is very evident, a volcanic vent fused into Shasta's northwest side. Shasta is so high that it often generates its own weather, wearing a mantle of clouds while the Shasta Valley basks in sunshine. It presents a particularly dramatic vision at sunup and sundown when its high snowfields are painted pink by the sun's long rays. Like a great beacon, it is the first to catch light in the morning and the last to lose it at sundown.

This tour begins on U.S. 97, which angles northeast from Weed to the Oregon border. If you're continuing from Tour Six, head east from Yreka through Montague on Highway 3, go south to Grenada on Montague-Grenada Road, then southeast on county road A-12 to U.S. 97. Otherwise, take the central exit from Interstate 5 in Weed and head northeast. Both routes gain altitude gradually, ascending Mount Shasta's broad foothills. The terrain will change from high, arid prairie and ranchlands to juniper, sage and piñon.

About fourteen miles from Weed (a mile from the A-12/Highway 97 junction if you're coming from Yreka), watch on your left for the **Veterans Living Memorial Sculpture Garden.** This distinctive drive-through complex of surrealistic bronze sculptures was crafted by artist Dennis Smith to honor veterans and victims of America's wars. It presents a striking picture in a low, brushy prairie with the great mass of Mount Shasta just beyond. Entering the complex, you'll first see "The Wall" inscribed with the names of hundreds of veterans. A short road leads to the garden's focal point, a dramatic sculpture of agonized human forms labeled "The Why Group." Short paths radiate from here, leading to six other sculptures. For a fee, veterans can have their names added to the wall, or one can contribute to the project by contacting: Living Memorial Sculpture Garden, P.O. Box 301, Weed, CA 96094; (530) 938-2218 or (530) 842-2477.

A couple of miles beyond the sculpture garden, a vista point on your left provides a grand view of Mount Shasta. RVers can spend the night here if they're self contained—providing an opportunity to watch the mountain at sundown and sunup.

Continuing a gradual climb, the almost-straight Highway 97 takes you into a conifer zone, over 5,101-foot Grass Lake Summit. From here, it drops into the broad, flat grasslands of Butte Valley, primarily a ranching area. Look in your rear view mirror and you'll see that Shasta is keeping an eye on you.

**Macdoel** claims 600 residents and offers fuel and a store. Larger **Dorris** has a thousand folks, and a couple each of motels, cafés and service stations. Just short of the Oregon border, turn east onto State Route 161 at the Tulelake sign. The highway fires arrow-straight across a once marshy basin between low hills. We say "once" because much of this area was drained in the early twentieth century, turning the region into a rich farming and ranching region. Prior to that, this was California and Oregon's largest wetland, covering 185,000 acres. Only twenty-five percent of the original marshlands remain, many of them shaped into squares as irrigation holding basins.

You'll shortly enter the Lower Klamath section of the **Klamath Basin National Wildlife Refuge.** Elements of the refuge are spaced over hundreds of square miles. The Lower Klamath Refuge is on the California-Oregon border, the Tule Lake and Clear Lake refuges are farther east in California and the Upper Klamath and Klamath Marsh sections are to the north in Oregon.

The surviving ponds of these once vast wetlands are still among the best places in America to see migratory and local birds. Officials estimate that *eighty percent* of migrating waterfowl on the Pacific Flyway stop here—hundreds of thousands of birds a year. (They once came by the millions.) Best bird-sighting time is October through December. The area also attracts America's largest concentration of bald eagles outside of Alaska, from December through February. Obviously, a good time to catch some of both is in December.

The highway follows a low levee through the Lower Klamath Refuge for several miles. Watch on your right for a turnout beside a marsh, where graphics will help you identify the various types of birds and other critters you'll see here.

If you you're in an RV and you'd like to spend the night in the area, **Stateline RV Park**, on your right just beyond the bird exhibit, has full hookups and showers; **$$$$**; (530) 667-4849. (Lava Beds National Monument, twenty miles away, has a campground with no hookups.)

You'll see more turnouts and roads leading into the refuge as you continue alongside this broad, flat pond. However, before you go wandering off, stop first at refuge headquarters for information and orientation. To get there—and eventually on to Lava Beds—watch for a right turn onto Hill Road, just short of Westside Store. A brown sign will indicate Lava Beds and the refuge visitor center, which is four miles away.

*Klamath Basin National Wildlife Refuge* • *Route 1, Box 74, Tulelake, CA 96134; (530) 667-2231. Visitor center open weekdays 8 to 4:30 and weekends 10 to 4; free.* ☐ The visitor center has several photos and displays on native flora and fauna and literature on the refuge. Ask to see a short orientation slide show which contains some very nice wildlife photos. An auto tour map available here will direct you to the best bird sighting areas on the refuge.

*Mount Shasta and Shastina—the nub on the right flank—rise majestically over rangelands near Highway 97. The cattle seem unimpressed by the view.*

Across the road from the visitor center, Discovery Marsh Trail leads to a pair of bird-watching blinds—one a few hundred yards away and the other about half a mile from the parking area.

From here, it's another eighteen miles to the visitor center of one of the more interesting yet least visited elements of the National Park system:

**Lava Beds National Monument** • *P.O. Box 8676, Tulelake, CA 96124; (530) 667-2282. Visitor center open daily 10 to 6; small entry fee. Adjacent Indian Wells Campgrounds has flush potties, with no hookups; well-spaced sites among the sage and junipers; $$.* ☐ Lava beds has two dramatic stories to tell—one concerning some of the most complex lava flows on the American mainland, and the other about one of America's last Indian wars.

In 1872, Modoc leader Kentipoos, known locally as Captain Jack, led several of his people off a reservation in Oregon and sought refuge in the rough lava flows south of Tule Lake. For nearly five months, his small band of fifty-two held off army units that eventually grew to a thousand men. During the siege, publicity-savvy Captain Jack held interviews with eastern newspaper reporters and won national sympathy. However, during an attempted peace negotiation, Army General E.C.R. Canby was killed. The Army intensified its attacks, isolating and starving the insurgents. Eventually, all members of the uprising were either killed or captured. Captain Jack and three of his lieutenants were hanged, and the rest were shipped off to a reservation in Oklahoma.

The Modoc War was the only major engagement between native people and settlers in California and one of the most costly Indian wars fought in the American West. It also was the only engagement in which such a high ranking officer was killed. (George Armstrong Custer was a colonel when he was done in by Sitting Bull's warriors, three years later at the Little Bighorn.)

The geological story of Lava Beds concerns an outerworldly, convoluted mix of lava flows and lava tubes in a high, barren desert that could be a setting for a *Star Trek* episode. Volcanoes have been spilling their lava here for a million years, with the most recent flows dating back about a thousand.

As you enter the monument, you'll see roads leading off to several lava tubes. These are formed when flowing lava cools and crusts over. This forms an insulating ceiling that allows the hotter lava beneath to continue flowing, leaving a long tube or cave. Unless you've come properly equipped, go to the visitor center before exploring any of these tubes. You can buy inexpensive plastic bump hats for low ceilings, and get loaner lights. At least two light sources are mandatory; you can really get lost in there! If you don't want to go bumping in the blackness, a small lava cave in front of the visitor center is lighted.

En route to the visitor center, pause at **Schonchin Butte,** a large cindercone with a hiking trail leading to the top. This is a pleasant hike, up through ancient twisted junipers eking out a living from the barren cindercone soil. Near the top, you can fork to the left and go up to a fire lookout perched dramatically atop a volcanic dike, or take the right fork and circle the butte. This route, more interesting and only slightly longer, also winds up at the fire lookout. The views of the tumbled lava landscape and distant wetlands are impressive from up here. If you arrive during the summer months, a fire-spotter will help you find interesting terrain features including—who else?—Mount Shasta.

---

*RV ADVISORY* ● Trailers aren't advised on the half-mile dirt road to the Schonchin Butte trailhead because parking and turnaround space are limited.

---

To see two other interesting elements of Lava Beds, go back the way you came in, but stay on the main park road instead of turning north onto Hill Road. You'll encounter **Captain Jack's Stronghold,** where you can hike among the twisted lava shapes that shielded the Indian insurgents from the invading army.

Beyond here, the road will take you out of the refuge and into the Tule Lake section of the Klamath Basin National Wildlife Refuge. Drive along the eastern edge of this squared lake on a levee road, then turn right at a stop sign and follow a gravel road two miles to **Petroglyph Point.** Hundreds of petroglyphs have been pecked into a sheer volcanic tufa cliff, although many have been vandalized so a fence has been erected to protect the rest. Drive a few hundred feet beyond the parking area and you'll find a trailhead for the **Petroglyph Bluff Trail.** A tough and mercifully short hike will deliver you to the top of this dike, where the view is dramatically different from the Schonchin Butte vista. You'll see a neat patchwork of farmlands, the blue basin of Tule Lake and Mount Shasta, of course.

A few hundred feet beyond the trailhead, you'll hit a paved county road. Turn left and you'll soon reach State Route 139 at the community of **Newell**, which has no services. A monument just beyond on Highway 139 marks the site of Tulelake Relocation Camp, one of ten such camps set up during the hysteria of World War II to imprison Japanese-Americans. Nothing remains of the site except a gutted wood frame building.

The town of Tulelake is a few more miles northwest, although it offers little of interest, unless you like horseradish or need food or fuel. (Tulelake calls itself the Horseradish Capital of the World.) Otherwise, you can head southeast on Route 139, following signs to Canby—bearing in mind that there are no service for the next forty miles. So if you need services:

## TULELAKE

**Population: 1,000**                                    **Elevation: 4,035 feet**

Despite prosperous surrounding farmlands and ranchlands, Tulelake is a rather battered old derelict of a town. Folks here relate more to next-door Oregon and do most of their shopping there, since that state has no sales tax. What little survives of downtown consists of a supermarket, restaurant, saloon and a mini-mart with a single fuel pump—which must make this the modern equivalent of a one-horse town.

If you need fuel, turn south from the highway onto Main Street. It swings to the left, taking you a few blocks through the shabby downtown area to that mini-mart with the lone gas pump, at Main and E streets. If you're a fan of horseradish or other interesting specialty foods, step across the street to **Mezzetta's Tulelake Horseradish Company** open daily 8 to 4:30. You can sample—and buy—a variety of food items made from the zesty parsnip, including horseradish mustard, salsas and sauces. The store also stocks a wide variety of other specialty foods.

If you're hungry for something other than horseradish, you have two choices. **Mike and Wanda's Coffee Shop** is back near the highway turnoff, on Modoc Street opposite the supermarket. It's kinda cute, with cattle brands burned into barnboard walls, and it has the usual chicken fried steak and such, plus pizzas and full bar service. It serves breakfast, lunch and dinner daily; $ to $$; (530) 667-3226. A bit more upscale, near Newell on the highway toward Canby is **Captain Jack's Stronghold Restaurant**, with American fare served in an old board and batten false front building. It's open for breakfast through dinner, Wednesday-Sunday, with full bar service; $$; (530) 664-5566.

If you're sleepy, you have one choice. **Park Motel** on Route 139 between Tulelake and Newell has modest rooms at modest prices, with TV and phones: P.O. Box 536, Tulelake, CA 96134; (530) 667-2913.

## Klamath Falls, anyone?

Since you're in the neighborhood, you might want to detour twenty-three miles northwest to Klamath Falls. This fair sized town has three museums, including the excellent **Flavel Museum,** one of the finest

archives of Western art you'll find anywhere. To learn about the town's offerings, contact: **Klamath County Tourism,** P.O. Box 1867 (1451 Main
St.), Klamath Falls, OR 97601; (800) 445-6728 or (541) 884-0666.

Meanwhile, heading southeast from Tulelake on Highway 139—don't
forget to wave goodbye to Mount Shasta—you'll travel through a mix of
high prairie and the pine woodlands of Modoc National Forest. At the
small town of **Canby**—no need to stop unless you need fuel—the highway merges with State Route 299. Nineteen miles east is a particularly
charming old town:

## ALTURAS

**Population: 3,300**                    **Elevation: 4,366 feet**

The brothers Dorris came to this high valley in 1870, built a way station and wooden bridge over the Pit River, and called their settlement
Dorris Bridge. Four years later, it was renamed Alturas, Spanish for "a
high place." The only town of any size for hundreds of square miles in this
thinly populated corner of California, Alturas is the seat and commercial
center for huge Modoc County. This is cowboy country and some of the
downtown buildings would fit into a Western movie set, with their classic
brick or wooden false fronts.

If you'd like information on Modoc National Forest, pieces of which are
scattered throughout this area, stop at the **Devils Garden Ranger Station** just outside of town on your left. It's open weekdays 8 to 4:30; (530)
233-5811.

Turn right at a blinking red light to merge with U.S. 395 and follow it
south half a mile into the downtown area. It's a rather curious scatter of
old brick and masonry nineteenth century buildings, with a few fifties and
sixties structures in between. Some of the older buildings are decorated
with historic murals.

Look to your right for the Spanish colonial style former railroad station
at 619 N. Main, now the **BPOE Temple.** This was headquarters for the
Nevada, California and Oregon Railroad, which locals called the "Narrow,
Cantankerous and Ornery Railroad." Another building worth a peek,
reached by turning left onto Fourth Street at a "Point of historical interest
sign," is the **Sacred Heart Church.** This small stone edifice occupying a
knoll was started in 1833 and not completed in 1910.

Continuing downtown on Main, you'll encounter another grand piece
of architecture, the 1909 white brick and balconied **Niles Hotel and Saloon** at Main and Modoc streets. This hostelry has been a showplace and
locals' hangout for decades, although it was closed when we passed
through, undergoing a change of ownership. If it's open when you arrive,
belly up to the bar in the saloon and admire the wonderfully cluttered
scatter of artifacts—assuming the new owners haven't turned the place
into a laundromat. The hotel restaurant, **Katie's Steakhouse,** was still
active when we last visited; see below.

For more sightseeing, turn left onto Modoc Street and go left again to
check out the 1915 beehive dome **Modoc County Courthouse.** Step
inside to admire its marble walls, stairways and leaded glass dome. Note
the bas relief and gold-leaf winged lion insets in the balcony balustrade.

Return to Main and drive another couple of blocks south to the **Alturas Chamber of Commerce** in an 1879 white clapboard cottage; open weekdays 9 to 5; (530) 233-2819. Next door is a fine local archive:

**Modoc County Historical Museum** • *600 S. Main St.; (530) 233-6328. Tuesday-Saturday 10 to 5 May through October. Free; donations appreciated.* ☐ This nicely arrayed archive exhibits a large weapons, native basket and pottery collection, plus a mock-up general store and assorted pioneer relics. The firearms display—a private collection donated to the museum—is particularly impressive, with weapons dating from the fifteenth Century. A big steam engine sits outside the attractive adobe brick museum building.

If you still haven't seen enough birds, head east on McDowel Avenue between the chamber and museum, following county roads 56 and 115 to **Modoc National Wildlife Refuge** adjacent to Dorris Reservoir. Open March through September, it's a good place to watch nesting waterfowl in summer. For details: Modoc National Wildlife Refuge, P.O. Box 1610, Alturas, CA 96101; (530) 233-3572.

## DINING

**Katie's Steakhouse** • *In the side of the Niles Hotel at 109 E. Modoc St. (Main); (530) 233-2600. American-continental; full bar service. Lunch weekdays, dinner Thursday-Monday and Sunday brunch. Major credit cards; $$$.* ☐ This stylish dining room has an appealing Gay Nineties look with brick interior walls, polished plank floors and ceilings, and maple furniture. The menu drifts from assorted steaks to Cornish game hens, lobster tails and shrimp bordelaise. Meals are ample, served with soup, salad and champagne sorbet. You can get lighter fare at an adjacent deli.

**Nipa's California Cuisine** • *1001 N. Main St.; (530) 233-2520. Asian-American; wine and beer. Lunch and dinner daily. MC/VISA; $$.* ☐ If this café serves California Cuisine, it's definitely from the Asian side of the state. It offers interesting variations on Southeast Asian fare such as red curry chicken in coconut milk, honey duck or chicken on a vegetable bed, and garlic and peppercorn prawns. The American side to the menu lists steaks, fried chicken, salmon and even hamburgers. Housed in a former car hop diner, this is a cheerful place, busy with potted and hanging plants, multicolored drop lamps and Thai artifacts. Nipa's is on the west side of Main Street, a block down from the highway 299/395 junction.

## RECLINING

**Dorris House** • *P.O. Box 1575 (County Road 57), Alturas, CA 96101; (530) 233-3786. Four rooms with private baths; expanded continental breakfast. No credit cards; $$ to $$$.* ☐ You'll have to travel into the country to find this turn-of-the-century ranch house, three miles east of Alturas near the wildlife refuge. Head out County Road 56, then go right on Road 57. Once there, you'll find an appealing inn with comfy rooms done in antiques, a family parlor and a very aromatic kitchen. From the grounds, you can watch the birds commuting to and from the nearby refuge. The inn's name comes from the founding Dorris brothers.

## Side Trip: Surprise Valley and Cedarville

Surprise Valley is one of those poorly-kept secrets about a special hidden place that most people overlook, so of course most visitors to Alturas go there. Travel guides such as this one see to that. It is an uncrowded area, since its isolation—tucked between the Warner Mountains and Nevada's Great Basin Desert—pretty much limits job prospects.

The only thing surprising about this ordinary looking farm valley is the charming little town of **Cedarville**, with a population of 800. Because of its alleged isolation, it still retains much of its late nineteenth century architecture. If you're into hot springs, there are several in Surprise Valley, all on private property. Local folks can tell you which are open and how to reach them.

To reach Surprise Valley, head northeast from Alturas on highways 299/395, then branch to the east on Route 299. You'll climb into the flanks of the Warner Mountains and top Cedar Pass at 6,305 feet. This is neither an awesome nor particularly challenging drive—just a sweeping climb up one side of the Warners and down the other, with a few ruggedly handsome cliff faces along the way. At the top of the pass, a sign announces that you've just entered the Great Basin. The view down to the twenty-mile-long green valley, accented by off-white ovals of dry alkali lake beds, is quite pleasing.

If you're looking for camping, there are Forest Service campgrounds just west and east of the pass. However, the western site, Cedar Pass Campground, was closed because of "tree hazards" when we drove through.

Highway 299 becomes Townsend Street as you enter Cedarville's pleasant tree-shaded suburbs. Watch on your right for a sign indicating **Cressler-Bonner Trading Post,** which is something of an overstatement. What you'll see is a small empty shell of a log cabin built by James Townsend in 1865 as the town's first structure. He was in business less than year before he was knocked off by native people, who were irritated at this Anglo intrusion. William T. Cressler and John H. Bonner bought the trading post, got along better with the Indians and became principals in the building of the town.

After a short distance, Townsend Street bumps into Main, and a right turn will take you past most of the old town's yesterday buildings. A few of them contain places to eat or sleep.

### DINING

**Country Hearth Restaurant** • *551 Main St.; (530) 279-2280. American; wine and beer. Breakfast, lunch and dinner daily. MC/VISA; $$.* ☐ Barnboard interior walls provide a pleasant setting for this cute early American café, where tasty meals of prime rib, steak, scampi and really good hamburgers are cooked over a wood stove. The Hearth also has a savory line of bakery goods.

**Tumbleweed Café** • *415 Main St.; (530) 279-6363. American-Mexican; full bar service. Breakfast through dinner Monday-Saturday and Sunday brunch. No credit cards; $$.* ☐ Tumbleweed occupies a squared log structure, although it's rather prim inside, with floral wallpaper, wainscotting and lace curtains. The menu features the usual steaks, chicken and chops, plus Mexican food four nights a week.

## RECLINING

**Drew Hotel** • *P.O. Box 193 (581 Main St.), Cedarville, CA 96104; (530) 279-2423. Fifteen rooms and a housekeeping unit. MC/VISA; $$.* ☐ This bright red wood frame hotel has been putting folks up since the turn of the century. Rooms are modest, with TV and early American accents. A suite with two bedrooms, kitchen and living room goes for a bit over $100 a night.

**J.K. Metzker House Bed & Breakfast** • *P.O. Box 630 (520 Main St.), Cedarville, CA 96104; (530) 279-2650. Three units with private baths; full breakfast. No credit cards; $$$$.* ☐ This early American home is one of the oldest structures in town, built in 1870 and certainly more attractive than the Cressler-Bonner Trading Post. It was, in fact, Cressler's home and it remained in his family until late in the twentieth century. Guest rooms feature print wallpaper and old fashioned bedsteads. A Franklin stove, TV/VCR and CD player make the downstairs parlor a comfortable place to hang out. If you need exercise, guest bicycles are available and the relatively flat valley with its uncrowded roads is ideal for peddling.

## Side trips: Fort Bidwell and Goose Lake

If you're still in an exploratory mood, you can drive twenty-six miles north from Cedarville, past Upper Alkali Lake to the tiny town of **Fort Bidwell**. It's *really* isolated because this is the only paved highway that reaches it. You'll find a traditional old general store busy with pioneer artifacts, and a few other late nineteenth century structures. If you want to spend the night, the **Fort Bidwell Hotel** is a bed and breakfast inn with modest rooms, and a restaurant serving dinner Thursday through Sunday and lunch on weekends; **$$**. For information: Fort Bidwell Hotel, Main and Garrison, Fort Bidwell, CA 96112; (530) 279-6199.

**Goose Lake**, about twenty miles north of Alturas on Highway 395, is one of California's largest natural lakes. It stretches for twenty-five miles along the highway into southern Oregon. This giant pale blue oval sits in a high prairie valley, rimmed by the rugged Warner Mountains to the east and a craggy wilderness area called Devils Garden to the west.

You can camp just over the border at Oregon's Goose Lake State Park, with RV and tent sites, water and electric hookups, a boat launch and picnic tables; **$$$**; MC/VISA. If you prefer to sleep indoors, continue on to the mile-high town of **Lakeview, Oregon,** which has several motels, cafés and two rather interesting museums.

☺ ☺ ☺

**Where do we go from here?** • From Alturas, a leisurely run southwest along State Route 299 will get you back to I-5 in Redding; see Tour Eight. Or you can stay with U.S. 395 and head south until you hit Carson City, where you can begin Tour Thirteen, the eastern Sierra.

*Tour Eight*

# PIT RIVER ROUTE
## ALTURAS TO REDDING ON HIGHWAY 299

This route through the grassy valleys, pasturelands and wooded mountain passes of north central California isn't particularly awesome. However, you will see—on a clear day—simultaneous views of Mount Shasta and Mount Lassen, since the highway passes between them.

And of course, if you've just taken Tour Seven in the previous chapter, this gets you back to Interstate 5. It's a bit like one of those repositioning cruises, when a ship ends its winter season of Caribbean cruises and sails to Alaska to begin its summer season.

Heading west from Alturas, Highway 299 follows a geological crease, seeking low points between the Klamath Mountains to the north and the Cascades below. The first portion of the trip takes you over a high prairie called the Modoc Plateau. Beyond Fall River Mills, you'll follow the twisting course of the Pit River, which has cut its way through a relatively recent lava flow. You'll see only small towns along this route and most have been hit hard by lumber industry cutbacks, so they don't look particularly prosperous.

To begin, head southwest from Alturas to **Canby**, a small town that offers little cause to pause. You'll soon leave a grassy high valley and be-

# TRIP PLANNER

**WHEN TO GO** ● Spring through fall are suitable times for this trip. Roads might get icy and passes may be temporarily closed by snow in winter.

**DRIVING DISTANCE** ● About 150 miles from Alturas to Redding.

**RV ADVISORY** ● There are no narrow, steep or twisting roads on this tour, except for the drive down to a generating plant on the Pit River.

**WHAT YOU'LL SEE** ● A twin panorama of volcanic peaks—Mount Shasta and Mount Lassen, Fort Crook Museum in Fall River Mills, Pit River Falls and Pit River gorge.

**WHAT TO DO** ● Angle for trout in Pit River Canyon and relax at the Pit River Lodge.

**TO BEGIN** ● Head southeast from Alturas on State Route 299.

## Useful contacts

**Burney Basin Chamber of Commerce**, P.O. Box 36 (37088 Main St.), Burney, CA 96013; (530) 335-2111.

**Fall River Valley Chamber of Commerce**, P.O. Box 475 (Heritage Building on Highway 299), Fall River Mills, CA 96028; (530) 336-5840.

## Pricing guidelines

**DINING:** Dinner entrée with soup or salad, without drinks or dessert for under $10 = **$**; $10 to $14 = **$$**; $15 to $25 = **$$$**; over $25 = **$$$$**.

**RECLINING:** A two-person room for $35 or less = **$**; $36 to $50 = **$$**; $51 to $75 = **$$$**; $76 to $100 = **$$$$**; more than $100 = **$$$$$**.

**CAMPING:** Under $10 = **$**; $10 to $14 = **$$**; $15 to $19 = **$$$**; $20 or more = **$$$$**

---

gin climbing into the pines toward **Adin Pass** at 5,173 feet. It's the highest point you'll reach on this route. Cruising down the other side, you'll encounter **Adin,** a pleasant, tree shaded old community in a high basin called Big Valley. The 1906 **Ye Olde General Supply Store**, downtown on your right, is worth a peek.

Hope for clear weather as you continue southwest from Adin, for you'll soon be able to see the snow-streaked peaks of **Mount Shasta** to the north and **Mount Lassen** to the south. The old towns of **Bieber** and **Nubieber,** nondescript except for their curious names, will come and go without incident. You'll then begin another climb and crest 4,603-foot Big Valley Summit. From this high perch, you'll get a grand view of Fall River Valley's vast patchwork of ranch lands and clusters of communities, with both Shasta and Lassen overseeing the vista.

As you drop down into the valley, watch on your right on the eastern edge of **McArthur** for pretty roadside floral gardens that extend in front of three homes. Downtown, check out the old style **McArthur Mercan-**

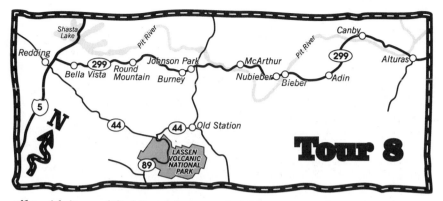

tile with its modified Dutch barn roof. Oddly, the town's low rise business district stands well back from the highway, as if shying away from traffic.

**Fall River Mills,** with 600 people, is widely scattered over the broad valley floor. What little survives of the town's old district is a small string of stores—many closed—reached by making a half-left off the highway onto Main Street at mid-town. The turn is just beyond a Forest Service office. The most interesting structure here is the weathered three-story **Fall River Hotel,** white stucco with burgundy trim and a curved false front façade. It has modestly priced rooms with breakfast; (530) 336-5550.

Continue through town on Highway 299 and watch on your right for an interesting museum complex on the west side:

**Fort Crook Museum** • *Highway 299; (530) 336-5110. May to October, Tuesday-Sunday noon to 4.* ☐ This extensive complex is nearly as big as downtown Fall River Mills. Several historic buildings have been dragged to this spot to form a pioneer village. They include Pitville School, fully furnished with blackboards and old fashioned inkwell desks; a mean-looking iron door jail; and a squared log cabin with rude pioneer furnishings. A large cinderblock building is filled with antique fire equipment, farm implements and wagons. The main museum, in a modern octagonal structure, exhibits a wide array of pioneer artifacts. Even if it's closed, you can wander the grounds and admire the old buildings.

West of Fall River Mills, you'll encounter the most dramatic portion of this route. A couple of miles out of town, watch on your left for a vista point above **Pit River Canyon** and **Pit River Falls,** which gushes as a multiple cataract hundreds of feet below. Volcanic eruptions several thousand years ago spilled down over this slope, blocking the Pit River, which managed to cut its way through. Continuing downhill from the vista point, the highway spirals along the north wall of the chasm. There are occasional wide spots on the opposite shoulder, where you can pull over and peer into Pit River Canyon's sheer basaltic cliffs.

At the bottom of the grade, watch on your left for a sign indicating "Pit River Campground." A winding, narrow road will take you to the lower end of Pit River Canyon, which offers three interesting elements—a recently restored 1920s resort, an ancient and still working generating plant, and a primitive campground. After winding downward for about a mile, a left turn will take you to Pit River Lodge, that powerhouse and a cluster of old buildings—all the work of Pacific Gas and Electric Company. The firm constructed a powerhouse here in 1921; it siphons water from the fast-flowing Pit River to turn its turbines. PG&E created a mini-company town here, with homes for the workers and a vintage hotel:

**Pit River Lodge** ● *P.O. Box 920, Fall River Mills, CA 96028; (530) 336-5005. Lodge rooms with share baths; $$ to $$$. Former company houses, fully furnished, also can be rented; $$$$$. The dining room serves breakfast through dinner Wednesday-Sunday; American fare, no alcohol; $$. MC/VISA.* ◻ This grand old lodge, not elegant but impeccably restored, sits beneath the shade of giant maples, cottonwoods and oaks. The front porch is an inviting place to spend a lazy afternoon. Rooms are simple and spotless; all have wash basins and down-the-hall bathrooms, except for the Bridal Suite, which has a full bath. The interior of the lodge is paneled in light woods and a fieldstone fireplace accents the early American style dining room. The menu lists halibut—a local favorite—plus honey glazed chicken, steaks and a few pasta dishes. Pit River Lodge is a peaceful retreat, except for the gentle hum of the powerhouse across from the park-like grounds.

There are no powerhouse tours, although you can stroll about the area and watch the water rushing through the tailrace. Do not drive across the bridge over the tailrace, since a departing worker may accidentally lock you in. You can walk over the bridge, then pick your way through the woods—no easy task—and find the main stream, which is very good for trout fishing.

A primitive campground, operated by the Bureau of Land Management, is about half a mile downstream from the powerhouse. Actually, primitive is an understatement; there are no designated campsites and the roads are terrible. The only facilities are pit potties. However, it's free, many of the sites are right over the river the place is quite popular. All the good sites were taken when we came through a summer weekday.

---

*RV ADVISORY* ● The drive down to the generating plant and campground is very winding, and interior campground roads are not maintained and deeply rutted. *Ickybod,* our 21-foot Winnebago, had no problems, but big rigs and trailers may have trouble maneuvering.

---

Back on the highway, continue a mile or so east and watch on your right for a nice little **Shasta County Park**, just after you cross Little Hat Creek. It has streamside picnic tables, barbecue pits and fishing access.

West of the park, Highway 299 becomes arrow straight, firing across a basaltic plain through sagebrush and piñon pines. At its intersection with State Route 89, you can go north briefly to **McArthur-Burney Falls Memorial State Park** or south to **Lassen Volcanic National Park**, both covered in Tour Nine in the next chapter.

Beyond the junction, you'll pass through a pair of strung-out towns. Although not models of urban planning, they are rather neat and tidy, compared with other hamlets along this route.

*Pit River Falls, seen through a telephoto lens from a viewpoint below Fall River Mills, cascades into a rugged basaltic gorge.*

## BURNEY & JOHNSON PARK

**Population: about 4,000**          **Elevation: 3,130 feet**

There's no border distinction between these two towns, scattered for several miles along both sides of Highway 299. Neither has any real character, since most of their low rise buildings are contemporary. Burney is the larger of the two, dressed up with a few outdoor murals. The twin towns offer several motels, service stations and cafés, including the first fast food joint you'll see since leaving Alturas. However, a couple of places are a cut above hamburger parlors:

### DINING

**Wiggy's** • *Highway 299 in Johnson Park; (530) 335-2120. American; no alcohol. Breakfast through dinner daily. No credit cards; $ to $$.* ☐ Watch on your right as you enter Johnson Park for this little barnboard cottage. It has tables out front and an appealing early American dining room with barnboard wainscotting and beam ceilings. The menu is essential American, with steak, chicken breast or chicken strips, pork chops and chicken fried steak. All but the steaks are under $10. Wiggy's has an even cheaper senior menu if you're willing to admit your age.

**Rex Club** • *Highway 299 in Burney; (530) 335-4184. American; full bar service. Lunch Thursday-Saturday, dinner nightly except Wednesday. MC/VISA; $$.* ☐ The Rex Club occupies a barnboard building on the left, just beyond Burney's second traffic signal. Its large Western style dining room issues steaks, assorted treatments of chicken, deep fried prawns, ravioli and spaghetti. A small, lively saloon is next door; it features live entertainment on Friday nights.

Pressing westward from Burney, State Route 299 continues through this basaltic prairie, threading its way easily between the Klamath and Cascade ranges. If you have a sharp geologist's eye, you may note the difference between the older layered sedimentary rocks of the Klamaths and the newer volcanic rocks and ash of the Cascades.

A couple of miles from Burney, a vista point provides a fine view of the rumpled, snow-streaked north face of Mount Lassen. You'll crest one final grade—4,368-foot Hatchet Mountain Summit, then begin a long descent toward Redding on Interstate 5. Tiny towns along the route—Hillcrest, Montgomery Creek, Round Mountain and Bella Vista—provide no reason to pause, except for their reduced speed limits.

☺ ☺ ☺

*Where do we go from here?* • Just about anywhere, since you're on I-5. Or you can stay on State Route 299 and dovetail into Tour Five, from Redding to Arcata.

## Tour Nine

# THE LASSEN ROUTE

## MOUNT SHASTA CITY TO MARKLEEVILLE

This pretty drive winds lazily through a mix of thickly wooded mountains, grassy valleys and alpine basins along State Route 89. The tumbled terrain was shaped as the Cascade-Siskiyou and Sierra Nevada ranges faulted and drifted apart, while volcanoes pushed their molten noses skyward. Lording above the northern end of this alpine landscape is 14,162-foot Mount Shasta.

Two other major geological features mark this route through northern California's mountain ranges. Although smaller than Shasta, Mount Lassen is equally dramatic, as one of the largest plug volcanoes in the world. And it could—like Washington's Mount St. Helens to the north—make headlines one day. It's sleeping, but it's not dormant; it last erupted in 1915.

Near the lower end of this scenic drive is Lake Tahoe, described by Mark Twain as "the fairest picture the whole earth allows." Not so fair as it once was and hardly uncrowded, this is still one of the world's grandest, highest and purest lakes. It sits well over a mile above sea level, measures seventy-one miles around and averages a thousand feet deep. We won't

# TRIP PLANNER

**WHEN TO GO** ● This is a summer through late fall drive, since the highway through Lassen Volcanic National Park is closed by winter snow, along with many park facilities. Also, many trails in the park don't open until summer—sometimes not until late July after a wet winter. Autumn color can be impressive in this area, particularly in Plumas County and the Feather River Canyon.

**DRIVING DISTANCE** ● About 340 miles, all paved. Allow two to three days for a leisurely trip, particularly if you plan to spend time in Lassen, or if you intend to do some fishing; there are plenty of lakes along this route.

**RV ADVISORY** ● You'll encounter some steep hills and tight turns, although the route is negotiable by large RVs or trailer rigs. Although Highway 89 travels through a forested area, much of the route is remarkably straight and level.

**WHAT YOU'LL SEE** ● Mount Shasta from assorted angles, McArthur-Burney Falls Memorial State Park, Lassen Volcanic National Park, Lake Almanor, the old mining town of Quincy, Plumas-Eureka State Park near Graeagle, rustic-trendy Truckee, the western edge of Lake Tahoe, appealing little Markleeville, and lots of pine trees.

**WHAT TO DO** ● Feed the fingerlings at Mount Shasta Hatchery; hike down to Burney Falls and up to the top of Mount Lassen; prowl the trendy shops of Truckee; take the waters at Grovers Hot Springs near Markleeville.

**TO BEGIN** ● Get to Mount Shasta City on Interstate 5, then head southeast on State Route 89.

## Useful contacts

**Chester-Lake Almanor Chamber of Commerce**, P.O. Box 1198, Chester, CA 96020; (800) 350-4838 or (530) 258-2426. (E-MAIL: almanor@psln.com)

**Lassen Volcanic National Park,** Box 100, Mineral, CA 96063-0100; (530) 595-4444.

**Mount Shasta Visitors Bureau**, 300 Pine St., Mount Shasta, CA 96067; (800) 926-4865 or (530) 926-4865.

**Plumas County Visitors Bureau**, P.O. Box 4120, Quincy, CA 95971; (800) 326-2247, (530) 283-6345. (WEB: www.plumas.ca.us)

**Truckee-Donner Chamber of Commerce**, 12036 Donner Pass Rd., Truckee, CA 96161; (530) 587-2757.

## Pricing guidelines

**DINING:** Dinner entrée with soup or salad, without drinks or dessert for under $10 = **$**; $10 to $14 = **$$**; $15 to $25 = **$$$**; over $25 = **$$$$**.

**RECLINING:** A two-person room for $35 or less = **$**; $36 to $50 = **$$**; $51 to $75 = **$$$**; $76 to $100 = **$$$$**; more than $100 = **$$$$$**.

**CAMPING:** Under $10 = **$**; $10 to $14 = **$$**; $15 to $19 = **$$$**; $20 or more = **$$$$**

focus heavily on Lake Tahoe; plenty of other guidebooks do that. Our route will brush the busy western shoreline then continue south and return to the quiet, crossing two low mountain passes, with a pause in tiny Markleeville, the smallest county seat in America.

## MOUNT SHASTA

**Population: 3,500**                    **Elevation: 3,554 feet**

This tour begins—as a good backroad tour should begin—by abandoning a freeway. From whatever direction you may be coming, take the central Mount Shasta city exit from Interstate 5, then head west away from town, following signs to Lake Siskiyou and the Sisson Museum. The road leads directly to a pair of attractions sharing a mutual campus.

**Mount Shasta Hatchery** is the oldest west of the Mississippi, established way back in 1888. Occupying the oldest hatchery building is the **Sisson Museum**, named for founders of the town of Sisson, which was the forerunner to Mount Shasta City. Justin Sisson settled here in 1853, then went back east a few years later to fetch a bride, Lydia. The couple provided the land for this still active hatchery. The museum is nicely arranged for a small-town archive, with pioneer photos and relics and a shiny 1915 Model-T Ford fire engine. An elaborate model railroad layout can be activated by punching the proper buttons. The archive is open 10 to 4 Monday-Saturday and 1 to 4 Sunday; (530) 926-5508.

At the adjacent hatchery, you can create a feeding frenzy by tossing a quarters' worth of fish food into the narrow rearing troughs. Available from vending machines, the stuff looks like tiny rabbit pellets—the food, not the poop. You also can wander through a large hatchery shed where thousands of tiny fingerlings squirm about. The hatchery grounds are open daily from 7 to sunset; (530) 926-2215.

If you seek a place to fish or camp, exit the museum-hatchery grounds, turn right and follow Old Hatchery Road past woodsy suburban homes to **Lake Siskiyou.** This 430-acre reservoir is appealing for its pine-rimmed setting and for the dramatic backdrop of Mount Shasta which, on a calm day, casts a mirror image in the blue water. You can drive down to water's edge for a dip or you can rent an assortment of small boats, kayaks, canoes and sea cycles at a marina. The main road winds around the lake and returns you to Old Hatchery Road, although it becomes a narrow dirt lane for the last few miles. You may have to pull over to allow oncoming traffic to shoulder past.

*Lake Siskiyou Camp Resort* • *P.O. Box 276, Mount Shasta, CA 96067; (888) 926-2618 or (530) 926-2618. (WEB SITE: www.mountshastaresort.com) Lodging units $$$ to $$$$; RV sites $$ to $$$$.* ☐ This lakeside resort has lodging in fully equipped trailers, plus tent and full hookup RV sites. Other facilities include a marina, boat launch, coin laundry, showers, playgrounds, barbecue and picnic area.

From Lake Siskiyou, return to the hatchery/museum entrance road, turn right, cross over the freeway and drive into downtown Lake Shasta on Lake Street. Just short of downtown, watch for two items of interest—**Black Bear Diner** on your right and the **Mount Shasta Visitors Bu-**

**reau** on your left. The bureau is open Monday-Saturday 9 to 5 and Sunday 9 to 3; (530) 926-4865.

## DINING

**Black Bear Diner** • *401 W. Lake St.; (530) 926-4669. American; wine and beer. Breakfast through dinner daily; open twenty-four hours on Friday and Saturday. Major credit cards; $$.* □ This neatly rustic diner serves hearty if not terribly creative portions of roast chicken, beef, turkey, pork, barbecued ribs, pot roasts and other stuff from grandma's kitchen. It's an attractive place, with historic Shasta photos decorating one dining room and sports memorabilia accenting another.

**Serge's Restaurant** • *531 Chestnut St. (left off Lake Street, a block east of Mount Shasta Boulevard); (530) 926-1276. French; wine and beer. Dinner Wednesday-Sunday plus Sunday brunch; closed Monday-Tuesday. Major credit cards; $$$.* □ This is a surprise for a town that's—well, a bit on the rustic side. French cuisine tilted toward the lighter side emerges from the kitchen and the grand bulk of Mount Shasta emerges outside; it's visible from the dining room and a deck. Serge's is noted for several vegetarian dishes in addition to Franco classics and it has a good wine list.

Shasta's old fashioned tree-lined Lake Street points directly toward the mountain. If you drive for eleven miles, swerving to the left onto Washington Drive/Everitt Memorial Highway, you'll wind up right in Shasta's lap, at the Bunny Flat trailhead. Most peak climbs begin here, although serious mountaineering equipment is needed. If you've somehow forgotten your ice ax, you can still follow trails to less challenging heights. (Permits are required for any ascent over 10,000 feet.) The views of Shasta's snow draped peak and the surrounding mountains are quite grand from the trailhead and its trails.

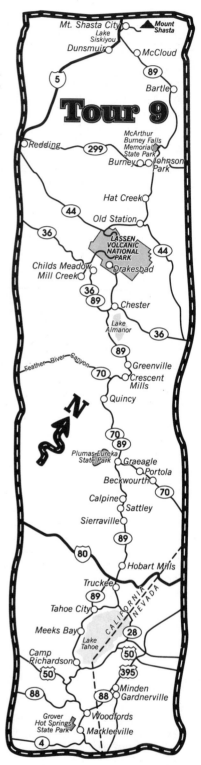

About four miles below Bunny Flat, **McBride Springs Campground** of Shasta-Trinity National Forest has wooded sites with tables and barbecues; no hookups; **$$**. Some have tree-filtered views of the mountain. You may find the place full on summer weekends.

---

**RV ADVISORY** • This route to Bunny Flat is a curving but gentle climb, with plenty of parking and turnaround space at the top, even for large motorhomes and trailer rigs.

---

Return to downtown, turn left onto Mount Shasta Boulevard and follow it south two miles to its juncture with State Route 89, near the south Mount Shasta offramp. Start heading east through a foothill area of manzanita and second growth pine. The great mass of Shasta will be looking over your left shoulder for much of the drive.

## McCLOUD

**Population: About 2,000**              **Elevation: 3,500 feet**

Several miles of surprisingly straight and flat highway will carry you to McCloud, an old company lumbering town that provides basic services and—for fans of early American architecture—some charming old false front and wood frame buildings. One has been converted into an inn. To find it and other old structures in the downtown area, follow a sign left from Highway 89 indicating the historic district:

***McCloud Bed & Breakfast Hotel*** • *P.O. Box 370 (408 Main Street), McCloud, CA 96057; (800) 964-2823 or (530) 964-2822. (WEB SITE: www.mchotel.com) Fourteen rooms and suites with private baths; full breakfast. MC/VISA, DISC; $$$$.* ◻ This 1915 colonial style wood frame hotel served lumber barons and their staff when McCloud was a company town. It has been nicely restored and furnished with early American antiques, including some canopy and four poster beds.

If you'd like to dine aboard lacquered wood and brass-trimmed railway cars and see fine scenery to boot, contact the folks at McCloud Railway Company about the **Shasta Sunset Dinner Train.** Following old rail logging lines, the train takes diners forty miles past Mount Shasta, Castle Crags and into the edge of the Trinity Alps. It runs from April to December; (800) 733-2141 or (530) 964-2141.

Continuing eastward on Highway 89, you might want to pause at the **McCloud Ranger Station** on the east side of town for area recreation information. It's open weekdays 8 to 5; (530) 964-2988. A few miles beyond, watch for a vista point that provides an unfettered view of The Mountain. It's one of the few places along this route where Shasta is completely free of foreground trees. This is a good photo spot—unless you like to frame your shots with foreground trees.

A bit beyond the viewpoint, Forest Road 13 will launch you on a convoluted although reasonably well marked 77-mile tour called the **Mount Shasta Loop.** It takes you completely around the mountain, ultimately delivering you to Weed on U.S. Highway 97. The first ten miles is paved to

*The ice cream scoop of Mount Shasta appears to be melting on the surface of Lake Siskiyou.*

the Ash Creek Mill site, then much of the rest is broken pavement or unpaved. It's bumpy and narrow, not suited for large RVs or trailer rigs. Even passenger cars and small RVs must be driven carefully. Inquire at the ranger station for conditions—and pick up a route map. Don't try this side trip in wet weather.

## To MacArthur Burney and Mount Lassen

Meanwhile, back on course, you'll whisk through **Bartle,** consisting of a café, mini-mart and a couple of gas pumps. Much more appealing, about ten miles beyond, is **Lake Britton,** a pine-fringed reservoir just below MacArthur Burney Falls State Park. A road angles sharply to the right, taking you down to a cozy little picnic area and fishing access. To get there from this direction, you have to overshoot the turnoff, make a marked U-turn just ahead and then come back.

---

*RV ADVISORY* ● The winding road down to the lake (not to mention the U-turn) would be a challenge for big motorhomes or trailer rigs.

---

Just down the highway, you'll see a sign to **Dusty Campground** which isn't really, since the interior roads are gravel. However, you will kick up a few clouds on the two-mile dirt lane that leads to this lakeside camping area, which is operated by Pacific Gas & Electric. It's a rather casual operation, with pit potties and no hookups, although it's cheap (**$$**) and there are several campsites right on the lake. Locals tend to fill it up on summer weekends.

**McArthur-Burney Falls Memorial State Park ●** *24896 Highway 99, Burney, CA 96013; (530) 335-2777. Modest day use fee; RV and tent sites with flush potties and showers; no hookups; $$$. For campsite reservations, call (800) 444-PARK; MC/VISA accepted. A souvenir shop and store is adjacent to the campground.* ☐ Although State Route 89 is a road less traveled, little 853-acre McArthur-Burney Falls State Park is not a place less visited. The campsites, shaded but rather closely tucked for a state park, are completely booked between Memorial and Labor Day weekends, so reservations are essential.

The reason for this popularity is an exceptionally pretty waterfall that drops in dozens of rivulets, 129 feet over a rough basaltic face. President Teddy Roosevelt was so taken by this multi-braided cataract that he called it the eighth wonder of the world—which may be a bit of an overstatement. A short zigzag trail will take you to the falls, where you can stand and enjoy the mist in your face, or drop a line into the burbling pool at the base. The trout fishing's good here, and the limit is two fish a day from the pool and from Burney Creek that trickles below it. A tree-canopied path follows the creek about two miles to Lake Britton. Incidentally, with all that mist, it can get chilly at the base of the falls, so take a wrap, even on a warm day.

A few miles below McArthur-Burney, the highway crosses State Route 299 and a right turn will take you five miles to the fused-together towns of **Burney** and **Johnson Park**. This lumbering and livestock trading center with a combined total of more than 7,000 residents provides a good assortment of restaurants, motels and stores. We stopped by here on Tour Eight, page 109. Pressing southward on State Route 89, you'll pass through the town of **Hat Creek,** occupying an agricultural valley. It has an interesting old cut stone general store with a couple of fuel pumps, and not much else.

A few miles below Hat Creek, a campground, mini-mart and café complex called **Rancheria** has tent sites and full hookups (**$$** to **$$$$**) around an attractive pond. Its rustic café serves tri-tips, honey dipped chicken and—as an occasional special—smoked trout. MC/VISA and DISC; (800) 346-3430 or (530) 335-7418.

Just beyond Rancheria, Mount Lassen will suddenly appear, probably wearing a mantle of snow unless it's been a dry year. It'll play hide and seek among the trees for the next dozen miles, until you enter the park. State Route 44 joins Highway 89 at the tiny town of **Old Station** and together they begin a leisurely twist up toward that grand volcano. Watch on your left for a vista point, where you'll get a fine view of the peak's ruggedly handsome north face. A display discusses Lassen's most recent eruptions; you'll learn that it belched more than 300 times between 1914 and 1921. A short nature trail takes you through a reforested burn area. The park entrance is seven miles beyond:

*Lassen Volcanic National Park* ● *Box 100, Mineral, CA 96063-0100; (530) 595-4444. Loomis Museum Visitor Center at Manzanita Lake open daily 9 to 5 in summer only. Southwest Information Station open daily 9 to 4 in summer only. Modest park entry fee. Food service at Manzanita Lake (north entrance) and Chalet Foods and Gifts (southwest entrance); general store, showers, laundry and fuel at Manzanita Lake. Camping at six campgrounds; some flush and some pit potties; tables and fire rings or barbecue grills; $ to $$. Lodging at Drakesbad Guest Ranch south of the park; see listing on page 120.* ☐

Until Mount St. Helens became a major media event in 1980, Mount Lassen held the spotlight as America's youngest active volcano. It had been sleeping fitfully for centuries until it began a series of grumbles, shakes and minor eruptions in 1914. A year later, it exploded with the vigor of the St. Helens blast, shooting a column of cinder, hot ash and smoke seven miles into the stratosphere. It remained restless for another six years, then it went back to sleep, leaving a torn landscape and a fascinating collection of geothermal features. By commuting between Lassen and St. Helens, the traveler can witness the slow process of post-eruption revegetation, sixty years apart.

With each visit, we continue to be amazed at the lack of crowds in this splendid national park. We found campsites available in all the park campgrounds in mid-July, although sites at Summit Lake and Manzanita Lake often book up on weekends and some summer weekdays.

We find Lassen to be more interesting than Mount St. Helens, offering more geothermal displays, better hikes and more awesome scenery. Much of what's appealing about this place can be seen from a series of turnouts along the park's only highway, State Route 89. It wraps sinuously around the mountain's northern, eastern and southern perimeters. However, you need to get out of your vehicle to really enjoy the park. Rangers conduct a variety of hikes and talks, and you can strike out on your own.

---

*RV ADVISORY* ● The park road twists like Christmas ribbon candy as it skirts the mountain, although it's well graded and navigable by a large motorhome or trailer rig.

---

Lassen has several required stops. At the **Devastated Area,** a short interpretive trail winds through a stark region still recovering from the big blast. From here, enjoy a leisurely drive around the mountain's flanks, then pull into the **Lassen Peak Trail** parking area just beyond the 8,512-foot road summit. You can hike part or all of the way to the top for absolutely splendid views of a grand convergence of the Sierra Nevada and Cascades. Mount Lassen marks the spot where the two mountain ranges meet. Get an early morning start, because you'll be gaining 2,000 vertical feet in a 2.2-mile grunt. The top of the peak is a rocky ridge and you'll have to scramble over giant boulders to attain the summit. It's difficult to define the trail here, although the best route is on the left side of the ridge. (Also, call ahead for trail conditions. The last time we visited, the peak trail still hadn't opened in mid-July.)

*Mount Lassen is as pretty as a Christmas card in winter. There's a snow play area near the southern entrance.*

Immediately beyond the parking lot, the road begins a quick downward spiral. Pause at a turnout for a gorgeous view of deep blue **Lake Helen**, backdropped by several serious peaks. We liked it so well that it wound up on the cover of this book.

Between Helen and Emerald Lakes is **Bumpass Hell**, the park's most popular stop. Here, a three-mile trail winds among an assortment of hissing, gurgling and burbling mudpots, hot springs, steam vents and other geothermal animations. The area's odd name comes from an unfortunate incident. Tour guide Kendall Bumpass lost a leg back in the 19th century when he fell into a boiling pool.

Near the southwest entrance station, you'll encounter the park's last significant feature. The **Sulfur Works** is a smaller area of thermal activity, reached by short trails and boardwalks. One whiff will tell you how it got its name. Just beyond, you can grab a bite to eat or pick up some souvenirs at the **Lassen Chalet**. And just beyond that is a campground and information station.

Lassen is mostly a summer place, yet it can be absolutely gorgeous in winter. Although the main highway through the park is closed, visitors can reach a snow play and informal cross-country ski area near the Chalet at the southern entrance. The Chalet is closed, although restrooms are open.

***Drakesbad Guest Ranch*** ● *Mailing address: California Guest Services, 2150 N. Main St., Suite 5, Red Bluff, CA 96080; (530) 529-9820. (E-MAIL: msilva@snowcrest.com) Nineteen rooms and cabins with private baths; $$$$$. MC/VISA. Rates include all meals.* ☐ Rustic and very popular, this is one place where you can't just drop in. Reservations for Drakesbad must be made months in advance, although you can call and hope for a cancellation. Built in the 1930s, this tree-shrouded resort in Lassen's foothills has simple accommodations. Amenities include a mineral pool, stables and fishing and hiking areas. Breakfast and lunch are buffet style— or you can order a picnic—while dinner is a multi-course affair with *nouveau* touches. With no room phones or television, this is a grand place for escaping civilization's crowds.

You have to leave the park to reach Drakesbad, which is at the end of Warner Valley Road, seventeen miles northwest of Chester. The ranch is inside Lassen's boundary, however. Hiking and riding trails will take you back the main part of the park along Highway 89, or into a wilderness of lakes, meadows and mountains in the eastern half of the preserve.

## To Chester and Quincy

Assuming that you don't have Drakesbad reservations, follow State Route 89 south through a steep-walled canyon. The road merges with Highway 36 and swings eastward. If you'd like a quiet place to camp, sleep or have a bite, drive three miles south on State Route 172 to **Mill Creek**, a summer home community. Its focal point is a combined resort, restaurant and campground with rather modest prices:

***Mill Creek Resort*** ● *#1 Highway 172, Mill Creek, CA 96061; (888) 595-4449 or (530) 595-4449. Nine housekeeping cabins $$$; camping and RV sites $$; restaurant $$. MC/VISA.* ☐ This homey complex includes a log main lodge, shaded RV sites and fully furnished cabins with kitchens. The old style café serves breakfast through early dinner, with wine and beer. Dinners are hefty affairs, featuring honey dipped chicken, steak and such, served with fries and biscuits.

## CHESTER

**Population: 1,200**                                      **Elevation: 4,525 feet**

Beyond the Mill Creek turnoff, the two roads separate. Route 89 continues south past the western shoreline of Lake Almanor while Highway 36 highway heads east through Chester. Although this low rise scatter of an old lumbering and ranching town isn't a tourist mecca, it has a couple of interesting restaurants and a cozy inn.

Heading into town on Highway 36, you'll pass the **Lake Almanor Ranger Station,** where you can gather information on woodsy areas of interest. The **Chamber of Commerce** is on the western edge of town at 529 Main Street; open weekdays 9 to 5; (530) 258-2426.

Continue through the small business district and you'll encounter those two restaurants, sitting side by side. Other than their juxtaposition, they have nothing in common. Beyond them, at the town's eastern edge, is an attractive bed & breakfast.

## DINING AND RECLINING

**Creekside Grill** • *278 Main St.; (530) 258-1966. American nouveau; wine and beer. Lunch and dinner daily in summer, Wednesday-Sunday the rest of the year. MC/VISA; $$.* ☐ Trendy dining in an old mill town? It started with the arrival of California Culinary Academy graduate Tracy Darue and her husband Don. They've decorated a comfortable old creek bank cottage with floral ceiling banners and bunting, giving its warm wood interior a cheerful look. The real cheer comes from the kitchen, where Tracy prepares such creations as grilled halibut steak with fresh mango kiwi salsa, and pork tenderloin with garlic mashed potatoes and glazed carrots. You can dine beside the aspen shaded creek on an outdoor deck or indoors, where large windows provide generous views.

**Knot Bumper** • *274 Main St.; (530) 258-3201. American; wine and beer. Lunch and dinner Monday-Saturday. MC/VISA; $.* ☐ The name says it. This is a good old boy restaurant in a rustic cottage, featuring beef dip, roast beef, thick steaks and several Mexican dishes. Most entrées are under $10. The interior is interesting in a Western sort of way, with wooden booths and knotty pine walls. It, too, has an outdoor dining deck.

**Bidwell House Bed & Breakfast** • *P.O. Box 1790 (One Main Street), Chester, CA 96020; (530) 258-3338. Fourteen guest rooms; mostly private baths; full breakfast. MC/VISA; $$$$.* ☐ Historians know the Bidwells as prominent early northern California pioneers; they built this mansion well over a century ago. It's been nicely restored and furnished with early American antiques. Some of the units have spa tubs and wood-burning stoves to add to their coziness and several have TVs and phones. If you're a traveling family, you can rent a cottage that sleeps six.

**Lake Almanor** hangs south of Chester in a shallow woodland basin. One of the largest freshwater reservoirs in the state, this brilliant blue pond covers more than fifty-two square miles. If you like to boat, water ski or fish, you may want to spend a day or more here. Most commercial resorts are on the eastern side and you can get a list from the chamber of commerce. Most campgrounds are on the wooded western shore, along our chosen route. Anglers can hook trout, bass and perch in these waters.

Pressing southward on Route 89, you'll enter Plumas County and a popular recreation area known as Feather River Country. (If you took high school Spanish, you know that "plumas" and "feather" are the same thing.) The highway takes you into Indian Valley and passes through two slightly dowdy but appealing old mining towns, **Greenville** and **Crescent Mills**. In Greenville, check out the cute combination justice of the peace and sheriff's office in a false front colonial structure on your right. If you're hungry, step into **The Way Station Dinner House** on the corner of Main and Highway 89. This funky old diner with bentwood chairs and wainscotting is open for dinner Wednesday-Sunday, serving essential American fare, with beer and wine; MC/VISA; (530) 284-6087.

And if you want linger longer in this area, check into the **Crescent Hotel Bed & Breakfast** in a restored 1927 lodge in Crescent Mills. Even if you don't need a room, check out the handsome lobby with its lacquered knotty pine walls, game trophies and fieldstone fireplace; it looks like a hunting club. The inn has seven rooms, mostly with shared baths; full breakfast. MC/VISA; **$$$**; (530) 284-0879.

Below Crescent Mills, the highway dips into pretty, boulder-strewn Indian Creek Canyon, then merges with State Route 70 at the confluence of Indian Creek and the Feather River.

## Side trip: The Feather River Canyon

Highway 70 through the Feather River Canyon has been designated as the Feather River Scenic Byway. It's a very pretty drive that will deliver you—after sixty miles of gentle turns and twists—to Oroville in the broad Central Valley. Longtime Californians will recall that the Feather River Project was conceived in the 1960s to divert northern California water to thirsty southern California; Oroville Dam is its cornerstone.

---

**RV ADVISORY** ● Although it passes through a steep-walled river canyon, Highway 70 is a surprisingly tame route, with few steep grades or tight turns. Any size rig should be able to make it.

---

This isn't an awesome drive, since the canyon is mostly a basic tree-cloaked, vee-shaped ravine. However, you'll encounter some steep rock-ribbed walls in the lower end. They're an interesting geological mix of dark pre-Cambrian serpentine and more recent granite deposited by ancient volcanoes. It's worth the detour if you have time on your hands. This is not wilderness drive; you'll encounter an occasional commercial RV park and small resort, plus several Forest Service campgrounds.

Perhaps the most interesting thing along this route is the tiny former mining town of **Belden,** reached by crossing a narrow steel bridge dating back to 1912. The town is even older, started when the Belden family found a bit of gold here back in the 1850s. It now claims a population of ten, and most of them are probably employed by the **Belden Resort**, consisting of a large western style, river view saloon with light food service, a mini-mart and a tree-shaded RV park; **$$**. You can sit and sip inside and try a game of pool or ping pong, or take your beer onto the porch and watch the river roll by. For information: Belden Town and Resort, 14785 Belden Town Rd., Belden (Oroville), CA 95915; (530) 283-2906.

Below Belden, the river becomes a series of liquid stairsteps, impounded by small dams and power plants operated by Pacific Gas & Electric. You'll alternately encounter stretches of rocky riverbed strewn with boulders larger than my first apartment, and flooded sections where dams have turned the stream into slender fjords. The canyon narrows dramatically through this area, so steep that the highway frequently tunnels through its rock walls.

If you continue on to Oroville, the highway swings away from the river. Just beyond the tiny town of **Yankee Hill**, it crests a ridge and provides a sudden and jarring view—the flat, vast and hazy expanse of the Central Valley. There's no reason to continue further, unless you're using this route to get back to civilization. There's plenty of it here; Route 70 becomes a busy four-lane highway and freeway passing through Oroville and Marysville. It eventually dissolves into State Route 99 that whisks travelers onto Interstate 5 and into Sacramento.

Meanwhile, back at the 89/70 junction, head south on the combined highways toward a picturesque mining town dating from the days of the great California Gold rush.

## QUINCY

**Population: 6,728**            **Elevation: 3,432 feet**

Every time we drive through Quincy, I think of my grandpappy, Walter C. Dallas. A lifelong wanderer, cowboy, hunter and wanna-be writer, he settled in these parts for a spell in the 1930s and 1940s. Never too fond of working for wages, he brewed moonshine and killed game to feed his family, which numbered around eleven as I recall. Like us, grandpappy didn't care much for crowds and this was one of California's least populated regions. It still is, with only 22,000 people in the whole county.

Quincy is a real charmer of a town with fine brick, stone and wood frame buildings, many decorated with historic murals. Several grand front-porch homes stand along residential streets shaded by trees older than my grandpappy. If you'd like to spend some time here—an easy temptation—stop at the **Plumas County Visitors Bureau** on the left as you approach town, near the airport. It's open weekdays 8 to 6 and Saturday 10 to 6; (530) 283-6345.

In the downtown area, the four-story 1921 **Plumas County Courthouse** dominates the low-rise business district like a misplaced Grecian temple. Step inside to admire its marble columns and staircase and massive glass and bronze chandelier. Immediately beyond, turn right onto Bradley Street for the town's nicely done archive:

*Plumas County Museum* ● *500 Jackson St. (Bradley); (530) 283-6320. Weekdays 8 to 5 the year around, plus weekends 10 to 4 from May to September.* ☐ Inside this prim white structure, you'll find nicely arrayed displays including an extensive bottle and crystal collection, a native peoples' bark shelter and an exhibit about a remarkable fellow named Jim Beckwourth. The son of a Southern white plantation owner and a slave mother, he was set free and spent most of his life as a Western America explorer and scout. In 1850, he found the lowest pass in the Sierra Nevada and blazed a trail through there, linking Plumas County with the rest of the world. He also founded the town of Beckwourth to the southeast.

A block below Main Street at Bradley and Lawrence Avenue, you'll find the town's most interesting restaurant:

*Moon's* ● *497 Lawrence St.; (530) 283-0765. Italian-Mexican-American; wine and beer. Dinner Tuesday-Sunday. MC/VISA, AMEX; $$.* ☐ An ancient stone and wooden building with a corrugated roof houses the four dining areas of this popular place. One also can nosh outside in warm weather, under a canopy of dangling plants. The versatile kitchen issues a hearty mix of Mexican and Italian fare, such as spicy chicken Monterey, calamari and pastas. It also serves some of the best pizzas in these parts, along with thick steaks and pork medallions.

## To Truckee and Lake Tahoe

Heading out of town on Highway 70/89, you'll soon encounter "new" Quincy—a short string of service stations, motels, fast food joints and markets separated from the historic district. Twenty-five miles later, at **Blairsden,** Highway 70 heads east to Nevada while our route continues south through the woodsy planned community of **Graeagle.** (The funny looking name is pronounced "Gray Eagle.") It originally was a lumbering town and several vivid red company buildings survive, housing boutiques and cafés. The old mill pond has become a park and picnic area.

## Side trip: Portola and Beckwourth

If you'd like to visit the town founded by that mountain man from the South, take Route 70 sixteen miles east to Beckwourth. En route, pause in **Portola** to check out the world's largest collection of diesel locomotives at the **Portola Railroad Museum.** It's open daily 10 to 5 and train rides are available in summer; (530) 832-4131.

Just east of Portola, watch for a sign to **Beckwourth Cabin** on Rocky Point Road. This reconstructed of an 1852 trading post and hotel built by Beckwourth doesn't keep regular hours; call (530) 832-4888 to see if you can get in. Otherwise, you can poke about the grounds. East of the cabin on Highway 70, only a few buildings remain in the town of **Beckwourth,** and one of them houses a grand old cowboy bar and café:

**Beckwith Tavern and Restaurant** ● *81059 Highway 70; (530) 832-5084. American; full bar service. Dinner Wednesday-Sunday, closed Monday-Tuesday. MC/VISA; $$.* ☐ Some say the famous mountain man's last name was Beckwith, then he got 'notional and decided to fancy it up as "Beckwourth." Beckwith Tavern carries the original name and it carries a lot of good old boy Western atmosphere as well. Local ranchers have sizzled their brands in the long bar, which looks like a set from a cowboy movie. Meanwhile, back in the kitchen, thick-cut pepper steaks sizzle on the grill. Assorted other steaks, prime rib and a few chicken and chop dishes round out the menu.

Back on Highway 89, between Blairsden and Graeagle, follow Johnsville Road (A-14) west to a state park that preserves elements of an old mining camp:

**Plumas-Eureka State Park** ● *310 Johnsville Rd., Blairsden, CA 96103; (530) 836-2380. Museum open daily 8 to 4 in summer; shorter hours the rest of the year. Campsites with showers and flush potties; $$$. The campground often fills during summer weekends although spaces generally are available on weekdays. It's not on the state park reservation system.* ☐ This park in a splendid alpine setting shelters the old mining town of Johnsville and its Eureka mine, which generated $25 million gold during the late 1880s.

You'll see a stamp mill where quartz ore was crushed into powder to separate the gold, a mining museum and an interesting scatter of machinery. Skiing figures in this area's history as well as mining. The first organized ski races in the Western Hemisphere were held in nearby Onion

Valley in 1861. Legendary Snowshoe Thompson, who packed mail over the wintertime Sierra Nevada on skis more than a century ago, often passed this way. His twenty-five-pound wooden skis—a far cry from today's composite slats—are on display in the museum, along with other early day skiing exhibits. The park encloses a striking slice of alpine wilderness—a 6,749-acre region of forests, glacier-shaped mountains and bejeweled lakes. Trails take hikers into the surrounding wilds.

As you continue south from Graeagle on Highway 89, the surrounding woods suddenly part to reveal pretty, green Mohawk Valley. Sitting at one end, with a nice view of the countryside, is a grand old stage stop now functioning as a country inn:

**White Sulfur Springs Ranch Bed & Breakfast** ● *P.O. Box 136, Clio, CA 96106; (800) 854-1797 or (530) 836-2387. (WEB SITE: www.graeagle.com/marketplace/whtssbb) Six units; one private and five shared baths; full breakfast. MC/VISA, DISC; $$$$.* ☐ Modern travelers now sleep at this inn instead of dusty stagecoach riders, although ghosts of those passengers might still recognize the place. It retains its early American look, with antiques and print wallpaper. The owners might look familiar too, since they're descendants of the McKenzie family that has owned the inn since 1867. Guests can browse through a relic-filled attic, dip into a heated mineral pool or just sit on the front porch and admire the view of Mohawk Valley.

The town of **Clio**, where White Sulfur Springs gets its mail, is just off Highway 89 north of the ranch, although it doesn't offer much of interest to travelers. Continuing southward, you'll leave Mohawk Valley and return to hilly tree country. Then the mountains open suddenly to reveal a most astonishing sight—a big slice of Nebraska, smack dab in the middle of the Sierra Nevada foothills. This is the **Sierra Valley,** a broad and remarkably flat pastureland discovered by Beckwourth/Beckwith in 1851. Settlers soon followed and it provided beef and produce for the gold mines of California and the Comstock Lode silver mines in next-door Nevada. The flat valley floor, nearly a mile above sea level, was created when a primeval lake soaked into the ground.

Highway 89 skirts the valley's southwestern edge, passing through the small ranching towns of **Sattley** (no services) and **Sierraville** (fuel, food and provisions). The latter is a neat scatter of wood frame buildings, including some rather imposing old farm houses. Beyond Sierraville, you'll roll through twenty-six miles of undulating and unpopulated woodlands. Several Forest Service campgrounds may tempt you to spend the night. Then suddenly, this road less traveled pops over a busy freeway and drops you in an historic town that has become the darling of ski bunnies and Tahoe-bound tourists.

## TRUCKEE

**Population: 2,400**                    **Elevation: 5,820 feet**

Interstate 80 carries travelers by the droves through a cleft in the Sierra Nevada called Donner Pass. Many hop off in Truckee to enjoy the summer scenery and winter sports of nearby Lake Tahoe. Just to the north is the large summer and winter resort of Tahoe-Donner. Thus, Truckee couldn't be a sleepy little mountain town even if it wanted to.

And it apparently doesn't want to. The town was founded in the 1860s as a Transcontinental Railroad construction camp and it evolved into a lively railroading and lumbering town. Many of its brick and cut stone buildings survive, although they shelter trendy boutiques and *nouveau* restaurants instead of batwing door saloons and bawdy houses. The ghosts of early settlers must be giggling at places like Truckee Tiffany's, the Tourist Club Bar and Bud's Sporting Goods and Ice Cream Parlor. (In case you never wondered, Truckee was named for the river that runs through it, which was named for Washoe Indian Chief Trokay.)

---

*RV PARKING ADVISORY* • Although the main street, Donner Pass Road, is usually thick with parked cars, RVs can find space on Jibboom Street, a block north and parallel.

---

It's fun to stroll along Donner Pass Road and poke your head into the brick-clad shops and cafés. The two-story brick and wooden balconied Truckee Hotel at Donner Pass and Bridge Street will catch your eye. And it's a fine place to pass the night. Trendy old Truckee offers some interesting restaurants as well, although you'll find more angel hair pasta and Cornish game hens than steak and potatoes.

## DINING

**O.B.'s Pub and Restaurant** • *10046 Donner Pass Rd. (opposite the fire station); (530) 587-4164. American; full bar service. Lunch and dinner daily. MC/VISA; $$.* ⊓ O.B.'s is housed in one of the venerable brickfronts, nicely dressed with café curtains, fluted chandeliers, brass and beveled glass. It follows the contemporary Truckee dining trend, featuring pepper whisky top sirloin (excellent!), ginger shrimp, honey glazed chicken and pork ribs.

**The Passage** • *In the Truckee Hotel at Bridge Street and Donner Pass Road; (530) 587-7619. American regional; full bar service. Lunch and dinner daily. MC/VISA, AMEX; $$$.* ⊓ You can get steak and potatoes in this stylish hotel restaurant, although it's tequila-marinated Black Angus top sirloin and garlic mashed potatoes. The Cornish game hens are here, too, along with other *chic* dishes. (During the Gold Rush, the Cornish miners from England ate meat and vegetable pies called pasties, which they warmed with their mining lamps. They probably never dined on Cornish game hens.)

**Wagon Train Coffee Shop** • *10080 Donner Pass Rd.; (530) 587-7574. American; wine and beer. Breakfast through dinner daily. MC/VISA; $ to $$.* ⊓ This is where you go if you don't like garlic in your mashed potatoes. Although the Wagon Train attracts lots of tourists, its remains an old fashioned café, serving liver and onions, leg of veal, young tom turkey and possibly even chicken fried steak. The breakfasts are ample and traditional, or you can stop by and grab a pastry from the bakery shelf. The place fits old Truckee quite nicely, with brick interior walls decorated with battered license plates, pioneer relics and historic photos. A toy train scoots around a track suspended above the dining counter.

### RECLINING

***The Truckee Hotel*** • *P.O. Box 884 (10007 Bridge Street), Truckee, CA 96160; (800) 659-6921 or (530) 587-4444. (WEB SITE: www.truckee-tahoe.com/truckeehotel) Thirty-seven rooms; some private and some shared baths; continental breakfast. MC/VISA, AMEX; $$$$.* ☐ Rebuilt in 1919 after fire destroyed the 1873 original, this old inn has been carefully restored, probably beyond its original appearance. The lobby parlor is a study in Victorian finery with brass and beveled glass, and a marble fireplace. Guest rooms have early American or European style furnishings, including beds with old fashioned headboards. The Passage restaurant is listed above.

Just west of Truckee off I-80, you may want to detour a pretty little lake which—ironically—marks one of the most dreadful episodes in America's great westward migration:

***Donner Memorial State Park*** • *On Donner Lake, two miles west of Truckee; (530) 582-7894. Modest day use fee; museum open daily 10 to 4. RV and tent sites with flush potties and showers; no hookups; $$$. For campsite reservations, call (800) 444-PARK; MC/VISA accepted.* ☐ This state park embraces Donner Lake, a near perfect blue oval as pretty as a turquoise pendant. In this sublime setting, the Donner-Reed emigrant party was trapped by an early snowfall on the wrong side of the Sierra in late 1846. Half the party perished during the savage winter and a few resorted to cannibalism to survive. However, most of this occurred not at the camp near Donner Lake, but within a group of men who had set out on foot to bring help from Sutter's Fort (now Sacramento). The park's Emigrant Trail Museum relates details of the Donner-Reed entrapment.

This same freeway exit will take you to the **Truckee-Donner Chamber of Commerce** at 12036 Donner Pass Road; it's open weekdays 9 to 5; (530) 587-2757.

## To Lake Tahoe and Markleeville

To continue your trek down Highway 89, take the North Lake Tahoe exit from I-80 and head south along the gurgling Truckee River. Certainly not a less-traveled road in this area, the highway passes the popular Squaw Valley Ski Resort and then skirts the western shoreline of Lake Tahoe. Although campsites are scarce in the Tahoe Basin in summer, we found vacancies at a couple of Forest Service campgrounds between I-80 and the lake.

The highway reaches the lake at **Tahoe City** although you won't see Mark Twain's "fairest picture" until you drive several miles south through roadside businesses and homes. This pale blue orb, cupped in paler blue mountains, begins peeking through the trees as you clear this alpine suburbia. Below **Meeks Bay,** as you enter **D.L. Bliss State Park,** the lake views become quite splendid.

As you drive, contemplate the enormity of this grand body of water. It's more than twelve miles wide and twenty-one miles long, and it's one of the world's highest large lakes, at 6,225 feet above sea level. Tahoe is the largest alpine lake in North America and the second deepest in the U.S., after Oregon's Crater Lake; the deepest point is 1,645 feet. Unlike volcanic-cupped Crater Lake, Tahoe was formed when faulting created a deep valley, then volcanic eruptions blocked one end to create a land-locked basin. Its natural outlet, now controlled, is the Truckee River.

Kit Carson and John C. Frémont were the first outsiders to see the lake, following the course of the Truckee in 1844. They named it Lake Bonpland, after a French explorer. It later was changed to Lake Bigler in honor of California's third governor. But John Bigler was a bit of a tippler and historian Hubert Bancroft once quipped:

*Nothing could have been in worse taste than in applying to a liquid so beautifully clear and cool the name of one who so detested water.*

Ultimately, the lake received an Anglicized version a Washoe Indian term *Da-ow-a-ga,* meaning big water or clear water. And it is indeed clear; sunlight-seeking water plants have been found growing 400 feet below the surface. Unfortunately, a frenzy of construction during the 1950s and 1960s literally muddied the waters and introduced nutrients that encouraged algae growth. The lake has lost about twenty-five percent of its original clarity.

It would be nice to picture this as a wilderness paradise. Unfortunately, eighty-five percent of the shoreline is privately owned and much of it has been grossly overdeveloped. The towns of Tahoe City, South Lake Tahoe and others have become ugly strip malls of service stations, motels and fast food joints. High rise casinos tower over the Nevada side of the south shore, where your best lake views are over steak Dianne and a good bottle of Cabernet at pricey rooftop restaurants.

However, you are now driving through a large protected slice of lake-shore as you follow twisting Highway 89 through Bliss State Park. You'll encounter several camping areas although sites are a tough ticket in summer. If you want to plan ahead—way ahead—call (800) 444-PARK for reservations. Most sites have flush potties, showers, picnic tables and barbecue grills, with no hookups; **$$$** to **$$$$**.

The finest gem in this jewel of a lake is **Emerald Bay**, everybody's favorite viewpoint. Several turnouts and a large parking area provide access to one of the most photographed sights in America—tiny, rocky Fannette Island cradled within a three-mile-long fjord-like bay. A one-mile hike will take you down to **Vikingsholm**, styled as a Viking fortress and built by a wealthy matron as a retreat in 1929. Guided tours are conducted every half hour from 10 to 4, weekends only from Memorial Day to mid-June, and then daily through Labor Day weekend. It's closed the rest of the year.

South of here, you can get recreation information at the well-equipped **Forest Service Visitor Center**. It's open daily 8 to 5 in summer, with shorter hours the rest of the year; (530) 573-2674. While there, check out the **Stream Profile Chamber,** providing an above-ground and underground look at a typical alpine stream.

A bit farther south are the 1920s resort complex of **Camp Richard-**

son and the **Tallac Historic Site**, where you can walk among grand old lakeside estates. Some are open to visitors and others are being restored; check at the visitor center for details.

And then, good grief! You're suddenly back in traffic-riddled civilization in the sprawling town of **South Lake Tahoe**. This ungainly strip of motels, resorts, service stations and cafés stretches six miles east to the Nevada border.

## Side trip: a dance around the lake

If this is your first visit to Lake Tahoe, we certainly recommend continuing around the rim drive; it's seventy-six road miles. After suffering through the scatter of South Lake Tahoe, you might want to pause at the south shore casinos of **Stateline**, and then head north on the Nevada side of the lake.

You'll again shed mankind's excess as you enter **Lake Tahoe Nevada State Park**, with campgrounds, vista points and lake access. Pressing northward, you'll drive through woodsy **Incline Village**, the only decently planned community on the lake. You'll then encounter more unrestrained development as you drive through **Crystal Bay** and **Tahoe Vista,** before completing your loop at Tahoe City.

Back on track and pressing southward on Highway 89 (which merges briefly with U.S. 50), you'll shed the human excess of South Lake Tahoe and begin a lazy climb toward **Luther Pass**. Although it tops out at 7,740 feet, the summit is a barely noticeable rise in the pavement. Below Luther, your woodland pathway merges with State Route 88, following the Carson River east through an attractive vee canyon. This is an exceptionally pleasing stretch, with the river cascading merrily over boulders the size of cargo trucks. You'll find several Forest Service campgrounds along here, and they rarely fill up.

At the point where the two highways separate, check out **Woodfords Station**, which dates from 1860 as a Pony Express stop. It's still a provisioning point for travelers through the Sierra Nevada, although it has burned down three times. The fourth incarnation is a properly rustic general store and deli that manages to avoid looking like a mini-mart. Hopefully, you can get essential provisions and light snacks. We say hopefully because a "for sale" sign was posted on the clapboard building when we last passed. From Woodfords, follow Highway 89 to an attractive streamside community that's pretty much cut off from the rest of California and probably doesn't mind too much:

### MARKLEEVILLE

**Population: 163**            **Elevation: 5,501 feet**

When we wrote our *Northern California Discovery Guide* in 1993, Markleeville's population was 165, so it's *almost* holding its own. In addition to rustic charm, it offers two interesting statistics: It's the smallest county seat in America and surrounding Alpine County is the least populated county in California, with about 1,200 residents. The courthouse is a hoot—a cut stone cottage not much bigger than our summer home in Columbia. You'll see it on the left on the far side of town.

This mountain hamlet was born in the 1860s when prospectors found a bit of gold in the Carson River and surrounding hills. When nearby Silver Mountain City's mines dried up in 1875, Markleeville's citizens took away the county seat and never gave it back. They also took Silver Mountain City's hotel. Since Markleeville is on the eastern side of the Sierra and winter snow closes the mountain passes above, residents relate more to Nevada than to California. The state line is only a dozen miles away, cutting through a cow pasture. Carson City is less than an hour's drive.

Other than the pint-sized county courthouse, downtown has two other buildings of note, including the **Alpine Hotel,** transported here from Silver Mountain City; see below. Just down the street is the old **Marklee-ville General Store** which looks properly weathered from without. Unfortunately, current owners have given the interior a mini-mart look, although there is a nice antique shop in back. You'll also find a couple of curio shops in the two-block-long business district.

### DINING AND RECLINING

*Alpine Hotel and Restaurant* ● *Main and Montgomery, Marklee-ville, CA 96120; (530) 694-2150. Breakfast through dinner daily; full bar service. Rooms and food $$. MC/VISA.* ☐ This clapboard inn was built in 1862 in Silver Mountain City. Then its boards were disassembled, numbered and moved here in 1886, where they were nailed back together. For more than a century, the Alpine has offered modest rooms and food. In the rather austere but congenial dining room, you can get fancy with chicken Chardonnay and scampi over rice pilaf, or old fashioned with pork chops or chicken fried steak. You can get a serious drink in the hotel's Cutthroat Saloon and don't panic; the name refers to a type of trout caught in the Carson River. If you decide to stay over, the Alpine country breakfast will get your engine started the next morning, featuring chicken fried steak, two eggs, potatoes, biscuits and gravy.

*Villa Gigli* ● *145 Hot Springs Road; (530) 694-2253. Italian; wine and beer. Dinner Friday-Sunday; reservations essential. No credit cards; $$.* ☐ Tuscany native Ruggero Gigli and his wife Gina operate this small café beside their home. The menu, as tiny as the cabin-style restaurant, has a "pasta of the day" (whose identity is posted on a sign out front) and a creative meat or poultry entrée, along with salad and dessert, and the food is exceptional. All pastas, sauces, breads and desserts are made from scratch, usually the same day they're served. On warm summer days, you can dine at picnic tables on a deck and watch the couple create over a barbecue grill. The little place is extremely popular, particularly in summer, so call for reservations.

To visit the nearby attractions, follow Hot Springs Road west from downtown. A right turn will take you uphill to the **Alpine County Historical Museum**, which does a nice job of preserving Markleeville's past. The collection includes assorted pioneer regalia and there's an old schoolhouse, log jail and stamp mill out front. The museum is open daily except Tuesday from noon to 5; closed in winter; (530) 694-2317, or call the Alpine County Chamber of Commerce at (530) 694-2475.

Villa Gigli (listed above) is bit farther along Hot Springs Road, also on the right. Press westward and Hot Springs Road will take you to an obvious destination:

**Grover Hot Springs State Park** ● *P.O. Box 188, Markleeville, CA 96120; (530) 694-2248. Fee for hot springs; open 9 to 9 in summer, then 2 to 9 weekdays and 9 to 9 weekends the rest of the year. RV and tent sites with flush potties and showers, no hookups; $$. For campsite reservations, call (800) 444-PARK; MC/VISA accepted.* ☐ You should reserve ahead for this popular little park, since many folks are drawn here for the mineral springs. The wooded setting is pleasant and the warm mineral water feels great, particularly on a chilly winter day when you can loll among the steam clouds. However, the concrete-lined pools are about as visually appealing as cattle troughs. No skinny-dipping, please; this *is* state property.

Continuing southeast from Markleeville, you'll follow the river for several miles through a pretty canyon. Frequent turnouts will tempt you to stop and soak your feet in the cool rush. Trout fishing is popular along here. After a few miles, Highway 89 swings away from the stream as it separates from Route 4. That road follows the river westward and eventually tops Ebbetts Pass; see Tour Twelve, page 171.

Highway 89 climbs toward 8,314-foot Monitor Pass, following the course of a cheerful little stream. The route to the pass—a slow, gently curving grade—isn't particularly impressive, although the downslope is awesome. As you crest Monitor Pass (marked by a stone monument) and begin a gentle downward spiral, you'll see an imposing panorama. The snow-streaked crests of the Sierra Nevada rise in the west and a convergence of the Pine Nut and White Mountains fill the eastern horizon. A bowl-shaped valley appears below and to your right—a glacial-carved basin cradled between jagged mountain ridges. To the east is the beginning of Nevada's Great Basin Desert, although it's patched with pasturelands here, irrigated by the Walker River.

The final descent takes you through a rock-ribbed canyon, then State Route 89 ends at U.S. 395 just above the tiny town of **Topaz**. If you need fuel, provisions or you want to gamble a bit, go four miles north to **Topaz Lake** on the Nevada border. You'll find two small casinos, a service station, mini-mart, RV park and a lakeside campground. We pass this way on Tour Thirteen, page 180.

☺  ☺  ☺

***Where do we go from here?*** ● You could take Tour Thirteen, following U.S. 395 south to Lone Pine. Another option is to take U.S. 50 east on Tour Twenty-three. Or you could backtrack from Topaz over Monitor Pass and do the Highway 4 (Ebbetts Pass) portion of Tour Twelve. Finally, you could just go on up to Reno and party for a while.

# TRIP PLANNER

**WHEN TO GO** ● Spring and fall are particularly nice in these coastal and mountainous inland areas. Winter's fine because there are no temperature extremes, although you might get wet. Summer is acceptable although Capitola may be crowded and it's awfully hot for hiking in the Pinnacles.

**DRIVING DISTANCE** ● It's about 165 miles from Capitola to Coalinga and another twelve to Interstate 5.

**RV ADVISORY** ● Nothing seriously challenges motorhomes and trailer rigs on this route, although you'll hit some kinky sections going over Hecker Pass. *Huge* motorhomes may have a problem since there's a 45-foot vehicle length limit.

**WHAT YOU'LL SEE** ● Charming little New England style Capitola, a grand view of coastal Santa Cruz County from Hecker Pass, well-kept downtown Gilroy and its vineyards, historic Mission San Juan Bautista, Pinnacles National Monument, Coalinga's nicely done historic museum.

**WHAT TO DO** ● Stroll on the beach and walk the Soquel Creek trail in Capitola; have a scenic lunch or dinner at Mount Madonna Inn; taste some good Zinfandel in Gilroy area wineries; hike among the fantastic shapes at Pinnacles National Monument; dig into a hefty steak at Harris Ranch Restaurant.

**TO BEGIN** ● Get yourself to downtown Capitola.

## Useful contacts

**Capitola Chamber of Commerce,** 716-G Capitola Ave., Capitola, CA 95010; (800) 474-6522 or (831) 475-6522.

**Gilroy Visitors Bureau,** 7780 Monterey St., Gilroy, CA 95020; (408) 842-6436.

**San Juan Bautista Chamber of Commerce,** P.O. Box 1037 (402-A Third St.), San Juan Bautista, CA 95045; (831) 623-2454.

## Pricing guidelines

**DINING:** Dinner entrée with soup or salad, without drinks or dessert for under $10 = **$**; $10 to $14 = **$$**; $15 to $25 = **$$$**; over $25 = **$$$$**.

**RECLINING:** A two-person room for $35 or less = **$**; $36 to $50 = **$$**; $51 to $75 = **$$$**; $76 to $100 = **$$$$**; more than $100 = **$$$$$**.

**CAMPING:** Under $10 = **$**; $10 to $14 = **$$**; $15 to $19 = **$$$**; $20 or more = **$$$$**

## Tour Ten
# INTO THE DIABLOS
### CAPITOLA TO COALINGA

**M**uch of west central California is shaped by low but rugged mountains that were named *El Diablo* by the Spanish because they're rather barren and they were the very devil to cross.

Today, the Diablo Range is breached in several places by east-west highways, including Route 152, coming in from the coast below Capitola. Between the Diablos and the Gabilan Mountains to the west, State Route 25 wanders through the rarely visited Paicines ranching and farming valley. This region has an ominous past, since it's creased by the San Andreas Fault, California's most active earthquake corridor.

However, we're not recommending this route because of its shake and quake past. It's an interesting drive that begins in Capitola, one of California's more appealing coastal towns. It then travels over a mountain pass to Gilroy, the garlic capitol of the world, also noted for fine wines issued by uncrowded wineries. From here, we'll lead you to San Juan Bautista, a charming old mission town, and then to quake-prone Hollister. We'll then head south on Route 25 through the Paicines Valley to Pinnacles National Monument. It's another of those federal preserves bypassed by most travelers. Our path then joins State Route 198, which travels through a rugged pass in the Diablo Range to Coalinga and on to Interstate 5.

## CAPITOLA

**Population: 10,200**                                      **Elevation: sea level**

Could we have taken a long, wrong turn and wound up on the New England seacoast? Capitola is a cute collection of Cape Cod style cottages and shops along the beach at the mouth of Soquel Creek. While certainly busy in summer, it is less known and thus less visited than more popular Santa Cruz to the north.

Despite its small size today—a fourth as large as Santa Cruz—Capitola was northern California's first beach resort. During the 1850s, folks pitched tents and built shanty resorts at "Camp Capitola" along Soquel Creek and on the ocean bluffs above. Those bluffs are now occupied by elegant homes, many of Victorian vintage, while cozy little cottages line Soquel Creek. Compact Capitola is a good walking city, so find a place to park and start doing so.

---

*RV PARKING ADVISORY* ● Downtown spaces are metered and marked, so there's no RV or trailer parking available. Drivers of such rigs will have to seek spots on nearby residential streets. We wouldn't advise bringing an RV into Capitola on a summer weekend, when *all* the streets are crowded.

---

Downtown is compressed into a few square blocks, busy with boutiques, galleries and cafés, and the crescent beach is but a short walk away. Also nearby is **Capitola Wharf,** a fine place for strolling above the scalloped surf. And while you're in a walking mood, take the Soquel Creek pedestrian path up a narrow, tree-shaded ravine past creekside homes.

### DINING

Capitola's "restaurant row" is along Esplanade and most cafés have decks over the beach. A perennial favorite, the Shadowbrook, is cantilevered into the bank of Soquel Creek, a few blocks from downtown.

**Margaritaville** ● *221 Esplanade; (831) 476-2263. Mexican; full bar service. Lunch and dinner daily. Major credit cards; $$.* ◻ Although Margaritaville is a franchise operation, this one occupies a fine niche between downtown and the beach, with cheerful tropical trim and an outdoor deck. In addition to conventional tortilla-wrapped things, the kitchen offers prawns in red sauce, and chicken breast with vegetables and herbs.

**Paradise Beach Grill** ● *215 Esplanade; (831) 476-4900. American; full bar service. Lunch and dinner daily. MC/VISA; $$$.* ◻ Another restaurant with a deck over the beach, Paradise Grill is bright and airy, with cathedral beam ceilings and flagstone floors. The menu suggests a creative kitchen, with entrées such as steak with pineapple anchiote butter, roasted chicken with honey chipotle jelly, and blackened ahi tuna steak.

**The Shadowbrook** ● *1750 Wharf Rd.; (831) 475-1511. American regional; full bar service. Dinner nightly and Sunday brunch. Major credit cards; $$$$.* ◻ Since 1947, the Shadowbrook has been a required stop for every visiting relative of every Santa Cruz County resident. One reaches its lush creekside setting by a delightful gimmick—a bright red funicular. Once there, explore its landscaped grounds, pause for a drink on the terrace, then adjourn to one of several intimate dining rooms. Although it's clearly a tourist draw, it has rather a fine kitchen, producing such fare as charbroiled swordfish with lime marinade and mango salsa, braised lamb shanks, and bacon wrapped prawns over polenta.

**Zelda's** • *203 Esplanade; (831) 475-4900. American; full bar service. Breakfast through dinner daily. MC/VISA; $$$.* ☐ Zelda will transport you to coastal New England and back to the Twenties with wainscotting, art deco touches, hanging plants and big windows to the beach. The menu is more contemporary, featuring sautéed scallops, fried prawns with coconut and basil, charbroiled salmon with parsley dill, plus steaks and pastas.

## RECLINING

**Capitola Inn** • *822 Bay Ave., Capitola, CA 95010; (831) 462-3004. Fifty-six rooms with TV and phones. Major credit cards; $$$$ to $$$$$.* ☐ This stylish inn has large, comfortable rooms and suites with view decks or patios. Some units have microwaves, fireplaces and spa tubs; several kitchenettes are available.

**Capitola Venetian Hotel** • *1500 Wharf Rd., Capitola, CA 95010; (800) 332-2780 or (831) 476-6471. Kitchen units and suites. Major credit cards; $$$ to $$$$.* ☐ Tucked between Soquel Creek and the wharf, this multi-colored inn was built in 1923 as America's first beachside condo. It's now listed on the National Register of Historic Places. All rooms have kitchen units and some suites have fireplaces.

**Inn at Depot Hill** • *250 Monterey Ave., Capitola, CA 95010; (800) 572-2632 or (831) 462-3376. (WEB SITE: www.innatdepothill.com; E-MAIL: lodging@innatdepothill.com) Twelve units with private baths; buffet breakfast. MC/VISA, AMEX; $$$$$.* ☐ This luxury resort, almost overdone with its lavish décor, was created from the town's turn-of-the-century railroad depot and an annex. Each room has a European theme, from Shakespeare's Stratford-on-Avon to Paris and on to Côte d'Azur. All rooms have TV/VCRs, stereo systems and marble-accented bathrooms; some offer patios and fireplaces.

## To the land of garlic and grapes

To depart downtown Capitola and begin this tour, head inland on Monterey Avenue. After a few blocks, turn right at a stop sign onto Park Avenue and follow it to the Highway 1 freeway. En route, you'll get filtered glimpses of a curving sandy beach through ranks of huge eucalyptus trees. To reach that beach, turn right just short of the freeway. It's part of two side-by-side state parks:

Small **New Brighton State Beach** has dozens of yards of strand, campsites, picnic areas and trails through inland eucalyptus groves. RV and tent sites have picnic tables and barbecue grills; with flush potties; no hookups; **$$$**; (831) 464-6330. Just to the south, reached by following McGregor Drive from New Brighton, is **Seacliff State Beach**. It has sites near the surf with hookups; **$$$$**; (831) 685-6442. The park's beachfront extends for more than a mile, in front of the coastal communities of Seacliff and Rio Del Mar. For campsite reservations at either New Brighton or Seacliff, call (800) 444-PARK; MC/VISA.

Follow the freeway a few miles south and take the State Route 152 exit into the midsize community of **Watsonville**, the commercial center for a fertile farming area. Highway 152 follows Main Street through the town's sturdy, well-kept Fifties style downtown, then it does a right-left-right turn to skirt around a one-way grid. Beyond the city, you'll pass through some of those fertile farmlands and you may want to pause a couple of roadside fruit and vegetable stands.

From here, you'll begin a lazily twisting drive to the top of Hecker Pass. The climb takes you into evergreen thickets, including a few second growth redwoods. Sitting atop the pass is a popular restaurant, and its lower parking lot provides a grand view of the sprawl of Santa Cruz County, with a thin blue line of the Pacific beyond.

*Mount Madonna Inn •*
*1285 Hecker Pass Hwy., Watsonville; phone (831) 724-2275. American; full bar service. Lunch Thursday-Saturday plus Sunday brunch; dinner Thursday-Sunday. Major credit cards; $$.* □ Although not as stylish as the Shadows, Mount Madonna inn also is a longtime local favorite and a required stop for visiting relatives. At night, the view from the window-walled dining room is splendid as a hundred thousand lights from a dozen cities sparkle below. The fare ranges from prime rib and chicken teriyaki to seafood.

You'll crest 1,039-foot **Hecker Pass** just east of the inn and a monument tells you that it was named in honor of Henry Hecker, who was instrumental in creating the "Yosemite to the Sea Highway" in the 1920s. Should you need a place to camp, **Mount Madonna County Park** is immediately beyond the pass, with nicely spaced and shaded sights tucked into the woods. It has flush potties with water and electric; **$$ to $$$$**.

---

**RV ADVISORY** • A sign at either end of Hecker Pass advises that the route isn't recommended for vehicles over forty-five feet.

---

As you crest the pass, you travel from Santa Cruz to burgeoning Santa Clara County, home to Silicon Valley. That electronic wonderland and the county seat of San Jose are many miles north, although its suburban sprawl is creeping into this rural area. Winding downhill from Hecker Pass, you'll note that a few subdivisions are sprouting among this region's vineyards. Fortunately, most of the wineries—noted particularly for their Zinfandels and other hearty reds—were still there when we last passed. Start looking for tasting rooms as the first vineyards appear. They're conveniently aligned along Hecker Pass Highway:

**Hecker Pass Winery** is on the left, with a simple and attractive wood-paneled tasting room, open daily 9 to 5; (408) 842-8755. It's owned by Italian immigrant Mario Fortino. His brother Ernie founded next-door **Fortino Winery,** an extensive complex with a tasting room, gift shop and deli. It's open daily 10 to 5; (408) 842-3305. Just beyond and to the right is **Thomas Cruse Winery,** a rather casual operation open weekends noon to 5; (408) 842-7016. A quarter of a mile below, also on the right, is **Solis Winery** with a modern tasting room open to the vineyards, 11 to 5; (408) 847-6306. The final tasting room, also on the right and just short of a traffic light that marks the suburban start of Gilroy, is **A. Conrotto.** This simple facility is open weekends 11 to 5; (408) 842-3053.

Between Solis and Conrotto, definitely worth a pause, is **Goldsmith Seeds,** a huge flower seed operation that presents a spectacular show of blooms in spring and summer. Visitors are welcome to walk among its Technicolor fields.

## GILROY

**Population: 31,500**                    **Elevation: 157 feet**

Once a small country town, the Garlic Capitol of the World is about to be swallowed up—garlic breath and all—by the Santa Clara County sprawl. Despite its surging suburbs, Gilroy is still the world's garlic center, producing more than ninety percent of America's supply of the "stinking rose." Tens of thousands of visitors are drawn to the annual Gilroy Garlic Festival, held the last weekend of July.

As you enter town, Hecker Pass Road becomes First Street; watch on your left for **Tassos' Old House** restaurant, which we recommend below. A few blocks beyond, First Street bumps into Monterey Street, which was U.S. 101 before a freeway bypass was built. We'll leave Route 152 here by turning right onto Monterey to pass through Gilroy's well-kept old downtown area. It has become a bit trendy these days, with a couple of boutiques and sidewalk cafés.

At Monterey and Fifth, stop at the **Garlic Festival Shop** where an amazing assortment of garlic specialty foods and garlic-theme items will— well—take your breath away; (408) 842-1625. A block to the left, at Fifth and Church streets, is the **Gilroy Historical Museum** in the old Carnegie library building, where you can learn more about the area's garlicky past. It's open weekdays 9 to 5 and sometimes on Saturday; (408) 848-0470. The second of our suggested restaurants, **Harvest Time**, is at Sixth and Monterey on your right. Just across the street, note the almost ridiculously ornate multi-gabled gingerbread-draped building, which houses the New Renaissance Center.

## DINING

***Harvest Time*** • *7397 Monterey St. (Sixth); (408) 842-7575. American; full bar service. Lunch and dinner daily. Major credit cards; $$*. ◻ This handsome Western style restaurant, with a horseshoe shaped bar as a focal point, features fresh local produce on its menu—including garlic, of course. Try the garlic calamari for an appetizer or, if you're serious about the stinking rose, a whole roasted garlic. Entrées range from pasta and seafood dishes to assorted steaks, herbal rack of lamb and *wienerschnitzel*.

***Tassos' Old House*** • *383 First St. (Hanna); (408) 847-7527. American; wine and beer. Lunch and dinner daily. Major credit cards; $$*. ◻ Housed in a white cottage with green trim, Tassos has a pleasing early American look. The menu is rather eclectic, dancing from chicken with prawns and artichoke hearts to peppered New York steak and—of course—breast of chicken with garlic.

From downtown Gilroy, turn left onto Tenth Street to reach the freeway or just stay on Monterey Street, which achieves the same result. A mile or so south, you'll see two more shops devoted to that breathy onion—**Garlic World** at 4800 Highway 101, (408) 847-2251; and **The Garlic Shoppé** at 4350 Highway 101, (408) 848-3646. Next door to the Garlic Shoppé is the **Rapazzini Winery** tasting room. Along with more conventional wines, it offers—are you ready for this?—*Château de Garlic*, a breathy white table wine. It's open daily 9 to 5; (408) 842-5649.

Working southward from Gilroy, you'll lose the Santa Clara County spread as you enter bucolic little San Benito County. Take the State Highway 156 exit and follow signs to an old mission town named for Saint John, the Baptist:

## SAN JUAN BAUTISTA

**Population: 10,650**                    **Elevation: 200 feet**

San Juan is two places—the old mission settlement, some of which is contained in San Juan Bautista State Historic Park; and the newer town, a couple of miles east and not very interesting.

To prowl the old town and its wonderfully rustic mission, take the first San Juan Bautista exit. After working through a pattern of old residential streets, you'll arrive at a large grassy plaza. It's rimmed by several state historic park buildings and the colonnaded Mission San Juan Bautista. Come on a weekday when the tourist crowds have thinned and you'll experience a kinder, gentler California. Visit the weather worn Victorian and whitewashed adobe buildings of the state historic park, walk the cool colonnade along the mission and step into its hushed interior.

Mission San Juan Bautista (not part of the state historic park) was founded in 1797 as one of the state's original padre outposts. The present church, built in 1812, has changed little. Unlike many missions, this has always been an active parish, so it was never abandoned and then rebuilt. However, it has been damaged occasionally. Those early padres didn't realize they were starting their mission complex atop the San Andreas Fault.

Most of old San Juan's storefronts are along Third Street, parallel to the mission. However, this is no longer a Spanish village; it's a Spanish-theme tourist village with ice cream parlors, a hot dog stand and a Christmas shop. Good grief, it doesn't even have a Mexican bakery! It does, however, have some interesting restaurants:

## DINING

**Doña Ester Restaurant** • *25 Franklin at Third; (831) 623-2518. Mexican; full bar service. Major credit cards; $$.* ◻ This appealing old café has a mix of Mexican and early American décor with Spanish tile floors, maple chairs and pretend Tiffany lamps. If the weather's nice, you can dine at a patio out back. It has the usual Mexican specialties plus a couple of spicy seafood dishes. For a filler-upper, try the all-chicken Doña Ester Special of an enchilada, burrito and taco.

**Felipe's California Cuisine** • *313 Third St.; (831) 623-2161. Mexican-Salvadoran; wine and beer. Lunch and dinner Wednesday-Monday. MC/VISA; $$.* ◻ Despite the name, Felipe's is more Mexican than Californian, with some interesting Salvadoran dishes added to the menu. Try the cheese-stuffed tortillas called *pupusas*, served with pickled cabbage called *curdito*. Another Salvadoran specialty is deep fried yucca root with pork chops. You also can choose more conventional Mexican fare or the *camarones rancheros*—sautéed shrimp with bell pepper, onions, garlic (are we still in Gilroy?) and tomato sauce. Felipe's is busily decorated with *Latino* trappings, historic photos and—a stuffed swordfish?

## RECLINING

**Posada de San Juan** • *P.O. Box 820 (310 Fourth St.), San Juan Bautista, CA 95045; (831) 623-4030. Rooms with TV and fireplaces. Major credit cards; $$$$ to $$$$$.* ◻ This new yet classic Spanish colonial style inn is within a brief walk of the Third Street shops and the mission plaza. The lobby is particularly handsome, with polished oak trim and Spanish arches. Rooms feature Latin décor, oversized tubs and fireplaces.

## Into earthquake country

Return to State Route 156 and continue northeast, past "new" San Juan Bautista. Just beyond, a right turn will take you on a steeply winding road (not recommended for large motorhomes or trailers) to **Fremont Peak State Park.** This little-visited preserve straddles several hundred acres of the Gabilan Range, including 3,170-foot Fremont Peak. It earned its name in 1846 when peripatetic General John C. Frémont, guided by Kit Carson, built a rough fortification here, expecting an attack by Mexican forces. It never came, so Frémont left. The park has primitive campsites, a picnic area, and hiking trails among the madrones, oaks and pines. A small observatory with a 30-inch telescope is open to the public occasionally. For information: Fremont Peak State Park, P.O. Box 1110, San Juan Bautista, CA 95045; (831) 623-4255; observatory (831) 623-2465.

A few miles beyond the Fremont Peak turnoff, you'll encounter the midsize town of **Hollister**. It sits in a farming valley surrounded by low hills the shape, color and texture of bread loaves. An exit to the right takes you into downtown. Or you can continue straight ahead to visit a former fruit stand that's become a tourist attraction and a large reservoir without a river.

### Side trip: Pacheco Pass and San Luis Reservoir

Highway 156 skims Hollister's edge, then after eight miles it ends at Route 152, which we left back in Gilroy. Here, it's called the Pacheco Pass Highway. Turn right (east) and you'll soon encounter a curious attraction:

**Casa de Fruta** ● *6680 Pacheco Pass Hwy., Hollister, CA 95023; (800) 548-3813 or (831) 842-9316. Motel units $$$; RV sites with full hookups $$$$. Restaurants serve American fare; breakfast through dinner; coffee shop open twenty-four hours; $$. MC/VISA.* ☐ Several decades ago, a local farming family named Zanger opened a fruit stand on the Pacheco Pass Highway and the dang thing just kept growing. Today, the "House of Fruit" includes a large specialty food and gift shop, a wine tasting counter, a motel, several restaurants, an RV park in a shady orchard, a service station, petting zoo, swimming pool, and an excursion train. This complex has become so—well, complex—that a shuttle bus scoots visitors around its 120 acres. A special favorite of ours is Casa de Fruta's chocolate-dipped dried fruit.

Beyond this complex, Highway 152 tops 1,368-foot Pacheco Pass and winds down into the vast flatness of the San Joaquin Valley. That mass of blue you see in the distance is **San Luis Reservoir,** which is surrounded by a state recreation area. The fake lake and its treeless shoreline aren't very interesting unless you have a boat or need a place to camp. There are two camping areas—**Basalt,** with water and electric hookups; and **San Luis Creek** without; $$$. For campsite reservations, call (800) 444-PARK; MC/VISA accepted.

Oddly, this giant pond isn't on a stream bed. The San Luis Dam was built across the end of a dry basin to create a storage pond for south-flowing aqueducts. Completed in 1967, it's a joint venture of the Central Valley Project and the California Water Project. This is the world's only major dam without a natural water source, and you can learn more at the Romero Visitor Center just off the highway; (209) 826-1196.

If you've taken the above detour, return to State Route 156 and then follow Highway 25 through Hollister. If you didn't do the detour, continue into Hollister and you'll soon link with Route 25 which—for some odd reason—is called the Airline Highway. (This rural farm community isn't served by any airline.) Hollister is a reasonably prosperous looking town with lots of sturdy brick and masonry in its old business district.

The town's most famous feature isn't visible, although it is frequently felt. Hollister was built smack dab across the San Andreas Fault and there's often a whole lotta shakin' goin' on; it has been damaged frequently by temblors. The worst thing that happened in the last quake—in 1985—was the loss of 20,000 gallons of decent wine at a nearby New Almaden Vineyards storage facility.

---

**FUELING ADVISORY** • At tiny Tres Piños just south of Hollister, a sign advises that you'll encounter no services for nearly a hundred miles, so respond accordingly.

---

From Hollister, State Route 25 travels the length of the Paicines Valley, a modestly attractive and quite remote basin cradled between the Gabilan and Diablo mountains. The highway sweeps lazily through this long and slender valley, initially past rich farmlands and vineyards, and then into beige grasslands where you'll encounter only an occasional ranch house and properly rustic barn.

The soft hills on both sides are inviting to hikers and to folks who simply like to sit on a rock and watch a hawk doing its requisite lazy circles in the sky. We like this region in the summer and fall when the grassy hills have turned to a tawny brown; their subtle shapes suggest the feminine curves of a well-tanned woman.

Thirty miles below Hollister, you'll be able to explore these hills, although the shapes will be considerably more masculine:

**Pinnacles National Monument** • *5000 Highway 146, Paicines, CA 95043-9770; (831) 389-4485. Modest admission fee. Bear Gulch Visitor center open daily 9 to 5. Private campground just outside the park; see below. RVs and trailer rigs can fit into a picnic parking area above the visitor center, which has several double-length spaces.* ☐

The Pinnacles is one of the most bizarre places on the planet. This ancient volcanic core, in startling contrast to the soft surrounding hills, has been eroded into every geological contour imaginable. No Hollywood set designer could have conceived a more grotesque variety of shapes—bulbous columns, spires, ridges, clefts and grottos. This is a hiking park, since the pinnacles themselves are some distance from the visitor center and parking areas.

The park gets busy on spring and fall weekends, although we found it uncrowded on an absolutely glorious October weekday. Summer days are usually hot and not pleasant for hiking, since there's very little shade up among the rocks. Any time of the year, you should pack plenty of water, for there is none once you leave the visitor center. The area around the visitor center is thick with oaks, madrones and brazen ground squirrels; it's a pleasant place to pause even if you don't plan to hike.

A network of trails winds among the park's formations, and you can see the best of the Pinnacles by following a 5.5 mile loop. Plan several hours up there, for you'll find yourself pausing frequently to stare in wonder at these amazing shapes. Pick up a brochure-map at the visitor center

*Strange, outerworldly shapes dominate the high ridges at Pinnacles National Monument.*

and take either the Condor Gulch Trail to the right of the parking lot or the Juniper Canyon Trail up through the picnic area. From either approach, you'll complete your loop by following the tough High Peaks Trail through the heart of the Pinnacles. It's a safe but difficult climb; part of the trail consists of steps hacked out of the rock, with handrails to help you steady your weary body. Views of great petrified waves of the surrounding mountain wilderness are impressive from up here.

Pinnacles National Monument has a matching visitor facility on the western side, the Chaparral area, reached by a winding road from U.S. 101 near Soledad. For the ultimate workout, hike from the Bear Gulch area across the High Peaks, down to Chaparral and back. Plan on most of a day, unless you can arrange a shuttle. On the return, you can swing wide on the Old Pinnacles Trail to avoid re-climbing the peak, although it's a five-mile trudge.

## CAMPING

**Pinnacles Campground** • *2400 Highway 146, Paicines, CA 95043; (831) 389-4462. (WEB SITE: www.pinncamp.com) RV and tent sites; electric hookups $$$$ on weekends and $$ weekdays.* ☐ This is a private campground just outside the park with electric hookups and nearby water, flush potties, showers and a swimming pool.

From the Pinnacles, continue another thirty-four miles south through the Paicines Valley. Highway 25 bumps into State Route 198 and a left turn will take you on a winding climb over the Diablo Range and into a high basin called Priest Valley. You can pause for provisions at a small café and mini-mart at **Priest Station** at the eastern side of the valley.

The final leg on this remote and scenic route is a winding descent through shallow, brushy and sometimes rock-ribbed Warthan Canyon. Then rather unexpectedly, you'll top a rise and downtown **Coalinga** pops into view. Although no tourist town, this mini-city of 10,250 is nonetheless rather appealing. Particularly tidy is the downtown shopping area and there's good reason. Much of the town was knocked flat by a 6.7 magnitude earthquake on May 2, 1983. The shaker destroyed or seriously damaged fifty businesses and 300 homes. Miraculously, no one was killed.

You can learn more about the quake and the rest of Coalinga's past at the **Baker Memorial Museum** downtown at 297 W. Elm Avenue. It's open weekdays 10 to 5, Saturday 11 to 5 and Sunday 1 to 5; (559) 935-1914. The museum's rather interesting collection includes mastodon bones found in nearby hills, several early day room groupings, plus native basketry and pioneer artifacts. And you'll learn how the town got its odd name. During the 1880s, a coal mine was operated briefly in the nearby hills and this was a loading site called "Coaling Station A." The owner lost his mine in a card game and it was closed down. However, oil was discovered in 1890 and it's still being pumped today.

From Coaling Station A, any of three routes will take you to Interstate 5 and beyond. If you're southbound, take Polk Street southeast from Coalinga's only stoplight, past a large K-Mart. You'll shortly pass a lockup with a rather benign name—Pleasant Valley State Prison—and hit the freeway a few miles beyond.

If you're northbound, follow Elm Avenue (Highway 198) through town and continue into the countryside. You'll pass several oil rigs, some with the pumper heads cleverly designed to look like animals. At the junction of routes 198 and 145, continue straight ahead onto Highway 145; you'll soon hit the freeway at the huge Harris Ranch cattle feedlot. If the wind's right, you'll smell it before you see it. If you'd like to stop at the very attractive Harris Ranch inn and restaurant complex (which smells considerably better), turn right at the 198/145 junction, staying with Route 198:

**The Inn at Harris Ranch** ● *Route 1, Box 777, Coalinga, CA 93210; (800) 943-2333 or (559) 935-0717. A hundred twenty-three rooms with TV movies, phones and honor bars; $$$$. Harris Ranch restaurant and adjacent cafe serve American fare; breakfast through dinner; full bar service; $$ to $$$. Major credit cards.* ◻ Harris Ranch owners proved that you can build a nice resort in the middle of nowhere and succeed, as long as it's on a busy highway—and a good three miles downwind of the feedlot. This elegant Spanish California complex has landscaped grounds, a tastefully appointed gift shop and even a butcher's mart, where Harris' famous beef is sold. The stylish restaurant and more casual café feature that beef on their menus, as well as a variety of other chicken and seafood entrées.

☺ ☺ ☺

**Where do we go from here?** ● Just about anywhere, since you're on California's major north-south artery. If you're following this book as we're writing it, head east across the San Joaquin Valley on Highway 198 to Hanford. Then go north on Route 41 to and through Fresno, to the beginning of the California gold country.

# PART II

# CALIFORNIA SIERRA

It was to become the greatest migration since the Crusades. Gold had been discovered in California! By the hundreds of thousands they would come, determined to strike it rich in this strange new land that many had heard about, but few had seen.

Problem was, a mighty mountain wall stood in their path, almost isolating California from the rest of the nation. The Sierra Nevada, Spanish for "snowy peaks," is the most dramatic mountain range in America. Although the Rockies may be better known to some, the Sierra Nevada is higher and more rugged. The range contains mainland America's tallest peak, 14,494-foot Mount Whitney, plus more than a dozen other peaks topping 14,000 feet.

Roughly separating California from Nevada—although the boundary line was drawn with a straight-edge—the Sierra is a great granite reef curving from north to southeast. From forty to eighty miles wide, it stretches nearly 450 miles from Mount Lassen in northern California to the Tehachapi Mountains east of Bakersfield.

Historian Oscar Lewis called the mountain range a "bulky, awkward and inconveniently high barrier." Particularly imposing is the towering eastern escarpment, which rises as much as 10,000 feet from the floor of Nevada's Great Basin Desert. Although hundreds of thousands of gold seekers were drawn to California, only a third braved the high, treacherous mountain passes of the Sierra Nevada. Most came the long way, by ship around Cape Horn, or across the malaria-ridden isthmus of Panama, hoping to find a San Francisco-bound ship on the other side. Others took the Overland Butterfield Stage route south through Texas, New Mexico, Arizona and northern Mexico, then worked their way up from southern California.

Eventually, wagon roads were cut through the Sierra Nevada and today, two year-around highways and four seasonal ones breech this mighty granite ridge. Ironically, that "bulky, awkward and inconveniently high barrier" has become one of California's favorite winter and summer playgrounds.

We'll thoroughly explore the Sierra Nevada in this section, first by visiting some of the lesser known gold rush camps in the western foothills. Next, we'll cross three high mountain passes, then we'll check out that great eastern Sierra escarpment, and finally, we shall poke about the mountain range's southern reaches.

HISTORICAL
DOWNTOWN
← MURPHYS
ᴗ HISTORICAL LANDMARK NO. 275 ᴗ

*Tour Eleven*

# THE GOLDEN CHAIN

## *CALIFORNIA'S UNDISCOVERED MOTHER LODE*

---

The California gold country, the region that inspired the famous 1849 rush to riches, stretches for more than two hundred miles along the western foothills of the Sierra Nevada.

Before California became American territory in 1848, Mexican miners had searched this region and found a bit of gold, although they never found the legendary main vein—*la veta madre* or "the mother lode." Although the gold country often is called the Mother Lode, it's unlikely that a main vein exists. Gold was distributed widely throughout the foothills, leached from the Sierra Nevada and carried downhill by dozens of rivers and creeks.

While Hispanic miners never made a big strike, an itinerant carpenter and handyman named James Wilson Marshall did. He'd been hired by early California entrepreneur John Sutter to build a water-powered sawmill on the American River. In late January of 1848, he found two nuggets "about the half the size and of the shape of a pea" in his millrace, and the word began to spread. California was still in Mexican hands, although Sutter had been granted permission to start an American colony near present-

# TRIP PLANNER

**WHEN TO GO** ● Any time of the year is a fine time to explore California's gold country. Autumn is nice because the weather's generally stable and you can encounter occasional touches of fall color. Summer's the best time to catch all of the museums open, and the lesser known towns aren't crowded even in peak season.

**DRIVING DISTANCE** ● The length of Highway 49 from Oakhurst to Vinton is 300 miles, and you'll need to toss in a few extra for frequent side trips.

**RV ADVISORY** ● Nothing on this route will challenge an RV or trailer, although a side trip from Downieville to Alleghany may not be suitable for big rigs.

**WHAT YOU'LL SEE** ● California State Mining and Mineral Museum in Mariposa, Hornitos, historic Big Oak Flat and Groveland, Columbia State Historic Park, charming old Murphys and its nearby wineries, Indian Grinding Rock State Historic Park and the town of Volcano, old Georgetown, Malakoff Diggins State Historic Park, mountain-rimmed Downieville and Sierra City, and the hidden town of Alleghany.

**WHAT TO DO** ● Have a drink in the Iron Door Saloon in Groveland; pan for gold or ride a stagecoach at Columbia State Historic Park; hang in mid-air at Moaning Caverns near Murphys and tour Mercer and California caverns; sip some good Zinfandel in the foothills; have a pastie in Grass Valley; go mountain biking near Downieville; pan for gold in the Yuba River.

**TO BEGIN** ● Get to Oakhurst via State Route 41 from Fresno or highways 145/41 from Madera, and start north.

## Useful contacts

**Downieville Chamber of Commerce**, P.O. Box 473, Downieville, CA 95936; (800) 720-7782 or (530) 289-3507. (WEB SITE: www.sierracounty.org)

**Calaveras Lodging and Visitors Association**, P.O. Box 637, Angels Camp, CA 95222; (800) 225-3764 or (209) 736-0049.

**Mariposa County Chamber of Commerce**, P.O. Box 425 (5158 Highway 140), Mariposa, CA 95338; (800) 208-2434 or (209) 966-2456.

**Tuolumne County Visitors Bureau**, P.O. Box 4020 (55 W. Stockton), Sonora, CA 95370; (800) 446-1333 or (209) 533-4420.

## Pricing guidelines

**DINING:** Dinner entrée with soup or salad, without drinks or dessert for under $10 = **$**; $10 to $14 = **$$**; $15 to $25 = **$$$**; over $25 = **$$$$**.

**RECLINING:** A two-person room for $35 or less = **$**; $36 to $50 = **$$**; $51 to $75 = **$$$**; $76 to $100 = **$$$$**; more than $100 = **$$$$$**.

**CAMPING:** Under $10 = **$**; $10 to $14 = **$$**; $15 to $19 = **$$$**; $20 or more = **$$$$**

day Sacramento. By the time word of the gold discovery reached the outside world, California had been ceded to the United States by the Treaty of Guadalupe Hidalgo. Thus, Mexico never profited from the first major gold rush in world history.

Hundreds of shanty towns were hastily erected as argonauts panned the gold-bearing streams that flowed from the high mountains. When the streams gave out, they dredged the gravel beds and then they began burrowing into the mountains themselves. These early mining camps were linked by primitive trails which eventually became wagon and stagecoach roads and ultimately—well into the twentieth century—a paved highway. In honor of the Great California Gold Rush, officials designated it as State Highway 49.

Within a few decades of Marshall's discovery, nearly all gold seeking efforts had been exhausted. What had once had been the most vibrant and most populated area of California became a quiet collection of weathered old towns. A few survived as trading and ranching centers; most simply withered back into the foothill soil from which they had sprung.

Gradually, tourists began poking about the area. Seeing the potential, surviving towns began preserving their historic buildings, opening ancient hotels to visitors and enshrining their gold rush memories in museums. Tourist promoters began calling narrow, lazily winding Highway 49 the "Golden Chain." In recent years, bed and breakfast inns have proliferated in the foothills like mountain lupine. Most of the rivers flowing out of the Sierra Nevada have been dammed to nourish thirsty flatland communities, and the resultant reservoirs are popular with boaters and fisherpersons.

Several state parks have been established to preserve the area's history. Columbia was designated in 1945 as California's first gold country historic park. Others followed—Malakoff Diggins near Nevada City, Empire Mine in Grass Valley, Marshall Gold Discovery in Coloma and Railtown 1870 in Jamestown.

Although still thinly populated—it's tough to make a living up here—the once sleepy gold country has become one of California's most popular tourist areas. Thus, Highway 49 is hardly a road less traveled. Many guidebooks provide abundant detail about attractions along this route, including our own *Best of the Gold Country.*

Instead of steering you to the obvious, this tour will guide you to lesser-known regions of the foothills. We'll take you off the Golden Chain to interesting historic sites and charming old mining towns that are overlooked by most travelers. And we'll pause in some of the Highway 49 towns the tourist tide often misses. We know this part of California well, for our summer home is in Columbia State Historic Park.

## Oakhurst to Coulterville

Highway 49, the Golden Chain, begins in **Oakhurst**, although that town had little to do with the gold rush. It was a farming and ranching center and it's now mostly a summer weekend refuge for residents of the hot San Joaquin Valley. Many pass through its strung-out business district headed for Bass Lake, a popular recreation area higher in the Sierra Nevada foothills.

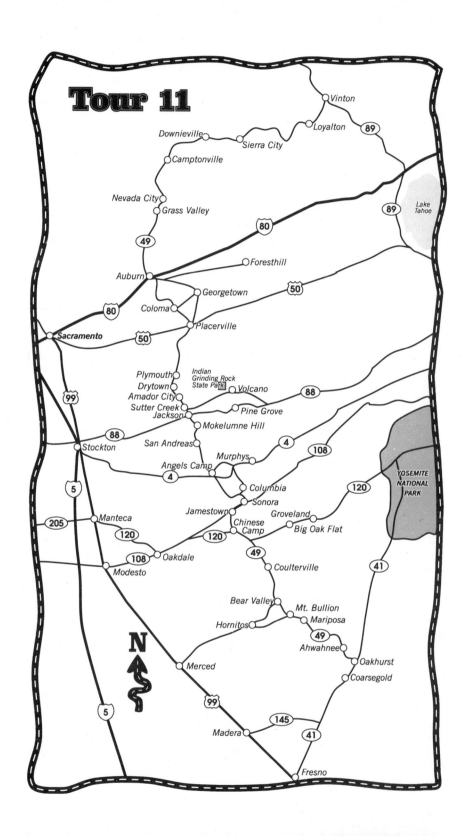

Heading north from Oakhurst on Highway 49, we'll pause for our first often-overlooked attraction—the **Wassama Round House** in the tiny hamlet of **Ahwahnee**. This is a classic Miwok Indian shelter and visitors can step into its cool interior, which is furnished only with a fire pit and a few low seats. Other elements of this compound are a sweat house, dance ring and three wikiups. The facility is open daily 11 to 4 and it's often the site of ceremonial dances. Call (559) 683-3631 or (559) 683-8194 for schedules.

**Mariposa,** the next town north, has all the early frontier character that Oakhurst lacks, with several false front stores, the oldest continually-used courthouse in California and an outstanding mineral museum. Although hardly a hidden attraction, the **California State Mining and Mineral Museum** south of town at the fairgrounds is a required stop. It has an outstanding collection of gems and minerals, plus fine exhibits on California's rich mining history. Hours are Wednesday-Monday 10 to 9 in summer and 10 to 4 the rest of the year; (209) 742-7625.

Once in town, you can learn more about Mariposa's historic sites, including its Mariposa County History Center, with a stop at the **Chamber of Commerce** at 5158 Highway 140, near Route 49; (209) 966-2456. That venerable courthouse, built in 1854 and still in use, is a block east of Highway 49 on Bullion Street. To get there, go east on Eighth and then north on Bullion.

## Side trip: Joaquin Murietta's Hornitos

One of the most colorful characters in the early California gold country was a Robin Hood style Mexican *bandito* named Joaquin Murietta. He supposedly took to outlawry after American tormenters tied him to a tree, beat him, abused is wife and killed his brother. (And ran over his dog?) Problem is, half a dozen Mother Lode towns claim this or a similar Murietta legend. The outlaw seemed to have been virtually everywhere in the Sierra foothills—often at the same time.

One of the earliest Murietta stories concerns the town of **Hornitos** a few miles west of Mariposa. If there were a Joaquin, this could have been his lair. It was one of the foothills' few Mexican villages, and one of the few gold country towns built around a classic Mexican plaza. Murietta supposedly robbed stagecoaches by day and slipped back into town at night to spend his loot on wicked ladies in the fandango halls. He allegedly used a tunnel under one of the saloons as an escape route when the posse came a-huntin'. However, sober-minded historians say the tunnel—which still exists—was used merely to keep the beer barrels cool.

Hornitos is an almost ghost town with a few interesting relics from Murietta's day—if he had a day. To get there, head north from Mariposa on Highway 49 about four miles through **Mount Bullion** and turn left (west) onto Old Toll Road. You'll travel downhill through a pretty landscape of green oak groves, ruby-barked manzanita and—in the spring—yellow-blooming wild mustard. If it's summer, you'll note that the temperature begins to rise as you lose altitude. Indeed, hornitos is Spanish for "little ovens." At 980 feet, it's one of the lowest mining towns in the Sierra foothills.

It also was one of the wildest, with as many as 15,000 citizens and an alarming number of fandango halls. Now shrunk to perhaps fifty residents, it's still rich in yesterday relics, including a mean looking granite block jail that must have been a *hornito* on a hot day, and the shell of the D. Ghirardelli & Co., general store. It was built in 1859 by forbearers of the still-active Ghirardelli Chocolate Company of San Francisco. From the plaza, head uphill to the 1862 St. Catherine's Church. This unusual wood frame structure with stone buttresses stands silent watch over the sleepy town.

From Hornitos, follow Bear Valley Road (J-16) about eleven miles to **Bear Valley** and resume your trek north on the Golden Chain. Seventeen miles up the highway is **Coulterville,** another appealing old mining camp. To get there, you'll have to wind down into "Hells Hollow," a thousand-foot-deep spiral into a canyon of the Merced River, and then twist back up the other side. It's not as scary as it sounds; it just has a lot of tight turns.

Tiny Coulterville is worth a pause for its fine regional museum and for a hotel whose history reaches back to the 1840s:

**Hotel Jeffery** ● *P.O. Box 440-B (Highway 49 at Main Street), Coulterville, CA 95311; (800) 464-3471 or (209) 878-3471. (WEB: www.yosemitegold.com/jefferyhotel) Twenty-one rooms and suites with private or share baths; $$$ to $$$$. Restaurant serves breakfast through dinner; $$. MC/VISA, AMEX.* ☐ One of the oldest buildings in the gold country, this green-trimmed structure with distinctive embossed tin siding was built in 1851 as a store, with a fandango hall upstairs. It was purchased by the Jeffery family a year later and converted to a hotel, and it's still operated by their descendants. Recently refurbished, it has rooms with period décor, the classic Western style Magnolia Saloon a handsome restaurant serving American fare.

**Northern Mariposa County History Center** ● *Highway 49 at Main Street; (209) 878-3015. Tuesday-Sunday 10 to 4 in summer and weekends and holidays the rest of the year.* ☐ Across the highway from the hotel, this weathered archive does a fine job of capturing the area's gold rush memories. The museum building, accented by cheerful flower beds, occupies portions of adobe structures dating from the 1850s.

If you go northeast on Main Street from the hotel and history center, you'll see several other interesting old buildings, including the still-intact 1851 Sun Sun Wo Chinese store.

## Coulterville to Columbia

Eleven miles north of Coulterville, Highway 49 merges with State Route 120 and a right turn will take you to Yosemite National Park. Even if you aren't planning a Yosemite visit, a brief and very twisting climb up Priest Grade will deliver you to a pair of interesting gold rush era hamlets. **Big Oak Flat** and **Groveland** offer a few wood frame and rough stone buildings that hug the narrow highway.

Particularly noteworthy is the **Iron Door Saloon** on the right in the upper end of Groveland. Built in 1852, it claims to be the oldest drinking establishment in California. Just beyond is another gold rush era hotel that's still in business:

**Groveland Hotel** ● *P.O. Box 289 (18767 Main St., Groveland, CA 95321; (800) 273-3314 or (209) 962-4000. (WEB SITE: www.groveland.com; E-MAIL: peggy@groveland.com) Seventeen rooms with private baths; continental breakfast; $$$$$. Restaurant serves dinner nightly; $$$. MC/VISA.* ☐ Beautifully restored, this historic inn features a mix of English and French furnishings, with print wallpaper and other late nineteenth century décor. The complex includes an 1850 stone and adobe structure and a 1914 Queen Anne style Victorian. The hotel restaurant, also dressed in nineteenth century finery, serves creative American fare.

Back on Highway 49 and pressing northward, you'll pass the large Don Pedro Reservoir and encounter tiny **Chinese Camp.** There's little left of this former Chinese mining community, although a left turn onto its main street will take you past an old Wells Fargo office and a few other historic buildings.

You're now in Tuolumne County, a growing commercial center and a gateway to Yosemite, so it's hardly an area less visited. Both **Jamestown** and **Sonora** have nicely preserved historic districts, rimmed by more contemporary suburbs.

To cruise Jamestown, turn right onto lower Main Street, which is lined with false front stores and a couple of old balconied hotels. At the upper end, Main blends back onto the highway.

To visit historic Sonora and remain on Highway 49, continue north and veer right and then left through an underpass, following signs to downtown Sonora and Columbia State Historic Park. After a one-mile uphill drive past suburban businesses and the Mother Lode Fairgrounds, you'll hit a stoplight at Washington Street. Turn left and follow Highway 49 through Sonora's historic district. (A block short of the stoplight, on your right at 55 W. Stockton Road, is the **Tuolumne County Visitors Bureau,** open weekdays 9 to 5:30, Saturdays 10 to 4 and Sundays 10 to 3; shorter hours in the off-season; (209) 533-4420.)

### Hail Columbia?

A few miles above Sonora, we'll suggest another detour from the Golden Chain, although—like Jamestown and Sonora—it's not a place less visited. Fork to the right onto Parrotts Ferry Road and follow it to **Columbia State Historic Park.** It's the most visited attraction in the California gold country, drawing 300,000 people a year. However, it's crowded only on summer weekends and it's certainly worth a stop if you haven't been there before.

Columbia is the only historic park in California that's also an individual community. (Some cities such as San Diego, Sacramento and San Juan Bautista have historic districts, but Columbia's entire townsite is an historic park.) Several blocks of the downtown area are closed to traffic, and you can stroll past grand old brick front buildings, catch a stagecoach ride at the Wells Fargo office, nibble some old time candy from Nelson's Candy Kitchen, pan for gold at the miner's shack and take a tour to a real gold mine. At the grizzled St. Charles Saloon, you almost expect a grizzled miner to come in, plunk down his bag of gold dust and demand four fingers of red eye. If Columbia looks familiar, it has been featured in dozens of movies, television shows and commercials, from the classic *High Noon* to the *Young Riders* and *Paradise* TV series. There's plenty to see here and two historic hotels invite you to spend the night:

**Fallon and City Hotels** ● *P.O. Box 1870, Columbia, CA 95310; (209) 532-7027. Rooms with private or share baths; full breakfast. MC/VISA; $$$ to $$$$$.* ☐ The two hotels reflect different eras in gold rush history. Following an $8 million restoration in 1986, the Fallon is one of the Mother Lode's finest lodgings, with an 1880s Victorian look. Guests at the City Hotel step in the 1860s, with Eastlake beds, floral wallpaper and early American furnishings. The City Hotel Restaurant, once featured in *Gourmet Magazine*, is easily the finest dining establishment in the gold country. It serves American regional cuisine in an opulent nineteenth century atmosphere, serving lunch and dinner with full bar service.

## Murphys, San Andreas and Mok Hill

From Columbia, continue following Parrotts Ferry Road, which spirals down to large New Melones Reservoir of the Stanislaus River, a good place for boating, water skiing and fishing. The road then climbs out of the Stanislaus canyon, headed for State Route 4 and Murphys. Before you get there, pause at **Moaning Cavern,** a large limestone cave reached by a spiral staircase. For an extra fee and an extra thrill, you can rappel down to the cave from a hole in the ceiling. One of the largest single caves in America, Moaning Cavern is open daily 9 to 6 in summer and 10 to 5 the rest of the year; (209) 736-2708.

Parrotts Ferry Road ends at State Route 4, which we take over Ebbetts Pass in Tour Twelve. For the moment, we'll take it only a few miles to Murphys, a real charmer of an old mining town. En route, watch on your right for the attractive tasting room of **Chatom Vineyards,** open daily 11 to 4:30; (209) 736-6500. This is one of several wineries in the area, since we've crossed into Calaveras County, a major Sierra foothill wine producing region. Foothill wineries are particularly noted for their Zinfandel. (For details on all gold country wineries, pick up a copy of our *Best of the Wine Country.* Ordering information is in the back of this book.)

## MURPHYS

Population: 1,850                                     Elevation: 2,171 feet

Our next "off the Golden Chain" town is a real charmer, with a fine collection of nineteenth century buildings basking under the shade of ancient locust and elm trees. It's one of the oldest towns in the Mother Lode, established in 1848 by two Irish brothers named Murphy, and thus the odd plural name. The youngest, 23-year-old John, made his fortune by paying local Miwok Indians with blankets and trinkets to do the digging. An early historian wrote:

*The camp of Mr. Murphy is in the midst of a small tribe of wild Indians, who gather gold for him, and receive in return provisions... They respect his person in part due to the fact that he has married the daughter of the chief.*

After a few months, the Murphys left California as happy millionaires—and left the chief's unhappy daughter behind.

*A reversal of fortunes? This sketch on the "Wall of Comparative Ovations" in Murphys questions who's the real jackass in the Great California Gold Rush.*

To do Murphys, turn left at the "Historic district" sign, then make a quick right onto Main and follow it into town. You'll soon encounter another wine tasting room on your right—**Milliaire Vineyards**, housed in a former service station. It's open Friday-Monday noon to 5; (209) 728-1658. Across the street, occupying one of Murphys' grand old mansions, is the **Dunbar House Bed & Breakfast Inn**, listed below.

Continue a few more blocks and you'll be in the heart of the historic district with its fine gathering of stone and brick buildings. Murphys looks more like a genteel old New England town than a gold rush survivor. A focal point is the imposing **Murphys Hotel** at Main and Algiers, which has been hosting the ordinary, the rich and the famous (including Ulysses S. Grant) since 1856. Across the street at Main and Sheep Ranch Road is the **Old Timers Museum**, an archive that houses Murphys' memories. It's open Friday-Sunday 11 to 4; (209) 728-2607. The museum's most curious feature is the Wall of Comparative Ovations, an historical and generally whimsical collection of plaques honoring early gold rush pioneers.

Most of Murphys' several curio shops, boutiques and cafés are in this area, so find a place to park and begin strolling. Other attractions around Murphys gallop off in three directions, so follow this driving route:

From downtown, head east on Sheep Ranch Road and you'll shortly see **Mercer Caverns,** an elaborate limestone cave with 45-minute tours through ten different underground chambers. It's open daily 9 to 5 from Memorial weekend through September, then weekends and school holidays the rest of the year; (209) 728-2101.

Cruising downhill from Mercer Caverns, you'll encounter **Stevenot Winery** in a pretty little basin surrounded by its own vineyards. Wines are tasted daily 10 to 5 in an intriguing sod roofed log cabin that more resembles an Alaskan sourdough's hut than a tasting room; (209) 728-3436.

Return to downtown and head west past the Murphys Hotel on Algiers Street. Appearing quickly on your left is **Maldevino Vineyards** tasting room in a white clapboard cottage, open daily 11 to 5. Just past the tasting room is a charming little community park with picnic tables, a gazebo and a gurgling stream. Continue a mile into the countryside and you'll reach the extensive and elegant **Kautz Ironstone Vineyards.** It's one of California's more elaborate winery complexes, with a tasting room, deli, art gallery and museum tucked beneath gnarled oaks, and aging cellars tunneled into a hillside. Kautz is open daily 11 to 5; (209) 728-1251.

Returning again to Murphys, head a couple of blocks north on Main to Murphys Grade and you'll find **Black Sheep Vintners.** Its rustic tasting room looks like a leftover from the gold rush; open weekends noon to 5; (209) 728-2157.

## DINING

**Café Soliel** ● *409 Main St.; (209) 728-2875. American regional; wine and beer. Lunch and dinner Tuesday-Saturday. MC/VISA, DISC; $$.* ☐ Sitting off the street behind its own courtyard, Café Soliel is a cozy restaurant serving tasty fare with Mediterranean and California *nouveau* accents. It features such entrées as grilled calamari steak, capellini pasta with fresh basil and Parmesan, savory lamb shanks and upscale pizzas.

**Grounds Restaurant and Coffee Bar** ● *402 Main St.; (209) 728-8663. American; wine and beer. Breakfast and lunch Monday, Wednesday and Friday-Sunday, dinner Wednesday-Sunday. MC/VISA; $$.* ☐ This simple little coffee bar with drop lamps and local art on its walls has a busy menu. The fare ranges from ribeye steak and shrimp Provencal to designer pizzas. Locals gather in the morning for its specialty coffees, pastries and hearty breakfast fare.

**Murphys Hotel Dining Room** ● *457 Main St.; (209) 728-3444. American-continental; full bar service. Breakfast through dinner daily. Major credit cards; $$$.* ☐ Contrasting the trendy Café Soliel and Grounds, the Murphys Hotel dining room is a classic, dressed in nineteenth century finery. The menu has an interesting mix of entrées, including whiskey steak with peppercorns and Bourbon, several seafood dishes, veal scaloppine and veal Marsala.

## RECLINING

**Dunbar House Bed & Breakfast** ● *P.O. Box 1375 (271 Jones at Main), Murphys, CA 95247; (209) 728-2897. Four units with private baths; full breakfast. MC/VISA, AMEX; $$$$$.* ☐ Listed on the National Register of Historic Places, this grand old 1880 Italianate mansion brims with early American and European antiques. However, rooms have modern amenities such as TV/VCRs and refrigerators. If the Dunbar House looks a bit familiar, it was featured in the short-lived *Seven Brides for Seven Brothers* TV series. (The town of Murphys frequently is used as a filming location.)

**Murphys Hotel and Lodge** ● *457 Main (at Algiers), Murphys, CA 95247-9628; (800) 532-7684 or (209) 728-3444. Nine rooms in the hotel with share or private baths and twenty in an adjacent motel unit with private baths; continental breakfast. Major credit cards; $$$ to $$$$$.* ☐ At the Murphys Hotel, you can sleep where President U.S. Grant slept and drink where notorious bandit Black Bart drank. Dating from 1856, it has been both renovated and preserved, furnished with American and Victorian antiques. Particularly attractive are the gold rush era saloon and the Victorian style Presidential Suite. The complex also has an nice lawn area and rose garden near an adjacent motel wing.

If you'd like to visit the old mining town of **Angels Camp** on Highway 49, the home of Mark Twain's famous jumping frog story, return to Highway 4 and head southwest. Otherwise, continue past Black Sheep Vintners and take Murphys Grade, which follows a pleasant little creek canyon downhill. After nine miles, you'll hit the northern end of Angels Camp, above the historic district.

A right turn onto Highway 49 will take you thirteen miles to the next foothill mining town, **San Andreas,** with 2,150 residents. Dating from 1848, it has been mostly modernized—at least to the 1950s. To see what little remains of the historic district, turn right at a blinking amber light onto Main Street. You'll immediately encounter—on your right—the fine **Calaveras County Museum and Art Gallery.** Behind the museum, you can peer into a jail cell where famous badman Black Bart was briefly held, awaiting transfer to San Francisco for trial. This old brick and cut stone building also houses the Calaveras County visitor center; it and the museum are open daily 10 to 4; (209) 754-6579.

Interested in exploring another cavity? Follow Mountain Ranch Road and then Cave City Road twelve miles east to **California Caverns.** It's the largest and most elaborate of several limestone caverns in the Sierra foothills. In addition to regular tours, you can sign up for special spelunking trips, including a fun and sticky mud crawl. (The management provides coveralls.) Regular tours are daily 10 to 5 in summer and 10 to 4 in fall; (209) 736-2708. Caves are closed from early winter through spring because of water seepage.

Meanwhile, back in San Andreas, if you remain on Main, you'll rejoin Highway 49 after about four miles. A few miles beyond is another town whose historic district, like that of San Andreas, is often overlooked by travelers. **Mokelumne Hill** was founded in 1848 and for a brief period it was one of the largest and wildest towns in California, with 15,000 citizens. "Saloons opened their doors, never to close for years," wrote historian Emmett P. Joy.

Mok Hill has shrunk to 560 residents and its historic district occupies about a dozen square blocks, downhill and to the right of Highway 49. To reach it, turn right just after you pass the Highway 26 junction. A few of these nineteenth century structures house curio and antique shops although most have ordinary stores or nothing at all. Mok Hill doesn't draw many visitors. Its main drawing card is one of the California gold country's oldest surviving lodgings:

*Hotel Leger* • *P.O. Box 157 (8304 Main St.), Mokelumne Hill, CA 95245; (209) 286-1401. Simply furnished rooms with private or shared baths; $$$ to $$$$. Restaurant serves dinner Thursday-Sunday and Sunday brunch; $$. MC/VISA.* ☐ Dating from 1851, this venerable hotel (pronounced *leh-ZHAY*) has a handsome lobby with nineteenth century furnishings. You'll also note something more contemporary yet still historic—a 1950s Wurlitzer jukebox. The dining room, dressed in period attire, serves early California fare such as chicken breast filet, assorted steaks and fish.

## Grinding rocks, a "volcano" and daffodils

Our next detour from Highway 49 begins in **Jackson**, ten miles north of Mokelumne Hill. At a four-way stop, turn right and head uphill on State Route 88 toward **Pine Grove.** (We also go this way on Tour Twelve, headed for Carson Pass.) Pine Grove doesn't offer much of interest, although a left turn from there onto Pine Grove-Volcano Road will take you to a couple of special lures.

*Indian Grinding Rock State Historic Park* • *14881 Pine Grove-Volcano Rd., Pine Grove, CA 95665; (209) 296-7488. Museum open weekdays 11 to 3 and weekends 10 to 4. Campground (reached from the first park turn-in from the highway) has RV and tent sites with flush potties; no hookups or showers. Or you can sleep in a traditional Miwok bark shelter. Camping reservations can be made directly with the park; $$$.* ☐ This state park preserves a huge bedrock mortar with more than a thousand holes ground by early Miwoks. The mortar cups were shaped as they used stones to pulverize acorns into a kind of pasty flour. The park also houses the excellent Chaw Sé Regional Indian Museum with fine exhibits on the history and lifestyles of these folks.

Just beyond Indian Grinding Rock is the scruffily charming old mining town of **Volcano.** It was established in 1848 and the odd name comes from the fact that the town rests in a high mountain basin. Residents, seeing early morning mist, fancied themselves in a caldera. Tiny Volcano has only a hundred or so residents, a couple of shops and cafés and one ancient hotel.

## DINING AND RECLINING

*The Jug and Rose Café* • *Main Street; (209) 296-4696. American; no alcohol. Breakfast through midafternoon weekends. No credit cards.* ☐ The Jug and Rose is noted for its all-you-can eat sourdough pancake brunch, which the management immodestly claims is the world's best. This cute little café with a turn-of-the-century soda fountain also serves light lunches and fountain treats. There are a few outdoor tables in back.

*St. George Hotel* • *P.O. Box 9 (16104 Main St.), Volcano, CA 95689; (209) 296-4458. (WEB SITE: www.stgeorgehotel.com; E-MAIL: st-george@volcano.net) Twenty rooms, some share and some private baths; $$$ to $$$$. Restaurant serves breakfast and lunch weekends and dinner Thursday-Sunday; $$. MC/VISA.* ☐ This three-story brick, double balconied hotel has been hosting folks since 1862. New owners have spruced it up and restored much of its early day finery. The restaurant serves rather *nouveau* cuisine for such a venerable establishment, such as grilled lamb loin with Zinfandel sauce, maple balsamic pork tenderloin and eggplant Napoleon with roasted peppers and goat cheese. A must-see is the adjacent saloon decorated with early day artifacts and hundreds of dollar bills pinned to calling cards on the walls and ceilings.

Three miles above Volcano is **Daffodil Hill,** where more than 300,000 daffodils bloom each spring. This private ranch is open to visitors and the best time to see the blooms is March through April.

## Through Amador County to Placerville

From Volcano, you can return to Highway 49 by following a road through a shallow wooded canyon to Sutter Creek, although the route is a bit rough and narrow. If you'd rather avoid the bumps and/or you want to visit historic **Jackson**, backtrack to Pine Grove and head downhill on Highway 88. Jackson's small historic district can be reached by turning left at a four-way stop.

If you continue north from downtown on Main Street, the route becomes Jackson Gate Road, taking you to **Kennedy Tailing Wheels Park.** It houses two surviving "tailing wheels," huge Ferris wheel shaped rigs that were used to move slurry from mines into settling basins. These were latter-day arrivals in the gold country, built in 1912 after a court ruling forbade dumping tailings into streams.

North of Jackson are three more mining towns, each smaller than the one before—**Sutter Creek, Amador City** and **Drytown**. They're busy with antique shops, boutiques and visitors, since Highway 49 runs right through their historic districts. Worth a pause is a beautifully restored hotel with a fine restaurant:

**Imperial Hotel** • *P.O. Box 195, Amador City, CA 95601; (800) 242-5594 or (209) 267-9172. (WEB SITE: www.imperialamador.com; E-MAIL: host@imperialamador.com) Six rooms with private baths; full breakfast; $$$$. Restaurant serves dinner nightly and Sunday brunch February through October; $$$. MC/VISA, AMEX.* ☐ Pause for a peek into the lobby or a drink in the classic saloon even if you don't intend to eat or sleep here. One of the most elegantly restored hotels in the gold country, the 1879 Imperial is dressed in old brick and fine Victorian antiques. Rooms have a mix of period and modern furnishings.

After passing through these three communities (and turning right to stay with Highway 49 at the State Route 16 junction), you'll hit **Plymouth,** another old mining town. It's better known as the gateway to the Shenandoah Valley, the largest wine producing area in the Mother Lode. Heading east from Plymouth, you can visit **Fiddletown**, another gold hamlet with a few nineteenth century buildings, then go north and prowl the Shenandoah Valley's fifteen or so wineries. For specifics, get a copy of the *Amador County Wine Country* brochure. It's available at area visitor centers or write: Amador Vintners, P.O. Box 667, Plymouth, CA 95669; (209) 245-4309.

Beyond Plymouth, a winding twenty-mile drive through lonely oak foothills will take you to **Placerville** and into the most congested part of the gold country. Placerville is fed by busy U.S. 50 and Auburn, the next major Highway 49 town, is served by Interstate 80. Since they're easily reached by the rest of California, they've become modernized and their suburbs have spread in every direction, although each has a small historic section. Between them, in a relatively unpopulated swatch of woodlands on Highway 49, is **Marshall Gold Discovery State Park**. It's the most important historic site—and thus one of the most visited areas—in the gold country. It was here, in tiny **Coloma**, that James Marshall had the dumb luck to find gold nuggets in the tailrace of the water-powered lumber mill he was building.

## To Georgetown, Coloma and Foresthill

A place that is *not* well known or heavily visited is **Georgetown,** high upon Georgetown Divide east of Coloma. To get there, follow Highway 49 through Placerville and across U.S. 50, then fork to the right onto State Route 193 about a mile north of town. A sixteen mile climb into the evergreens will deliver you to Georgetown, which boomed as a mining center in the 1850s. It has shrunk to a handful of residents, although it has several appealing brick and wood frame gold rush survivors. Two of them provide places to eat and/or sleep:

### RECLINING AND DINING

**American River Inn Bed & Breakfast** ● *P.O. Box 43 (Main at Orleans streets), Georgetown, CA 95634; (800) 245-6566 or (530) 333-4499. Eighteen rooms with some share and some private baths; full breakfast. MC/VISA, AMEX; $$$$ to $$$$$.* ◻ This three-story board and batten hotel is particularly alluring for its extensive selection of giftwares, antiques and collectibles that ramble through several downstairs rooms. Beyond the stuffed critters and curios, note the fine Victorian and early American furnishings, particularly in the breakfast area. This structure was built as the American Hotel in 1853.

**Georgetown Hotel and Parra's Mexican Restaurant** ● *Main Street, Georgetown, CA 95634; (530) 333-2848. Simply furnished rooms $$ to $$$. Parra's Mexican Restaurant serves lunch and dinner daily except Monday; $ to $$. MC/VISA.* ◻ While not elegant, the Georgetown is worth a visit for its classic old bar filled with game trophies, antiques and other regalia. The hotel has had a hectic career. The original was built atop a gold mine in 1849; it burned and was rebuilt in 1852, and again was scorched and rebuilt in 1896. That version still survives. Parra's Restaurant is in the rear, dressed in bright Mexican accents. It serves a variety of smashed beans and rice dishes, plus a couple of steaks.

If you've not visited Coloma, head downhill from Georgetown, following signs to and through Garden Valley. However, if you've been there and done that, continue north from Georgetown on Highway 93 to busy Auburn. Before you hit the town itself, a turn right will take you up the American River Canyon, along a top-of-the-world ridge to **Foresthill.** This old town doesn't have much of an historic district, although its setting among great stands of evergreens is nice.

Heading back downhill toward Auburn, you'll cross the lofty **Foresthill Bridge**. It's one of the highest in California, a dizzying 800 feet above the American River Canyon. It was built to span the reservoir that would have flooded this beautiful chasm after completion of the Auburn Dam. That project, hotly disputed by environmentalists, is on indefinite hold so the bridge spans 800 feet of empty air. If you'd like to experience that lofty feeling and stare into the canyon far below, the bridge has pedestrian walkways.

With more than 10,000 residents, **Auburn** is the largest town in the gold country, scattering itself in all directions. You'll have to wade through several miles of this sprawl as you continue northward on Highway 49. (If you've detoured to Foresthill, you can re-join the Golden Chain by going south briefly on Interstate 80, then exiting and following signs toward Grass Valley.)

### Pause for a pastie

After twenty-five miles, mostly on a four-lane highway and even a slab of freeway, you'll reach Grass Valley and Nevada City, two very popular stops on the Golden Chain. In addition to an historic district and the Empire Mine State Historic Park, **Grass Valley** is noted for its Cornish pasties (pronounced *PAHS-stees*). These spicy meat and vegetable pies were introduced by Cornish miners during the town's heyday as a hardrock mining center, and three bakeries still produce them.

The best pasties come from **Mrs. Dubblebee's** at 251-C South Auburn. It's an easy reach from the freeway; take the historic downtown exit onto Auburn Street and go right for half a block. (The historic area is to the left, under the freeway.) The pastie place is in a prim little cottage on your left. You can enjoy your treat on a porch dining area or take several along for meals-on-the-go. Mrs. Dubblebee's is open daily from mid-morning to late afternoon; (530) 272-7700.

Just up the freeway from Grass Valley, **Nevada City** is the darling of the tourist crowd, noted for its fine Victorian buildings and trendy shops and restaurants. It's worth a stop if you haven't been there. However, this tour is about less visited places. We're about to leave the busiest section of the Golden Chain and enter the least visited and most scenic.

### Sierra County and the end of the chain

North of Nevada City, the freeway ends and a left turn will keep you on Highway 49, taking you into Sierra County, a pristine area of sparkling streams, thick evergreen forests and high mountain lakes. Covered mostly by national forest, it's one of the least populated and prettiest counties in California. **Nevada City Ranger Station,** on your right just after you leave the freeway, can provide you with material on the area. It's open weekdays 8 to 5; (530) 265-4531. Winding into the woods, you'll soon spiral down to a pretty stream crossing in **South Yuba River State Park.** This relatively new park has few facilities other than a river recreation area popular for sunbathing, swimming and fishing.

Just beyond, watch for a turnoff to North Bloomfield and **Malakoff Diggins State Historic Park.** It preserves a strange moonscape in a river canyon, created by years of hydraulic mining. Late in the gold rush, after all the stream gold was panned out, mining companies began using powerful water hoses called monitors to blast gravel loose from river and creek banks and even from dry ravines. This slurry was then run through long "toms" or troughs to separate the gold from the gravel. However, the runoff muddied downstream rivers, caused floods and silted up farmers' fields. The practice was stopped in 1884 when Judge Lorenzo Sawyer handed down the first environmentally-based ruling in American history. It forbade mining companies from dumping their tailings into a stream. This put Malakoff and its North Bloomfield Gravel Mining Company out of business. The park preserves the wildly eroded mining area and the old town of North Bloomfield. An adjacent campground has RV and tent sites with flush potties; no hookups or showers. For campsite reservations, call (800) 444-PARK; MC/VISA accepted.

Winding northward on Highway 49, you'll pass thorough small and somewhat scruffy **North San Juan**, followed by **Camptonville**, then you'll spiral down into the thickly wooded **Yuba River Canyon.** This is an idyllic area for RVers and tenters since half a dozen Forest Service campgrounds line its banks. The stream is popular for fishing and gold panning.

## Side trip: Goodyears Bar and Alleghany

This sixty-mile loop takes you to a pair of historic mining towns missed by the majority of gold country travelres. Several miles beyond Camptonville, turn right onto Mountain House Road. You'll soon reach **Goodyears Bar**, an old mining camp with a few tattered buildings. Follow Mountain House as it pirouettes steeply down a pretty creek canyon and then back up the other side of a ridge.

After several miles of bumps, you'll arrive at **Forest,** another tiny mountain town comprised of a handful of weather-worn wood frame buildings. Just beyond, go left on Ridge Road and wind town to **Alleghany**, a near-ghost town with a couple of dozen old buildings and perhaps that many residents and stray dogs. A hardrock mine called Sixteen-to-One was Alleghany's *raison de entrée* for decades, and it's still being worked on a part time basis. If you'd like to disappear from the world for a few days, check into the town's only lodging:

**Kenton Mine Lodge** ● *P.O. Box 942 (Foote Crossing Road), Alleghany, CA 95910; (800) 634-2002 or (530) 287-3212. Nine cabins and bunkhouse units; $$$$ per couple with two meals or $$ without meals. MC/VISA.* ⌑ This rustic hideaway is fashioned from an old miners' boarding house. Accommodations are basic and intriguing; you can stay in a bunkhouse or in simple cabins with hand-made furniture. Meals are served family style in an old cookhouse. Guests can peer into a mine tunnel, check out an ancient stamp mill, pan for gold in Kanaka Creek, play volleyball or croquet on a lawn area or just loaf in the sun.

From Alleghany, you can retrace your route through Goodyears Bar or choose a couple of alternates. All-paved Ridge Road follows the gentle curves of a high ridge and joins Highway 49 above North San Juan. Henness Pass Road, which is prettier but bumpier than Ridge Road, joins Highway 49 in Camptonville.

---

**RV ADVISORY** • The road through Goodyears Bar is dirt, bumpy and steep, as is Henness Pass Road back out of the steep canyon that shelters Alleghany. Small RVs can make it in good weather with the discomfort of a lot of bumps. Drivers of big rigs and trailers may prefer to go in and out of the Alleghany area on Ridge Road above North San Juan.

---

Back on Highway 49, retrace your route northeast from Camptonville, following the relatively level course of the Yuba River north to our second favorite gold country town, after Columbia:

## DOWNIEVILLE

**Population: 400**                          **Elevation: 2,899**

William Downie led a group of miners into this wilderness in 1849 and stopped to make camp at the confluence of two rivers. According to campfire talk, a member of the party caught and boiled a salmon and found gold in the bottom of the pot. The group went no further; a gold camp was established on the spot.

Downieville is right where those miners left it, sitting prettily among the trees at the merger of the Yuba and Downie Rivers. Many of its brick, rough stone and wood frame buildings date from the gold rush era. A recent state and federally funded project to remove all overhead utility lines makes this tiny town particularly appealing.

### ACTIVITIES

**Gold panning** • A genteel version of the gold rush is still alive here. The two rivers flowing through town are open to public panning and about fifty ounces of glitter are taken out by visitors each year.

**Mountain biking** • Several nearby Forest Service roads and trails are popular for mountain bikers. Two outfits offer bike rentals and repairs, tours and shuttle service: Coyote Adventure Company at 123 Nevada St., (530) 265-6909 or (530) 289-0109; and Downieville Outfitters in the old Claycroft building at Main and Commercial; (530) 289-0155.

**Whitewater rafting** • Swift runoffs on the Yuba River provide conditions for lively whitewater trips from spring through early summer. Tributary Whitewater Tours of Grass Valley has one and two-day outings; (530) 346-6812 or (800) 6-RAFTING.

### DINING

**Downieville Diner** • *Main Street; (530) 289-3616. American; wine and beer. Breakfast and lunch daily; dinner Thursday-Sunday. MC/VISA; $$.* ☐ This old fashioned café has a contemporary menu, featuring port wine linguine, teriyaki chicken, steaks and seafood, plus a wide sandwich selection. It sits between Main Street and the river, with a rear deck overlooking the stream.

**Downieville Bakery and Café** • *Main and Commercial; (530) 289-0108. American; no alcohol. Breakfast and lunch daily in summer and Wednesday-Sunday the rest of the year; $.* ☐ This is the breakfast gathering spot for locals, in the rough cut stone 1852 Claycroft building. Try savory baked goods and assorted coffees to begin the day and a variety of sandwiches for lunch.

**Riverview Pizzeria** • *Main and Nevada streets; (530) 289-3540. Pizza and other light fare; wine and beer. Lunch through dinner daily. MC/VISA; $.* □ It's not often that we list a pizza joint among our preferred dining spots, although the pizza is excellent here. The Riverview has a variety of other offerings, including inexpensive spaghetti or ravioli dinners, calzones, gyros, hamburgers and tasty oven baked sandwiches.

### RECLINING

Two small motels are in downtown Downieville, and a really fine hideaway is a few miles north, perched above the cascades of the Yuba River.

**Dewarts Riverside Inn** • *P.O. Box 176 (206 Commercial St.); Downieville, CA 95936; (530) 289-1000. Rooms with TV; rates include continental breakfast. MC/VISA, DISC; $$$ to $$$$.* □ This motel sits alongside the Downie River and each unit has a river-view balcony. It also has a barbecue area and a streamside patio; kitchen units are available.

**Downieville Inn** • *P.O. Box 128 (117 Main St.), Downieville, CA 95936; (530) 289-3243. Rooms with TV. MC/VISA; $$$.* □ Sitting at midtown, this small motel has an attractive lawn and barbecue area; kitchen units are available.

**Sierra Shangri-la** • *P.O. Box 285 (Highway 49, three miles north), Downieville, CA 95936; (530) 289-3455. Eleven units including three B&B rooms with continental breakfast; all with private baths. MC/VISA; $$$$ to $$$$$.* □ Picture a cozy cottage with a pot-bellied stove, in a forest glen and perched on the bank of a cascading stream. Shangri-La, indeed; this is one of the most idyllic getaways in the gold country. Facilities include three bed & breakfast units in the main building and eight cabins with kitchens, decks and barbecue areas.

### CAMPING

Nearly a dozen Forest Service campgrounds are alongside the Yuba River, both above and below Downieville. They have the usual shaded sites; some flush and some pit potties; no hookups; $ to $$$. These are great places for fishing and gold panning, since many of the campsites are within a few feet of the stream.

## SIERRA CITY

**Population: 100**                                    **Elevation: 4,187 feet**

Twelve miles upstream from Downieville, Sierra City is another tree-shrouded mining town. Founded in 1850, it occupies a particularly dramatic site, between the Yuba River and an ancient and craggy volcanic dike called the **Sierra Buttes**. A brief side trip from Bassetts north of here will get you closer to those ramparts; see below.

The fine **Kentucky Mine Park and Museum** is a couple of miles north of town on Highway 49. It provides two appeals—a virtually intact nineteenth century ore processing mill and a museum that preserves artifacts of Sierra County's past. In the stamp mill, visitors can view the wicked looking jaw crushers that broke gold ore into pebbles and the "stamps" that pulverized them to dust. The museum is open Wednesday-Sunday 10 to 5; (530) 862-1310.

## RECLINING AND DINING

**Buckhorn Lodge and Restaurant** ● *Main Street, Sierra City, CA 96125; (800) 991-1170 or (530) 862-1170. Cabins and rooms; $$$ to $$$$. Restaurant serves American fare; full bar service. Dinner nightly in summer, Thursday-Sunday the rest of the year; $$. MC/VISA.* ☐ This restored stone and wood complex in downtown Sierra City has a variety of rooms, suites and housekeeping cabins. The restaurant, with beam ceilings and maple furniture, serves steak, lamb chops, charbroiled chicken breasts and pastas. *Al fresco* fans can adjourn to a courtyard and a patio.

**Bush & Herringlake Country Inn** ● *P.O. Box 68 (downtown on Main Street), Sierra City, CA 96125; (530) 862-1501. Four units with spa tubs. MC/VISA; $$$$.* ☐ This attractively furnished inn occupies an 1871 brick and stone building that once housed a Wells Fargo Express office. Owners have kept the wide plank floors and cedar walls, added modern conveniences and decorated the inn with early American furniture.

**Holly House** ● *P.O. Box 350 (119 Main St.), Sierra City, CA 96125; (530) 862-1123. (WEB SITE: www.hollyhouse.com). Six units, some private and some shared baths; full breakfast. MC/VISA; $$$$ to $$$$$.* ☐ This Italianate home on the southern edge of Sierra City was remodeled and fashioned into an inviting B&B in 1998. Nicely appointed units feature Victorian and early American décor, with amenities such as spa tubs, oversized brass beds and love seats.

## CAMPING

**Sierra Skies RV Park** ● *100 Carrier Circle, Sierra City, CA 96125; (530) 862-1166. RVs only; full hookups $$$$.* ☐ The attraction of this park is that it's near downtown, yet in a shaded area alongside the Yuba River. It has showers, a coin laundry and horseshoe pits.

Several Forest Service campgrounds surround Sierra City. Particularly appealing is **Wild Plum**, just above town on **Haypress Creek**, with some sights near the rushing water. Many other campgrounds are in the Lakes Basin Recreation area behind the Sierra Buttes; see below.

## To the end of the Golden Chain

Above Sierra City, Highway 49 winds still higher into this splendid land of rivers and forests. At **Bassetts,** a former stage stop and now a country store, you can turn left and follow Gold Lakes Road north into the **Lakes Basin Recreation Area,** an imposing region of lakes and high mountain meadows. It more resembles the Great North Woods than the Sierra Nevada, with jeweled lakes gleaming through protective rings of evergreens, and boggy meadows where you expect to see a moose solemnly chewing marsh grass. However, the bold and jagged Sierra Buttes dominate the horizon, proving that you haven't taken a wrong turn and wound up in northern Minnesota.

Our favorite alpine pond here is Sardine Lake, whose placid waters reflect the jagged profile of the Sierra Buttes. It has a small pine-shaded resort and marina and you'll also find several Forest Service campgrounds in the region. Trails from here lead high into the ramparts of the buttes.

If you continue north on Gold Lakes Road, you'll crest a craggy pass, then drop downhill and connect with State Route 89 just below the resort community of **Graeagle**. We passed this way on Tour Nine. If you didn't take that route, a trip north from Graeagle to **Plumas-Eureka State Park** is definitely worth the brief detour; see page 124.

Meanwhile, continuing north from Bassets on Highway 49, you'll soon reach the highest point in the Golden Chain—6,701-foot Yuba Pass. Just over the ridge, you can pause at a turnout for a view down into Sierra Valley, that strange slice of Nebraska we mentioned in Tour Nine, page 125. A graphic points out that mountain man Jim Beckwourth, a freed black slave, discovered the valley in 1851 while blazing a trail through this area. It served a vital role in providing beef, vegetables and lumber to mines in the region.

The highway descends into Sierra Valley, briefly intersects State Route 89, then passes through the little farm hamlets of **Sattley, Sierraville** and **Loyalton.** And finally, 300 miles from its beginning in Oakhurst, the Golden Chain comes to and end in tiny **Vinton** on State Route 70. This village offers no gold rush history and no real reason to pause.

☺ ☺ ☺

**Where to we go from here?** ● If you turn east onto Highway 70 in Vinton, you'll soon hit U.S. 395. You can drop down through Reno and Carson City to Minden-Gardnerville, where you can start Tour Thirteen. Or drive up to Virginia City, jump ahead to the Nevada section of this book and run Tour Twenty-two backward. Another choice is to backtrack to Highway 89 in Sattley and run a piece of Tour Nine either north or south.

HOPE YOU ENJOYED
YOUR VISIT
PLEASE COME AGAIN

*Tour Twelve*

# TRIPLE PASS PLAY
## THREE HIGHWAYS OVER THE SIERRA NEVADA

O nce a formidable barrier to migration, the Sierra Nevada range is now one of California's favorite playgrounds. Dozens of high mountain lakes, scores of campgrounds, miles of hiking trails and most of the state's major ski resorts draw several hundred thousand summer and winter visitors. However, we're going to guide you over three passes that lure only a fraction of that number.

Until the discovery of gold in 1848, the Sierra barrier discouraged settlement of northern and central California. Then as mining camps grew into communities, quick passage through the Sierra Nevada became an economic necessity. The first wagon trails were hacked over Sonora and Donner passes and Echo Summit, just south of Lake Tahoe. When the Pony Express was established in 1860, the swift riders chose the latter route. A few years later, engineers of the transcontinental railroad blasted and burrowed their way through Donner Pass.

During the latter half of the nineteenth century, more passes were cut through the mountains. With the coming of the horseless carriage, all eventually were improved to carry automobile traffic, and this opened the Sierra Nevada to tourism. Some of the state's oldest resorts still lure summer and winter visitors and we'll visit a few of them in this chapter.

# TRIP PLANNER

**WHEN TO GO** • The only time you can do this drive is from late spring through late fall, since all three mountain passes are closed by winter snow. However, roads to the ski resorts are kept open from the California side. Generally, the passes are open from mid-May or early June until sometime in November, although most of the summer resorts shut down by October. Some popular campgrounds may fill up on summer weekends, although the area is uncrowded otherwise. Autumn is nice when aspen and cottonwoods lining streams on the eastern slopes present a fall color show.

**DRIVING DISTANCE** • More than 300 miles total, depending on where you start. **Individual distances**—SONORA PASS: Sonora to U.S. 395 above Bridgeport is eighty miles. EBBETTS PASS: Markleeville to Angels Camp is seventy-eight miles. CARSON PASS: Jackson to Minden-Gardnerville is ninety-seven miles.

**RV ADVISORY** • Large motorhomes and trailer rigs are *not* advised to attempt Sonora and Ebbetts passes, since they have hairpin turns and steep grades up to twelve percent. Carson Pass can be negotiated easily by trailers and motorhomes.

**WHAT YOU'LL SEE** • Mostly lots of splendid high Sierra scenery, plus several old mountain resorts and chalets, Bear Valley winter and summer resort, Kirkwood resort, and Calaveras Big Trees State Park.

**WHAT TO DO** • Swim, boat and fish in high mountain lakes, including Pinecrest (Sonora Pass), Lake Alpine (Ebbetts Pass), and Bear Valley and Silver Lakes (Carson Pass); hike sections of the Pacific Crest Scenic Trail; ski at Dodge Ridge (Sonora Pass), Bear Valley (Ebbetts Pass) and Kirkwood (Carson Pass).

**TO BEGIN** • This triple pass tour starts in the Gold Country town of Sonora. It's easily reached by taking freeways 580 and 205 east from the San Francisco Bay Area, then picking up State Route 120 in Manteca, which is a popular approach to Yosemite National Park. Instead of continuing to Yosemite, branch northward on Route 108 just below Sonora.

## Pricing guidelines

**DINING:** Dinner entrée with soup or salad, without drinks or dessert for under $10 = **$**; $10 to $14 = **$$**; $15 to $25 = **$$$**; over $25 = **$$$$**.

**RECLINING:** A two-person room for $35 or less = **$**; $36 to $50 = **$$**; $51 to $75 = **$$$**; $76 to $100 = **$$$$**; more than $100 = **$$$$$**.

**CAMPING:** Under $10 = **$**; $10 to $14 = **$$**; $15 to $19 = **$$$**; $20 or more = **$$$$**

Two of these high mountain trails—over Donner Pass and Echo Summit—have become Interstate 80 and U.S. Highway 50. Vital east-west links, both are kept open the year around, except for temporary closures from winter storms. However, the four lower passes are closed by the first good snowfall and they remain that way until spring thaw.

The best known of these is Yosemite National Park's Tioga Pass, the highest in California at 9,945 feet. With the popularity of Yosemite, this route—Highway 120—is often crawling with travelers. The other three passes draw fewer visitors since they offer only seasonal traffic and they don't have the draw of a major national park. If you don't mind lots of twists and turns and occasional cliff edge exposures, you can turn our triple pass route into a grand high Sierra outing.

You will note as you drive over these passes that the western and eastern slopes of the Sierra Nevada are quite different. The mountain range was formed by the same collision of Pacific Ocean plates that triggers California's earthquakes. Since the mountain-building pressure comes from the west, the western slope is a long, rumpled series of foothills, like a scuffed green carpet. The eastern slope, where the strata was pushed upward and fractured, is dramatically rugged and steep. Further, because the Sierra range blocks rainstorms sweeping over California from the Pacific, the eastern slope is much more arid than the west. This lack of precipitation—called the rainshadow effect—creates the vast Great Basin Desert that covers much of Nevada.

## Highway 108 over Sonora Pass
### SONORA WEST TO U.S. 395

We'll begin with one of the most spectacular Sierra Nevada crossings. This route rivals Highway 120 over Yosemite's Tioga Pass as the most scenic trans-Sierra drive.

Sonora Pass is the oldest emigrant route through the Sierra Nevada, first crossed in October of 1841 by the 34-member Bartleson-Bidwell party. Packing their belongings on mules, horses and oxen, they were the first American settlers to make a mountain crossing into California. The first wagon crossing of Sonora Pass wasn't accomplished until 1852, and it was a tough passage. Mountain man Grizzly Adams, coming over the pass in 1854, noted in his journal:

*On all sides lay old axle trees and wheels...melancholy evidence of last season's disasters.*

These disasters were reduced when the route was improved in 1865 to become the Sonora-Mono Toll Road. Even then, it took a six-horse wagon team three weeks to make the round trip between Sonora and Bridgeport. The drive is considerably easier today, although it's still a bit of a challenge. Sonora Pass has the steepest grades of any Sierra crossing, up to twelve percent, so don't try this with a tired engine or bad brakes.

To begin, follow Washington Street through Sonora's handsome old downtown area, headed toward the hills. If you're coming from the San Joaquin Valley or Bay Area on Highway 120/108, you can take the Sonora bypass and pick up the route above the downtown area, although you'll miss the historic district. It's certainly worth a peek, with its well-cared-for

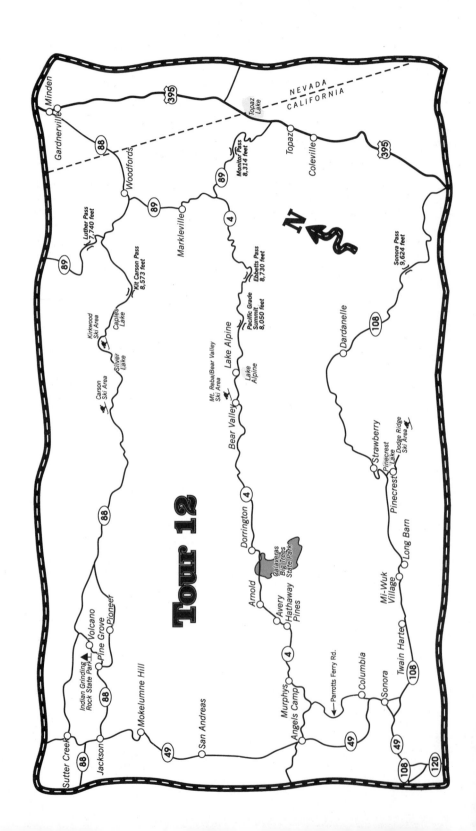

brick and masonry buildings left over from the gold rush. Many of them contain shops, boutiques and cafés.

As you head uphill from downtown, Washington Street becomes Mono Way, which swings eastward toward the Sierra Nevada. You'll soon leave most of what's interesting about Sonora and travel through its ordinary eastern end, where folks live and work and shop at Wal-Mart. After passing a couple of shopping centers, turn left at a somewhat confusing intersection to stay with Highway 108 toward Pinecrest. (If you've taken the Sonora bypass, you'll pick up the Sonora Pass route at this point.)

Following a brief four-lane climb, you'll pass a community with a silly name. **Twain Hart** was named by its promoters for Mark Twain and Bret Hart, who once wrote about this area. Neither, of course, ever set foot in their double-namesake town, since it wasn't created until long after their departures. It's an attractive mountain village, and a left turn will take you to its alpine style shopping area called Twain Hart Village.

Beyond here, you'll enter serious pine tree country; two other smaller planned communities—**Sugar Pine** and **Mi Wuk Village**—will come and go in a blink. Just above, you'll encounter a place with real history and personality.

**Long Barn** dates back to the turn of the century, when it was developed as a provisioning center for travelers over Sonora Pass, and as a recreation area for summer and winter tourists. Many of its wood frame buildings with their steep snow-shedding roofs are still intact. So is its original tourist facility:

**Long Barn Lodge** ● *P.O. Box 100, Long Barn, CA 95335; (800) 310-3533 or (209) 586-3533. (WEB SITE: www.longbarn.com; E-MAIL: info@longbarn.com) Thirty-eight lodge rooms and furnished cabins with TV, refrigerators and microwaves; $$$. Restaurant serves American fare; breakfast and dinner weekends only; $$; food available daily at the snack bar. Major credit cards.* ☐ To confirm the vintage of this grand old lodge, note the black and white photos near the entry—with Model-T's and Model-A's parked in the snow out front. It has changed little since then except for occasional refurbishments. The dining room is particularly nice, with rough polished log walls, lace curtains and tulip chandeliers. Long Barn is more popular in winter, since it has a large ice skating rink, and it's only a few miles from the Dodge Ridge ski area. At outdoor pool is open in summer.

A few miles above Long Barn, you'll encounter **Pinecrest,** the busiest place on the mountain. This is definitely not your thing if you're trying to avoid crowds. Its focal point is Pinecrest Lake, a large Stanislaus River reservoir that bustles with summer boaters and waterskiiers. A large, tree-shaded Forest Service campground (flush potties, no hookups) sits alongside the lake and its sites are rather close together. Pinecrest looked a bit chaotic when we passed through on a summer weekend. However, it's very popular with families, who come for the water play and a variety of Forest Service-sponsored activities. The area also has an alpine home development, although it has few commercial services.

**Pinecrest Lake Resort** has an assortment of cabins and condos and a restaurant; P.O. Box 1216, Pinecrest, CA 95364; (209) 965-3411. Just up a short road is **Dodge Ridge,** a fine winter sports area that underwent a major expansion in 1998. It offers a good mix of beginner, intermediate and challenging advanced runs; (209) 965-3474.

Above Pinecrest, two tiny towns appear and disappear before the highway begins its steep climb toward Sonora Pass. **Strawberry** is comprised mostly of a large strawberry-colored log general store. The interior is a pleasing mix of old fashioned general mercantile and contemporary mini-mart. From Strawberry, the route dips into a classic glacial carved valley then, after nineteen miles, it passes through **Dardanelle**, with an old lodge, store, service station and RV park. The woodsy village boasts a population of two.

---

**RV ADVISORY** • Beyond Dardanelle, a sign warns that trailers aren't advisable, although it gives no length limit for vehicles. Considering the steep corkscrew turns ahead, we wouldn't recommend attempting it in anything much longer than twenty-five feet.

---

Above Dardanelle, watch on your left for the **Donnell Vista** rest area. A short trail takes you to an impressive viewpoint high above Donnell Reservoir in the great granite gorge of the Stanislaus River Canyon. Continuing upward, Highway 108 gets down to some serious climbing, with tight switchbacks, some exposed edges and grades up to twelve percent. If you want to enjoy the scenery, find a place to pull over!

And the scenery is splendid. Approaching the top of the pass, you'll be up near the treeline. Great terraces of granite rise about you like free-form pyramids; steep walls of the Stanislaus River Canyon fall away far below. Just short of the crest, a mountain stream—a Stanislaus tributary—appears at roadside and cascades wildly downhill.

When you finally pop over **Sonora Pass** at 9,624 feet, you'll definitely have that top of the world feeling, since you're sitting on the second highest paved mountain pass west of the Rockies. An historic marker on the north side of the highway provides some background on this famous alpine crossing.

Having accomplished the top, you'll practically fall down the other side. The road spirals steeply, with ten to twelve percent grades. You'll shortly pick up a tributary of the Walker River gushing alongside. The stream falls away and, as you reach the crest of a wide valley, it reappears as a tiny thread meandering far below. Highway 108 skims down the north side of the canyon and settles on the valley floor, called Pickle Meadows. Soon, you'll encounter the orderly barracks, outbuildings and military regalia of the U.S. Marine Corps Mountain Warfare Center.

Note the dramatic change in vegetation as you cruise past the military base, from thick forests above to thin pine forests mixed with sagebrush. You're seeing a classic rainshadow effect. To the east, the valley sheds the last of its pines and empties into Nevada's Great Basin Desert. A few miles from the Marine base, Highway 108 dissolves into U.S. 395. A seventeen-mile drive southeast would take you to Bridgeport, the end of the old Sonora-Mono Toll Road.

# Highway 4 over Ebbetts Pass
## FROM U.S. 395 EAST TO ANGELS CAMP

This is an unusual rite of mountain passage because you'll crest two passes—Ebbetts Pass and Pacific Grade Summit—with pretty Summit Valley cradled between them.

If you've just finished Sonora Pass, head north on U.S. 395 through a shallow, attractive canyon of the Carson River, then go west on Highway 89 over 8,314-foot Monitor Pass. It's not a difficult climb and the view back down into the Great Basin is quite impressive. (See Tour Nine, page 131 for more details.) You'll pick up State Route 4 just below Markleeville; head west through an appealing rocky chasm carved by the cottonwood-lined Carson River. After a few miles, the highway picks up a tributary, Silver Creek, and continues its march toward Ebbetts Pass.

These streams, coursing merrily along tumbled beds of gravel and boulders, may tempt you to pause, and frequent turnouts permit you to do so. Informal camping is popular along this stretch, and it's a favored fly fishing area. Incidentally, Mother Nature didn't stir up all that gravel. The Carson and Silver Creek stream beds were heavily dredged by goldseekers during the nineteenth century. You may still see occasional dredges, attended not by tattered prospectors in battered hats, but by wetsuited "recreational miners."

The canyon begins to narrow farther upstream and aspens replace the cottonwoods as you climb higher. Incidentally, the area puts on a fine fall color show. Soon, Highway 4 swings away from Silver Creek and begins a serious upward spiral toward the pass.

---

*RV ADVISORY* ● At the beginning of the steepest part of the climb, a sign advises that nothing over twenty-five feet should attempt this route.

---

This is a spectacular ascent as the highway twists between forest-cloaked granite walls of the Sierra Nevada. Up ahead, you can see domes and spires stretching above the treeline. The road narrows and the centerline disappears so you'll need to stay alert. Just short of the crest, you'll encounter a pretty little alpine lake rimmed by ponderosa pines and granite boulders. If you'd like to stroll a few miles on the **Pacific Crest Scenic Trail,** you'll find a trailhead parking area nearby.

As you top 8,730-foot **Ebbetts Pass,** a sign explains that this was a supply route between California and the Nevada silver mines, not an immigrant route. The last major pass chopped through the Sierra Nevada, it was opened in 1864 and named for Major John Ebbetts.

Spiraling quickly down from the pass, you'll level off somewhat and meander through the pines of 7,060-foot Summit Valley. You'll find a Forest Service campground here, in case you'd like to linger longer in this sky high alpine basin. A crooked climb out of the basin—actually steeper and twistier than the Ebbetts Pass approach—will deliver you over 8,050-foot **Pacific Grade Summit.** Just beyond is a tiny alpine pond infinitely more appealing than its name—Mosquito Lake.

*Lake Alpine on Highway 4 shimmers at sunset; it's one of the larger and more attractive of the Sierra Nevada lakes.*

Heading downhill, you'll soon encounter somewhat larger **Lake Alpine**, the most popular playground up here. Expect it to be a bit busy on summer weekends with canoes, kayaks, other boats and fisherpersons. (Although motorboats are permitted, there's a ten mile-per-hour speed limit.) A rustic resort across the highway offers the only developed facilities in this high mountain reach:

**Lake Alpine Lodge ●** *P.O. Box 5300, Bear Valley, CA 95223; (209) 753-6358. Off-season address: Lake Alpine Lodge, P.O. Box 579, Big Sur, CA 93920; (831) 667-2424. (WEB SITE: www.lakealpinelodge.com; E-MAIL: lalpinelodge@aol.com) Open May 1 to mid-October. Tent cabins $$; housekeeping cabins $$$$. Restaurant serves breakfast through dinner, daily in summer then weekends only in spring and fall; full bar service; $$. MC/VISA.* ☐ Dating from the 1920s, this log and shingle-sided resort has fully furnished cabins, tent cabins with outside fire pits and picnic tables, a dining room, a small saloon and mini-mart. Step into the Old West style main lodge and admire the varnished, rough-hewn lodgepole pine ceiling posts and the huge stone fireplace. The front porch is a fine place to sit—with a drink or lunch—and watch folks play in the lake across the way. If you want to play as well, the lodge has rental boats and mountain bikes.

A large Forest Service campground rims part of the lake's northern shore, with flush potties and no hookups; **$$**. You generally can get a spot on summer weekdays, although it can fill on weekends.

Three miles west of Lake Alpine is **Bear Valley**, the largest summer and winter ski resort in this part of the Sierra Nevada. This 7,000-foot-high retreat has a fair-sized collection of woodsy homes and condos, with

Bear Valley Lodge as its activity center. It's primarily a winter resort, with both downhill and cross country areas; call (209) 753-2301 for winter sports information. However, it does have an active summer program, including biking (rentals available), fishing, horseback riding, tennis and volleyball. It can get a bit busy during the annual Bear Valley Music Festival, from late July through early August, although the rest of the summer is relatively uncrowded.

## RECLINING AND DINING

**Bear Valley Lodge** ● *P.O. Box 5440, Bear Valley, CA 95223; (209) 753-BEAR. Fifty-three rooms and suites with TV, phones and other amenities. Major credit cards; $$$ to $$$$$.* ◻ Rustic modern best describes this four-story shingle-sided lodge. It has the full range of resort amenities including dining (see below), a cocktail lounge, health spa, pool, hot tubs and a mini-mart.

**Creekside Dining Room** ● *At Bear Valley Lodge; (209) 753-2325. American; full bar service. Dinner nightly; breakfast and lunch avilable in other lodge restaurants. Major credit cards; $$.* ◻ The appealing café matches the lodge's rustic modern look with beam ceilings, barnboard walls with print wallpaper accents and maple chairs. Menu offerings include ribeye steaks, prawns and rack of lamb.

Highway 4 unkinks considerably at Bear Valley and the run downhill to Angels Camp will be relatively fast unless you get stuck behind a logging truck or pokey RV. Several miles and two thousand feet below Bear Valley, you'll encounter the old lumber town of **Dorrington**. It consists mostly of a saloon, mini-mart and one of the oldest resorts in the Sierra foothills:

**Dorrington Hotel and Restaurant** ● *P.O. Box 4307 (3431 Highway 4), Dorrington, CA 95223; (209) 795-5800. Five rooms with share baths and a cabin with a private bath; continental breakfast; $$$$. Restaurant serves Northern Italian fare; wine and beer; dinner only, Thursday-Monday; $$$. MC/VISA.* ◻ This clapboard, pitched roof hotel dates from the 1852 when it was a stagecoach stop. New owners have done a fine job of renovating the place. Check out the Victorian lobby with its dark woods, beveled glass, wainscotting and tulip chandeliers. The cabin has a stone fireplace, spa tub and kitchen unit. The restaurant menu features veal parmigiana, scaloppini and a good assortment of pastas.

Just below is one of California's favorite state parks, so don't expect to find it uncrowded, particularly on summer weekends.

**Calaveras Big Trees State Park** ● *Highway 4, Arnold; (209) 795-2334. Modest day use fee. RV and tent sites with potties and showers, no hookups; $$$. For campsite reservations, call (800) 444-PARK; MC/VISA accepted.* ◻ This 6,000-acre park preserves some of California's finest sequoias, as well as virgin stands of huge pines. It receives more than 250,000 visitors a year so the park's main North Grove is often crowded. However, you can shed the crowds rather easily by taking a one-mile hike along a brushy trail to the South Grove. If you'd like to camp at Calaveras

Big Trees, reservations are essential in summer, although you generally can get in during the off-season.

Below the state park, you'll pass through the nondescript community of **Arnold** and then **Murphys** which *is* very inviting and quite historic. For specifics, see Tour Eleven, page 152. From here, a nine-mile run takes you to Highway 49 and **Angels Camp,** made famous by a travel writer much older than I.

## Highway 88 over Carson Pass
### JACKSON WEST TO MINDEN-GARDNERVILLE

If you're looking for an easy route over the Sierra Nevada, follow the one chosen by legendary mountain man Kit Carson. He led John C. Frémont's federal surveying party through this low cleft in 1844. It's the second oldest Sierra Nevada crossing, after Sonora Pass. Although it's relatively high—8,573 feet—the approach from either direction is surprisingly gentle. Drivers often crest Carson Pass without realizing they've done so.

Having driven all of the Sierra Nevada passes, we've wondered why more pioneers and explorers didn't use this easy route. The Bartleson-Bidwell party had to struggle over rugged Sonora Pass with their mules and oxen in 1841, and the Donner party suffered horribly in the winter 1846-47 because an early season snowstorm trapped them below the difficult pass that now bears their name.

The Carson Pass route begins in Jackson, another of California's historic gold rush communities. If you've just finished the Ebbetts Pass tour, drive north on Highway 49 from Angels Camp and turn eastward onto State Route 88. The most direct approaches to Jackson from the rest of California are on Highway 88 from Stockton or Route 16 from Sacramento.

East of Jackson, you'll encounter **Pine Grove,** a community of 2,100 that's stretched for a couple of miles along the highway. This ordinary town offers no cause to pause unless you need fuel or supplies. However, three interesting attractions—the old mining town of Volcano, Indian Grinding Rock State Park and Daffodil Hill—are nearby. These are covered in Tour Eleven, starting on page 156.

Pine Grove eventually blends into **Pioneer,** essentially more of the same commercial sprawl. At the far end of town, you'll see what supports these two communities—the huge C&M Cedar Products Mill; it smells great. A mile or so beyond the mill, an **El Dorado National Forest** visitor center can provide information on the mountain area you're about to enter; it's open weekdays 8 to 5. And beyond that is the most interesting café we found in this string of alpine commercialism:

**O.K. Corral Restaurant** ● *27065 Highway 88; (209) 295-4883. American; full bar service. Lunch and dinner Friday-Sunday. MC/VISA; $$.* ☐ To find this country style café, look for a building with a buckboard sitting on its roof. Then step into the rather plain dining room for ribs, pasta, steaks, seasoned filet mignon or tequila lime chicken. The Western style saloon is more attractive, with truss beam ceilings and a free-standing metal fireplace. Ask if they'll serve you in there.

Several miles above Pioneer, after you've finally shed this alpine suburbia, go right for a couple of miles to a small resort that appeals primarily to boaters, fisherpersons and families who want to play on the water:

**Bear River Resort** • *40800 Highway 88, Pioneer, CA 95666; (209) 295-4868. Cabins $$$$; RV sites with full hookups $$$$. Restaurant serves breakfast and lunch daily and dinner nightly except Sunday; $$. MC/VISA.* ⯐ This small resort on Bear River Reservoir has fully furnished cabins with kitchens, and RV sites with water and electric hookups. Other facilities include a saloon, marina, coin laundry, video parlor, and rentals of fishing boats, canoes and paddle boats.

If you'd like a nice view of the rock-ribbed Bear River Canyon, drive beyond the resort and cross a small concrete dam. About a mile beyond, you'll hit a Forest Service campground with shaded sites and pit potties; **$$**. Not much more than a 21-footer will fit in here.

Beyond Bear River Reservoir, Highway 88 continues its gradual climb, following a ridge that provides pleasing views of distant granite peaks. After topping a small crest, you'll get a vista of **Silver Lake** with a massive terraced ridge rising from its southeast shore. Drop downhill from this vantage point, turn right and follow a two-mile paved but somewhat bumpy road to an historic mountain retreat beside the lake:

**Plasse's Resort** • *30001 Plasse Rd., Silver Lake, CA 95666; (209) 258-8814. RV and tent sites with water, tables and fire rings; $$$. Restaurant serves breakfast through dinner nightly in summer; $$; bar adjacent.* ⯐ This rustic retreat was established as a trading post by Ramon Pierre Plasse in 1853. Still operated by his descendants, it's one of America's oldest family resorts. One of the original squared log cabins now houses a video game parlor—a sign of changing times. Plasse's facilities include a general store, kids play area, horseshoe pits, game courts, coin showers and a laundromat. Among its recreational offerings are fishing, water sports and horseback rides.

Beyond the resort turnoff, the highway brushes the edge of the lake, crosses a small spillway and passes between two campgrounds. The Forest Service's **Silver Lake Campground** has pit potties and no hookups; **$$**. Across the way is Pacific Gas and Electric Company's **Silver Lake West Campground** with flush potties; **$$$**. Both have nicely spaced, shaded sites. PG&E has several reservoirs in this area, with more than half a dozen campgrounds. For information, call (415) 972-5552.

Beyond Silver Lake, you'll encounter another historic resort, although it has been modernized into a popular ski area. **Kirkwood Village** is composed primarily of alpine condos and cabins, with the ski slopes above. Call (209) 258-6000 for downhill ski information and (209) 258-7248 for cross-country skiing.

If you continue past the turnoff to the village, you'll encounter a wonderfully rustic restaurant—all that's left of the pioneer settlement:

**Kirkwood Inn** • *Highway 88, Kirkwood; (209) 258-7304. American; full bar service. Breakfast through dinner daily. MC/VISA.* ⯐ The café is housed in a squared log structure dating from 1864, when Zachary Kirkwood started a trading post and settlement here. Although the ski area just to the west is *Gortex moderne*, this restaurant is grandly rustic with rough-hewn beam ceilings, plank floors and pioneer gear hanging from the walls. It's the most appealing café we found on this three-pass drive. From the kitchen emerges babyback ribs, sesame chicken, lemon and dill halibut, pot roast and assorted pastas. A lively saloon shares the cabin with the restaurant.

Beyond Kirkwood, you'll pass large Caples Lake, then begin the final climb toward 8,573-foot **Kit Carson Pass.** As we said above, the approach is surprisingly gentle. At the crest, a Forest Service information center has exhibits and material on the surrounding mountains. Several hiking tails lead from here, and many serious backpackers like to trek into the adjacent Mokelumne Wilderness.

Just down the other side of the pass, a turnout provides a view of tree-rimmed Red Lake and informational plaques on the history and topography of this area. Continuing a gentle downhill spiral, you'll pick up the creek-sized Carson River and follow it through a pretty rock-lined canyon.

Toward the lower end of this small ravine, at the junction of State Route 89, the highway passes **Woodfords Station,** once a Pony Express stop; see Tour Nine, page 129. Beyond Woodfords, Route 88 begins a long, rather straight descent into the pasturelands of the Carson Valley. You'll cross into Nevada and hit U.S. 395 at the twin communities of Minden and Gardnerville. If you have some spare change you'd like to shed, the rather pleasant **Carson Valley Inn** offers all the usual Nevada games of chance, plus lodging and an RV park; (800) 321-6983 or (775) 782-9711. For specifics, see Tour Thirteen, page 179.

*Where do we go from here?* ● Since Highway 395 is a major north-south route, you have several options. You can drive into the next chapter, heading south along the dramatic eastern ramparts of the Sierra Nevada on Tour Thirteen, or pick up State Route 89 in Markleeville and run Tour Nine backward. If you haven't done the other segments of this chapter, head west from Markleeville and take Highway 4 over Ebbetts Pass, or pick up Highway 108 south of here and run the Sonora Pass route in reverse.

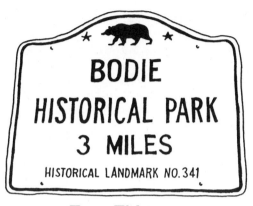

BODIE
HISTORICAL PARK
3 MILES
HISTORICAL LANDMARK NO.341

*Tour Thirteen*

# EASTERN SIERRA
### *MINDEN-GARDNERVILLE TO LONE PINE ON U.S. 395*

Welcome to the highest and most dramatic mountain escarpment in America. Every time we need our spirits renewed—to soar as high as the crests of California's tallest peaks—we head for the eastern slope of the Sierra Nevada.

Most high mountain ranges are fronted by tumbled foothills. However, the Sierra's eastern escarpment reaches abruptly skyward, rising as much as ten thousand feet from the Great Basin Desert. This is the highest mountain face on the North American continent and of course Mount Whitney is the tallest peak in mainland America, at 14,494 feet. Amazingly, the continent's lowest point is just 100 miles away, 282 feet below sea level at Badwater in Death Valley. (See Tour Twenty-one page 278.)

As we pointed out in the beginning of this section, this great mountain face was a difficult obstacle for gold seekers and settlers headed for California. Still today, no road crosses the Sierra Nevada for 200 miles between Lee Vining east of Yosemite and Kernville in southern California.

Even though Highway 395 is thousands of feet below the Sierra crests, you'll still be cruising at high altitudes, so this area is relatively cool country in summer and downright cold in winter. You'll travel around 7,000

# TRIP PLANNER

**WHEN TO GO** ● This is a late spring through late fall trip, since elevations are high and you're likely to encounter snow in winter. Of course if you want to ski at Mammoth Mountain, you'll *want* to encounter snow. Fall offers the best weather, with splashes of color in foothill canyons. An *Eastern High Sierra Fall Color Guide* is available from Bishop and Mammoth Lakes visitor bureaus. Spring vistas can be awesome, when the Sierra Nevada crests are still heavily mantled with snow. However, you won't be able to reach Devil's Postpile National Monument or take side trips to Glacier Lodge or Whitney Portal because of snow pack.

**DRIVING DISTANCE** ● About 260 miles, including side trips.

**RV ADVISORY** ● RVs will suffer three miles of bumps en route to Bodie, and some tight turns and steep grades on side trips to Devil's Postpile, the bristlecone pines area and Whitney Portal.

**WHAT YOU'LL SEE** ● The awesome escarpment of the Sierra Nevada, Topaz and Mono Lakes, Mono County Museum in Bridgeport, Bodie State Historic Park, Devil's Postpile National Monument, Laws Railroad Museum near Bishop, and the Eastern California Museum in Independence.

**WHAT TO DO** ● Walk about the weathered ruins of Bodie State Historic Park; stroll among the tufa formations at Mono Lake; follow a trail to the top of Devil's Postpile; sample goodies at Erick Schatts Bakerÿ in Bishop; prowl among the rocks of the Alabama Hills west of Lone Pine; and hike—with advance permits—the high country around Mount Whitney.

**TO BEGIN** ● Pick up U.S. 395 at any point around Reno, Carson City or below, and head south to Minden-Gardnerville.

### Useful contacts

**Bishop Area Chamber of Commerce**, 690 N. Main St., Bishop, CA 93514; (760) 873-8405.

**Big Pine Chamber of Commerce,** P.O. Box 23 (126 Main St.), Big Pine, CA 93513; (760) 938-2114.

**Bridgeport Chamber of Commerce**, P.O. Box 541, Bridgeport, CA 93517; (760) 932-7500.

**Carson Valley Chamber of Commerce**, 1512 Highway 395, Gardnerville, NV 89401; (702) 782-8144.

**Lone Pine Chamber of Commerce**, P.O. Box 749 (126 S. Main), Lone Pine, CA 93535; (760) 876-4444. (WEB SITE: www.cris.com/lpc)

**Mammoth Lakes Visitors Bureau**, P.O. Box 48, Mammoth Lakes, CA 93546; (888) GO-MAMMOTH or (760) 934-2712. (WEB SITE: www.visitmammoth.com; E-MAIL: mmthvisit@qnet.com)

### Pricing guidelines

**DINING:** Dinner entrée with soup or salad, without drinks or dessert for under $10 = **$**; $10 to $14 = **$$**; $15 to $25 = **$$$**; over $25 = **$$$$**.

**RECLINING:** A two-person room for $35 or less = **$**; $36 to $50 = **$$**; $51 to $75 = **$$$**; $76 to $100 = **$$$$**; more than $100 = **$$$$$**.

**CAMPING:** Under $10 = **$**; $10 to $14 = **$$**; $15 to $19 = **$$$**; $20 or more = **$$$$**

feet in the northern reaches of this drive, and then drop down to 4,000 feet in the Owens Valley.

A small *caveat* before we begin: Highway 395 is a major north-south artery and not a "road less traveled" in the usual sense. In fact, it's four lane much of the way. Further, Mammoth Lakes is a major winter and summer resort, drawing tens of thousands of visitors, mostly from Southern California. However, the area is sparsely populated, with only a few small towns along this lengthy drive. Compared with other popular tourist routes, U.S. 395 is not heavily traveled, particularly in spring and fall.

## A Nevada beginning

The twin towns of **Minden** and **Gardnerville** in Nevada's Carson Valley provide a good staging area for this drive. With a combined population of nearly 6,000, they offer a fair selection of restaurants, service stations and motels. You'll find the **Carson Valley Chamber of Commerce** at 1512 Highway 395 in an old fashioned building painted with historic murals. It's open weekdays 8 to 5, plus Saturday 10 to 3 in summer; (702) 782-8144.

About two blocks beyond, in a large brick former high school is the fine **Carson Valley Museum**. Notable among its exhibits are game trophies presented in a men's den setting, a workable model ore processing mill, a full sized Washoe Indian bark shelter and assorted pioneer artifacts. It's open daily 10 to 5; (775) 782-2555.

### RECLINING AND DINING

If you feel the need to gamble away some spare change and perhaps spend the night, one establishment has full facilities:

**Carson Valley Inn** ● *1627 Highway 395, Minden, NV 89423; (800) 321-6983 or (775) 782-9711. (WEB SITE: www.cvinn.com; E-MAIL: cvinn@aol.com) Midsize casino complex with 230 rooms and suites with TV and phones; $$$ to $$$$. Restaurant and coffee shop open twenty-four hours; American fare; full bar service; $$. RV park has full hookups with showers and laundry; $$$. Major credit cards.* ☐ Although compact, this well maintained resort is versatile, offering a full casino, three restaurants and a glass-enclosed spa. Rooms are in the main inn and a nearby motel.

Nevada is noted for its Basque restaurants that serve huge multi-course style meals at modest prices. One of the more historic is in Gardnerville:

**Overland Hotel** ● *691 Main St.; (775) 782-2138. Basque-American; full bar service. Lunch Tuesday-Sunday and dinner nightly. MC/VISA; $$.* ☐ Brace yourself for a friendly onslaught of food at this former Basque boarding house. Huge dinners, served family style, include unlimited quantities of soup, salad, French bread and at least two meat entrées, accompanied by drinking glasses filled with a sweet red wine. The meal ends with dessert, hot tea and comfortable groans from overstuffed diners.

## To Bridgeport, Bodie and Mono Lake

From Gardnerville, Highway 395 brushes the edge of the Pine Nut Mountains and travels through high desert terrain. It leaves Nevada at small gaming resort complex above the treeless shores of Topaz Lake:

*Topaz Lodge & Casino* •
P.O. Box 187, Gardnerville, NV
89410; (800) 962-0732 outside
Nevada or (775) 266-3338. Motel
style rooms with TV and phones;
*$$*. RV park with full hookups;
*$$$*. Dining room is open 24 hours
with all-you-can-eat buffets on
weekends; full bar service; *$$*.
MC/VISA. ⬜ This busy little com-
plex above Topaz Lake includes a
small casino, seasonal pool, gen-
eral store and service station. The
casino, dining room and some
lodging units have lake views. The
RV park often fills up in summer,
although spaces generally are
available the rest of the year.

Just to the north of Topaz
Lodge, a road leads down to the
lakeshore and **Topaz Lake Rec-
reation Area**, operated by Dou-
glas County. It has campsites
within steps of the shoreline with
flush potties, showers, water and
electric hookups; *$$*. The facility
also has picnic areas and a boat
launch. Topaz Lake is noted for
yielding large cutthroat trout.

---

*FUELING NOTE* • Top off
your tank at Topaz Lake (or Gardnerville), for fuel is limited and expensive for the next fifty or so
miles.

---

South of Topaz Lake, Highway
395 travels through a wide ranching valley, passing the tiny towns
of **Topaz** and **Coleville,** which
have no services. **Walker,** claim-
ing 300 citizens, has a couple of
small motels and restaurants and a
country store with fuel. Below
Walker, the highway meanders
through shallow Walker River
Canyon, following the course of
the small, swift-running stream.

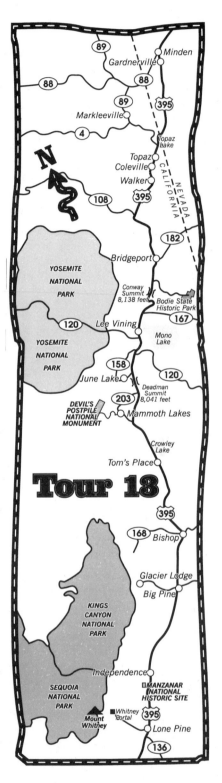

Several pullouts offer inviting places for a streamside picnic or casual camping, and you'll encounter a couple of Forest Service campgrounds near the canyon's southern end. The Walker is a popular trout fishing stream, and its cottonwoods and aspens present a gorgeous display of yellow in the autumn.

Pressing southward, you'll swing away from the Walker River and travel through the wide, sagebrush-studded Antelope Valley. The snow-patched crests of the Sierra Nevada, which had been shielded by foothills, now present themselves in their towering grandeur. These lofty peaks, like giant gnomes hunched shoulder to shoulder, will accompany you for most of the rest of the trip. Although this is rolling desert terrain, you're still high in the sky here, at more than 6,000 feet. Then the highway climbs into the evergreens, crests 7,519-foot Devil's Summit and spirals down to the first of several small eastern Sierra ranching communities:

# BRIDGEPORT

**Population: 500**                          **Elevation: 6,645 feet**

Mostly a small collection of motels and service stations, Bridgeport has an old fashioned business district with a few masonry and wood frame false front stores.

Note the elaborate façade of the still-active 1880 **Mono County Courthouse** with its squared belltower. A block behind and to the left of the courthouse is the **Mono County Museum** in a small city park. It occupies an 1880 schoolhouse and displays the usual pioneer artifacts, with a few rusting farm implements out front. It's open May through late September, 10 to 4 daily, with an hour lunch break. At midtown, you'll encounter an historic inn on your right:

**Bridgeport Inn** • *P.O. Box 426, Bridgeport, CA 93517; (760) 932-7380. Eleven modestly furnished inn rooms with share baths and fifteen motel units with private baths; $$$ to $$$$. Dining room serves breakfast through dinner; American fare; full bar service; $$. MC/VISA.* ☐ Built in 1877, this white shingle-sided inn is nicely dressed in Victorian and early American furnishings. The restaurant is particularly appealing, with bentwood chairs, lace curtains, ceiling fans and tulip chandeliers. A Western style saloon and cozy parlor with a potbellied stove complete this pleasant yesterday setting.

The **Chamber of Commerce**, downtown on Main Street, is open weekdays 9 to 5; (760) 932-7500. South of town, you'll pass the **Bridgeport Ranger Station**, where you can stock up information on hiking, camping, fishing and exploring the next-door Sierra Nevada. It's open weekdays 8 to 5; (760) 932-7070.

A few miles below Bridgeport, a left turn will take you thirteen miles over high desert to a town that boomed, went bust and is now being held in a state of arrested decay:

**Bodie State Historic Park** • *P.O. Box 515, Bridgeport, CA 93517; (760) 647-6445. Park open daily 9 to 7 in summer and 9 to 4 the rest of the year. Modest entry fee per vehicle.* ☐ "Goodbye God, I'm going to Bodie," a little girl wrote in her diary in the late nineteenth century. It would not be hard to believe that God had forsaken this lonely windswept town terraced against a desert hillside. However, despite hot summers and bitterly cold winters at this 8,000 foot altitude, the town thrived for decades after gold was discovered in 1859. Thirty years later, it boasted a population of ten thousand, with the usual ration of saloons, fallen angels and hustlers. Of course, the gold eventually gave out and Bodie was abandoned.

California designated it as a state historic park in 1962. Instead of restoring it, officials decided to leave it just the way they found it—unpainted, ramshackle and sagging. Basically, the state's role is to keep it from collapsing.

There are no facilities here except a small visitor center, drinking water and potties. One can spend a fascinating couple of hours wandering the streets and peering through dirt-streaked window panes into empty buildings. Although only five percent of Bodie remains, the ghost town is surprisingly large, with several dozen structures on this lonely hillside, and a large ore processing mill above.

---

**RV ADVISORY** • A sign advises that the road to Bodie is not recommended for anything over thirty feet. However, the first ten miles of the road is paved and we found few tight turns. The last three miles, although wide enough for any size rig, are dirt and extremely rough; RVs will want to travel at a crawl. Once there, you'll be directed to a special RV parking area.

---

Continuing south on U.S. 395, after you top 8,100-foot Conway Summit, you'll see the huge pale blue-gray orb of **Mono Lake**, more than 1,300 feet below. It's an unlovely lake with a barren shoreline, yet it's strangely fascinating, staring upward from the Mono Basin like a giant blind eye. Because the lake has no outlet, it's too salty and alkaline for fish. In fact, its more than twice as salty as the average ocean and eighty times as alkaline. However, it's home to trillions of brine shrimp which, in turn, attract thousands of seagulls and migratory birds. Mono is an important migration stop on the Pacific Flyway.

You can pause at a vista point about a quarter of a mile down from the summit to study this strange alkaline pond, which is the focal point of one of California's longest running water wars.

Early in this century, the Los Angeles Department of Water and Power bought, grabbed and otherwise acquired water rights to the Owens Valley south of here. It sparked a series of battles that became known as the Owens Valley Water Wars. In 1941, not satisfied with drying up the once agriculturally rich valley, L.A. officials began diverting water from streams that fed Mono Lake, and the great salt pond began to disappear. Environmentalists came to the aid of local residents and another long water conflict began. Then in 1983, the California Supreme Court placed Mono Lake under laws that protect waterways from excessive diversion that threatens their biosystems. By that time, its level had dropped by forty-eight feet; it had lost half its water and doubled its salinity. After another eleven years of negotiations, all parties agreed to raise the water level by

*A tufa formation rises like a ghost ship on the surface of Mono Lake as a storm brews in the Sierra Nevada range beyond.*

nineteen feet. Finally in the mid-1990s, cutbacks in the diversion began.

One of the curious results of water diversion has been the appearance of scores of tufa formations. These are calcium carbonate cones and spires formed below the surface when calcium-laden freshwater springs come into contact with alkaline lake waters heavy in carbonate. Many have been exposed as the lake level has dropped. This region has been designated as the Mono Lake State Tufa Reserve and these strange outerworldly shapes can be seen at several places along the shoreline. They range from a foot to more than a dozen feet high.

After dropping down from Conway Summit, the highway skirts the lake's western shore. You'll pass several access points where you can see tufa shapes, take a dip in the buoyant waters and camp at a couple of primitive campgrounds. (Your dip won't last long; the highly alkaline water is rather harsh on the body.)

If you'd like to view the lake in comfort, pause at **Mono Inn Restaurant** just beyond the turnoff to Mono Lake County Park. The inn's big-windowed dining room serves dinners nightly except Tuesday, plus Sunday brunch, with full bar service. It accepts major credit cards; **$$**; (760) 647-6581. Sharing the same building is the **Ansel Adams Gallery**, displaying works of the famed California photographer; noon to 9 Monday-Saturday and 10 to 9 Sunday, closed Tuesday; (760) 647-6161.

A bit beyond the restaurant, the multi-agency **Mono Lake Information Center** has interpretive exhibits about the lake and a vista point thereof. It's open daily 9 to 7 in summer, with shorter hours in the off-season; (760) 647-6572.

Just beyond the information center is **Lee Vining,** a small collection of motels, restaurants and service stations. It lacks the character of Bridgeport, and it serves primarily as a fueling stop for travelers on Highway 395 and State Route 120. The state highway reaches west over Tioga Pass into Yosemite National Park and east into Nevada.

If you follow Highway 120 five miles east, you can visit Mono Lake's **South Tufa Reserve,** which has the area's best collection of these odd pockmarked, pale gray shapes. Exhibits discuss their formation and the wildlife that inhabits the area—mostly birds, brine shrimp and harmless black alkali flies. A trail system leads among these strange spires, cones and ridges, which suggest a forest of misshapen gnomes. (Because of cutbacks in water diversion and recent years of heavy rain, the lake is rising so quickly that sections of the trail have to be re-routed to keep walkers' feet dry.)

Although it's interesting to walk among the tufa gnomes, it's more fascinating to paddle among them. Caldera Kayaks trips (see below) launch from nearby Navy Beach and cruise among several offshore formations. If you have a motorless boat aboard, you can put in there as well, and you can pick up navigational maps of the lake from a kiosk.

## ACTIVITY

*Mono Lake tours* ● If you'd like to paddle about the lake, **Caldera Kayaks** offers guided natural history tours, plus rentals of single and double kayaks and kayak lessons. For information, contact: Caldera Kayaks, P.O. Box 726, Mammoth Lakes, CA 93546; (760) 935-4942. (WEB: www.calderakayak.com; E-MAIL: info@calderakayak.com)

## Scenic loops: June and Mammoth Lakes

Immediately beyond the east Highway 120 junction, State Route 158 heads west toward the Sierra Nevada foothills on the **June Lake Loop.** This is a pleasant if not awesome drive that takes you along the shoreline of several ponds and into the pines. Most of its appeal is for boaters and fisherpersons as it brushes the edges of Grant, Silver and June lakes. The small **June Mountain Ski Resort** is up here, with downhill and cross-country facilities; (760)648-7733. This is not a wilderness loop, incidentally. The lake shores are busy with small resorts, campgrounds and RV parks. The town of **June Lake** has only 600 year-around residents, although it's wall-to-wall motels, resorts, cafés and service stations.

The June Lake Loop returns you to Highway 395 and about nine miles later, a second turnoff takes you to a larger and better known resort area. **Mammoth Lakes Scenic Route** isn't really, unless you define a highway lined with second growth pines as scenic. It leads to the busy resort town of **Mammoth Lakes** with nearly 5,000 residents and **Devil's Postpile National Monument.** To visit these elements, follow the drive several miles until it hits a T-intersection. Turn right and drive uphill on Minaret Road toward **Mammoth Mountain Ski Resort** which also is a popular summer play area; (800) 367-6572 or (760) 934-2571. This route now becomes scenic as those second growth pines give way to imposing vistas of high Sierra crags.

*Like tumbled stones from an ancient temple, basaltic columns are scattered below Devil's Postpile.*

**_Devil's Postpile National Monument_** • *Phone (760) 934-2289 in summer and (760) 872-4881 the rest of the year. Shuttle bus fee for entry* ☐ Although Devil's Postpile is a national monument, it's part and parcel to Mammoth's summer recreation program. The resort provides bus service into Reds Meadow, a pretty, rock-ribbed valley of the San Joaquin River where the "postpile" is located. Because of winter snow, the road into the valley is open only from early summer to the end of October. And because the monument is popular and road is very narrow, visitors can't drive their cars into the valley from opening day until just after Labor Day Weekend. However, those with camping permits can drive to their valley campsites. (See "Camping" below, on page 186.) After Labor Day, all visitors can drive to the monument until the road closes for the winter.

---

*RV ADVISORY* • The road into the valley is very steep, narrow and winding. Although we saw no posted restrictions on RV or trailer sizes, big rigs need to be handled with care. You'll have to seek out wide spots for passing, since much of the road is single lane.

---

Buses operate daily 8 to 5:30, every fifteen to twenty minutes from the Mammoth Mountain Inn; tickets are on sale in the lobby. The trip down is quite impressive, with pauses along the way to admire the Sierra Nevada crest and valley vistas. Once into the valley, the buses stop at pretty alpine lakes, campgrounds and trailheads. Visitors can ride the shuttle bus free among the various stops within the valley.

The national monument is one of ten stops on the bus route. A quarter-mile trail leads to the "postpile," a wall of nearly vertical fused-together flat-sided basaltic columns formed by cooling lava. Just short of the postpile, a trail leads to the crest of this strange formation, where the tops of the posts resemble the rough tile floor of an ancient ruin. The trail continues a couple of miles to Rainbow Falls, a cataract in a forest canyon. There are several other interesting hiking trails in the area and you can learn about them at a small visitor center near the shuttle bus stop.

# MAMMOTH LAKES

**Population: 4,800**                    **Elevation: 7,860**

After returning from the postpile, follow Minaret Road into the town, where you'll find a good selection of restaurants, lodgings and other services, many in attractive alpine style buildings.

Continue through town and turn left at a traffic signal onto Main Street. As you clear the business district, you'll see the large, well-equipped **Mammoth Visitor Center**, set back off the road on your left. Jointly operated by the Mammoth Lakes Visitors Bureau and U.S. Forest Service, it's open daily 8 to 5; (760) 934-2712.

## ACTIVITIES

Although Mammoth is noted primarily as a ski resort, it has a variety of summer activities. Two lifts at the ski area provide scenic rides in summer and several local firms have bike and sports equipment rentals. Scheduled summer activities include conducted hikes, mountain bike camping trips, outdoor concerts and rock climbing. To learn more, get a copy of the *Mammoth Vacation Planner* from the Mammoth Lakes Visitors Bureau. If you're here in autumn, ask for a copy of the *Eastern High Sierra Fall Color Guide*.

## RECLINING AND DINING

**Cinnamon Bear Bed & Breakfast** ● *P.O. Box 3338 (Main and Center streets), Mammoth Lakes, CA 93546; (800) 845-2873 or (760) 934-2873. (WEB SITE: www.cinnamonbearinn.com; E-MAIL: cinnabear1@aol) Twenty-two units with TV, phones and private baths; full breakfast. Major credit cards; $$$$.* ☐ This chalet style inn features New England colonial furnishings, including four-poster canopy beds. Units with fireplaces, spa tubs and kitchen facilities are available. The inn occupies a wooded setting near downtown and the ski area.

**Mammoth Mountain Inn** ● *P.O. Box 353, Mammoth Lakes, CA 93546; (800) 228-4947 or (760) 934-2581. (WEB SITE: www.mammoth-lodging.com; E-MAIL: the-inn@mammoth-mtn.com) Large resort with 213 rooms and suites; TV movies and phones; $$$$$. Mountainside Grill and Yodler serve breakfast through dinner daily; $$ to $$$. MC/VISA, AMEX.* ☐ "Alpine modern" best describes this exceedingly handsome lodge adjacent to the Mammoth ski area. It's dressed in rich wood paneling, cathedral beam ceilings and stone accents. Rooms and suites are comfortably

*The Minarets, a dramatic sawtooth ridge, can be seen at the far left in this photo of the Sierra Nevada range from the Mammoth Lakes area.*

furnished and fifty kitchen units are available. The Mountainside Grill serves antelope medallions, prawns Madagascar, Long Island duckling and other American-continental fare. The more casual Yodler Bar & Pub features chicken satay, pizzas and sandwiches.

**La Sierra's** • *Upper Main near Minaret; (760) 934-8083. Mexican-American-Italian; full bar service. Lunch weekdays and dinner nightly. MC/VISA; $$.* ☐ The look is Hispanic-trendy with splashes of Mexican color, wrought iron and thick ceiling beams. The menu dances all over the place, from tortilla-wrapped things and designer pizzas to garlic chicken and assorted pastas. It's a popular local hangout, with live entertainment.

**Matterhorn Restaurant** • *680 Minaret Rd. (in Alpenhof Lodge); (760) 934-3369. European-American; wine and beer. Breakfast through dinner daily. MC/VISA, AMEX; $$ to $$$.* ☐ This Swiss chalet café fits its alpine surroundings, with a cozy fireplace and oil lamps. Wild game is a specialty, and it also has several seafood dishes, plus European fare such as *wienerschnitzel, cordon bleau* and veal with apple slices.

### CAMPING

Several Forest Service campgrounds are in Reds Meadow along the San Joaquin River near Devil's Postpile, with the usual shaded sites and flush or pit potties, with no hookups; **$$.** You'll need a camping permit to drive to your site in summer. Check at the ranger kiosk near Mammoth Mountain Inn, the Minaret entry kiosk above Reds Meadow or the Mammoth Lakes Visitor Center on the highway out of town; see above.

If you continue downhill past the Mammoth Lakes Visitor center, you will soon blend back into U.S. 395. Pressing southward, you'll crest 7,000-foot Sherwin Summit and then begin a gradual roll downhill. By the time you reach Bishop in the Owens Valley, you will have shed 3,000 vertical feet.

A few miles below Sherwin Summit, as you begin the main descent into the valley, watch for a "Point of historical interest" sign indicating a vista point to your right. You're looking into what was once a rich agricultural valley, extending a hundred miles south from Bishop. Since the Los Angeles Department of Water and Power took most of its water, much of it is a desert basin, although it still has a few ranches and pasturelands. The valley was named in 1845 by western explorer and cartographer Captain John C. Frémont, in honor of one of his officers, Richard Owens.

## BISHOP

**Population: 3,680**                                    **Elevation: 4,140 feet**

As the major commercial center for the eastern Sierra, Bishop is a rather scattered community. It has neither the alpine charm of Mammoth Lakes nor the frontier look of Bridgeport. However, it's in an impressive setting, saddled between the eastern escarpment of the Sierra Nevada and the little-known but imposing White Mountains. California's second highest mountain range with several peaks over 14,000 feet, this is home to a large bristlecone pine forest. "Large" is a misleading term, for these are centuries-old trees dwarfed by the severe conditions of their alpine environment. (See "Side trip" on the next page.)

Before you reach Bishop, you can visit the interesting **Laws Railroad Museum** by turning east onto U.S. 6 and driving five miles toward the White Mountains. Stroll through old railroad cars and poke into a general store, medical office and other pioneer stores. Laws was a busy railroading center, with trains running between California and Nevada, until the line died during the 1930s Owens Valley Water Wars. The museum is open daily 10 to 4; (760) 873-5950.

Back on Highway 395 and continuing toward town, you can shed a few dollars if you wish at the **Paiute Palace Casino**, which has a few slot and video machines, table games and a small café. More authentic to native custom is the **Paiute-Shoshone Indian Cultural Center** at 2300 West Line Street. This fine little archive presents exhibits on the arts, crafts and lifestyles of the Paiutes, with a gift shop selling native artifacts. It's open weekdays 9 to 5 and weekends 10 to 4 in summer and weekdays 10 to 3 in the off-season; (760) 873-4478. To reach it, turn right onto Line Street (Highway 168 at a traffic light) at the south end of town and drive about a mile west.

As you enter town from the north, the **Mount Whitney Ranger Station** of Inyo National Forest is on your left at 798 North Main. It's a good place to gather information about the Sierra Nevada high country and a bristlecone pines visit. Hours are 8 to 5 weekdays; (760) 873-4207. A bit beyond, in an A-frame at 690 North Main, is the **Bishop Area Chamber of Commerce**. It's open weekdays 9 to 5 and weekends 10 to

4; (760) 873-8405. If you're here in autumn, ask for a copy of the *Eastern High Sierra Fall Color Guide.*

Across the street is **Erick Schatts Bakkerÿ**, in business since 1907 and famous for its round-loaf sheepherders bread. It sells an incredible array of other baked goods. You can satisfy your sweet tooth with American, Dutch and Scandinavian pastries, cakes and specialty breads, or build lunch at a large deli. (Try a Dagwood deli sandwich on garlic cheese bread.) Dine indoors or take your lunch on the road. The bakery is open daily from 7, with various closing hours; (760) 873-7156.

### OTHER PLACES TO DINE

**Amigo's** • *285 N. Main St.; (760) 872-2189. Mexican; wine and beer. Lunch and dinner Monday-Saturday, closed Sunday. MC/VISA.* ☐ Amigo serves typical Mexican fare, plus interesting items such as crab Vallarta with white wine sauce. It's cheerfully decorated with *serape* table trim and *sombreros* gracing the wood paneled walls.

**Whiskey Creek** • *524 N. Main St.; (760) 873-7174. American; full bar service. Breakfast through dinner daily. MC/VISA; $$.* ☐ This is an appealing "modern early American" style restaurant with lots of polished wood, maple furniture and folk artifacts. A saloon, outdoor deck and folk craft shop are part of the complex. The menu features assorted chickens, steaks and chops, plus a few spicier dishes like Caribbean shrimp and chicken *caliente.*

Sixteen miles south of Bishop, you'll encounter **Big Pine,** a community of 1,500. It doesn't offer much of visitor interest, although it has the requisite service stations, mom and pop motels and cafés. A pair of side trips from here are definitely interesting and you can pick up information at the Chamber of Commerce **Visitor Center** mid-town on the left at 126 S. Main St.; (760) 938-2114

## Side trip: Bristlecone pines

The route to the bristlecone pines of the White Mountains is long, slow, winding and steep, so check your water and radiator coolant and pack a lunch. To begin, drive east from Big Pine on State Route 168 for about thirteen miles, then turn north on White Mountain Road, just below Westgard Pass. You'll soon pass **Grandview Campground** at 8,500 feet, which is free, with pit toilets and no water.

At 10,100-foot **Schulman Grove** on the edge of the bristlecone preserve, you can pick up material on the pines at a seasonal ranger station, and perhaps join a ranger-led outing. The short Alpha Trail leads to the nearest grove and a 4.5-mile hike through this thin air delivers you to the **Methusaleh Grove,** home to the most ancient of these ancients. To protect it from vandals, no sign identifies the 4,700-year-old Methusaleh Tree, the world's oldest living thing.

A rough 11-mile drive takes you to the **Patriarch Grove,** a strangely desolate lunarscape at 11,000 feet. Lichen, tiny flowers, scattered bristlecones and passing hawks are all that prevail at this altitude. You're on one of the highest roads in California and if you insist on going higher, a seven-mile hiking trail takes you to the top of **White Mountain** at 14,246 feet. That's just 250 feet lower than Mount Whitney.

This strange "Paradise Lost" of the bristlecones is a chilly and harsh land of icy winds, bare rock, poor limestone soil and little water. This place is either starkly bleak or hauntingly beautiful, depending on your poetic state.

---

**RV ADVISORY** ● Although White Mountain Road to Schulman Grove is paved, it's very steep and winding and not recommended for large RVs or trailer rigs. The unpaved road to Patriarch Grove is *definitely* not advised for large rigs. You may have second thoughts about taking the family sedan to Patriarch as well; inquire at Schulman about the road's condition.

---

### Side trip: Glacier Lodge

Glacier Lodge is an appealing mountain retreat at the upper end of pretty Big Pine Creek, west of Big Pine. Facilities include a lodge, rustic cabins and an RV park. The original chalet, dating from 1917, burned down in early 1998 but should be rebuilt by the time you get there.

Even if you don't plan to stay at the lodge or RV park, this is a nice drive to an interesting region. **Big Creek Recreation Area** below and around the lodge site has several shaded campgrounds, picnic areas and fine places to fish or splash the in burbling creek. To get there, turn west at the blinking light in downtown Big Pine and make a bee-line for the Sierra Nevada foothills. It's a rather straight, easy-to-negotiate road.

This region offers a curious botanical blend. The hills rising steeply above the creek are brushy and beige, while the heart of the canyon shelters thick evergreen groves. At the upper end, however, you'll be surrounded by woodlands, within the canyon and above. From the higher reaches, you'll get splendid views of the Sierra's lofty granite spires. What appears to be just another patch of snow way up there is the southernmost glacier in America.

**Glacier Lodge** ● *P.O. Box 370, Big Pine, CA 93513-0370; (760) 938-2837. Six chalet style lodge rooms and ten rustic cabins; $$$$. RV park with water and electric hookups; $$$. MC/VISA.* ⊔ This complex has the essentials for a pleasant mountain getaway. You can buy staples at a mini-mart and a barbecue café is open for lunch through early dinner, with everything under $10.

For more rustic camping, the Forest Service's Big Pine Creek Campground is within walking distance of the lodge complex, with tables and barbecue grills, no hookups; **$$**. Several other Forest Service campsites are along the highway coming up.

### Big Pine to Lone Pine and Whitney Portal

You'll enjoy some of the Sierra Nevada's most dramatic vistas on the forty-three mile stretch of Highway 395 between Big Pine and Lone Pine. About midway, you'll hit another eastern Sierra town with a bit of charm:

# INDEPENDENCE

**Population: 1,000**                    **Elevation: 3,925 feet**

Little Independence has several false front stores and a few motels, service stations and cafés, plus an historic inn, an interesting courthouse, a nice little museum and the former home of a slightly famous author.

For a quickie town tour, stop first at the Spanish colonial style **Winnedumah Hotel**, listed below. Across the street, admire the Greek federalist **Inyo County Courthouse**, more than a century old and still in use. Now, turn right on Center Street beside the hotel and drive three blocks to the **Eastern California Museum** at 155 N. Grant. Occupying a low cinderblock building, it's relatively organized and uncluttered, displaying an interesting assortment of pioneer artifacts. You can visit a scatter of old farm equipment out front. The museum is open daily except Tuesday, 10 to 4; (760) 878-0258.

From here, go a block south on Grant, then a block east on Market to Webster and you'll see the semi-famous writer's residence on your left. The two-story Dutch-style **Mary Austin Home** sheltered the author *Land of Little Rain*, a book about life in the eastern Sierra. It's privately owned, although there's a marker out front about Ms. Austin and her tenure here.

## RECLINING AND DINING

**Winnedumah Hotel** ● *P.O. Box 147, Independence, CA 93526; (760) 878-2040. (WEB SITE: www.qnet.com/~winnedumah; E-MAIL: winnedumah@qnet.com) Twenty-four rooms with private or share baths; extended continental breakfast; $$$. Restaurant serves prix fixe multi-course dinners Fridays and Saturdays; $$$.* □ Dating from 1927, this Spanish colonial wood frame hotel has modest lodgings and a rather attractive dining room with bentwood chairs and plate rails. The lobby, nicely done in early American décor, was a bit musty when we visited, although it may be spruced up by the time you arrive.

Six miles south of Independence, you'll pass the remnants of one of the saddest chapters in American history. **Manzanar Relocation Center** was one of ten concentration camps where Japanese-Americans were imprisoned during World War II. More than 10,000 people lived here in cold, leaky wood and tar paper shacks from 1942 until 1945. Little remains except a pair of stone sentry posts with pagoda roofs that seem to be a cruel joke, a large and tattered auditorium and a cemetery.

Manzanar was designated a national historic site in 1992. It isn't staffed, although elaborate interpretive facilities are planned for the future. Meanwhile, you can walk around this desolate patch of land—once made green by the Japanese—and look up at the contrasting beauty of the Sierra Nevada. Tours and programs are conducted periodically; check with the Eastern California Museum for schedules; (760) 878-0258. *Farewell to Manzanar*, a book by former internee Jeanne Wakatsuki Houston, helped bring national attention to the place. Her book is on sale at the Mount Whitney-Death Valley Interagency Visitor Center; see below.

## LONE PINE

**Population: 2,060** **Elevation: 3,773 feet**

This gathering of late nineteenth century buildings is our favorite town along the eastern Sierra. It's both charming and functional, with a couple of interesting restaurants and a truly dramatic setting. Further, it occupies a significant crossroads in this grand land east of the Sierra Nevada. Heading west, you can zig-zag up to Whitney Portal, one of the most dramatic enclaves in the entire mountain range. Here, people set out to climb the highest mountain in mainland America. Go east and you'll drop into Death Valley, ultimately reaching the lowest point in the country.

There are no museums or other special attractions here. Lone Pine is simply a pleasant little place for hanging out and watching the light and shadow shows on the White Mountains and Sierra Nevada each morning and evening. And if you wanna play cowboy, head for the Alabama Hills just west of town, where dozens of old hayburner movies were shot. A film festival is held every October, featuring special showings of those cowboy classics; call (760) 867-4314 for information.

To learn more about Lone Pine and its surrounds, stop at the **Chamber of Commerce** at 126 S. Main. It's on your left as you drive south, set back off the street near the town's only traffic light; open weekdays 7 to 4; (760) 876-4444.

The fine **Mount Whitney-Death Valley Interagency Visitor Center** is a mile south of town and briefly east on Highway 136. It has lots of information on the surrounding wilds, a picnic area and a good stock of books on the Owens Valley Water Wars and Manzanar. It's open daily 8 to 4:50; (760) 876-6222.

Incidentally, many folks have trouble spotting Mount Whitney, since it's mixed in with several other peaks, including some mountains in the foreground that appear taller. At the Interagency Visitor Center, a display inside and a marker outside will help you spot that modest-appearing yet lofty wedge.

### DINING

***Merry Go Round Dinner House*** • *212 S. Main St.; (760) 876-4259. American; wine and beer. Dinner nightly. Major credit cards;* ***$$***. ◻ This is a surprise in remote Lone Pine—a restaurant with a clever merry-go-round theme. No, the room doesn't spin. However, the dining area is octagonal, the walls are mirrored and ceiling is hung with tapestry to give you that carousel feel. Settle into a snug booth and try the chicken breast, assorted steaks, barbecues and seafood entrées.

***Mount Whitney Restaurant*** • *277 S. Main at Post; (760) 876-5751. American; wine and beer. Breakfast through dinner daily. MC/VISA;* ***$*** *to* ***$$***. ◻ The knotty pine walls of this attractive café are busy with cowboy photos—not real cowboys but stars of the more than 300 horse operas filmed in the nearby Alabama Hills. The fare is appropriate to the setting—steaks, chicken fried steak, meat loaf and such. The Alabama Hills hamburger is particularly tasty.

## Side trip: Whitney Portal

The steep and winding thirteen-mile drive to Whitney Portal is worth the effort even if you don't plan to stay at one of the most dramatically situated campgrounds in America.

From the town's only traffic light, head west on Whitney Portal Road. It first passes through the rugged Alabama Hills, a Bureau of Land Management recreation area. Movies such as *Gunga Din* and *Bengal Lancers* were filmed here, along with scores of Western movies and TV films. About a mile beyond a sign marking the BLM recreation area, look on your right for a monument that discusses this area's Hollywood past. It was dedicated in 1990 by Roy Rogers, who made his first movie here in 1938. From the monument, a dusty drive called Movie Road takes you past tumbled boulders and ragged ridges where Ken Maynard, Tom Mix, John Wayne, Gene Autry and "Hopalong Cassidy" fought for truth, justice and the American way. (Can you imagine a present day movie hero calling himself "Hopalong?" It sounds like a crippled rabbit.)

Continuing west on Mount Whitney Road, you'll pass the Forest Service's easy-to-reach **Lone Pine Campground** in sagebrush foothills. Most of its sites provide views of the steep face of the Sierra Nevada. It has water, pit potties and no hookups; **$$**. Sites can be reserved by calling (800) 280-CAMP; MC/VISA accepted.

Beyond the campground, you'll begin a serious zig-zag climb to Whitney Portal. Views of the steep face of the Sierra escarpment ahead and the Owens Valley behind are most impressive. **Whitney Portal Campground** is installed in a narrow canyon beneath sheer granite walls hundreds of feet high, with a creek gushing merrily past the campsites. The terrain is so steep that most of the sites are terraced. Facilities include tables and barbecue pits, with chemical flush potties and no hookups. Campsites go quickly in summer, since they're popular with people planning to climb Mount Whitney, whose main trailhead is just above. They can be reserved by calling (800) 280-CAMP; MC/VISA accepted.

---

***WHITNEY HIKING ADVISORY*** • To avoid crowds on the popular eleven-mile trail to Mount Whitney, departures are limited to fifty hikers a day. When we last checked, reservations could be made six months in advance, although permits go *very fast*. Officials begin taking reservations at 8 a.m. on the "eligible day" and they're usually all gone within fifteen minutes. The best method is to begin dialing furiously at the stroke of eight—with credit card in hand. For details on the program, contact the Inyo National Forest Reservation Service, P.O. Box 430, Big Pine, CA 93513; (888) 374-3773 or (760) 938-1136; FAX (760) 938-1137. (WEB SITE: www.sierrawilderness.com)

---

***WHERE DO WE GO FROM HERE?*** • You can continue south on Highway 395 and begin Tour Fourteen, crossing under Sierra Nevada range to Kernville and Sequoia-Kings Canyon. Or head southeast into Death Valley National Park and run Tour Twenty-one in reverse.

# TRIP PLANNER

**WHEN TO GO** ● Spring through fall is best for the southern Sierra and Sequoia-Kings Canyon National Park. The road into Kings Canyon is closed during winter.

**DRIVING DISTANCE** ● About 235 miles from the U.S. 395 Inyokern Junction to the heart of Kings Canyon, plus thirty-six miles from there back to Grant Grove Village.

**RV ADVISORY** ● Small RVs should have no problems with this route, although it involves several areas of tight turns and steep climbs. A sign advises that rigs over twenty-two feet shouldn't attempt the long climb into Sequoia National Park from Three Rivers. However, park officials told us that vehicles and trailer rigs with a combined length up to forty feet are permitted on the road. Anything over that should use alternate routes; see details below for other approaches.

**WHAT YOU'LL SEE** ● An interesting Joshua tree forest on the extreme southern edge of the Sierra Nevada range, Isabella Lake and quaint Kernville with its fine historical museum, the murals of downtown Exeter, and the scenic beauty of Sequoia and Kings Canyon national parks.

**WHAT TO DO** ● Stroll among the big trees; climb the stairs up Moro Rock and hike part of the High Sierra Trail in Sequoia National Park; pay your respects to the General Grant Tree in Grant Grove; take the tour through Boyden Cave en route to Kings Canyon; walk the Zumwalt Meadow nature trail and do some hiking in the Cedar Grove section of Kings Canyon National Park.

**TO BEGIN** ● The route starts near the Inyokern Junction on U.S. 395, although you can approach from several directions; see details below.

## Useful contacts

**Kernville Chamber of Commerce,** P.O. Box 397, Kernville, CA 93238-0397; (760) 376-2629.

**Lake Isabella Chamber of Commerce,** Box 567, (6117 Lake Isabella Blvd.), Lake Isabella, CA 93240-0567; (760) 379-5236.

**Sequoia and Kings Canyon National Parks,** Three Rivers, CA 93271; (559) 565-3341.

## Pricing guidelines

**DINING:** Dinner entrée with soup or salad, without drinks or dessert for under $10 = **$**; $10 to $14 = **$$**; $15 to $25 = **$$$**; over $25 = **$$$$**.

**RECLINING:** A two-person room for $35 or less = **$**; $36 to $50 = **$$**; $51 to $75 = **$$$**; $76 to $100 = **$$$$**; more than $100 = **$$$$$**.

**CAMPING:** Under $10 = **$**; $10 to $14 = **$$**; $15 to $19 = **$$$**; $20 or more = **$$$$**

## Tour Fourteen

# SOUTHERN SIERRA
## OWENS VALLEY TO SEQUOIA-KINGS CANYON

The stars of this road show are Sequoia and Kings Canyon national parks. Sequoia gets a fair amount of summer traffic, yet Kings Canyon is visited only lightly, although it was described by John Muir as equal in beauty to the Yosemite Valley. Both were formed in the same manner, by glacial actions that widened once narrow river canyons.

We recommend this as a late spring to fall drive and it's particularly appealing in autumn. We visited during early October weekdays and found only a handful of people in Sequoia and even fewer in Kings Canyon. The areas do get busy on summer weekends of course, since they're within a few hours' drive for several million Californians. This tour won't work in winter because the highway into Kings Canyon is closed by snow; roads into Sequoia can be shut down temporarily by storms.

Our reasons for the rather convoluted approach to Sequoia-Kings Canyon are twofold. First, it takes you across the southern tip of the Sierra Nevada range, through Joshua tree desert highlands that have their own special appeal. The charming old community of Kernville with its adjacent Kern River and Isabella Lake are inviting as well.

Second, this route across the Sierra Nevada bottom is an easy transition from Tour Thirteen in the previous chapter. If you're approaching from elsewhere, you can get on course by following State Route 178 northeast from Highway 99 in Bakersfield. Or head north from southern California on either U.S. 395 or State Route 14. If you approach from Bakersfield, we recommend staying on Highway 178 until you crest Walker Pass to get a look at that impressive Joshua tree forest.

## Owens Valley to Kernville

If you're dovetailing from the previous tour, head south through the Owens Valley on U.S. 395 to its junction with State Route 14 just above Inyokern. Continue straight ahead to blend onto Highway 14, following the "Los Angeles" sign. Eleven miles later—you don't really want to go to L.A., do you?—turn right onto State Route 178.

You're curling around the southern toes of the Sierra Nevada range here, although you'll initially pass through the hilly mesquite terrain of the upper Mojave Desert. Then as Highway 178 climbs toward Walker Pass, you'll enter an intriguing "forest" of Joshua trees. Neither tree nor cactus,

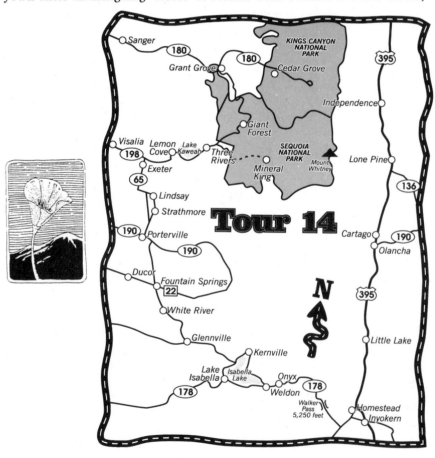

this strange plant can grow up to forty feet tall; some have a tangled web of branches that suggest leafless, hairy-limbed oaks. They were named by early Mormons, who pictured them as men with arms extended to heaven.

The climb up 5,250-foot Walker Pass is rather gentle, through a shallow vale flanked by rocky hills. You'll then begin a lazy spiral into the **Kern River Valley,** a virtual desert botanical garden of Joshua, junipers, sage and yellow-blooming rabbit brush.

Almost ignored by most guidebooks, this little-visited area is quite appealing, flanked by steep and rocky hills that form the Sierra Nevada's southern perimeter. At its upper end is Isabella Lake, one of California's largest reservoirs. If you like to fish, it's noted for yields of bass, crappie, bluegill and catfish, while the Kern River is a good trout stream. Three towns occupy the Kern River Valley—Lake Isabella and Wofford Heights, which aren't very interesting, and Kernville, which is as cute as a bug.

As you drive through Kern River Valley, you'll first encounter the hamlet of **Onyx,** which has a couple of small general stores dating from 1851. About a mile apart, they're now thinly disguised mini-marts. Beyond **Weldon,** with more than a thousand residents but no business district, you'll see large slices of blue, marking the beginning of **Isabella Lake.** Follow the shoreline and you'll shortly encounter the town of **Lake Isabella** with a population of 3,428. This ordinary looking berg is interesting mostly because of its lakeside location. At a four-way stop, a right turn will put you onto Highway 155 bound for Kernville. However, if you want to learn more about this area, continue straight ahead for half a block and you'll see the **Visitor Information Center** of Lake Isabella on your right. It's in a tiny cinderblock cottage decorated with murals; open weekdays 8 to 5; (760) 379-5236.

Heading toward Kernville, you'll pass through sections of Sequoia National Forest, with several campgrounds either in the thin woods above the lake or down near the water. The Forest Service's **Lake Isabella Information Center** is on your right just beyond the town of Lake Isabella. It's open daily 8 to 5 in summer with shorter hours the rest of the year; (760) 379-5646. A short distance beyond are the earthfill dam that forms Isabella Lake and **French Gulch Marina** with docks, a boat launch and boat rentals; (760) 379-8774.

You'll then leave the national forest and encounter **Wofford Heights,** an uninteresting collection of stores and homes terraced uphill from the lake. After a few more miles, you'll hit a town worth a pause:

## KERNVILLE

**Population: 1,860**                    Elevation: **2,651 feet**

A former mining camp dating from the 1850s, Kernville has dressed itself in Western style false front buildings. Most are new and made to look old; many house boutiques, cafés and antique shops. Well-groomed **Riverside Park** on the Kern River adds to the town's appeal.

Although it has that proper pioneer look, the town's main draw is the Kern River, which offers short stretches of wild rapids and other sections suitable for tubing. Kernville is abrim with outfits selling river trips; see "Activities" below. Since it's within easy reach of Los Angeles and Bakersfield, it gets very crowded on summer weekends, so try to plan your visit around that problem.

For a quickie tour of Kernville, turn left onto Berlando Drive at the south edge of town and you'll encounter the **Kernville Ranger Station**; (760) 376-3781. Now go right onto Whitney Drive for a block and then right again onto Big Blue Road and you'll be in front of the **Kern Valley Historical Museum.** Housed in a Western style wood frame building, it has a gift shop, art gallery and nicely arranged displays concerning the history of the area. Many movies have been shot in this region and exhibits focus on the films of Gene, Roy, Joel, Hoppy, Hoot and the Duke. The museum is open Thursday-Sunday 10 to 4; (760) 379-5895.

Back on the main drag—Kernville Road—if you continue through town, cross the Kern River and take an immediate right, you'll be in **Frandy Park.** Not pretty and green like **Riverside Park,** Frandy is the major launch point for river trips and three outfitters have offices there.

## ACTIVITIES

*Rafting and Tubing Trips* ● Whitewater and float trips on the Kern River are short and usually modestly priced. Generally, you can get booked without advance reservations, although they may be filled up on summer weekends.

**Mountain and River Adventures** books river trips and a variety of other activities from its outdoor adventure store near the bridge at 11113 Kernville Rd.; (800) 861-6553; (760) 376-6553.

The three outfits based in Frandy Park are **River Place**, (760) 379-4616; **Kern Outdoor Center**, (800) 488-RAFT or (760) 376-8806; and **Whitewater Voyages**, (760) 379-4444.

## RECLINING AND DINING

*Kern River Inn Bed & Breakfast* ● *P.O. Box 1725 (119 Kern River Dr.), Kernville, CA 93238; (800) 986-4382 or (760) 376-6750. (E-MAIL: kernriverinn@lightspeed.net) Six rooms with private baths, some with fireplaces; full breakfast. MC/VISA, AMEX; $$$$.* □ This beautifully appointed country style inn is opposite Riverside Park and the Kern River, and its rooms provide views thereof. Although built in 1991, it has an early American look, with brass beds, ceiling fans and print wallpaper. The parlor is equipped with books, a TV/VCR and table games.

*Cheryl's Diner* ● *11030 Kernville Rd.; (760) 376-6131. American; no alcohol. Breakfast through dinner daily. MC/VISA; $.* □ This family style diner serves inexpensive dinners including chicken fried steak, baby beef liver and fried chicken, plus breakfast omelettes and hot sandwiches for lunch. It's housed in a cozy cottage near the river, with an outdoor patio.

*That's Italian* ● *9 Big Blue Rd. (Kernville Road); (760) 376-6020. Italian-American; wine and beer. Lunch Friday-Sunday and dinner nightly. MC/VISA; $$.* □ The name doesn't match the setting, since this restaurant is housed in a rustic barkwood cottage that dates from 1920. However, the inside look is strictly Italian, with red checkered tablecloths, hanging plants and floral wall murals. The fare runs from chicken cacciatore and veal Parmagiana through assorted pastas.

## CAMPING

**Frandy Park** • *Off Kernville Road on the Kern River. RV sites; $$.* ⊓ The park has informal dirt sites with no hookups; showers and flush potties. It's near town and three river runners have offices here; see above.

**Sequoia National Forest** • Several Forest Service campsites are on the shores of Isabella Lake and alongside the Kern River. Many are on the National Recreation Reservation System and sites can be reserved up to a year in advance with a MasterCard or VISA by calling (800) 280-CAMP.

### Sequoia: How do we go from here?

There are two ways to get from here to Three Rivers, the gateway to Sequoia National Park. The first is roundabout and mostly on straight highways; the second is more direct but busy with hills and curves.

Option one adds about twenty-five miles to your tour. Head southeast from Lake Isabella to Bakersfield, go north on Highway 99 to Tulare, take State Route 63 to Visalia and then go east on State Route 198 to Three Rivers. Much of this is freeway or four-lane highway.

---

**RV ADVISORY** • The first option may be preferable for RVers since you'll encounter a wearying amount of curves and hills on the more direct approach. However, RVs and trailer rigs with a combined length over forty feet aren't permitted on the climb from Three Rivers into Sequoia National Park, so they must use yet another approach. (A sign on the park road is more conservative, advising against anything over twenty-two feet.) Big rigs should take the Bakersfield route to Visalia, then stay on Highway 63 until it hits Highway 180, and follow this east into Grant Grove. From there, you can go south into Sequoia and then north and east into Kings Canyon.

---

Option two—the direct approach—is for those who like woodland settings and don't mind a lot of curves, so get a good grip on your steering wheel. From **Wofford Heights**, head northwest on State Route 155 toward Alta Sierra and Glennville. You'll face twenty miles of tight twists and turns, topping 6,102-foot Greenhorn Summit and then spiraling down the other side. (A sign advises that large trucks shouldn't attempt this route; thus the good news is that you aren't likely to encounter any.)

As you wind down the far side of Greenhorn Summit, you'll enter an attractive, hilly oak-chaparral woodland flanked by rocky foothills. Narrow roads lazily follow the gentle contours of this land that is surprisingly remote, despite its nearness to central California population centers. Occasional ranches break up the pleasant monotony of this landscape.

The only town you'll hit on this route—and it is tiny—is **Glennville** at the base of the Greenhorn grade. Fork to the right at a Porterville sign, then go right again at a second sign indicating Porterville, White River and Fountain Springs. Several miles beyond, just after you enter Tulare County, take a left to stay your Porterville course. Twenty-two miles from Glennville, you'll encounter the crossroads of **Fountain Springs**, not a town but an old Western style saloon and restaurant. If all that driving has worked up an appetite, you can get lunch or dinner in the restaurant, which is in a pool room off the bar, with a few tables. (When we were there, the lady bartender also was the cook and waitress.) The menu consists of hamburgers, a sizable chili size and three kinds of steak.

From Fountain Springs, continue straight through the crossroad. After a few miles, the oak-chaparral woodland unexpectedly yields to citrus groves and fashionable country homes. About thirteen miles after leaving Fountain Springs, you'll hit a traffic signal on State Route 190 on the edge of—where else?—**Porterville.**

---

**NAVIGATIONAL NOTE** ● If you're running this route in reverse, follow Highway 65 south through Porterville, take Highway 190 east, then go right (south) at the second stoplight, which is Plano Road. This will take you to the Fountain Springs intersection.

---

A town of 34,000, Porterville is the commercial center of a large citrus, vineyard and farming area. However, it doesn't offer much visitor appeal so we'll suggest skimming its fringes and continuing toward Sequoia. Arriving from Fountain Springs, go left (west) on Highway 190 for about two miles and then head north on State Route 65, a freeway that skims Porterville's western edge. You'll soon pass the equally uninteresting communities of **Strathmore** and **Lindsay**.

After the highway's four-lane section ends, turn right at a four-way stop to stay with Route 65, headed for **Exeter.** It's a tidy and appealing little community with several historic murals on its well-tended downtown buildings. To see them, take a half left onto D Street shortly after you enter the city limits (at a "Business district and city park" sign). After several blocks, turn left onto Pine Street, which takes you through the heart of downtown. If you'd like to learn more about Exeter, pause at the **Chamber of Commerce** in a Spanish colonial railroad depot on your right at Pine and F. It's open weekdays 9 to 5; (559) 592-2929. There's not much of interest beyond here, so do a U-turn and stay on Pine until it blends back onto Highway 65. Use the tall, slender Exeter water tower as your landmark.

After a couple of miles, Route 65 bumps into Highway 198; turn right and head for Sequoia. You'll pass through a pleasant foothill area of groves and farmlands that surround the prim little town of **Lemon Cove.** Watch on your right for an imposing anti-bellum style mansion, now a country inn:

**Mesa Verde Plantation Bed & Breakfast** ● *33038 Highway 198, Lemon Cove, CA 93244; (800) 240-1466 or (559) 597-2555. (WEB SITE: www.plantationbnb.com; E-MAIL: rekax@plantationbnb.com) Eight rooms with some private and some share baths; full breakfast. Major credit cards; $$$$ to $$$$$.* ☐ This late nineteenth century ranch surrounded by orchards indeed suggests a southern plantation mansion, with its columns and second story balconies. Each of the guest rooms is decorated with an

Old South theme and named for one of the characters from *Gone With the Wind*. Amenities include a swimming pool, hot tub and a video library.

Beyond the inn, Highway 198 sheds groves and farmlands and climbs into beige, rocky foothills. The U.S. Army Corps of Engineers' **Kaweah Reservoir** has boat launching areas, picnic sites and other recreational lures. Its **Horse Creek Campground** has paved interior roads and shaded, well-spaced sites with picnic tables and barbecue grills, showers and flush potties; no hookups; **$$**.

## THREE RIVERS

**Population: 2,600**                              **Elevation: 800 feet**

Above the reservoir, Highway 198 becomes Sierra Drive as it enters Three Rivers, a typical pre-national park community with motels, service stations and small cafés. It stretches for several miles through foothill woodlands, finally ending just short of Sequoia National Park's Ash Mountain entrance station.

If you'd like to nip a bit of the grape, watch on your right just as you enter town for the **Bullene Vineyards** with a tasting room, deli and gift shop. It's beside the highway at 40220 Pierce Drive; open daily 10 to 6; (559) 561-9463.

The former **Kaweah Colony**, a nineteenth century commune that once made international headlines for its utopian ideals, is three miles north of Three Rivers. If you're curious, turn left across the Kaweah River onto North Fork Drive in the lower end of Three Rivers. The short trip will take you past comfortable country homes and a couple of horse stables to the only surviving element of the colony—a post office housed in a tiny barnboard ivy covered cottage.

The colony was established in 1886, then it folded after six years due to internal bickering and because colonists couldn't get title to their land. Kaweah today is primarily a retirement community.

### DINING

**Angelina's Family Dining Room** ● *41891 Sierra Dr. (mid-town, on the left); (559) 561-0114. American-Italian; wine and beer. Breakfast through dinner daily. MC/VISA; $$.* ☐ Housed in a quaint red cottage with white trim, Angelina features rural American cookin' such as fried chicken, chicken fried steak and liver and onions, plus several pasta dishes. The décor is early American and the place is only slightly musty; fresh air folks can adjourn to a lattice patio out back.

**Three Rivers Restaurant and Bakery** ● *43368 Sierra Dr (upper end of town, on the right).; (559) 561-4761. American; no alcohol. Breakfast through mid-afternoon daily. No credit cards; $.* ☐ Also in a red and white cottage, this café is appealing primarily for its patio, shaded by a giant oak and decorated with several flower beds and gurgling garden fountains. It's a pleasant place to enjoy rich muffins, giant stickybuns and other pastries, or breakfast omelettes, luncheon hamburgers and assorted sandwiches.

*This is the classic look of a giant Sequoia—with a thick trunk and high canopy. It's shorter, chubbier and has more mass than a coast redwood.*

**Sequoia and Kings Canyon National Parks** ● *Three Rivers, CA 93271; (559) 565-3341. (WEB: www.nps.gov/seki or www.r5.fs.fed.us/sequoia) Lodging information and reservations: (888) 252-5757 for Sequoia and (888) 335-5500 for Kings Canyon, or (559) 335-5500 for either. Campground reservations: (800) 365-CAMP in the park (up to three months in advance) and (800) 280-CAMP in Sequoia National Forest (up to a year in advance). MC/VISA accepted for both;* **$$ to $$$.** *Supplies, restaurants and lodging are at Lodgepole and the new Wuksachi Lodge in Sequoia; and at Grant Grove and Cedar Grove in Kings Canyon. Most lodgings are in the* **$$$$ to $$$$$** *range. There are two visitor centers in each park: Foothills above Three Rivers and Lodgepole near Giant Forest in Sequoia; and Grant Grove and Cedar Grove in Kings Canyon. They're generally open daily 8 to 5, although hours can vary. Modest entry fee is good for both parks. Cedar Groves section of Kings Canyon is closed in winter.* ☐

Jointly administered yet with separate borders and identities, Sequoia and Kings Canyon national parks are among our favorite places in California. Sequoia is home to several groves of *sequoia giganteum*, the world's largest living thing. It also shelters the wildest and most rugged sections of the Sierra Nevada, including Mount Whitney, the mainland's tallest peak.

Kings Canyon is home to a smaller sequoia grove and one of the deepest and most beautiful chasms in America. Both parks are noted for their high Sierra hiking trails which, even in summer, are rarely busy. (Incidentally, the sequoia or big tree is shorter, chubbier and heavier than its coast redwood cousin. It's distinctive for its rough cinnamon colored bark, prettier we think than the brown bark of the coast redwood.)

---

*RV & FUELING ADVISORIES* ● For environmental reasons, both service stations at Sequoia-Kings Canyon have been closed, so fuel up in Three Rivers. No vehicle or trailer rig over forty feet is permitted on the long, twisting climb from Three Rivers to Giant Forest. An alternate approach for big rigs is State Route 180 to Grant Grove; see details on page 199 above. The rest of the parks' main roads, including the long spiral into the Cedar Grove area of Kings Canyon, are less challenging. Call (559) 565-3341 for current road conditions.

---

Your trip into the park begins not among big trees but in the same oak-chaparral zone you've been seeing since Kernville. Just inside the Ash Mountain entrance, you can pause at the **Foothills Visitor Center** for more specifics on the two parks. From here, enjoy a leisurely and winding sixteen-mile climb that delivers you to **Giant Forest,** home to four of the world's largest trees and once the park's main activity center.

If you've not been here for a few years, you won't recognized the place. To lessen human impact on the sequoias' root systems, Giant Forest's lodgings and campgrounds were removed recently. They're nearly all gone—the market, the rustic cabins, the pizza parlor... The sole survivor is the former store building, being concerted into a museum. Thus, nothing remains of Giant Forest except the most awesome trees you'll ever see.

From here, a side road leads to a pair of popular park features. **Moro Rock** is a massive granite monolith providing great views of this region of California. Look east for splendid vistas of the Great Western Divide—the high, sawtooth ridges of the Sierra Nevada. Look west and you'll see the flat expanse of the San Joaquin Valley. From this vantage point, the human impact on the earth's atmosphere becomes perfectly unclear. On a good day, the skies above the Great Western Divide are sunny and crisp, perhaps with a few puffy clouds. On virtually all days, the skies over the San Joaquin Valley are hazy, overlain with a dirty blanket of smog.

Just beyond Moro Rock, **Crescent Meadow** is a peaceful glen rimmed by sequoias, other evergreens and aspens. This also is the start of the High Sierra Trail, which takes you eleven miles to Bearpaw Meadow. It's a wilderness camp perched on the brink of a great granite bluff, with lofty peaks soaring all about. With reservations, you can spend the night in simple shelters and dine on hearty dinners and breakfasts. Call (888) 252-5757 or (559) 335-5500—well in advance—for Bearpaw Meadows lodging. Otherwise you can, with a wilderness permit, backpack into the area and sleep under the stars.

If you aren't ready to tackle eleven miles of the High Sierra Trail, a hike of less than a mile will take you to a splendid Great Western Divide viewpoint. Then as you return, you can fork to the right and follow signs to Tharp's Log, a burned out sequoia trunk that an early resident had fashioned into a one-room cabin. From there, a trail leads back to Crescent Meadow. A wooded area near the Crescent Meadow parking lot is popular for picnickers and thus popular for bears; be wary as you munch your salami sandwich and mind the warning signs posted about.

Continuing north from Giant Forest on the Generals Highway, you'll shortly come upon the **General Sherman Tree**. Two hundred seventy-five feet high and with a waistline of 103 feet, it's considered the world's largest living thing. Just beyond is **Lodgepole,** where the park's main visitor facilities have been shifted from Giant Forest. Here, you'll find a market and souvenir shop, restaurant, large campground and another visitor center. The sleek yet rustic new Wuksachi Lodge, opened in 1999 to replace Giant Forest lodgings, is just beyond.

From here, you'll follow the leisurely winding Generals Highway twenty-five miles to Grant Grove in Kings Canyon National Park. En route, the road leaves Sequoia National Park and travels through a swatch of Sequoia National Forest, where you'll pass a couple of campgrounds and a hideaway resort:

*Montecito-Sequoia Lodge* • *8000 Generals Highway; (800) 227-9900 or (559) 565-3388; (WEB SITE: www.montecitosequoia.com; E-MAIL: msrservations@montecitosequoia.com). Mailing address: 2225 Grant Rd., Suite 1, Los Altos, CA 94024. Thirty-six lodge rooms with private baths and thirteen cabins with nearby bathhouses. American plan with breakfast and dinner buffets; $$$$ per person. MC/VISA.* ☐ This rustic hideaway a mile off the highway features a lake, swimming pool, spa and a four-season activity program, with planned family activities in summer and cross-country skiing in winter. The large, spacious main lodge isn't elegant, but it's well maintained and comfortable. Overstuffed couches before fireplaces in the dining area and an adjacent bar are cozy spots for relaxing.

**Grant Grove** occupies the tip of a Kings Canyon National Park peninsula, sitting like an upside-down Italy on the northwest flank of Sequoia National Park. It's home to a major sequoia grove, plus a woodsy modern complex that includes lodging, a market and gift shop, an attractive early American style restaurant and a park visitor center with a museum. There's also a campground nearby. The area's most noted feature is the **General Grant Tree**, third largest in the park, at 267 feet high. Folks from the San Joaquin Valley come up to conduct Christmas services every year and General Grant has been designated as the Nation's Christmas Tree. No, they don't decorate the upper branches with colored lights.

## Into Kings Canyon

From Grant Grove, it's all downhill into the main part of Kings Canyon National Park—the region that inspired its name. The canyon is a deep ravine carved by the south fork of the Kings River. This grand gash is one of the deepest in the world, nearly 8,200 feet down if you cheat and measure from the highest of the surrounding peaks.

*This dramatic pinnacle is part of Windy Cliffs, opposite Boyden Cave in the heart of Kings Canyon.*

Most of the route into the canyon is through Sequoia National Forest, until you reach the bottom of the chasm in the Cedar Grove section of the national park. The thirty-six-mile drive—surprisingly gentle for a drop into a ravine—is the most dramatic canyon descent in California. It takes you from evergreens through oak-chaparral, into a near desert environment and then back into confers—mostly cedars—as you reach the shelter of the canyon floor. As you spiral downward, you'll enjoy vistas of this awesome abyss and of the Sierra Nevada crests on the far horizon. And you will encounter two developments en route, both offering fuel:

**Hume Lake,** ten miles from Cedar Grove, has a Forest Service campground and a Christian retreat center with lodgings and family activities. Visitors—even heathens like us—are welcome to shop at the store and fuel up at the gas pumps. To learn about the center, contact: Hume Lake Christian Camps, 64144 Hume Rd., Hume, CA 93628; (559) 335-2881.

**Kings Canyon Lodge,** quite different from the Christian retreat, is a small and rustic getaway near the bottom of the drive into the canyon. It has comfy cabins with fireplaces, a restaurant, cowboy style bar and fuel. The main lodge- dining room is decorated with game trophies, critter skins and mountain man regalia. Note the two classic gravity-feed fuel pumps outside the lodge; it's almost worth topping off your tank to watch one of them work. (At this remote spot, fuel prices are necessarily high.) For information: Kings Canyon Lodge, P.O. Box 820, Kings Canyon National Park, CA 93633; (559) 335-2405.

Beyond the lodge, you'll encounter **Boyden Cave,** a small but impressive limestone cavern. Forty-five-minute tours will take you past a good assortment of stalactites, stalagmites, columns, drapes and such. Particularly impressive are the "Wedding Cake" which more resembles a melting leaning tower of Pisa, and a scalloped limestone column that suggests a Christmas tree layered with snow. The fee is modest and tours are conducted daily, 9 to 5 from road opening through Labor Day, then 11 to 5 until the road closes in the fall.

At Boyden Cave, you've reached the floor of the canyon, a narrow, rock-walled chasm still being carved by the tumultuous Kings River. Following the dancing stream, you'll re-enter Kings Canyon National Park at **Cedar Grove,** where the narrow chasm has been widened by primeval glaciers. It's easy to agree with John Muir's comparison to Yosemite Valley. Granite walls and monoliths rise 4,000 feet from the canyon floor, rivaling the great shapes of Yosemite. Facilities here consist of several campgrounds, a small store and gift shop, lodgings and a ranger station. All of this shuts down in winter and only one campground, Sentinel adjacent to Cedar Grove, is kept open in the fall. No more are needed; campsites rarely fill up here, even in summer.

Beyond Cedar Grove, there isn't much more than stunning scenery. The highway continues a few miles to a spot appropriately called Roads End, where trails spin off into the wilderness. En route, take time for the mile and a half nature walk through **Zumwalt Meadow** alongside the Kings River. A trail guide (available at the visitor center) matched to markers will give you a good understanding of the flora and geology of this most amazing canyon.

A monument at Roads End discusses John Muir's efforts to have this place preserved. He first proposed a park in 1891, yet it wasn't accomplished until 1940 and this section of Kings Canyon wasn't included until 1965. The main part of the canyon, through which you just passed, is still national forest land—a political hedge for possible future development of a dam site. Hopefully, that will never occur.

A few hundred feet behind the monument is Muir Rock, a large and remarkably flat granite slab extending into the Kings River. This is a pleasant place to pause, stare up at the imposing monolith of the Great Sentinel and reflect on Muir's rather flowery yet urgent words:

*Let our law-givers make great haste before it is too late to set apart this surpassingly glorious region for the recreation and well-being of humanity, and all the world will rise up and call them blessed.*

☺ ☺ ☺

*Where do we go from here?* • You mean we have to leave? It's all uphill from here, back to Grant Grove. From there, you can drop quickly into the hazy San Joaquin Valley by following Highway 180 west to Fresno or Route 245 southwest toward Visalia. If you take State Route 41 north from Fresno to Coarsegold, you can start exploring the lesser known reaches of the California gold county on Tour Eleven.

*PART III*

# CALIFORNIA SOUTH

**T**wo out of every three Californians live in the region that
many like to call the Southland. Thus, finding roads less traveled
can be a bit of a challenge in this most congested area of the state.

However, southern California also contains vast expanses of desert and much of this so-called "wasteland"—such as Joshua Tree
and Death Valley national parks—is quite fascinating. We've also
discovered interesting routes in the south central coast area and we
even found an uncrowded wine country where you can get a decent
Chardonnay, way down near San Diego.

The southland also has several mountain ranges. Our drives will
take you into the Santa Ynez Range above Santa Barbara; to San
Gabriel Mountains, where you can look down upon crowded Los
Angeles; and to the San Bernardino Mountains that separate busy
Riverside and San Bernardino from the Mojave Desert.

*Southern California isn't all smog and traffic. Areas such as the Mojave Na-
tional Preserve, with its strange Joshua tree forests, are free of crowds.*

# TRIP PLANNER

**WHEN TO GO** ● Any time of the year is fine for this two-county area, which is noted for its benign climate. However, expect Avila and Pismo beaches, Solvang and Santa Barbara to be crowded on summer weekends.

**DRIVING DISTANCE** ● Our pleasantly erratic path through the south central coast covers about 130 miles.

**RV ADVISORY** ● There are no limitations on RVs or trailer rigs on this route, except for a brief side trip in the mountains above Santa Barbara.

**WHAT YOU'LL SEE** ● Old 1930s style resort towns of Avila and Pismo Beach, rustic Port San Luis, La Purisima Mission, the fine murals of downtown Lompoc, tourist-busy Solvang and its Mission Santa Inés, a great view of the Santa Barbara coast from San Marcos Pass, and the seaward side of Santa Barbara.

**WHAT TO DO** ● Play in the sand and stroll the piers at Avila, Pismo and Port San Luis; drive the hard-packed sands of Pismo State Beach; hike to Nojoqui Falls in Nojoqui Falls County park; shop until your credit card screams in Solvang; taste the wines of the Santa Ynez Valley.

**ADVENTURE PASSES** ● A pilot program requiring the purchase of an "Adventure Pass" for southern California national forests was started as we went to press. It may still be in effect as you read this. The pass must be displayed any time a vehicle is parked within one of the national forests. The fee was $5 per day when we last checked, and passes are available at forest service offices and many local businesses. If you fail to display a pass, you'll get what amounts to a "fixit ticket," requiring that you purchase one. Refusal to play the game can result in a fine up to $100.

**TO BEGIN** ● Exit U.S. 101 Freeway below San Luis Obispo, headed west for Avila Beach.

## Useful contacts

**Pismo Beach Chamber of Commerce,** 581 Dolliver St., Pismo Beach, CA 93449; (805) 773-4382.

**Santa Barbara Visitor Information Center,** #1 Santa Barbara St., Santa Barbara, CA 93101; (800) 927-4688 or (805) 965-3021.

**Solvang Conference & Visitors Bureau,** P.O. Box 70, Solvang, CA 93464; (805) 688-6144.

## Pricing guidelines

**DINING:** Dinner entrée with soup or salad, without drinks or dessert for under $10 = **$**; $10 to $14 = **$$**; $15 to $25 = **$$$**; over $25 = **$$$$**.

**RECLINING:** A two-person room for $35 or less = **$**; $36 to $50 = **$$**; $51 to $75 = **$$$**; $76 to $100 = **$$$$**; more than $100 = **$$$$$**.

**CAMPING:** Under $10 = **$**; $10 to $14 = **$$**; $15 to $19 = **$$$**; $20 or more = **$$$$**

## Tour Fifteen
# SOUTH CENTRAL COAST
### AVILA BEACH TO SANTA BARBARA

The south central coast is a region unto itself. Although it's geographically part of southern California, its residents don't identify with the great Los Angeles-to-San Diego sprawl below them.

This region is comprised primarily of two counties—San Luis Obispo and Santa Barbara, each with a county seat of the same name. These mid-size cities provide sufficient commercial, leisure and cultural facilities to keep residents of this area quite content. The counties are blessed with benign climates, scenic mountains, pretty seacoasts and even fine wines. What more could a populace want? This self-sufficient region is generally overlooked by the California mainstream—a fact that undoubtedly pleases most of the locals.

While not heavily populated, these are not uncrowded areas. The city of San Luis Obispo has 42,000 residents; Santa Barbara has twice that number and it's a major tourist destination. However, our route through these two prosperous counties will steer you away from heavy traffic and crowds—particularly if you run this course on a weekday. Even in peak summer, we didn't encounter excessive traffic.

## AVILA BEACH AND PORT SAN LUIS

**Population: About 1,000**                    **Elevation: sea level**

We'll begin with a seaside resort just south of San Luis Obispo that was—until recently—a charming vision in art deco. Avila Beach was established in the 1880s as a tiny coastal retreat. Then in the 1930s, it became a virtual company town of Union Oil, used as a major petroleum shipping terminal. Because its south-facing beach was sheltered from chilly winds, its popularity as a resort continued. However, most of the beach crowds were drawn to the more famous Santa Barbara and Pismo Beach, so Avila has remained small and quaint.

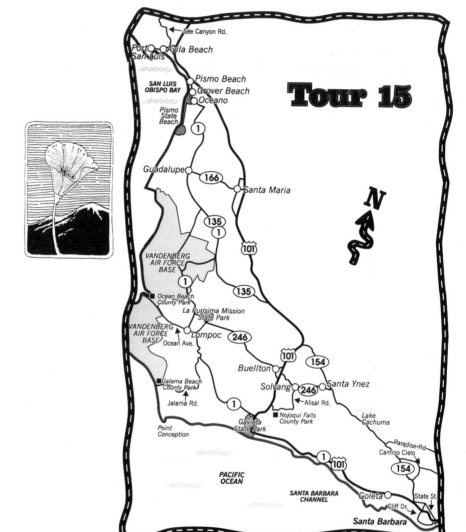

Several years ago, residents learned to their dismay that pipelines leading to the loading piers had been leaking for decades, creating a bog of oil-soaked soil beneath the town. A study conducted in 1997 confirmed that no immediate health hazards exist and Unocal has agreed to spend millions to clean up its mess. The cleanup requires the removal of several 1930s style buildings along the seafront, since they sit atop the oil bog. This process began in 1998 and structures are being replaced as the soil is cleaned. (The area also has a second environmentally questionable tenant, the Diablo Canyon nuclear generating plant. However, it has thus far caused no problems.)

Despite its dilemma, Avila Beach is still an appealing place for visitors. Many old seafront shops and cafés are still here and hopefully the replacement buildings will retain the quaint 1930s look. The long curving beach—declared free of any health risks—is as warm and inviting as it has been for generations. Just north of that beach is Port San Luis, another charming old settlement. It has not suffered an oil soaking so life there continues as usual.

To reach the Avila Beach-Port San Luis area, take San Luis Bay Drive if you're coming from the north on Freeway 101, or Avila Beach Drive if you're coming from the south.

## Brief side trip: See Canyon

If you're here in the fall, turn north from San Luis Bay Drive onto See Canyon Road and you'll encounter several apple ranches that sell fresh-off-the-tree fruit. This a pretty drive any time of the year, through thickly wooded oaks, madrones and orchards. The road is rather narrow and winding for large motorhomes and trailer rigs, and you'll hit gravel after about five miles. However, the apple outlets are on the paved section.

Back on the main road, you'll soon arrive in appealing little Avila Beach, with its modest pastel colored wood frame and stucco homes, cafés and shops. A concrete promenade rims its crescent bay.

Charmingly funky old Port San Luis is a couple of miles north. Not really a town, it's a small working seaport with a pier, a couple of fish processing plants and a commercial fishing fleet. Stroll out onto the pier and you'll encounter a fine seafood restaurant, fish markets and a public fish cleaning station. Expect to see an occasional sea lion bobbing about in the water below.

If you'd like to discover a really private beach—during low tide at least—scramble along the rocks to the right of the main Port San Luis parking lot. You'll soon encounter a small bit of sand sheltered from the rest of the world. There's also great tidepooling areas in the rocks. Check tidal charts, since the beach can disappear during high tide.

---

***RV PARKING ADVISORY*** ● Parking slots are angular on Avila Beach's Front Street so RVs won't fit, although there's plenty of parking on nearby streets. Port San Luis has a large parking area with room for RVs and trailer rigs. Cars can drive onto the pier, but it won't accommodate RVs or trailers and turn-around space is limited.

---

## DINING

**Fat Cats Restaurant** • *Port San Luis; (805) 595-2204. American; wine and beer. Open twenty-four hours. MC/VISA, AMEX.* ☐ Across the parking lot from the pier, this small Spanish style cottage specializes in huge servings of fish and chips, plus fried clams, prawns or scallops, hamburgers and assorted sandwiches. Try the *huevos rancheros* to start your day, or the special dessert of graham cracker crust cheesecake with boysenberry topping to end it. The "Cat" has an attractive outdoor patio.

**Louie's on the Pier** • *Port San Luis pier; (805) 595-7089. American; mostly seafood; wine and beer. Lunch to early evening daily except Tuesday; $.* ☐ Handy for quick bites, this small café features fish, calamari or shrimp & chips, and combinations thereof, plus hamburgers and several tortilla-wrapped items. You can take your food to picnic tables outside and watch life on the pier.

**Olde Port Inn** • *Port San Luis pier; (805) 595-2515. American; mostly seafood; full bar service. MC/VISA, AMEX; $$$.* ☐ This long established nautically styled restaurant is earning raves for its fine fare. The California Writers Association recently named it one of the state's top ten seafood restaurants. Specialties include cioppino, blackened fresh fish, bacon wrapped and cheese stuffed prawns, and spicy Mexican prawns sautéed in with olive oil, garlic and jalapeño peppers. The nautically attractive café has three dining areas—upstairs with good aquatic views, downstairs before an open kitchen and on a wind-sheltered deck.

## RECLINING

**The Inn at Avila Beach** • *P.O. Box 328 (256 Front St.), Avila Beach, CA 93424; (805) 595-2300. Rooms and suites with TV/VCRs and phones. MC/VISA; $$$$ to $$$$$.* ☐ This small, inviting Mediterranean style inn is just a few paces from the sand in downtown Avila Beach. Most units have bay views and many have kitchenettes or refrigerators and private decks. The décor is Mexican-Mediterranean.

**San Luis Bay Inn** • *P.O. Box 189, Avila Beach, CA 93424; (800) 438-6493 or (805) 595-2333. Condo style units with full kitchens; $$$$$. Mulligan's Bar & Grill serves breakfast through dinner; full bar service; $$$. Major credit cards.* ☐ Sitting on a bluff above Avila Beach and Port San Luis, this attractive Spanish style inn has been converted to timeshare condos. However, non-members can rent the units as well. Facilities include a pool, spa and gym, salon and an 18-hole golf course with a pro shop. The restaurant, which offers bay views, serves American fare ranging from breast of duck to currently fresh fish.

**Sycamore Mineral Springs Resort** • *1215 Avila Beach Dr., San Luis Obispo, CA 93405; (800) 234-5831 or (805) 595-7302. (WEB SITE: www.sycamoresprings.com; E-MAIL: info@smsr.com) Luxury units with phones, TV, mineral spa tubs and private decks or balconies; rates include breakfast credit; $$$$$. Gardens of Avila Restaurant serves California and continental fare; full bar service; (805) 595-7365; $$$. Major credit cards.* ☐ A landmark since 1897, this once rustic mineral spa between Avila

*Seagulls of a feather flock above the Port San Luis pier, a sign that a fishing boat is probably offloading its catch.*

Beach and Highway 101 has re-emerged as a gorgeous Spanish style resort. Tucked against a thickly wooded hillside, the lushly landscaped complex includes a swimming pool, spa and gift shop. Suites have VCRs, refrigerators and microwaves. Among restaurant specialties are seafood pasta with clams and scallops, halibut encrusted with fresh herbs and grilled salmon with jambalaya.

## CAMPING

RVs can park on a dirt lot just outside of Port San Luis, paying at a self-service fee station; **$$$**. There are no hookups or facilities other than a small deck, although the view of the bay is nice.

***Avila Hot Springs*** • *250 Avila Beach Dr., San Luis Obispo, CA 93405; (800) 332-2359 or (805) 595-2359. RV and tent sites; full hookups* **$$$$**. *Major credit cards.* ☐ This old, relatively well-kept resort has a large mineral pool, mini-mart, snack bar and rec hall. It's located just off Highway 101.

# Avila Beach to Solvang

From Avila Beach, we'll steer you on a rather convoluted route that generally follows Coast Highway 1. We'll keep you off busy Freeway 101 and away from crowds—at least until you hit the popular Danish style community of Solvang.

Head west on Avila Beach Drive and, just short of the freeway, turn right onto Palisades Road. It soon becomes Shell Beach Road and takes you past rows of prim seaside homes. For a look at the beachfront and some quite elegant mansions, turn right at a stop sign onto Vista del Mar, follow it several blocks to Ocean Boulevard and swing left. The boulevard passes a couple of blocks of open ocean with parking areas and beach access, then swings inland past some quite posh seaside homes. This brief beach loop turns left again, taking you back to Shell Beach Road.

Continuing south, you'll shortly enter the old fashioned resort of **Pismo Beach,** famous for its clams, although it's just about clammed out. However, it's still popular as a family vacation spot. For a look at its 1930s art deco style beach area with its surf and swimsuit shops, fish and chips cafés and souvenir stores, turn right down one-way Pomeroy Avenue. This takes you to the old Pismo Pier and a public parking lot.

---

*RV PARKING ADVISORY* • Double-length spots in the parking lot can accommodate RVs and trailer rigs, but don't expect to find much space in summer, particularly on weekends.

---

Pass through the parking lot, turn left and return to the main drive, which has now become Dolliver Street and State Highway 1. Immediately on your right is the **Pismo Beach Chamber of Commerce,** open Monday-Saturday 9 to 5 and Sunday 10 to 4; (805) 773-4382.

About a mile beyond, you'll encounter the campground for **Pismo State Beach,** which has well-spaced and shaded sites just across a wooded dune area from the seashore. It has flush potties and no hookups; **$$$**. Sites fill up in summer and on most weekends the year around, although they can be reserved by calling (800) 444-PARK; MC/VISA.

Pressing southward on Highway 1, you'll hit **Grover Beach,** where you can follow Grand Avenue west to another section of Pismo State Beach. This is the **Oceano Dunes State Vehicle Recreation Area,** where folks can drive on the hard-packed beach sand. In fact, they can drive several miles down the beach and exit at the town of Oceano.

---

*BEACH DRIVING ADVISORY* • Beach driving is "not recommended for highway vehicles," according to a sign, although all sorts of rigs including motorhomes are driven onto the sand. Once out there, you can camp in designated areas for a very modest fee. Beach driving should be done only on hard packed sand. If you get stuck in loose sand—and plenty of people do—it's rather expensive to get towed free. AAA tow trucks won't go out there; the park service has a contract with a local towing firm and it's rather expensive.

---

South of Grover Beach you'll encounter—either via the beach drive or Highway 1—quaint little **Oceano,** which has a few surf shops and cafés. On the south side of town, watch on your right for a cleverly fashioned restaurant:

**Rock 'n' Roll Diner** • *1300 Railroad Ave. (Highway 1); (805) 473-2040. American; wine and beer. Lunch through dinner weekdays; breakfast through dinner weekends. Major credit cards; $$.* ◻ Not just another nostalgic diner, the Rock 'n' Roll is housed in a pair gleaming stainless steel rail passenger cars. It's back to the Fifties inside with Marilyn and Elvis posters, Naugahyde booths and chrome rimmed tables and chairs, trimmed in cheerful red and white. The menu is more contemporary, featuring—in addition to 'burgers and shakes—pork chops with lemon and garlic, popcorn shrimp, and a barbecue combo of tri-tip, fried chicken and beef ribs. There's a small patio in the rear.

Below Oceano, the highway swings away from the coast and travels through a patchwork produce farming area backgrounded by low, tawny hills. You can tell by the smell that most of the produce produced here is cabbage. **Guadalupe** is a predominately Mexican agricultural community with a mix of Spanish and turn-of-the-century American architecture. On the far side of town, note the old fashioned Hispanic cemetery with elaborate statues and tombstones over the graves.

About ten miles below Guadalupe, this little-traveled highway becomes a freeway, although the traffic doesn't appear to warrant it. Perhaps it was built to provide quick access to **Vandenberg Air Force Base**. It covers much of the coastal bulge of Point Conception to the west and south of here. Vandenberg is a major missile testing center and area residents often are treated to night visions of fiery launches.

Stay with Highway 1 as this odd little freeway complex makes a couple of twists and turns. Then, about two miles after you've brushed past Vandenberg's main gate, leave Route 1 at a freeway interchange, following signs to the left toward La Purisima Mission. The freeway ends and becomes Purisima Road.

**La Purisima Mission State Historic Park** • *2295 Purisima Rd., Lompoc, CA 93436; (805) 733-3713 or 733-1303. Daily 9 to 5; modest admission fee.* ☐ This is one of California's most authentically preserved Spanish missions—for a curious reason. Abandoned and in ruins, it was restored from 1934 through 1941 as a project of the Depression era Civilian Conservation Corps. Workers used tools similar to those employed by Indians who had built the original mission under padre supervision. As a result of the extensive restoration, it's the largest mission complex in the state, yet it's one of the least visited. Facilities consist of two whitewashed adobe outbuildings with museum exhibits (including a display concerning the "CCC boys"), and a main mission quadrangle with two chapels, several shops and sleeping quarters.

For your day's workout, follow a trail from the right side of the parking lot about a third of a mile up to *Vista de la Cruz,* a hilltop cross. It provides an overview of the mission and a fine vista of a neat patchwork quilt of produce and flower fields beyond. This area is noted for its commercial flower farms, which present a brilliant show from spring through summer.

As you exit the state park, go straight across the highway onto Mission Gate Road. Drive about a mile past some of the floral fields, then turn right (southwest) onto State Route 246. It becomes Ocean Avenue as it heads for **Lompoc**, where you'll rejoin Highway 1. This city of 41,000 residents—many of them working at Vandenberg—is not a tourist mecca. However, its old fashioned downtown area is worth a look for its fine historic murals. In fact, it's one of the best collections we've seen in Western America. The tree-shaded Spanish style city center is quite prim and inviting, although it has lost most of its business to the suburbs.

If you'd like to pause for refreshment, the **Southside coffee Shop** at H Street (Highway 1) and Ocean Avenue has the usual specialty coffees, bagels and such. Its interior appears to be an extension of the surrounding antique shops, busy with collectibles and old posters.

A nine-mile drive west on Ocean Avenue will take you through a corridor of Vandenberg Air Force Base (no stopping, please) to **Ocean Beach County Park**. This is a day use area with picnic tables and small wetland at the mouth of the Santa Ynez River, usually populated by several waterbirds. A short walk across a railroad track takes you to a long sandy beach.

Our next stop is the Danish village of Solvang, which can be reached by heading eastbound on Highway 246, from Lompoc through Buellton. However, we'll go the long way around, on a scenic drive through more of this hilly and oak-clad headland of Point Conception.

Return to Lompoc on Ocean Avenue, following Highways 1 and 146 west through town, then take Highway 1 south. Several miles from town, a winding fourteen-mile drive will take you to **Jalama Beach**, a very isolated yet thoroughly equipped county park. The drive itself is appealing—through rumpled, oak-clustered beige hills, past pasturelands and isolated ranches. The park is tucked into the base of a headland, nicely landscaped and with a crescent beach beyond. Its extensive facilities include a small store and café, showers and recreation areas. Despite its remoteness, it's quite popular and reservations are recommended. Contact Jalama Beach County Park, Star Route, Lompoc, CA 93436; (805) 736-3504; WEB SITE: www.sbparks.com. Water and electric hookups **$$$$**; tent sites **$$$**.

Back on Highway 1, another scenic fifteen miles will deliver you to busy U.S. 101 freeway. Unless you want to visit large **Gaviota Beach State Park** just to the south, take the northbound on-ramp. After two and a half miles, watch for a small brown "Nojoqui Park" sign and turn right. This puts you on Alisal Road, a winding lane often canopied with oaks, which are bearded with Spanish moss.

At pleasant little **Nojoqui Falls County Park**, you can follow a short trail to Nojoqui Falls, a silvery thread spilling over a rock face. It's often dry from summer through fall, although the walk alongside an oak-shaded creek bed is pleasant. From the park, the road passes the elegant **Alisal Ranch Resort**. The route then follows the resort's gorgeous creekside golf courses into the mountain-rimmed Santa Ynez Valley, and into the side door of its most famous attraction:

## SOLVANG

**Population: 3,500**                                    **Elevation: 495 feet**

It started innocently enough. In 1911, a group of Danish immigrants came to farm, build a community and establish a folk school to preserve their old world heritage. Tourists began coming to little Solvang—which means "sunny field"—drawn by its Scandinavian architecture. So of course, residents opened bakeries, restaurants and European import shops to lure more visitors.

The tourists kept coming and the shops kept opening and today, Solvang probably the most visited "theme town" in California. It's all here, in wonderful Scandinavian excess—scores of shops in cross-timbered buildings, Scandinavian style service stations and motels, restaurants overflowing with *smorgasbord* and *aebleskivers*, and Danish windmills that pump no water. With its growing popularity, the Scandinavian atmosphere has been intensified and yet diluted. You can dine at the Bit O' Denmark Café or the Big Bopper; you can shop in places that sell Copenhagen crystal or T-shirts.

If you followed us through the town's side door, you missed the **Solvang Visitor Bureau.** To reach it, continue on Alisal Road to Mission Drive (Highway 246) and turn left. The visitor center is about five blocks west, in a small but imposing circular brick building on your right, at Mission and Fifth Street. It's open daily 10 to 4; (805) 688-6144. If you're here in summer, you'll also find a visitor kiosk in Solvang Park on Mission and First. In addition to its shops and cafés, Solvang has three specific lures:

**Elverhoj Museum** • *1624 Elverhoy Way; (805) 686-1211. Wednesday-Sunday 1 to 4; modest admission charge.* ☐ Occupying the former home of a prominent Solvang family, this fine museum is located in a residential area a few blocks from the shopping district. You can get directions at the visitor center. Exhibits include several furnished rooms, Danish artifacts and a gallery of works by local artists. Particularly striking is a traditional Danish country kitchen with hand-painted floral designs on its wall panels and cabinet doors.

**Hans Christian Andersen Museum** • *In the Book Loft at 1680 Mission Dr.; (805) 686-9770. Daily 9 to late afternoon; free.* ☐ A small but nice exhibit concerning the great Danish storyteller is upstairs in the this combined book store and coffee house near the heart of town. Displays include original photos (old Hans was rather homely), early editions of his books and graphics about his life.

**Old Mission Santa Inés** • *1760 Mission Dr.; (805) 688-4815. Daily 9 to 7 in summer and 9 to 5:30 the rest of the year. Modest admission fee.* ☐ Historical coincidence placed this Spanish mission next door to the Danish style village. The mission came first of course. It's one of California's original twenty-one, founded in 1804. Now completely rimmed by the town, it has a museum with early church artifacts and an elegantly simple chapel that provides welcome retreat from the Solvang hubbub.

## DINING

When in Denmark—? Although you can get Chinese, Italian and trendy American nouveau fare in Solvang (not to mention 'burgers at the Big Bopper), we come here for Danish food. These are our favorites:

**Bit O' Denmark** • *437 Alisal Rd.; (805) 688-5426. Danish and American; full bar service. Breakfast through dinner daily. MC/VISA; $$.* ☐ Well of course it's touristy, but it's also the oldest and perhaps the best Danish restaurant in town. Try the traditional *aebleskivers* (muffin-like pancakes) for breakfast and *smorgasbord* (open faced sandwiches) for lunch. At dinner, you can choose from a few American dishes or Danish meatballs, roast duck with sweet and sour cabbage and other Scandinavian fare. And of course the restaurant has that appealing old world Danish look.

**Little Mermaid** • *1846 Mission Dr. (near Fourth); (805) 688-6141. Danish and American; wine and beer. Breakfast through dinner daily. MC/VISA; $$.* ☐ This charming little café serves the best *aebleskivers* in town. You can watch them being made in the morning at an *aebleskiver* booth in a corner of the dining room. For dinner, try the roast pork with red cabbage and applesauce, or steak with onions and pan-fried potatoes. Meals here are ample and rather inexpensive.

**Solvang Bakery** • *460 Alisal Rd.; (805) 688-4939. Danish and American; mostly bakery goods; no alcohol. Breakfast through early evening daily. MC/VISA; $.* ☐ More of a bakery than a café, this savory place is packed with diet-wrecking goodies. They range from traditional Danish cookies and candied fruit bread rings to every kind of cake, pastry, cookie and specialty bread that your taste buds can imagine. A small and quite cute dining area serves light Danish and American fare, or you can order bakery savories, accompanied by coffee or tea.

### RECLINING

Solvang has a score or more motels, with predictable names like Kronborg Inn, King Frederik Inn and Svendsgaard's Danish Lodge. If you're an AAA member, you'll find a long list in the California/Nevada TourBook. If not, you can get a longer list from the visitors bureau. Beyond the half-timbered motels, two places are particularly appealing:

**Alisal Guest Ranch and Resort** • *1054 Alisal Rd., Solvang, CA 93463; (800) 425-4725 or (805) 688-6411. (WEB SITE: www.alisal.com) Seventy-three elegantly furnished studios and suites with fireplaces and full resort amenities. MC/VISA, AMEX; rates include breakfast and dinner; $$$$$.* ☐ This 10,000-acre spread dates from the 1700s as a land grant to a Spanish conquistador. It's now one of California's most opulent hideaways, with two golf courses, tennis courts, swimming pool and spa, a private fishing lake and even a ranch petting zoo. And of course, you can saddle up and head into the hills. The Ranch Room restaurant serves California *nouveau* fare; lunch and dinner daily; full bar service.

**Storybook Inn Bed & Breakfast** • *409 First St. (Oak), Solvang, CA 93463; (800) 786-7925 in California or (805) 688-1703. Nine units with private baths and TV; continental breakfast. Major credit cards; $$$$ to $$$$$.* ☐ A short walk from downtown, this large tile-roofed European style inn is elegantly furnished with antiques. Individually decorated rooms have canopy, sleigh or four-poster beds; eight have fireplaces.

### CAMPING

**Cachuma Lake County Park** • *Highway 154 on Lake Cachuma; (805) 686-5055. RV and tent sites; hookups $$$$. MC/VISA, DISC.* ☐ This large county park has shaded sites—some well-spaced and some rather snug—with tables and barbecue grills, flush potties and showers. It also offers boating, boat rentals, a general store, gift shop and service station. Although it often fills up in summer, we found plenty of space on a fall weekend.

*Santa Ynez Recreation Area* ● *In Los Padres National Forest above Solvang. RV and tent sites; $$. Sites can be reserved with a MC/VISA by calling (800) 280-CAMP.* ☐ The Santa Ynez Recreation Area along Paradise Road has several campgrounds with shaded sites, picnic tables and barbecue grills. Some have flush and some have pit potties.

## A valley of wine

In recent decades, the Santa Ynez Valley has become a serious wine producing area. Nearly a dozen wineries with tasting rooms are within a short drive of Solvang. You can pick up a detailed map-brochure at the Solvang Visitor Bureau, or contact: Santa Barbara County Vintners' Association, P.O. Box 1558, Santa Ynez, CA 93460; (800) 218-0881 or (805) 688-0881. You also can stop by the association's office at 3669 Sagunto Street in Santa Ynez, just east of Solvang.

Our statewide winery guide, *The Best of the Wine Country*, lists all of the wineries with tasting rooms in the Santa Ynez Valley and elsewhere in the south central coast. It's available at book stores or it can be ordered directly; see the back of this book for details.

## Into the hills: Solvang to Santa Barbara

This is certainly a region of contrasts. The Danish-style community of Solvang is surrounded by ranches and vineyards, and just to the west are the oak and pine-thatched Santa Ynez Mountains.

To complete this wandering itinerary through the south central coast, head east from Solvang on Highway 246 into the heart of the Santa Ynez Valley. You'll pass the small town of **Santa Ynez** and shortly intersect with State Route 154. A right turn will take you high into the Santa Ynez Mountains and to the ragged blue oval of **Lake Cachuma**. Watch on your left for a vista point that provides a view of the lake and its earthfill Bradbury Dam. Continuing onward and upward, you'll pass **Cachuma Lake County Park**; see above.

The road rims the lake for several miles. Just beyond water's end, a turn left onto Paradise Road will take you into Los Padres National Forest's **Santa Ynez Recreation Area** with hiking trails, several campgrounds and picnic sites; see above. Pressing upward, you'll cross Cold Spring Canyon on Cold Spring Arch Bridge, which is much higher than it appears from a vehicle's vantage point. If you'd like to follow the squiggly "pre-bridge" spiral into the canyon, pick up Stagecoach Road back at the Paradise Road junction. It parallels Highway 54 for a couple of miles and then twists down into ravine. Taking this route, you'll understand why the bridge was built. At the bottom is delightful **Ye Cold Spring Tavern,** once a stagecoach stop and now a pleasingly funky restaurant with a rather contemporary menu; (805) 967-0066.

Squirming back up the other side, you'll rejoin Highway 154 and soon crest 2,224-foot San Marcos Pass. This vantage point provides a splendid vista of the Santa Barbara coastline and—on a good day—the Channel Islands far out to sea. This view will stay with you for much of the winding route down out of the mountains.

---

*RV ADVISORIES* • Stagecoach Road down to Ye Cold Spring Tavern is narrow and twisting, not recommended for large motorhomes or trailers. This goes double for the road to Painted Cave (below), which is very skinny, steep and winding with many hairpin turns. It's not advised for any rig much over twenty feet and definitely not for trailers or fifth wheel units. Further, it's not recommended for timid drivers in any sort of vehicle!

---

## Side trip: Chumash Painted Cave

Just beyond San Marcos Pass, Camino Cielo, a road as twisty as a stepped-on snake, follows the crest of the Santa Ynez Mountains, passing dozens of tucked-away forest homes. After two miles, a right turn onto Painted Cave Road will take you to **Chumash Painted Cave,** an undeveloped state historic park. Within the cave—just over a mile down the road on your right and not easy to spot—are several rock paintings done centuries ago by the Chumash Indians.

The narrow, coiling road provides grand views of Santa Barbara and the Channel Islands as it hugs the outer slope of the mountains. After a few more miles of twists and turns, it re-joins the highway.

At the bottom of Highway 154's steep descent from the Santa Ynez Mountains, you'll enter the side door of **Santa Barbara.** One of the most popular tourist spots on the West Coast, and with a population of more than 87,000, this is hardly a place less crowded. We won't cover its many attractions, restaurants and resorts here, since an abundance of information is available on this handsome Spanish style city from other sources. However, we will spell out an interesting driving route through this city—not necessarily traffic-free—that will show off some of its best features.

## Driving Santa Barbara

As you approach on Highway 154, cross over 101 freeway and go left onto State Street. Now, cross back over the freeway, go right onto La Cumbre Road and cross the freeway yet another time by staying straight ahead on La Cumbre. (This is less complicated than it sounds.) La Cumbre blends into Las Palmas Road, which takes you through **Hope Ranch**, a headland that houses a contemporary edition of the landed gentry. (This isn't how the other half lives. This is how the top one tenth of one percent of multi-millionaires with the good sense to choose Santa Barbara live.)

The road descends from this thickly wooded headland and heads for the Santa Barbara beachfront. The attractive enclave of **Arroyo Burro Beach,** a county park on your right, has a parking area and beach access. If it's mealtime, pause at the adjacent **Brown Pelican Restaurant** with tables practically over the sand. It's open for breakfast through dinner daily; (805) 687-4550.

Continue past Arroyo Burro for a few blocks to a stop sign and blend onto Cliff Drive. After one mile and two traffic signals, go right on Meigs Road, which drops down few blocks toward the beach. Swing left onto

*Santa Barbara occupies one of the prettiest settings on the California coast, with a palm lined beachfront and bold mountains rising beyond.*

Shoreline Drive, which is Santa Barbara's grand beach promenade. It's flanked by a walking and biking trail and by Shoreline Park on a bluff above the ocean. After a few blocks, the street drops down to beach level and becomes Cabrillo Boulevard. Incidentally, if the sun seems to be in the wrong place, Santa Barbara's beach faces due south, twisted around by the bulge of Point Conception. Like the south-facing Avila Beach, it enjoys rather benign weather.

Depending on reconstruction progress, you may or may not be able to explore **Stearns Wharf,** a public fishing pier with seafood restaurants and curio shops. This longtime Santa Barbara landmark was destroyed by fire in late 1998. If it has been rebuilt when you arrive, it's a great place to stroll above the surf without getting your feet wet. You'll enjoy views seaward to the Channel Islands and landward to Spanish tile-roofed Santa Barbara hugging its coastal shelf, beneath green-clad mountains.

Continuing along Cabrillo Boulevard, you'll pass **Santa Barbara Zoological Garden** on your left, followed by three upscale beachfront hotels—Santa Barbara Inn, Cabrillo Inn and the Radisson Hotel Santa Barbara. Beyond these digs, Cabrillo swings away from the beach, wraps around the opulent Four Seasons Santa Barbara Biltmore, and then hits a four-way stop. You can jump onto the freeway here, or go for one final stretch of Santa Barbara elegance. To do so, continue straight ahead and drive through the upscale commercial and residential area of **Coast Village.** After less than a mile, you finally must surrender to the freeway and drive out of this chapter.

☺  ☺  ☺

***Where do we go from here?*** ● U.S. 101 is a major north-south freeway, so pick a direction. By staying southbound, you'll wind up in Ventura County and our next tour.

# TRIP PLANNER

**WHEN TO GO** • Ventura County is another all-year destination. Its best times are fall through late spring, since refugees from Los Angeles tend to crowd the area in summer.

**DRIVING DISTANCE** • Our amble around Ventura County, including a side trip up Wheeler Gorge, covers about eighty miles.

**RV ADVISORY** • Nothing on this route will inhibit an RV.

**WHAT YOU'LL SEE** • The artsy resort community of Ojai and its Ojai Valley Museum, Santa Paula Union Oil Museum, historic downtown Ventura and its Mission San Buenaventura, Ventura Harbor and Channel Islands National Park Visitor Center, and Channel Islands Harbor.

**WHAT TO DO** • Rent a boat and play on Lake Casitas; explore the Sespe Mountain wilderness; watch the "Pink Moment" in the Ojai Valley; stroll the Ventura pier; play in the surf and sand at one or more the county's many state beaches; catch a tour boat to Channel Islands National Park.

**ADVENTURE PASSES** • A pilot program requiring the purchase of an "Adventure Pass" for southern California national forests was started as we went to press; for details, see Tour Fifteen, page 208.

**TO BEGIN** • Get south of Santa Barbara on U.S. 101.

## Useful contacts

**Greater Oxnard and Harbors Tourism Bureau,** 200 W. Seventh St., Oxnard, CA 93030-7154; (800) 2-OXNARD or (805) 385-7545. (E-MAIL: oxtour@west.net) Ask for a copy of the *Scenic Coastal Drive,* which follows much of the route in this tour.

**Greater Ventura Chamber of Commerce,** 785 S. Seaward Ave., Ventura, CA 93001; (805) 648-2875.

**Ojai Visitors Center,** P.O. Box 1134 (150 W. Ojai Ave.), Ojai, CA 93024; (805) 646-8126. (WEB SITE: www.the-ojai.org; E-MAIL: the-ojai@jetlink.net)

**Santa Paula Chamber of Commerce,** Tenth and Santa Paula streets, Santa Paula, CA 93060; (805) 525-5561.

## Pricing guidelines

**DINING:** Dinner entrée with soup or salad, without drinks or dessert for under $10 = **$**; $10 to $14 = **$$**; $15 to $25 = **$$$**; over $25 = **$$$$**.

**RECLINING:** A two-person room for $35 or less = **$**; $36 to $50 = **$$**; $51 to $75 = **$$$**; $76 to $100 = **$$$$**; more than $100 = **$$$$$**.

**CAMPING:** Under $10 = **$**; $10 to $14 = **$$**; $15 to $19 = **$$$**; $20 or more = **$$$$**

## *Tour Sixteen*

# VENTURA VENTURE

### *EXPLORING A COMPLEX COUNTY*

---

**V**entura County is an appealing region of interesting towns, wilderness mountains and sunny seacoasts. It is greatly coveted by millions of Los Angelinos desperately seeking respite from smog and traffic. It also is a thriving, growing area and—like San Luis Obispo and Santa Barbara counties in the previous tour—it is not a place uncrowded. On summer weekends, when those Los Angelinos pour down the Ventura Freeway, it's definitely a place *crowded.*

However, the huddled Los Angeles masses leave poor Ventura County alone during much of the year. Residents then breathe a sigh of relief and go about their business of living the good life in this land of beaches, marinas, mountains and citrus groves.

I'm well acquainted with this area, having lived in Ventura for five years while working for a county newspaper. In something of a departure from the rest of the tours in this book, we have fashioned for you a Ventura County scenic drive. It doesn't always avoid crowds although it takes you to the kinds of places that Venturans themselves enjoy.

Don't try this on a summer weekend.

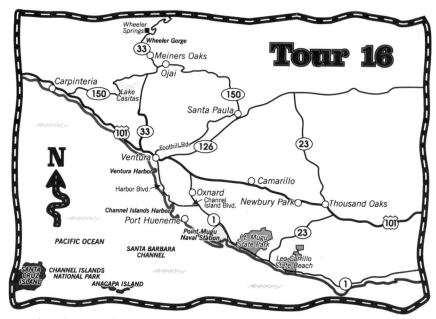

Tour 16

If you've just finished Tour Fifteen, you can blend easily into this one. Heading south from Santa Barbara on U.S. 101, take the State Route 150 exit toward Ojai, following a shallow creek canyon into low hills mantled with oaks and orange groves. About fifteen miles into the drive, you'll crest a ridge and see below—rimmed by thick woods—a very convincing looking mountain lake. However, it's an artificial pond and it had its fifteen minutes of fame in 1984 as the rowing venue for the Los Angeles Olympics. Continue along this wooded route and you'll shortly arrive at the entrance:

**Lake Casitas Recreation Area** • *11311 Santa Ana Rd., Ventura, CA 93001; (805) 649-2233; camping reservations (805) 649-1122. Modest day use fee; tent sites $$$; water and electric sites $$$$.* ❑ Lake Casitas spreads its liquid fingers through acres of hilly woodlands, providing lots of hidden bays for boaters and fisherpersons. Facilities include several camping sites among gnarled oaks, a snack bar, bait and tackle shop, boat launch and rentals and lakeside picnic areas. Campgrounds fill up most weekends, including spring and summer; reservations are recommended.

A couple of miles beyond the recreation area turnoff, Highway 150 blends into State Route 33, which takes you into an idyllic town that once was a stand-in for Shangri-La. For many residents, it's the real thing:

## OJAI

**Population: 7,905**                    **Elevation: 750 feet**

This art colony occupies a mountain-rimmed valley that film producer Frank Capra supposedly used in his long shots as the setting for *Lost Horizons* in 1937. Some historians dispute this, although it would have been appropriate, for the mythical Shangri-La was a land of eternal youth.

Since its founding in the 1870s, Ojai has attracted health-seekers, meta-physical muses and other esoteric types.

Among the organizations tucked into the valley's orange groves and oak forests are the Krotona Institute of Theosophy, the Krishnamurti Foundation and the Happy Valley School, which was founded by Aldous Huxley. The Krotona and Krishnamurti facilities are open to visitors; you can get hours and directions from the Ojai Visitor Center; see below.

Historians disagree on the meaning of Ojai's odd name, which may be a Chumash Indian word either for "the nest" or "the moon." Enthusiasts have capitalized on this dispute by calling Ojai "the place of the nesting moon," which is a bit overdone. Actually it's the sun—more specifically the sunset—that gives the Ojai Valley its best moment, and it's even pink. The fading sun's rays strike the face of a bold promontory called Topatopa, turning it to a soft blush, particularly in fall and winter. Many residents pause each evening to stare at the bluffs and enjoy their "Pink Moment."

With nesting moons and pink moments, Ojai obviously is a place for utopian thinkers. For the casual visitor, it's simply a nice place to walk around and enjoy. The tree-shrouded town is rich in Spanish and Moorish architecture and you can pick up a walking tour guide at the **Ojai Visitor Center**. It's downtown at 150 W. Ojai Avenue; weekdays 9:30 to 4:30 and weekends 10 to 4; (805) 646-8126.

Highway 33 becomes Ojai Avenue as it enters town and some of the best architectural examples are right on the main stem. Note the California-mission style former Catholic church on your left at 130 West Ojai Avenue, now housing the **Ojai Valley Museum.** It features displays on the area's history and exhibits of local artists. Most notable among these are the lustrous glazed pottery and whimsical figurines of local and international art legend Beatrice Wood, who died in 1998 at the age of 102. The museum is open Wednesday-Sunday 1 to 4; (805) 646-2290.

A couple of blocks beyond is Ojai's classic landmark, a Moorish domed structure that houses—of all things—the post office. Across the street is the block-long mission revival style Arcade, lined with boutiques and galleries. Both the post office and Arcade were built in 1917 to give the town a Mediterranean look. Another interesting stop, noted not for its architecture but for its huge book selection, is **Bart's Books,** northwest of downtown at Cañada and Matilija. This large indoor-outdoor book store has more than 100,000 titles lining tree-sheltered shelves.

A fine time to visit is during the Ojai Music Festival in late May or early June. Held in an outdoor bowl in Libby Park, it features works ranging from classics and *avant-garde* to jazz; (805) 646-2094.

## DINING

*Boccali's Pizza and Pasta* ● *3277 E. Ojai Ave. (two miles east of town); (805) 646-6116. Italian; wine and beer. Lunch and dinner Wednesday-Sunday and dinner only Monday-Tuesday. No credit cards.* ☐ The Boccali family has been serving hefty pasta dinners and tasty pizzas in this country cottage restaurant for a many decades. Locals crowd into the cozy interior and spill onto a large patio to devour pounds of raviolis, spaghetti, eggplant Parmesan and lasagna.

*The Moorish dome of the post office building is a popular landmark in the art colony of Ojai*

**Gaël's Café-Restaurant** • *423 E. Ojai Ave.; (805) 646-8235. American regional; wine and beer. Lunch and dinner daily. MC/VISA;* ***$$****.* ⌑ This trendy looking bistro with Southwest style salmon and turquoise décor offers an interesting and varied menu. It ranges from trout stuffed with crab meat and veal osso bucco to barbecued pork ribs. Gaël's has two dining rooms, one open to the street and another balconied above a cozy cocktail lounge, plus a few sidewalk tables.

**The Ranch House** • *South Lomita Avenue at Besa Road; (805) 646-2360. (WEB SITE: www.theranchhouse.com) Eclectic menu; wine and beer. Dinner Wednesday-Sunday, plus Sunday brunch; reservations essential. Major credit cards;* ***$$$$****.* ⌑ Hardly a ranch house, this is a casually elegant restaurant tucked into a lush jungle of ferns, palms and flowering plants, with a meandering garden stream and even a smiling Buddha. It features a changing, mixed menu that may wander from spicy Indonesian style beef and creatively prepared fresh fish to chicken in coconut milk.

**Sea Fresh Seafood** • *535 E. Ojai Ave.; (805) 646-7747. American; mostly seafood. Lunch and dinner daily. MC/VISA;* ***$$****.* ⌑ While not fancy, this combination fish market, restaurant and sushi bar lives up to its name, for the owners operate a fishing boat off the nearby coast. In addition to fresh fish of the day—which you can select from a seafood case—it features crabcakes, hot and spicy shrimp, seared *wasabe* crusted tuna and coconut prawns. It has seating indoors and on a heated patio.

For quick bites, try **Jim and Rob's Fresh Grill** adjacent to Sea Fresh Seafood, serving Mexican fare, including chili colorado and carnita asada; with patio seating; (805) 640-1301; MC/VISA; **$$**. For a light breakfast, try **Bill Baker's Bakery** at 457 E. Ojai Avenue, featuring German and American breads, pastries and cookies, plus specialty coffees. It has few tables inside and out; (805) 646-1558.

### RECLINING

**The Oaks at Ojai** • *122 E. Ojai Ave., Ojai, CA 93023; (800) 753-6257 or (805) 646-5573. (WEB SITE: www.oaksspa.com) Forty-two rooms, suites and cottages with phones and TV. MC/VISA, DISC; $$$$$ per person, including all meals.* ☐ Want to eat right, take off a few pounds and get in shape—right in downtown Ojai? The Oaks spa has comfortable rooms, a complete fitness program and all meals, starting under $150 per person. This fitness resort in the heart of town has a landscaped swimming area, spa and sauna, a pretty pink and salmon dining room and a cheerful floral-decorated lobby with a fireplace.

**Ojai Valley Inn and Spa** • *Country Club Road, Ojai, CA (800) 422-6524 or (805) 646-5511. (WEB SITE: www.ojairesort.com) Luxury resort with 207 rooms and suites with TV movies, phones and many amenities; $$$$$. Oak Café and Vista Dining Room serve American-continental fare; full bar service; breakfast through dinner and Sunday brunch; $$$. Major credit cards.* ☐ The largest and most stylish of several Ojai valley resorts, this long established retreat offers golf, tennis, a large health spa, hiking and biking trails, fishing and horseback riding. Dating from 1923 and recently renovated, the inn is surrounded by dozens of lushly landscaped acres.

### CAMPING

**Camp Comfort** • *Hermosa Road, off Highway 33 southwest of town. RV and tent sites; $$ to $$$.* ☐ Rather rustic, this small park and campground has close-together shaded sites with tables, barbecues, flush potties, a picnic area and playground. To reach it, go southeast from west Ojai Avenue for about a mile, then drive briefly right.

**Dennison Park** • *Four miles east of town on Highway 150; (805) 656-6753. RV and tent sites; no hookups; $$$.* ☐ This wooded park on Sulfur Mountain above the Ojai Valley has shaded, rather snugly spaced sites with flush potties, picnic tables and barbecue grills. Operated by the local Lions Club, it's just beyond the crest of Dennison Grade, on the right side of the highway.

**Los Padres National Forest** • Several Forest Service campgrounds are in the mountains north of Ojai. Particularly appealing is Wheeler Gorge Campground, set among gnarled oaks alongside a babbling brook, about eight miles north of Ojai on Highway 33. It has RV and tent sites with flush potties and no hookups; **$$$**. It fills up in summer and on many spring and fall weekends. Sites can be reserved with a Mastercard or VISA by calling (800) 280-CAMP.

## Side trip: Wheeler Gorge and the Los Padres wilds

The northern two-thirds of Ventura County is occupied by the mountainous and thickly wooded Los Padres National Forest, a popular playground for hikers, backpackers, campers and fisherpersons. State Route 33 winds through this area, eventually emerging into San Luis Obispo County. Thirty-seven miles up the highway, Lockwood Valley Road branches to the right and travels through this mountain wilderness for another thirty-four miles. It connects with Interstate 5 near Lebec, north of Los Angeles. The route is rather winding but all paved, and it can be handled by RVs and trailer rigs.

Tucked into a wilderness corner of this national forest is the Sespe Condor Sanctuary. Here, forestry officials and the National Audubon Society are attempting to save the last of the California condors, majestic if ugly birds with six-foot wingspans. They've just about died out and the few survivors were taken several years ago to the San Diego Wild Animal Park, where they're thriving and even having chicks. It's obviously a much better life than flying around, looking for dead things. The sanctuary isn't open to the public because some of the condors have been re-introduced.

If you'd like to sample a nice slice of Los Padres National Forest without committing to a major excursion, you can make a scenic sixteen-mile round trip from Ojai through Wheeler Gorge. Head north on Highway 33 from the western edge of town. You'll pass through an attractive suburb of Spanish style businesses and homes, followed by ordinary-looking **Meiners Oaks.**

Beyond here, the route follows Matilija Creek up a vee canyon that narrows dramatically as you press northward. After a few miles, the highway squeezes through steep-walled Wheeler Gorge, crawling through three tunnels along the route. Just north of the last tunnel is **Wheeler Gorge Campground,** the Forest Service site listed above under "Camping." You've seen the best of Wheeler Gorge, so this is a good turn-around point, unless you want to press higher into the Las Padres wilderness.

## Ojai to Santa Paula and Ventura

Back in town, head eastward on State Route 150 (Ojai Avenue) which travels through an appealing stretch of orange groves. At the base of Dennison Grade is the country cottage of **Boccali's Pizza and Pasta** that we recommended above. After a brief, winding climb, watch for a vista point on your right. It provides a fine view of the Ojai Valley's neat grid of orange groves and red-tile roofs and the distant mountains. This, according to a stone marker, is the very spot where Ronald Coleman stood—with Frank Capra at the camera—to stare in awe at his Shangri-La.

Just beyond, you'll crest the grade and pass **Dennison Park**, listed above, under "Camping." The highway then passes through a high, mountain-rimmed basin decorated with more orange groves, other fruit orchards and horse ranches. As you travel through this pretty valley, you'll get a closer look at those stratified Topatopa bluffs of Pink Moment fame.

The highway then begins a downhill spiral toward Santa Paula. At the start of the descent, you can see tar oozing from steep banks on the right side of the road. Supposedly, Chumash Indians gathered this seepage to make their boats water tight for cruising to the offshore Channel Islands.

This is indeed petroleum country; Union Oil Company—now Unocal— was founded just below in **Santa Paula.** However, the nearest drilling activity is farther east. Actually, the boom that launched Santa Paula in the late 1800s has subsided and most of the former oil lands are now covered with citrus groves.

As you descend into this modest, well-tended town of 11,000 folks, the highway swings slightly left to become Tenth Street. You'll soon see the **Santa Paula Chamber of Commerce** (weekdays 9 to 5) and adjacent Santa Paula Art Gallery (Thursday-Sunday noon to 4). They're both housed in a cute red former railway station. A couple of blocks beyond, you'll hit Main Street and an archive that tells the town's story:

**Santa Paula Union Oil Museum** ● *1001 E. Main St.; (805) 933-0076. Wednesday-Sunday 10 to 4. Free; donations appreciated.* ◻ The Union Oil Company began here in 1890 and this fine old red brick structure now houses a city-run museum. Much of the display focuses on Unocal, of course, with everything from old gasoline pumps to some early TV commercials. (Did you know that Marilyn Monroe once hyped for Union Oil?) One display concerns not the oil business, but one of America's greatest disasters. The St. Francis Dam above Santa Paula burst in 1928, sending a wall of water down the Santa Clara river bed through this and several other communities. Hundreds of homes were lost and 400 people died; it still stands as America's worst flood, in terms of lives lost.

From the museum, turn right onto Main Street and cruise through this low-rise mix of generally well-preserved old Spanish and American Fifties buildings. After about a mile of Santa Paula suburbs, Main Street T-bones into Peck Road. Go right and uphill for less than a mile and make a 90-degree left turn onto Foothill Road.

This aptly named country lane will carry you almost nonstop into **Ventura,** a handsome coastside community that is home to the county seat and one of California's earliest missions. However, this mini-city of 89,000 isn't the largest community in Ventura County. That distinction belongs to sprawling, ungainly but prosperous **Oxnard,** with nearly 145,000 residents. (The town's dumb name comes from Henry T. Oxnard, who started the sugar beet industry in the county a century ago.)

Your Foothill Road route takes you past orange groves and ultimately into Ventura suburbs, with views of the blue Pacific and the Channel Islands in the distance. (The paralleling Santa Paula Freeway will accomplish this trip, although it's not very interesting.) After more than ten miles of Foothill, turn left and downhill briefly on Seaward Avenue, then go right onto Main Street.

This takes you two miles through the heart of Ventura's well-tended downtown area and ultimately to the elegantly simple **San Buenaventura Mission** on your right. It will be difficult to imagine, as you admire this well-groomed structure surrounded by bustling Ventura, that it once

*A fancy carriage awaits a wedding party at the simple yet elegant Mission San Buenaventura.*

stood on a lonely meadow above the ocean. San Buenaventura ("The good venture") was the last outpost established by California's peripatetic mission father, Junipero Serra. He planted the holy cross here in 1782 and much of the present mission structure dates from 1809. The complex includes a nicely restored church, a small museum and Catholic school. The chapel and museum are open Monday-Saturday 10 to 5 and Sunday 10 to 4; (805) 648-4496.

Across the street is the city's main archive, housed—appropriately—in a mission style structure:

### Ventura County Museum of History and Art ● *100 E. Main St.; (805) 653-0323. Tuesday-Sunday 10 to 5; modest admission charge.* ☐ This professionally done museum traces the county's past from the native Chumash to the coming of the padres, oil and agriculture. Particularly impressive, although not related to the area, is a large exhibit of dressed miniature figurines of heroes, heroines and scoundrels of world history, done by local artist George Stuart. Out back is a collection of old farm machinery, labeled so that city folks can tell a bean cutter from a beet plow.

From the museum or mission, turn left onto any nearby side street, drop down to Thompson Avenue and go left again. After a few blocks, cross over the freeway on California Street, turn left yet again and continue southeast on Harbor Boulevard. The route takes you first past waterfront businesses, then along a sandy beachfront and finally to the elongated **Ventura Pier.** To reach it, you'll have to overshoot and double back on a frontage road to a parking lot for **San Buenaventura State Beach**. (The lot will accommodate RVs, for a special fee.) The pier has a couple of curio shops and the nautically trendy **Eric Ericsson's Restaurant**, which we've listed below, under "Dining." Much of this area is part of the state beach and the parking fee you just paid gives you access to a couple of miles of smooth sand and semi-active surf.

Continuing southeast along Harbor Boulevard, you can catch a glimpse of Ventura's original beach settlement by turning right onto Seaward Avenue. It still retains a pleasing 1930s Spanish-California look. Several small storefronts contain chowder houses, bikini shops and espresso cafés. From the end of the street, one can stroll out onto the sand without paying a fee. It's a grand little corner of Ventura, but them I'm showing favoritism since I once lived here, able to start and end my days with a beach walk.

Moving right along Harbor Boulevard, you'll pass a compact beach community called Ventura Keys and shortly reach **Ventura Harbor.** Pass in front of the harbor, then turn seaward (right) onto Spinnaker Drive and follow it about a mile past marinas, shopping complexes and restaurants. The largest shopping area is **Ventura Harbor Village** and our favorite restaurant here is **Frullati's,** which we list below. At the end of Spinnaker Drive, you'll encounter the visitor center for one of America's most unusual national preserves:

### Channel Islands National Park ● *1901 Spinnaker Dr., Ventura, CA 93001-4354; (805) 658-5730. Visitor center open weekdays 8:30 to 4:30 and weekends 8 to 5.* ☐ The national park consists of five offshore islands—Anacapa, Santa Cruz, Santa Rosa, San Miguel and Santa Barbara. These are splendid aquatic and wildlife sanctuaries, and they protect some creatures that are unique to these isolated bits of land. A total of eight islands, which are seaward extensions of the Santa Monica Mountains, are strung like a green and beige necklace along this southwest-facing coast. The national park was established in 1980 after a fierce battle among conservationists, some private landowners and would-be developers. Three of the islands remain in private hands.

### Getting out there

One can't simply swim out to Channel Islands National Park, of course. However, you can book a variety of natural history trips with **Island Packers,** whose offices are adjacent to the visitor center. Trips to one or more islands can vary from a few hours to all day, or one can arrange for camping drop-offs. A night or so on one of the Channel Islands is a grand experience. The trips aren't expensive. When we last checked, a half-day cruise to Anacapa—the nearest island—was less than $25 per adult; all-day trips started under $40 and camping trips were under $90. For details contact: Island Packers, 1867 Spinnaker Dr., Ventura, CA 93001; (805) 642-1393. (WEB SITE: www.islandpackers.com; E-MAIL: ipco@isle.net) The office is open daily 9 to 5. If you're planning an excursion in summer, it's a good idea to call ahead.

Meanwhile, landlubbers can enjoy exhibits at the visitor center and browse through a good selection of natural history and regional guidebooks. Displays include a "floating" three-dimensional topo map of the islands, stuffed versions of the critters living out there and a simulated tidepool. An upstairs viewing tower provides nice vistas—on a good day—of the islands, and of green-clad Ventura, crawling up low coastal hills.

Our next stop in this Ventura venture is the county's second public harbor. To get there, continue southeast on Harbor Boulevard for several miles, passing tidal flat agricultural fields, subdivisions and three more state parks—**McGrath, Mandalay** and **Oxnard Beach.** All offer lots of sand and surf, and McGrath has camping areas with tables, barbecue grills and showers; no hookups; **$$$.** Sites can be reserved with a MasterCard or VISA by calling (800) 444-PARK. Incidentally, a bike route follows level Harbor Boulevard for several miles.

**Channel Islands Harbor** was dredged between two old shoreside communities, Hollywood Beach and Oxnard Beach, which date from the 1920s. (When they were first developed, beachfront lots sold for $50!) The harbor has three sections—the seaward Harbor Boulevard/Hollywood Beach side, the Peninsula and the Oxnard Beach-Silver Strand area. Two of Ventura County's most durable seafood restaurants are out here—the **Whale's Tale** off Harbor Boulevard and the **Lobster Trap** at the end of Peninsula Road. Both go back at least thirty years, when I lived here; they're listed below. A second office of **Island Packers** also is out here, at 3600 Harbor Boulevard; (805) 382-1779. You can catch Channel Islands National Park trips from here as well as from Ventura Harbor.

Harbor Boulevard will take you into the seaward side of the harbor and Hollywood Beach. To visit the harbor's other two "legs," retreat from Hollywood Beach, turn right onto Channel Islands Boulevard, then go right again onto Peninsula Drive. (The Lobster Trap is here.) Backtrack and go right again for the Oxnard Beach-Silver Strand side of the harbor.

We'll suggest two final Ventura County stops, if you're interested in boats or naval history. From the east side of the harbor, scoot up Victoria Boulevard a short distance to the **Ventura County Maritime Museum.** It traces the history of men and their ships through models, paintings and nautical artifacts, with a particular focus on California coastal shipping. The museum is open from 11 to 5, daily in summer and Thursday-Monday the rest of the year; (805) 984-06260.

The U.S. Naval Construction Battalion Center is immediately east of the harbor, adjacent to the town of **Port Hueneme.** If you follow Channel Islands Boulevard east past the front of the base, you can turn right onto Ventura Road for a visit to the **CEC/Seabee Museum.** It traces the history of the Naval Civil Engineer Corps and those "Fighting Seabees." You first must pause at the Ventura gate for a pass and you'll need proof of vehicle insurance. The museum is open weekdays 8 to 4:30, Saturday 9:30 to 4:30 and Sunday 12:30 to 4:30; (805) 982-5163.

## DINING IN COASTAL VENTURA/OXNARD
### In order of appearance

**Eric Ericsson's** ● *On the Ventura Pier at 668 Harbor Blvd.; (805) 643-4783. American; full bar service. Lunch and dinner daily. Major credit cards; $$$.* ⧠ This large restaurant has a trendy cathedral ceiling-exposed steam pipe look. It has window walls to the sea and the town, and an upstairs bar with a deck over the pier. The menu is what you'd expect for a place on a pier—shellfish, shrimp scampi, scallops and seafood pastas. Among specialties are a "clam bake" of crabs, clams, mussels and scallops in a tarragon broth; and—only in southern California—Mexican cioppino.

**Frullati's** • *In Ventura Harbor Village at 1559 Spinnaker Drive; (805) 658-9153. Italian; full bar service. Lunch and dinner daily except Tuesday; breakfast on weekends. MC/VISA; $$.* ☐ We like this place because it's *not* a typical harbor seafood restaurant. The look is nautical, although the temperament and kitchen are Italian. Homemade pastas dominate the menu, along with classics such as veal piccata, chicken marsala and chicken Alfredo. Can one get fish in this portside place? Certainly; try the pesto and prawns or filet of salmon with fettuccine and capers. Diners can dine inside beneath a lacquered wooden boat hanging from the ceiling, or on an outside deck, where a guitar player entertains on weekends.

**The Whale's Tail** • *Channel Islands Harbor at 3950 Bluefin Circle; (805) 985-2511. American; full bar service. Lunch weekdays, dinner nightly and Sunday brunch. Major credit cards; $$$.* ☐ This large, open two-story complex has fine harbor views, particularly from its upper deck. It has a good seafood menu as well, featuring fried shrimp in beer batter, seafood skewer, garlic shrimp and lobster linguine, plus prime rib, steak and lamb chops for the landlubbers. This long established place, going on its fourth decade, has a good selection of white wines by the glass—essential for a proper seafood restaurant.

**The Lobster Trap** • *Channel Islands Harbor at 3605 Peninsula Rd.; (805) 985-6361. American; full bar service. Lunch and dinner daily. Major credit cards; $$$.* ☐ One of the coast's more handsome restaurants, the "Trap" has a sleek modern look with white nappery and maple chairs; the dining area is terraced to enhance harbor views. While seafood accents the menu, it doesn't dominate it. In addition to garlic Thai shrimp, clam linguine, cioppino and such, one can get tournedos of beef, New Zealand rack of lamb, herb roasted prime rib or saffron chicken.

☺ ☺ ☺

**Good grief, how do we get out of here?** • It may appear that you're miles from a main highway, although escape from coastal Ventura County is relatively easy. If you'd like to pursue scenic Highway 1 southeast to Malibu and Santa Monica, continue east on Channel Islands Boulevard. You'll encounter an interchange after a couple of miles. On the other hand, if you want to reach U.S. 101, go north from here on Ventura Road (opposite the Seabee base entrance) or on Victoria Avenue (past the Maritime Museum). The freeway is about three miles up.

# TRIP PLANNER

**WHEN TO GO** ● Spring and fall are the best times to explore the mountainous woodlands above Los Angeles. Unfortunately, Mount Wilson Observatory is open only on weekends, when the mountains are most crowded. The region can become quite congested in summer, and thousands come up for snow play in winter. For winter road conditions, call (800) 427-7623.

**DRIVING DISTANCE** ● The Angeles Crest Highway (State Route 2) from La Cañada to Cajon Junction at Interstate 5 is about sixty-five miles, including a side trip to Mount Wilson Observatory.

**RV ADVISORY** ● Motorhomes and trailer rigs should be able to negotiate this route, although it does have some tight turns, particularly on the Mount Wilson road.

**WHAT YOU'LL SEE** ● Mount Wilson Observatory, and mostly lots of trees and some pretty mountain scenery, with plenty of hazy overviews of the Los Angeles Basin.

**WHAT TO DO** ● Hike some of the many trails of Angeles National Forest; take a tour of the Mount Wilson facilities; grab a chili cheese dog at Newcombe's Ranch Family Restaurant; or enjoy Chinese-Malaysian fare at Wrightwood's Crystal Island Restaurant.

**ADVENTURE PASSES** ● A pilot program requiring the purchase of an "Adventure Pass" for southern California national forests was started as we went to press; for details, see Tour Fifteen, page 208.

**TO BEGIN** ● Get to La Cañada on Freeway 210 on the northern edge of greater Los Angeles.

## Useful contact

**Headquarters, Angeles National Forest**, 710 N. Santa Anita Ave., Arcadia, CA 91006, (818) 574-1613; or **Arroyo Seco Ranger District**, Oak Grove Park, Flintridge, CA 91001, (818) 790- 1151.

## Pricing guidelines

**DINING:** Dinner entrée with soup or salad, without drinks or dessert for under $10 = **$**; $10 to $14 = **$$**; $15 to $25 = **$$$**; over $25 = **$$$$**.

**RECLINING:** A two-person room for $35 or less = **$**; $36 to $50 = **$$**; $51 to $75 = **$$$**; $76 to $100 = **$$$$**; more than $100 = **$$$$$**.

**CAMPING:** Under $10 = **$**; $10 to $14 = **$$**; $15 to $19 = **$$$**; $20 or more = **$$$$**

*Tour Seventeen*

# THE SAN GABRIELS

## *ABOVE THE SMOG: THE ANGELES CREST DRIVE*

**W**e didn't expect to find an uncrowded yet interesting road in Los Angeles County until we drove the Angeles Crest Highway, within view of California's largest city. Although it was hardly deserted—we cruised it on a fall weekend—it wasn't at all crowded.

Two large mountain ranges loom over southern California's cities, separating them from the Mojave Desert—the San Gabriels above Los Angeles and the San Bernardino range above San Bernardino and Riverside. In fact they form a rainshadow that helped *create* the Mojave. Each is covered by a national forest and each of course is a major recreation area for southern Californians. Except for their highest reaches, these aren't lushly forested, since the mountains are rather far south. Their rocky foothills are semi-arid yucca, oak and chaparral woodlands, with pine and fir forests in the upper elevations.

As we explored these areas for this tour and the next, we noted an irony. The woodlands above huge Los Angeles are relatively undeveloped, with Wrightwood as the only town, while the alpine region above the less populated San Bernardino-Riverside is busy with little towns and resorts, notably Arrowhead and Big Bear.

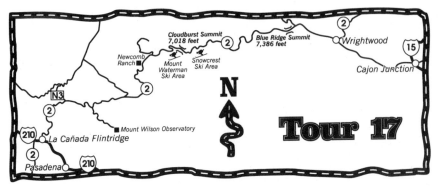

## The forest of angels

The 1,000-square-mile Angeles National Forest, covering much of the San Gabriel Mountains, receives 32 millions visitors a year. These are mostly repeat customers from Los Angeles, who come primarily in the summer, and on winter weekends to play in the snow. However, we found no crowds when we visited this area on a sunny fall weekend.

Often, as we explored these mountain wilds, we had this sense of being a thousand miles from nowhere, yet we were practically in the smoggy alpenglow of the largest city in the most populous state in America. The city is out of sight much of the time, then its great sprawl will appear quite dramatically at a bend in the highway. On a good day—and these are unfortunately rare—you can see all the way to the Pacific Ocean. The best vistas are from the Mount Wilson Highway.

The Angeles Crest Highway (State Route 2) runs the length of the San Gabriels, spiraling upward from La Cañada. Since there are no towns up here except Wrightwood on the far end, this is primarily hiking and camping country. More than 500 miles of hiking trails twist through rocky, oak-studded woodlands and higher evergreen forests. More than fifty Forest Service campgrounds dot the area. Sites generally are available in fall and spring, although they often fill up in summer and on off-season weekends.

An irritating problem we encountered was dozens of motorcyclists who use this highway as their personal speedway on weekends, whizzing along the twisting roads at an alarming clip.

"We scrape them off the pavement every now and again," a forest service official told us, pointing out that there were several fatal accidents each summer. There is talk of putting the brakes on these young racers, so their ranks may have thinned by the time you make the drive. Also, there are fewer hell-for-leather bikers on weekdays.

---

**FUELING ADVISORY** ● You'll encounter no fuel stops for fifty-five miles after leaving the freeway, so you may want to tank up. There are service stations at the La Cañada interchange.

---

To begin your trek, follow I-210 to La Cañada, take the Angeles Crest Highway exit and head north. You'll begin climbing immediately, first through La Cañada suburbs and then into oak chaparral foothills. You'll probably experience a sudden surge of relief as you shed freeway traffic and retreat into the hills. A good place to load up on information—and get your required National Forest Adventure Pass—is at the **Clear Creek ranger station**, a few miles into the drive.

Immediately beyond is the trailhead for a hike up **Colby Canyon**—a good workout to start your day in the mountains. It's quite a versatile trail, first following a pretty, boulder-strewn creek ravine and then zig-zagging steeply upward through thick brush to a grand vista point beside a ridgetop cistern. If you don't want to tackle the entire two-mile trudge to the cistern, you can hike less than a mile to a creek crossing at a sylvan glen with a beautiful little pool. The creek was still running and the glen was lush and green when we made the trip in the fall. And we encountered only a handful of other hikers.

On the road again, you'll shortly reach the turnoff to **Mount Wilson Observatory** and **Skyline Park.** Open only on weekends from 10 to 4, the observatory is at the end of a twisting five-mile road. Free tours are given at 1 p.m. For information, call (626) 440-1136.

Even if the observatory is closed, it's worth the drive for the spectacular vistas of the Los Angeles basin. The observatory and park complex are rather short on directional signs, so follow our lead to find your way around:

After you encounter a steel forest of radio and TV antennae, swing left and drive through a gate to the main parking lot. This gets you to the observatory complex and its surrounding Skyline Park. Immediately beyond and above the lot is a pavilion with picnic tables, where you can enjoy that great L.A. view. Just to the left of the pavilion, you can stroll a paved road to the observatory buildings. You'll first encounter the small Mount Wilson Museum with the usual sky photos and astounding astronomical statistics about light years and numbers of stars in the galaxies. Opposite the museum is the 150-foot high Tower Telescope, used only for studying the sun. It's not open to visitors.

Follow a path past a dome enclosing a 50-inch telescope and you'll soon arrive at the star of this starry place. The Hooker Telescope, with a 100-inch mirror, has made some of the most significant discoveries in the history of astronomy, starting with the fact that we are not alone. Using this lens, astronomers discovered that there are many galaxies beyond ours, with untold billions of stars. This was the world's largest telescope when it was put into service in 1917, until the installation of the 200-inch Hale telescope on Mount Palomar three decades later. Forty-five steps will take you up to a gallery where you can see the dimly lit 'scope suspended in a huge steel harness.

Back on the Angeles Crest Highway, you'll encounter **Charleston Flats Recreation Area** with lots of camping and picnic areas. Just beyond and to your right is a viewpoint on for Devil's Canyon, a great steep-walled abyss thinly coated with pines. A trailhead on the far side of the turnout takes hearty backpackers into the canyon's 35,000-acre San Gabriel Wilderness Area.

After a short distance, watch on your left for the **Chilao Visitors Center,** the most complete forestry complex in these mountains. It's open

*Resembling a space age fire lookout, the Tower Telescope at Mount Wilson Observatory is used to study the sun.*

daily, generally from 8 to 5; (626) 796-5541. You'll find exhibits on the flora and fauna of this area, and a display concerning the Gabrielino Indians who once lived in these wilds. Two short interpretive trails lead from the center. One passes a series of outdoor displays concerning lifestyles of the Gabrielinos. A nature trail leads to a typical turn-of-the-century forest ranger's log cabin; this one was built in 1900 at a cost of $75. The rude furnishings—a bunk, cast iron stove and saddle racks—reminds us that Smokey Bear's buddies lived a rather rough life in those days.

Just beyond Chilao is **Newcombe's Ranch Family Restaurant and Saloon,** part of an 1891 homestead and operated by descendants of the founders. Grab a 'burger and a glass of suds and admire the rustic museum-like interior of this weathered diner. It's open Friday-Sunday 8 to 7: (626) 440-1001. This is a favorite hangout for the bikers who zoom about the mountains. You'll probably discover as we did that they're nice kids; they just go too damned fast.

From Newcombe's, the highway meanders in pleasant alpine monotony for more than a dozen miles, passing small ski areas, vista points, campgrounds and picnic sites. You'll hit the highway's high point at 7,901-foot Dawson Saddle and then begin a gradual downward spiral to the only town up here:

# WRIGHTWOOD

**Population: 3,300**              **Elevation: 6,960 feet**

Appearing smaller than its population figure suggests, Wrightwood is an appealing alpine community of summer and winter homes. Nearby ski areas of Big Pines (760-249-6590) and Wrightwood (760-249-3830) make it a popular place in winter. The town's brief business and residential areas are sloped uphill to your right, where you'll find a couple of interesting restaurants. Both are less than a block from the highway:

**Blue Ridge Inn** • *6060 Park Dr.; (760) 249-3440. American; full bar service. Lunch and dinner daily. MC/VISA; $$$.* ☐ Dating from 1948, this comfortable café now has a "mountain modern" look with warm woods and table lamps in its dimly lit dining room. An attractive bar is adjacent. Menu offerings include grilled swordfish with lemon and dill sauce, sautéed scallops, steak and such.

**Crystal Island Restaurant** • *5995 Cedar (at Laurel); (760) 249-6515. American, Chinese and Malaysian; wine and beer. Lunch and dinner daily except Tuesday. MC/VISA. MC/VISA; $$.* ☐ This restaurant fits no mold and that's part of its charm. Housed in a shingle-sided cottage, it has an early American look with tulip chandeliers, antiques and overstuffed couches. Yet the menu is a contemporary American-Asian mix. It features peppercorn steak, shrimp Marsala, ginger beef, steamed jumbo shrimp, and crispy fried pork with vegetables and red chilies.

For quick bites, try **Cinnamon's Bakery** in a shopping complex to the left, at 1350 Highway 2. Open from early morning to early afternoon, it issues specialty coffees, baked goods and sandwiches; (760) 249-5588.

☺ ☺ ☺

**Where do we go from here?** • From Wrightwood, the Angeles Crest Highway drops quickly toward a desert environment. It ends after nine miles at State Route 138, which continues the desert descent to Interstate 15 at Cajon Junction. If you want to blend seamlessly into Tour Eighteen, simply stay aboard Highway 138, cross the freeway and head into the San Bernardino Mountains.

# TRIP PLANNER

**WHEN TO GO** • Like the previous tour, this one is best taken in spring or fall, since it's busy with southern Californians in summer. They're also drawn to several ski areas in winter. For winter road conditions, call (800) 427-7623. Fall is a fun time, since both Lake Arrowhead and Big Bear Lake celebrate Oktoberfests, with activities on weekends from mid-September to mid-October.

**DRIVING DISTANCE** • You'll cover about 115 miles if you follow state highways 138, 18 and 38. These take you from Cajon Junction through Lake Arrowhead and Big Bear Lake to Interstate 10 east of Redlands.

**RV ADVISORY** • The steep twisting climb into the mountains from Cajon Junction on State Route 138 is not advised for trailers. Folks with trailer rigs and large motorhomes will have an easier time of it if they approach on Highway 18 from San Bernardino.

**WHAT YOU'LL SEE** • Three large alpine lakes—Silverwood, Arrowhead and Big Bear, grand vistas of the San Bernardino-Riverside flatlands, upscale Lake Arrowhead Village, Big Bear Discovery Center and cutely rustic Fawnskin.

**WHAT TO DO** • Play on the lakes; shop the trendy boutiques of Lake Arrowhead Village; ride the *Arrowhead Queen* or *Princess* on Lake Arrowhead; hike the Cougar Crest Trail above Big Bear.

**ADVENTURE PASSES** • A pilot program requiring the purchase of an "Adventure Pass" for southern California national forests was started as we went to press; for details, see Tour Fifteen, page 208.

**TO BEGIN** • Continue across Tejon Junction on Highway 138 from Tour Seventeen. If you have a big motorhome or trailer, head for San Bernardino and take State Route 18 north.

## Useful contacts

**Lake Arrowhead Communities Chamber of Commerce**, P.O. Box 219 (Arrowhead Village), Lake Arrowhead, CA 92353; (800) 337-3716 or (909) 337-3715. (WEB SITE: www.lakearrowhead.net)

**Big Bear Lake Resort Association**, P.O. Box 1936 (630 Bartlet Rd.), Big Bear Lake, CA 92315; (800) 4-BIGBEAR or (909) 866-4608. (WEB SITE: www.bigbearinfo.com; E-MAIL: bbira@bigbearinfo.com)

**San Bernardino National Forest: Arrowhead Ranger Station** at 28104 Highway 38 (P.O. Box 350), Skyforest, CA 92385, (909) 337-2444; **Big Bear Discovery Center** at 41397 North Shore Dr. (P.O. Box 290), Fawnskin, CA 92333; (909) 866-3437.

## Pricing guidelines

**DINING:** Dinner entrée with soup or salad, without drinks or dessert for under $10 = $; $10 to $14 = $$; $15 to $25 = $$$; over $25 = $$$$.

**RECLINING:** A two-person room for $35 or less = $; $36 to $50 = $$; $51 to $75 = $$$; $76 to $100 = $$$$; more than $100 = $$$$$.

**CAMPING:** Under $10 = $; $10 to $14 = $$; $15 to $19 = $$$; $20 or more = $$$$

## Tour Eighteen
# THE SAN BERNARDINOS
## THE RIM OF THE WORLD DRIVE

---

**I**f Angeles National Forest, which we explored in the previous tour, is primarily a wilderness playground, then next door San Bernardino National Forest is simply a playground. Visitors here can ride a fake paddlewheeler, take summer ski lifts, water ski, jet ski, parasail, go on trail rides and catch jeep excursions.

Folks came to this area early—and stayed. Gold was found in the Holcomb Valley north of Big Bear in 1859, then ranchers and loggers followed after the gold gave out in 1875. Later in the century, streams were dammed to create Lake Arrowhead and Big Bear Lake, and so of course tourists followed. Early in the twentieth century, privately-developed Lake Arrowhead became a hideaway for Hollywood's elite and it still is, although you'll more likely find business tycoons than film stars in the region's forest mansions. The Bavarian style Lake Arrowhead Village, busy with trendy shops, is a favorite stop for visitors.

Although this mountain area may seem awfully civilized, the surrounding 660,000-acre San Bernardino National Forest still offers typical hiking-backpacking-camping lures. It has more than twenty campgrounds and at least that many picnic sites.

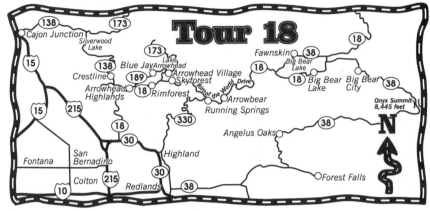

The cliff-hanging and aptly-named Rim of the World Drive is the main highway through the San Bernardinos. Notched into the mountains' southern flanks, it provides almost constant vistas of the valley below. Views are more impressive than those from the Angeles Crest Highway because this region isn't as hazy and smoggy. Also, Rim of the World Drive is lower than Angeles Crest, providing considerable detail of the great suburban sprawl of San Bernardino and Riverside. With a good lens, you can pick out individual houses or stores.

If your binoculars pick up a set of Golden Arches, you might like to know that San Bernardino is the birthplace of fast food. McDonald's restaurant, featuring pre-cooked fifteen-cent hamburgers, was started in the late 1940s by Richard and Maurice "Mac" McDonald. They were bought out by Ray Kroc in 1961 and the original McDonald's Restaurant no longer exists. It was under Kroc's ownership that McDonald's expanded into a major chain, with "billions and billions" of grams of fat sold.

## Doing the rim

The highways through the San Bernardino Mountains aren't exactly uncrowded since they link the area's many communities. However, they're rarely congested, except on summer weekends.

To begin doing the rim, continue on State Route 138 from the previous chapter, or if you're approaching from Interstate 5, take the exit marked Palmdale-Silverwood Lake and head east. You'll twist and wind through a brushy desert for a few miles and then level off as you enter San Bernardino National Forest.

The silver sliver of **Silverwood Lake** will appear after a few miles. This good sized reservoir in a brushy basin is rimmed by **Silverwood Lake State Recreation Area,** with fishing, boating, waterskiing, swimming and camping. Nice oak-shaded sites have tables and barbecue grills, flush potties and showers. Campsites can be reserved with a MasterCard or VISA by calling (800) 444-PARK.

Just above is the **Cottonwood Ranger Station** of San Bernardino National Forest, where you can pick up your National Forest Adventure Pass, assuming the program is still in effect. Immediately beyond, the highway begins a steep, twisting spiral into the mountains and a sign advises that trailer rigs shouldn't attempt it; see "Trip planner" above.

Near the top of the climb, you'll encounter the scattered mountain village of **Crestline,** sitting at 4,720 feet, with about 8,600 residents. Primarily a forest home community, it doesn't offer much for the casual visitor. To stay on course through its sometimes confusing road patterns, keep following Highway 138 signs. Just beyond the small business district, you'll drop briefly downhill and catch your first look at the impressive sprawl of San Bernardino and Riverside. You'll soon hit a curious three-level interchange—although this isn't a freeway. Highway 138 ends here and you'll blend into Route 18, the Rim of the World Drive.

---

*NAVIGATIONAL NOTE* ● If you decided to approach this area from San Bernardino on Highway 18, this is the point where the two routes merge.

---

Heading eastward on Rim of the World, you'll note that the highway definitely was built for the views, with frequent turnouts to allow motorists to enjoy them. If you'd like to dine with that view, a restaurant perched over the precipice comes up shortly:

**Cliffhanger Restaurant** ● *Highway 18 at Lake Gregory Drive, Arrowhead Highlands; (909) 338-3397. American and continental; wine and beer. Lunch and dinner daily. MC/VISA.* □ This chalet style restaurant's dining room consists mostly of large windows to draw in the panorama from below, with a glass enclosed deck for even better views. It's particularly impressive during dinner, when a million lights twinkle from the valley. The menu is mostly American, with beef, chicken, seafood and pasta.

Beyond the Cliffhanger, you'll pass the hamlet of **Rimforest.** A left turn onto State Route 173 will take you three miles downhill to the most stylish community up here, sitting beside its namesake lake.

## LAKE ARROWHEAD

**Population: 6,300**                    **Elevation: 5,191 feet**

This popular pond started out as Little Bear Lake in 1891 when three Ohio businessmen dammed a small creek to form a reservoir. In the 1920s, they were bought out by a Los Angeles syndicate that raised the dam and renamed the reservoir Lake Arrowhead, after a natural rock formation on the face of San Bernardino Mountain.

The company created a private Bavarian style community that thrives to this day, although it has gone through several ownerships and a couple of receiverships. Its centerpoint is Lake Arrowhead Village, an attractive shopping complex wrapped around an arc of the lake. In 1979, the village was completely burned—as part of a fire training exercise—then rebuilt.

Although carefully groomed and without neon, Lake Arrowhead Village has succumbed to the temptation of fast food, offering one of the few McDonald's in America with lakeside dining. The **Arrowhead Communities Chamber of Commerce** is on the second floor of the main shopping complex, above Subway, another fast food joint. It's open weekdays 9 to 5; (909) 337-3715.

The lakeside Arrowhead Village shopping complex is attractively dressed in Bavarian architecture

The village is worth a brief stroll, particularly along the waterfront, where you can rent a boat, catch a lake cruise or just sit and watch folks feed the ducks.

## ATTRACTIONS AND ACTIVITIES

**Ice skating** • *Iceoplex Ice Castle, Highway 189 and North Bay Road in nearby Blue Jay; (909) 33-SKATE. Various hours; modest admission fees.* ⊓ This public rink has skating lessons, hockey workouts and general skating. Saturday night "Rock 'n Skate" dancing sessions are popular.

**Lake Arrowhead Children's Museum** • *Lake Arrowhead Village; (909) 336-1332 or (909) 336-3093. Daily 10 to 6 in summer and 10 to 5 the rest of the year; modest admission charge.* ⊓ This small, nicely done *kindermuseum* features a nature and science center, puppet theater and a special toddler play area.

**Lake cruises** • *Arrowhead Queen Co., dockside at Lake Arrowhead Village; (909) 336-6992. Daily; hours vary.* ⊓ Two cruise boats, the pretend paddlewheeler *Arrowhead Queen* and the sleek varnished wood 1930s style *Arrowhead Princess* speedboat provide sightseeing trips around the lake.

**Rim of the World Historical Society Museum** • *Lake Arrowhead Village adjacent to the kids' museum; (909) 336-1322. Daily 10 to 6; small admission fee.* ⊓ This new museum traces the area's development from native folks to early logging to the creation of the resort and planned community. Nicely done and uncluttered, the archive has lots of historic photos and select artifacts.

## DINING

**Belgian Waffle Works** ● *On the lakefront at Lake Arrowhead Village; (909) 337-5222. American; wine and beer. Breakfast through early evening. Major credit cards; $$.* ◻ Sitting just off the lake, this appealing European style café is a good place to start an Arrowhead day. Try the calorie-ridden Belgian waffles with their assorted fruit toppings, chased with a cappuccino. A specialty—probably not available in Belgium—is a waffle stuffed with Swiss cheese and turkey. Designer coffees, sandwiches, chilies and salads complete the menu.

**Garibaldi Grille** ● *Lake Arrowhead Village; (909) 337-1171. Italian; full bar service. Lunch and dinner daily. MC/VISA; $$$.* ◻ Head for the Grille on a warm summer afternoon or evening, when you can dine on a deck beside a marina. The interior's nice, too, with beam ceilings, floral wall paintings and comfy booths. The menu is traditional *Italiano*—osso bucco, cioppino, veal Parmigiana and chickens cacciatore and Marsala.

**Woody's Boathouse** ● *On the lakefront at Lake Arrowhead Village; (909) 337-2628. American; full bar service. Lunch and dinner daily plus Sunday brunch. Major credit cards; $$$$.* ◻ This large, nautically modern restaurant offers lake views from its dining areas, which are decorated with varnished woods, boating scenes and model boats. The menu wanders from garlic seasoned scampi over angel hair pasta and chicken pesto to babyback ribs, charbroiled chicken breasts and assorted fish.

## RECLINING

Dozens of resorts and several bed & breakfast inns are tucked into the trees around the lake, and you can almost always find room in spring and fall. This is but a small sampler:

**Bracken Fern Manor** ● *P.O. Box 1006 (815 Arrowhead Village Rd.), Lake Arrowhead, CA 92532; (909) 337-5557. (WEB SITE: www.lakearrowhead.com/brackenfernmanor) Ten rooms with private baths and breakfast. MC/VISA; $$$$ to $$$$$.* ◻ Dating from 1929, this handsomely refurbished inn occupies a Bavarian style building with "an eclectic collection of international antiques." Each room bears a woman's name, in honor of "Gibson girl" hopeful starlets who came here in the Twenties and Thirties, sometimes on the arm of a Hollywood wolf. Facilities include a library, art gallery, game room, wine tasting cellar, garden hot tub and a sauna.

**Chateau du Lac Bed & Breakfast Inn** ● *P.O. Box 1098 (911 Hospital Rd.), Lake Arrowhead, CA 92352; (800) 601-8722 or (909) 332-6488. (WEB SITE: www.lakearrowhead.com; E-MAIL: chateau@js-net.com) Five rooms with TV, phones and private baths; full breakfast. Major credit cards; $$$$$.* ◻ This tree-shrouded Victorian style home occupies a bluff, with views of Lake Arrowhead. Rooms are individually furnished, with French country décor; some have fireplaces and spa tubs.

**Gray Squirrel Inn** ● *P.O. Box 377 (326 Highway 173), Lake Arrowhead, CA 92352; (888) 719-3563 or (909) 336-3602. Nine units with TV and phones. MC/VISA; $$$.* ◻ Simple and affordable, this chalet style inn has rooms, family units with kitchenettes and two honeymoon suites.

**Lake Arrowhead Resort** • *P.O. Box 1699 (on the lake at Arrowhead Village), Lake Arrowhead, CA 92352; (800) 800-6792 or (909) 336-1511. One hundred sixty-one rooms and suites with TV movies, phones and many amenities; $$$$$. Dining room serves American and continental fare; full bar service; breakfast through dinner; $$$. Major credit cards.* ☐ The largest lodge at the lake, Arrowhead Resort has a health spa, pool, racquetball courts and a lakefront beach. Most rooms have lake views and the complex recently was renovated.

**Saddleback Inn-Arrowhead** • *P.O. Box 1890 (just outside the village entrance), Lake Arrowhead, CA 92352; (800) 858-3334 or (909) 336-3571. Thirty-four rooms and suites, most with large spa tubs, refrigerators and gas fireplaces; $$$$$. The Tapestry Restaurant serves American fare; breakfast through dinner; wine and beer; $$$. Major credit cards.* ☐ Elaborate early American décor brightens this historic inn, with print wallpaper, polished woods and wainscotting. One of Lake Arrowhead's oldest resorts, it dates from 1919 and has been completely refurbished.

## Arrowhead to Big Bear

Back on the Rim of the World Drive, you'll see the **Arrowhead Ranger Station** on your left; open daily 8 to 4:30; (909) 337-2444. Next door is the hamlet of **Skyforest,** with a few curio shops, cafés and stores. A few miles beyond, **Running Springs** is a disorganized scatter of homes and small businesses. It collides with **Arrowbear,** a smaller version of the same thing.

Beyond Running Springs/Arrowbear, you'll finally shake this string of pine tree suburbs and enter national forest lands. However, you'll still see plenty of civilization far below as your cliff-hanging highway meanders slowly uphill. Half a mile east of Arrowbear is **Children's Forest,** a new Forest Service facility with a kid-oriented visitor center, special learning activities and interpretive trails. The nearby Keller Peak Lookout, of interest to both kids and adults, is open daily from 9 to 5 in summer. For information, call (909) 337-5156. Thirteen miles from Running Springs, a right fork will take you this area's other major resort town:

## BIG BEAR LAKE

Population: 6,200                    Elevation: 6,754 feet

Although slightly smaller in population than Arrowhead, the town of Big Bear Lake seems larger, perhaps because it has a bigger commercial area. The lake *is* considerably larger than Lake Arrowhead, about eight miles long; it's the major play pond in these mountains.

While Arrowhead is a planned community, Big Bear Lake is a more conventional town that just happens to be in the mountains. It slowly evolved after folks came to this high basin, first to seek gold and then to log and farm in the late 1800s. While it lacks the woodsy chic of Lake Arrowhead, it does have a nice little Bavarian style shopping area and some very attractive lakeside homes.

After you've driven through a couple of miles of suburbs, continue straight ahead under "The Village" sign onto Village Drive. This takes you into that *faux* Bavarian district with shops, boutiques and a gallery or two.

At mid-village, go left for a block down Bartlett Road; you'll find a large parking lot suitable for RVs, plus the Big Bear Lake **Chamber of Commerce** and Resort Association offices. They're open weekdays 8 to 5 and weekends 9 to 5; (909) 866-4608.

## ATTRACTIONS AND ACTIVITIES

**Big Bear Discovery Center** • *41397 North Shore Dr. (P.O. Box 290), Fawnskin, CA 92333; (909) 866-3437. Daily 8 to 4:30; free.* ◻ Opened in 1998, this large woodsy modern complex has exhibits on the flora, fauna and geology of the area. It's operated by the Forest Service and serves as an info center both for surrounding forest lands and nearby communities. Picture windows provide nice views of the lake.

**Tours** • Big Bear Jeeps run two to four-hour excursions into the hills, including the site of the old mining town of Holcomb, daily 9 from to 5, May through October; (909) 878-5337. A free self-guiding auto tour map to the Holcomb Valley is available from the Big Bear Discovery Center.

**Lake cruises** • A 40-passenger trimaran departs Pine Knot Landing on 80-minute tours of the lake daily from 10 to 6, April through November; (909) 866-2628.

**Water park** • Alpine Slide at Magic Mountain near Big Bear has several downhill water courses, plus groomed sledding slopes in summer; (909) 866-4626.

**Winter sports** • Bear Mountain ski resort has full facilities for skiers and snowboarders, plus a golf course and scenic chair lift for summer visitors; (800) BEAR-MTN or (909) 585-2519. Another downhill area is at Snow Summit, (909) 866-5766. It has a scenic sky chair, mountain biking and hiking trails in summer. Cross-country trails are groomed near the Big Bear Discovery Center.

## DINING

**Boo Bear's Den** • *572 Pine Knot Ave.; (909) 866-2162. (E-MAIL: boobears@bigbear.com) American; full bar service. Breakfast through dinner daily. MC/VISA; $$.* ◻ This casual, locally popular place has a sunny country style dining room with a fireplace and high backed booths, and a large garden dining area with umbrella tables. Combination dinners are a specialty, like steak and shrimp or chicken and ribs. It also features several pasta dishes.

**Iron Squirrel** • *646 Pine Knot Ave.; (909) 866-9121. American-continental; wine and beer. Dinner nightly. MC/VISA; $$$.* ◻ Elegant in a woodsy sort of way, the Squirrel has stained oak floors, tulip chandeliers and—a nice touch—booths separated by seat backs and lace curtains. The rather creative kitchen issues steaks, lamb chops with garlic, braised lamb shanks over fresh vegetables, orange roast duckling and veal Marsala.

**Stillwell's Restaurant** • *At Northwoods Resort, 40650 Village Dr.; (909) 866-3121. (WEB SITE: www.northwoodsresort.com; E-MAIL: info@northwoodsresort.com) American; full bar service. Lunch and dinner daily; breakfast in the coffee shop. Major credit cards; $$.* ◻ The most appealing restaurant on the mountain, Stillwell's is nicely attired in natural woods, polished log rafters, antler chandeliers and mountain man artifacts. One can dine on an outside deck over a small moat. The menu is versatile, featuring seafood pot pie, pork ribs, ostrich filet and sea bass.

### RECLINING

Lodgings generally are less expensive here than at Lake Arrowhead. They consist mostly of motels, small chalet style resorts and a few B&Bs. One facility is rather imposing:

**Northwoods Resort ●** *P.O. Box 2943 (40650 Village Dr.), Big Bear Lake, CA 92315; (800) 866-3121 or (909) 866-3121. (WEB: www.north-woodsresort.com; E-MAIL: info@northwoodsresort.com) One hundred forty-one rooms and suites with TV, phones and other amenities. Stillwell's Restaurant listed above. Major credit cards; $$$$ to $$$$$.* ◻ Sitting at the entrance to Big Bear Village, this large rustic-modern complex has a pool and spa, a "semi-moat" duck pond, gift shop and sports equipment rental shop. Ski packages are available for Bear Mountain and Snow Summit. Even if you don't plan to stay here, step inside to admire the polished log beam ceilings, natural wood paneled walls and—in Stillwell's—unusual antler chandeliers.

### CAMPING

**San Bernardino National Forest ●** The surrounding forest lands have more than twenty campgrounds and some are on the National Forest reservation service. Sites can be reserved with a credit card by calling (800) 280-CAMP. Nearest campground to Big Bear Lake is **Serrano,** near the Big Bear Discovery Center. Check there for other campsite locations.

## Around the lake and outta here

From Big Bear Village, drop down to Big Bear Boulevard, the main commercial street. Head eastward and you'll shortly clear town. Before leaving the area, however, we suggest a loop drive around the lake, which is quite scenic in spots.

To do so, turn left at a traffic signal onto Stanfield Cutoff. Before doing this, you might want to continue through the signal to the recently developed **Stanfield Marsh Wildfowl Preserve**, just across the intersection. It's essentially a small park with benches where you can sit and watch the birdies in a marshy area at this end of Big Bear Lake. There were no interpretive signs when we visited and all we saw was a few mudhens, although things should improve.

Back on Stanfield Cutoff, head north, following "North shore resort" signs. After crossing a viaduct over the lake's eastern end, turn left at a stop sign onto North Shore Drive (State Route 38). The **Big Bear Discovery Center** will soon appear on the right; see "Activities" above. Beyond, you'll finally shed civilization and cruise along the most interesting side of the lake—less populated and more wooded than the south shore.

For your day's workout, watch on your right for the **Cougar Crest** trailhead; it's about a quarter of a mile beyond the discovery center. This hike is a moderate four-mile round trip through a thin pine forest to a ridge that offers a panorama of Big Bear Lake. The first mile is fairly level, and then you climb a series of gentle switchbacks. The trail goes behind Cougar Crest, then climbs to its top at a trail junction. For the best lake view, continue a few hundred feet beyond the ridge until you reach a rocky slope with no obstructing trees.

Returning to Highway 38, you'll encounter **Fawnskin,** a forest hamlet with many homes right on the water. Beyond, you'll pass more Forest Service facilities—trailheads, lakeside picnic areas, boat launches and roads to nearby campgrounds. And soon you'll be at the junction with Highway 18 at the lake's west end. To close the loop, it's faster—despite heavier traffic—to follow Route 18 back through Big Bear Lake. Of course, the winding North Shore Drive is more scenic.

A few miles east of Big Bear Lake, you'll encounter **Big Bear City.** Off the lake and more of a working community, it doesn't offer much of interest. It does, however, offer choices for getting down off the mountain. Highways 18 and 38 merge here and then separate. If you'd like to go north into the deserts, take Route 18 toward Victorville and Barstow.

If, however, you'd like to complete a wide sweeping loop of the San Bernardino Mountains, stay with Highway 38. It forks to the right on the east side of town, climbs a slight rise and finally sheds Big Bear City's suburbs. Beyond here, the highway is well engineered and very lightly traveled, taking you on wide, easy turns to the eastern edge of San Bernardino National Forest and then sweeping west again. This area is virtually unpopulated, and busy with Forest Service campgrounds. At least one, **San Gorgonio,** remains open in the off season. It's quite nice, with paved interior roads and pads, and flush potties.

You'll encounter only one town on this forty-two mile drive from Big Bear City—tiny **Angeles Oaks** with fuel, a café and cabins. From here, you'll gradually drop a couple of thousand feet to a dry riverbed, where you'll leave the trees behind. A sharp left turn will take you to a Christian retreat called **Forest Falls.** There's not much of interest back there, unless you're a retreating Christian. Highway 38, now pointing west and unkinked, follows the riverbed, headed for **Redlands** and Interstate 10.

***Where do we go from here?*** • If you'd like to pick up Tour Nineteen, you have two choices—one simple and longer, the other complicated and more direct. Your first choice is to follow Route 38 west to Redlands, then continue west on I-10 to Colton and take I-215 south to I-15 and Temecula, where the next tour begins.

For the much shorter rural route, turn south from Highway 38 onto an unnamed road at a sign indicating **Yucaipa.** (The turn is seven miles west of the Forest Falls junction.) After five miles of nondescript Yucaipa suburbs, turn right (west) onto Avenue L, a block before the road ends. Cruise down Avenue L a mile or so to Calimesa Boulevard in **Calimesa.** Go left and you'll shortly see signs indicating Interstate 10. Follow the freeway eight miles southeast to the second **Beaumont** exit and take State Route 79 south. Stay with this highway as it merges with Route 74 in **Hemet.** Seven miles west of Hemet, the two highways separate; follow Route 79 south toward I-15 and **Temecula.** You'll hit the town's quickly expanding suburbs before you reach the freeway. Go southeast briefly on I-15 and take the Rancho California Boulevard exit.

ENTERING

# JULIAN

HISTORIC DISTRICT

HISTORICAL LANDMARK NO. 4I2

*Tour Nineteen*

# INLAND SAN DIEGO
## *TEMECULA TO JULIAN & CUYAMACA STATE PARK*

This tour mostly concerns inland San Diego County, although it begins in Temecula in southern Riverside County. It's a region full of surprises, particularly for those who stereotype San Diego County as a land of beaches, Spanish tile roofs and palm trees.

That image is proper for the coast and certainly for San Diego itself, California's second largest city. However most of San Diego County—which is huge—is comprised of low mountain ranges and deserts. It's home to the world's second largest telescope, charming old missions and a venerable mining town that seems to have shifted southward from the California gold country. It is a place of both apples and oranges and—except on sunny weekends—it is surprisingly uncrowded.

### *TEMECULA*

Population: 27,000                                    Elevation: 1,006 feet

If you haven't been to Temecula in the past twenty years, you will be stunned by what you see. The personification of southern California growth explosion, it has evolved from a quaint cowtown into a thriving planned community of pink tile roofs and flagstone patios.

# TRIP PLANNER

**WHEN TO GO** ● This is an any-time-of-the-year route since the weather in San Diego County is rather benign. Summer is all right because this area isn't crowded with visitors, although winery tasting rooms in the Temecula Valley and the shops and boutiques of Julian can get busy on summer and fall weekends.

**DRIVING DISTANCE** ● It's eighty-four miles from Temecula through Julian and Cuyamaca State Park to I-8 at Descanso.

**RV ADVISORY** ● A sign advises that the twisting grade up to Palomar Observatory is not recommended for large trucks, so it might be a challenge for very large motorhomes or trailer rigs.

**WHAT YOU'LL SEE** ● Old Town Temecula, Mission San Antonio de Pala, Palomar Observatory, Lake Henshaw, Santa Ysabel Mission, the old fashioned towns of Santa Ysabel and Julian, and oak-mantled Cuyamaca Rancho State Park.

**WHAT TO DO** ● Sip good Chardonnay in the Temecula Valley, sample the products of the Julian Pie Company, taste fresh Julian apples in the fall, explore trails of Cuyamaca Rancho State Park.

**TO BEGIN** ● Get to Temecula on Interstate 15. If you're coming down from Tour Eighteen, see the end of the previous chapter for specifics.

## Useful contacts

**Julian Chamber of Commerce**, P.O. Box 413 (2129 Main St.), Julian, CA 92036.

**Temecula Valley Chamber of Commerce**, 27450 Ynez Rd., Suite 104, Temecula, CA 92591; (909) 676-5090.

## Pricing guidelines

**DINING:** Dinner entrée with soup or salad, without drinks or dessert for under $10 = **$**; $10 to $14 = **$$**; $15 to $25 = **$$$**; over $25 = **$$$$**.

**RECLINING:** A two-person room for $35 or less = **$**; $36 to $50 = **$$**; $51 to $75 = **$$$**; $76 to $100 = **$$$$**; more than $100 = **$$$$$**.

**CAMPING:** Under $10 = **$**; $10 to $14 = **$$**; $15 to $19 = **$$$**; $20 or more = **$$$$**

Temecula, an Indian word for "valley of joy," began in 1884 as a stagecoach stop and a provisioning center for the huge Vail Ranch, which covered most of the Temecula Valley. The town changed little until the late 1960s, when Kaiser Development Company bought the ranch and started building the planned community of Rancho California. Today, the combined population of Temecula and Rancho California is approaching 50,000—and growing.

This area also is home to California's newest wine country. In the 1970s, vintners found that the mild, sunny climate was ideal for the production of Chardonnay and other white wines. Four thousand acres of grapes and several tasting rooms now share the valley with fancy horse ranches and country estates.

Meanwhile, old Temecula sought survival by becoming a Western style tourist shopping complex. After two decades of slow conversion, it recently underwent a complete facelift. Utility lines went underground, boardwalks replaced sidewalks and "old" false front buildings emerged on vacant land. The result is a cowboy theme village that looks about as authentic Disney's Frontierland. Can officials really be serious about preservation when they permit a McDonald's restaurant in their historic district, even if it does look like an old train station?

To tour Temecula old and new, take the Rancho California exit from I-15 and follow signs to Old Town along Front Street. You'll find plenty of parking—except on summer weekends—at a large lot at Front and Sixth, beside that train station McDonald's. RV and trailer rigs can fit here if it isn't too crowded. A large mural at one end of the lot may be the most impressive thing down here, tracing the town's transportation history from a stage coach through a steam train to a hot air balloon above the vineyards.

You can pick up a copy of the *Temecula Valley Visitors Guide* at the **One Song Shop** in Butterfield Square at Front and Third streets; it serves as an unofficial visitor center. The official one, Temecula Valley Chamber of Commerce, is buried in a new shopping center somewhere out there on the flats.

## Into the vineyards

If you'd like to sample some of the Temecula Valley's fine wines, return to Rancho California Road, cross the freeway and pass through the pink stucco and turquoise planned business and residential areas. The suburban spread ends quite abruptly, for growth fanatics had the good sense to protect the valley's vineyards with an agricultural zone.

Most of the wineries are along Rancho California Road, starting with **Hart**

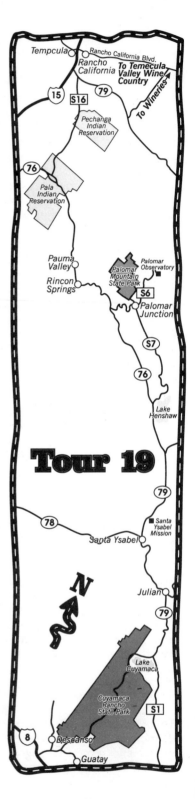

**Winery** on your left; open daily 9 to 4:30; (909) 676-6300. The imposing **Thornton Winery** housed in a French style château is just beyond on the right; daily from 10 to 5; (909) 699-0099. It produces sparkling wines as well as table wines, and it houses the attractive Café Champagne listed below. On the left is **Callaway Vineyard and Winery**, the oldest and largest of the valley's wineries, dating from 1974. Hours are 10:30 to 5 daily; (909) 676-4001.

The new **Stuart Cellars** is on the right, just up from Thornton; daily 10 to 5; (909) 676-6414. Across the way is **Mount Palomar Winery**, tucked behind a ridge; open daily 9 to 5; (909) 676-5047. On the right side of Rancho California is the **Baily Winery** tasting room, housed in a hilltop bungalow; daily 10 to 5; (909) 676-9463.

Beyond Baily, the next two wineries are to the left and to the right of Rancho California on Calle Contento. **Temecula Crest** is on the left at 40620 Calle Contento; daily 10 to 5; (909) 676-8231. A right turn gets you to **Cilurzo Vineyard and Winery** at 41220 Calle Contento; daily 9:30 to 5; (909) 676-5250. Founders Vincenzo and Audrey Cilurzo share vineland seniority with Callaway; they planted the valley's first vines in 1967 and opening their winery in 1978.

Back on Rancho California Road, the easternmost facility is **Wilson Creek** on the left near the junction of Glenoaks Road. It specializes in wines and weddings, open daily 10 to 5; (909) 693-9463. If you turn right onto Glenoaks and then right again on De Portola Road, you'll encounter the valley's other two wineries with tasting rooms. **Filsinger**, on the right in a Spanish colonial style building, is open weekends 10 to 5; (909) 676-4594. Two miles beyond, also Spanish style and on the right is **Keyways Winery and Vineyard,** open weekends 10 to 5; (909) 676-1451.

**NOTE:** For more detail on these vintners and their wines, get a copy of our *Best of the Wine Country*. It's available at major book stores or you can order directly; see the back of this book.

## DINING

Three of our chosen restaurants are in Old Town—places that have survived the Hollywood cowboy conversion. The fourth is an appealing café at Thornton Winery.

### The Bank of Mexican Food ● *28645 Front Street in Old Town;*
*(909) 676-6760. Mexican; wine and beer. Lunch and dinner daily. Major credit cards; $ to $$.* ☐ The name is silly, although this place is rather inviting, housed in old brick and brightened by a few Mexican artifacts. It was built in 1912 as the Temecula Bank, called the "Pawn Shop" by local ranchers. It now serves tasty Mexican fare instead of foreclosure notices.

### Café Champagne ● *At Thornton Winery, 32575 Rancho California*
*Rd.; (909) 699-0088. American nouveau; wine and champagne. Lunch daily, dinner nightly except Monday. MC/VISA; $$$.* ☐ This stylish restaurant, done in light woods with a vineyard theme, offers dining indoors and out. The changing menu focuses on regional fare, seasoned by herbs from its own garden. And of course, it has a good wine list. The café is very popular for weekend lunches and dinners, so reservations are advised.

San Antonio de Pala is the only California mission still serving native peoples. This is the campanario or bell wall.

**Rosa's Cantina** ● *28636 Front Street in Old Town; (909) 695-2428. Mexican; wine and beer. Lunch and dinner daily plus weekend brunch. Major credit cards; $.* ☐ This cheerful cantina is appealing for its sunny courtyard. Here, you can devour tasty, hearty and quite inexpensive smashed beans and rice dishes while watching the passing tourist parade on Front Street. The indoor dining area is dressed with piñatas, serapes and such.

**Swing Inn Family Café** ● *28676 Front Street in Old Town; (909) 676-2321. American; wine and beer. Daily from early breakfast through dinner. MC/VISA; $.* ☐ Temecula's oldest café, this false front classic dates from 1927 and its prices haven't changed too much since then. Calling itself "world famous," this simple diner advertises—on huge outdoor banners—biscuits and gravy for a dollar, liver and onions for $4 and steak and eggs for $5. Prices may have increased by the time you get there, but probably not by much. We hope Swing Inn survives the area's rhinestone cowboy gentrification, since it's about the only authentic thing left there.

## To Pala, Julian and Cuyamaca

From Temecula, go briefly south on I-15 to the Highway 79 exit and cross east under the freeway. After a few blocks, fork right at a traffic signal, leaving State Route 79 and following signs south to the Pechanga Indian Reservation and Pala. You'll soon shed Temecula's sprawl and enter a pleasant oak woodland on a highway that sees little traffic. If you need to shed your loose change, the **Pechanga Casino** comes up on your right after a couple of miles.

You'll soon cross into San Diego County and, about nine miles from Temecula, enter the Pala Indian Reservation and the quiet village of **Pala.** You'll hit a stop sign at Pala Mission Road; go left (east) briefly to **Mission San Antonio de Pala.** This is one of the most appealing of California's missions, with hand-painted decorations on its whitewashed adobe walls and a classic *campanario* (bell wall). Step inside the simple chapel, with rough log beam ceilings and a tile floor worn smooth by the sandals of nearly two centuries of worshipers. Pala was established in 1816 as an *asistencia* (sub-mission) to Mission San Luis Rey southwest of here. It carries a special distinction as the only California mission still ministering to the native people. The chapel, a small museum and gift shop are open Tuesday-Sunday 10 to 4 from April through October and 10 to 3 the rest of the year; (760) 742-1600.

Just past the mission, you'll join State Route 76, headed eastward into the **Pauma Valley.** This is rather a pretty basin, adorned with dark green citrus groves that begin at roadside and extend high into the flanking mountains. As the highway starts climbing out of the grovelands, fork to the left onto County Road S-6, heading up Palomar Mountain to the world's most famous optical device.

---

*RV ADVISORY* ● The grade up Palomar Mountain has many tight turns, although they're well engineered. Alertly driven RVs and trailer rigs should be able to negotiate the road, although a sign advises that it's not recommended for large trucks.

---

After nearly seven miles of twists and turns, during which you'll get occasional glimpses back to the Pauma Valley citrus groves, you'll arrive at a junction with County Road S-7. **Palomar Mountain General Store** here has grocery staples, curios and souvenir T-shirts. Next-door **Palomar Mountain Restaurant** is open daily in summer and Friday-Monday the rest of the year, from mid-morning through late afternoon, serving light American fare.

A left turn onto Road S-7 will take you three miles up to **Palomar Mountain State Park,** essentially a high hillside swatch of oaks, pines and spruce trees. Its Silver Crest picnic area is rather pleasant, with a monster spruce tree in its middle. Other than this, we found no pressing reason to go up there, unless you need a place to camp. The very attractive oak-shaded campground has flush potties and showers, with no hookups; **$$$**; (760) 742-3462. Sites can be reserved with a MasterCard or VISA by calling (800) 444-PARK.

Back at the junction, continue north on County Road S-6 toward the observatory. En route, you'll pass the **Observatory Campground** of Cleveland National Forest, a bit cheaper than the state park, but with pit potties and no showers. Just beyond is the star of Palomar Mountain:

**Palomar Observatory** • *Palomar Mountain; (760) 742-2119. Museum open daily 9 to 4; gift shop open daily in summer and weekends only the rest of the year. Picnic area nearby.* ☐ More interesting and better arranged than the Mount Wilson Observatory (Tour Seventeen), Palomar houses the world's most honored starfinder. The 200-inch Hale telescope unveiled in 1948 is no longer the world's largest, having been eclipsed by a 236-inch Russian lens. However that instrument has never worked quite right and the Hale is still considered the world's best gatherer of starlight.

Astronomers at Palomar no longer sit within the telescope's giant framework and squint into the eyepiece. Stellar images are now videotaped in a modern control center that looks capable of launching a space shuttle. Linked to computers and spectrographs, the great Hale telescope continues to make significant discoveries.

You can watch a video in the visitor center about the telescope's development, peer at sky photos and be dazzled by the usual astounding astronomical figures. You may or may not want to know, for instance, that a light year is six trillion miles. Our nearest galaxy, Andromeda, is two million light years away and—well, you get the idea. From the museum, a short walk takes you into the Hale telescope's dome, where a couple of nicely done graphics describe how it works.

Return to the junction and take Road S-7 east, following signs toward Lake Henshaw. A short distance from the junction, a left turn at a fire station will take you to a rustic hideaway in the village of Palomar Mountain:

**Palomar Mountain Lodge** • *P.O. Box 122 (22228 Crestline Rd.), Palomar Mountain, CA 92060; (760) 742-8744. (WEB SITE: www.netpage.com/palomarlodge) Simple lodge rooms $$$. Restaurant serves lunch and dinner Tuesday-Saturday, and breakfast and lunch Sunday; wine and beer; $$. MC/VISA.* ☐ This handsomely weathered 1920s squared log inn is worth a look even if you don't plan to recline or dine. Step inside to admire its great stone fireplace and rough beam ceilings, and inhale the heady aroma that suggests an old trapper's cabin. Antler chandeliers dangle from the ceiling and game trophies and skins decorate the walls. On a clear day, from umbrella tables out front, you can see across San Diego County to the ocean.

Palomar Mountain's east grade is not as snake-like as County Road S-6 coming up from the Pauma Valley, and you'll quickly and easily descend to State Route 76. That pale orb below, sitting in a featureless beige basin like a giant blue hand print, is **Lake Henshaw.** It's rather a homely pond with a barren shoreline, although it yields good catches of bass, crappie, bluegill and catfish. You can learn all about that at small resort across the highway:

**Lake Henshaw Resort** • *26439 Highway 76, Santa Ysabel, CA 92070; (760) 782-3487 or (760) 782-3501. Housekeeping cabins with kitchens; $$$; RV park with hookups; $$$, without $$. MC/VISA.* ☐ This somewhat scruffy resort has rustic cabins, an RV park, boat rentals, a store and a small café serving breakfast through dinner, with wine and beer. Across the highway, a short road leads to the lake and a boat launch.

About four miles beyond the resort, the highway blends into State Route 79, headed for Santa Ysabel and Julian. After seven miles, watch on your left for the tiny and charming **Santa Ysabel Mission,** founded in 1818. Weathered yet tidy, the complex includes a whitewashed chapel built in 1924, a small museum and picnic tables beneath gnarled oaks. This exceedingly pleasant retreat is open daily 8 to 5:30 in summer and 8 to 4 the rest of the year.

Just below is the tiny old town of **Santa Ysabel.** Most of its structures are occupied by shops and galleries, a spillover from nearby Julian. On your right as you enter town are the **Julian Pie Company** and adjacent **Julian Pie Company Restaurant.** The bakery, in a cheery red building, offers exceptionally tasty pies, plus other baked goods, specialty coffees and ice cream. The apple pies are worth writing to Mom about. Also savory are "apple memories," small, feather-light cookies made of cinnamon-dusted pie crust. The adjacent restaurant, with an early American menu and décor, serves breakfast through dinner daily; major credit cards **$$**; (760) 765-2400.

From here, follow Highway 79 into thickly wooded hills past apple orchards and roadside fruit stands. The largest and oldest—dating from 1916—is **Farmers Fruit Stand and Bakery**. It has a large selection of apples and apple pies, plus specialty foods, breads, bakery goods and apple cider. Next door is the **Codarossa Winery** "tasting saloon" in a tiny false front store.

## JULIAN

**Population: 1,300**                                          **Elevation: 4,220 feet**

Promoters of Julian have exercised more restraint than those in Temecula. Or perhaps they just have a smaller budget. Instead of constructing phony Western style buildings, the folks here make do with what they have, preserving the original look of this old mining town.

The Julian area offers a curious mix—not apples and oranges but apples and gold. Prospectors found gold in these hills in the late 1880s, but it soon ran out and the town was on the verge of dying. Then folks realized that the high altitude was ideal for apple production and Julian got its second lease on life. Then came the tourists, and they're still coming. You might want to avoid Julian on summer and fall weekends. (The town celebrates the autumn apple harvest with festivities that draw major crowds.)

The first thing of interest you'll see as you approach town is the **Julian Pioneer Museum** at Washington and Fourth. It's nicely done, with pioneer artifacts and photos displayed on wood panel walls. Other exhibits include an entire surrey, saddles and a horse-drawn sleigh. It's open daily 10 to 4 April through November, and weekends only the rest of the year; (760) 765-0227.

From the museum, head uphill on Main Street to prowl the shops and boutiques of this old town. Although most buildings are original, no tourist lure has been left unturned. The former town hall is a venue for weekend melodramas; the Julian Drugstore is a working pharmacy and a pharmaceutical museum; the next-door Miners Diner has red checkered tablecloths, an old fashioned soda fountain and fare to match. There's another Julian Pie Company outlet just below the heart of downtown at 2225 Main, in an old cottage with a shaded patio out front; (760) 765-2449.

## DINING

We liked two restaurants in Julian—one trendy and cozy; the other downright corny.

**The Julian Grille** • *2224 Main St.; (760) 765-0173. American; full bar service. Lunch daily, dinner nightly except Monday, Sunday brunch. MC/VISA; $$.* ☐ Housed in a tree-shaded cottage, the Grille has a kind of folksy-trendy look, with bentwood chairs, ceiling fans, hanging plants and white nappery. One can dine indoors or in a pleasant garden area. The menu features chicken Jerusalem, shrimp scampi and tempura, spicy fisherman's stew, and tomato herb pasta. A tasty specialty is "Sweet Georgia Peach"—chicken breast sautéed with pecans and topped with peaches.

**Rongbranch Restaurant** • *2722 Washington; (760) 765-2265. American; full bar service. Lunch and dinner daily. Major credit cards; $$.* ☐ The silly spelling tells you that this false front place is targeted to tourists. The inside look is predictable—knotty pine walls and cowboy regalia. It does occupy one of the town's old corrugated roof buildings and its serves hefty helpings of good old American grub, plus several pasta dishes. "Down home dinners" include honey dipped chicken, buffalo steak, and liver and onions. The Boars Head Saloon in the rear is a good place to retire with a drink while your travel mate is browsing the boutiques.

## RECLINING

**Julian Gold Rush Hotel** • *P.O. Box 1856 (2032 Main St.), Julian, CA 92036; (800) 734-5854 or (760) 765-0201. (WEB SITE: www.julianhotel.com; E-MAIL: b&b@julianhotel.com) Fifteen rooms and cottages with private baths; full breakfast. MC/VISA, AMEX; $$$$.* ☐ Julian's oldest hotel has been restored and dressed in early American finery, including print wallpaper, scalloped drapes and old fashioned bedsteads with country style spreads. The sitting room is particularly comfy, with overstuffed furniture and a cast iron stove. The complex also includes a couple of cottages. The hotel was started in 1897 by freed Missouri slaves Albert and Margaret Robinson.

Pressing south from Julian on State Route 79, you'll reach Cuyamaca Rancho State Park (pronounced *kwey-uh-MAK-uh*). This former Spanish ranch contains 25,000 acres of oak, chaparral and pine woodlands, more than a hundred miles of hiking trails and several campgrounds.

About three miles from Julian, before you enter the park, watch on your left for a vista point. It provides an impressive panorama of the Anza-Borrego Desert, which we've scheduled for a visit in the next chapter.

A bit farther along is small **Lake Cuyamaca** with a store, café, tackle shop, boat rentals and RV hookups. Its lake view restaurant serves Austrian fare such as smoked pork chops and *wienerschnitzel*, plus American steaks, chicken and chops. It's open for breakfast through dinner; MC/VISA; $$; (760) 765-0700. The state park is just beyond:

**Cuyamaca Rancho State Park** ● *12551 Highway 79, Descanso, CA 91916; (760) 765-0755. Attractions include hiking trails, picnic sites and an historical museum. RV and tent sites, no hookups; $$$. Two of its campgrounds have flush potties and showers—Paso Picacho in the northern end and Green Valley Falls to the south. Reservations advised in summer and on fall weekends by calling (800) 444-PARK; MC/VISA accepted.* ☐

As you enter the park's lush woodland, look to your left for 5,730-foot Stonewall Peak, a green clad conical mountain with a bald knob. A few miles below, turn left at the park headquarters sign and drive about a quarter of a mile to an attractive three-story stone structure. One of the original ranch buildings, it now houses a visitor center and museum open weekdays 8:30 to 4:30 and weekends 10 to 4. The museum has exhibits about the native Kumeya'ay people, plus the flora, fauna and geology of the park and historic photos of the ranch. This complex also has a small store open 10 to 4, daily in summer and weekends only the rest of the year. Several hiking trails begin at the visitor center area.

Below the visitor center, you'll travel through more oak and chaparral woodlands, and then hit Interstate 8 near **Descanso Junction.**

☺ ☺ ☺

**Where do we go from here?** ● Interstate 8 provides quick deliverance west and east. However, if you plan to blend into the next tour to Anza-Borrego Desert, reverse your route through the park—the scenery's nice in either direction—then head east from Julian on State Route 78. Or you can seek new scenery on the return route by taking rambling County Road S-1 north. This twenty-three mile route climbs and twists through the Laguna Mountains of Cleveland National Forest east of Cuyamaca and links with Highway 79 below Julian.

As you drive downhill from Julian toward the Anza-Borrego Desert, you'll drop quickly from a temperate to a desert climate zone—something to contemplate if you're planning this trip in summer.

HOPE YOU ENJOYED
YOUR VISIT
PLEASE COME AGAIN

## Tour Twenty

# DESERTS & DATES

### ANZA-BORREGO TO JOSHUA TREE NATIONAL PARK

**A** massive oval chunk of southeastern California once was considered a desert wasteland. It's still desert, although it's hardly wasted. It contains two national parks, a national preserve, California's largest state park, several resort communities including the famous Palm Springs, and nearly all of America's date palm groves.

This region, which extends west from the Tehachapi Mountains to Death Valley and then south to the Mexican border, covers about 35,000 square miles. That's nearly the size of Indiana. The landscape ranges from "high desert"—the Mojave, often over a mile above sea level and rich with cactus gardens, to "low desert"—the Colorado, covered mostly by creosote bush and mesquite. And you can't get any lower than Death Valley, the bottom point in North America.

Californians have been concerned about their deserts ever since there have been Californians—going back to the first Spanish settlers. Their initial concern was to avoid them. Father Junipero Serra, arriving in 1769 to establish the first missions, stayed close to the coast to miss the inland deserts. In 1775, Juan Bautista de Anza led a group of San Jose-bound colo-

# TRIP PLANNER

**WHEN TO GO** ● Since these are desert areas, this tour is best taken from fall through spring. If you love fresh dates, do the trip in fall or early winter, when date palms in the Coachella Valley ripen.

**DRIVING DISTANCE** ● The route from Julian through Anza-Borrego Desert State Park, along the Salton Sea and north through Mojave National Preserve covers about 160 miles, with another ten miles to reach Twentynine Palms.

**RV ADVISORY** ● The only advisory on this route is to take plenty of water.

**WHAT YOU'LL SEE** ● The vast and arid expanses of Anza-Borrego Desert State Park, the briny Salton Sea, the date gardens of the Coachella Valley and the cactus gardens and wild landforms of Joshua Tree National Park.

**WHAT TO DO** ● Hike into Borrego Palm Canyon at Anza-Borrego Desert State Park; try a date shake at Valerie Jean's; dip your toe—but not much else—into the Salton Sea; hike through the stunning formations of Joshua Tree National Park, particularly on the Arch Rock and Skull Rock trails.

**TO BEGIN** ● Head downhill from Julian from the previous tour. If you didn't take it, drive north from Interstate 8 through Cuyamaca Rancho State Park to Julian.

## Useful contacts

**Anza-Borrego Desert State Park** ● *P.O. Box 299, Borrego Springs, CA 92004-0299; (760) 767-4684.*

**Borrego Springs Chamber of Commerce,** P.O. Box 420 (622 Palm Canyon Dr.), Borrego Springs, CA 92004; (800) 559-5524 or (760) 767-5555. (WEB SITE: www.borregosprings.com; E-MAIL: borspcoc@znet.com)

**Joshua Tree National Park,** 74485 National Park Dr., Twentynine Palms, CA 92277-3597; (760) 367-5500. (WEB SITE: www.nps.gov/jotr)

## Pricing guidelines

**DINING:** Dinner entrée with soup or salad, without drinks or dessert for under $10 = **$**; $10 to $14 = **$$**; $15 to $25 = **$$$**; over $25 = **$$$$**.

**RECLINING:** A two-person room for $35 or less = **$**; $36 to $50 = **$$**; $51 to $75 = **$$$**; $76 to $100 = **$$$$**; more than $100 = **$$$$$**.

**CAMPING:** Under $10 = **$**; $10 to $14 = **$$**; $15 to $19 = **$$$**; $20 or more = **$$$$**

---

nists across San Diego County's Anza-Borrego Desert—and didn't stop. A group of Fortyniners headed for the gold fields nearly died crossing Death Valley. Once the deserts had been crossed, the next temptation was to irrigate and cultivate them. Construction of a diversion dam on the Colorado River near Yuma in 1905 led to a levee break that turned a low desert basin into the Salton Sea. It's still there, growing mostly brine shrimp. However, tens of thousands of acres of desert have been irrigated and cultivated, particularly in the Coachella Valley and south through El Centro to the Mexican border.

After people began using the deserts, the conservationists came, determined to help save what remained. They were concerned, and rightfully so, about general abuse of this so-called wasteland. Under the loose control of the Bureau of Land Management, much of the desert has been open to off-road vehicles, hunting, uncontrolled grazing and mining. A major conservation step was achieved in 1994 when Congress passed the California Desert Protection Act. This created the Mojave National Preserve and upgraded Death Valley and Joshua Tree from national monument to national park status, while adding additional acreage to both.

We shall explore California's desert—including those three federal preserves—on the next two tours. The first thing you'll notice, if you haven't been here before, is that deserts aren't vast swatches of sand. In fact, sand dunes are rather a novelty. Mostly, California's deserts are thick with vegetation and quite mountainous. They contain some amazing landforms. Incidentally, except for resorts such as Palm Springs, these deserts are almost always uncrowded.

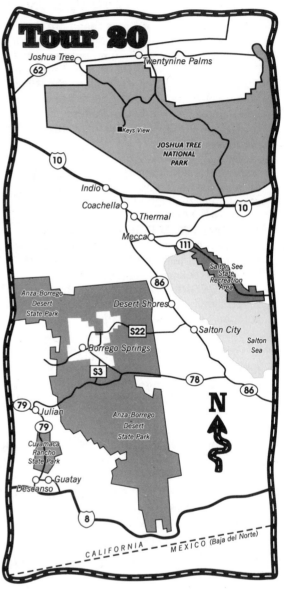

## Julian to Anza-Borrego

From Julian, spiral quickly downhill on State Route 78, through a vee-shaped valley cradled by green-clad hills. The route levels off briefly in a high basin, then it loses more altitude until it reaches a beige desert. Welcome to America's largest state park:

**Anza-Borrego Desert State Park** ● *P.O. Box 299, Borrego Springs, CA 92004-0299; (760) 767-4684. Modest day use fee is collected at park headquarters in Borrego Springs. Main campgrounds are at Tamarisk Grove several miles inside the west entrance and at Borrego Palm Canyon, near the visitor center above Borrego Springs. Both have tables, barbecue grills and flush potties; no hookups; $$.* ☐

Anza-Borrego Desert is interesting although not awesome. The same can be said for Borrego Springs, the town surrounded by this huge state park. Although the adjacent mountains are imposing, particularly in late light, there are much more dramatic desert settings and more attractive desert towns in California. Mostly, Anza-Borrego is *big*, covering 600,000 acres—nearly half of San Diego County. Much of the park is in the Colorado Desert that extends westward from the Colorado River. It's generally under a thousand feet above sea level, so it doesn't have the rich cactus gardens of some of the higher desert areas.

However, Anza-Borrego does have its moments. Some areas offer impressive spring wildflower blooms from mid-February to early April, and the park has one of the largest native palm groves in California. It has several dramatic land formations such as the Borrego Badlands and Split Mountain, and this is a serious hikers' park, with more than thirty trails and nature walks. The double-jointed name, incidentally, honors De Anza's trek through here and the desert's elusive bighorn sheep. *Borrego* is Spanish for a yearling sheep or lamb.

Several miles after you've entered the park on Highway 78, turn left onto County Road S-3 toward Borrego Springs. **Tamarisk Grove Campground** is near the junction, with nicely spaced sites shaded by silvery-limbed tamarisk trees. Across the highway, the short **Cactus Loop Trail** will provide an introduction to local plant life; pamphlets are available at the trailhead. Beyond Tamarisk Grove, the highway climbs a low, rocky ridge and then descends into a broad desert basin. In the middle is the only town in California completely surrounded by a state park:

## BORREGO SPRINGS

**Population: 2,989**                         **Elevation: 780 feet**

Road S-3 forks to the right at the edge of town and carries you into the heart of this scattered, low-rise community. However, you might want to pause first at the intersection to admire **La Casa del Zorro,** a strikingly elegant desert resort; listed below.

Continuing toward town, you'll encounter a landscaped traffic disc called Christmas Circle. Do a three-quarter turn and spin off onto Palm Canyon Drive to pass through the heart of Borrego Springs. Don't expect a Palm Springs; this is a rather simple little community. On your right about midtown is the **Borrego Springs Chamber of Commerce** at 622

Palm Canyon Drive, open weekdays 9 to 5; (760) 767-5555. Across the street is the town's main shopping area, simply called The Mall. Incidentally, nearly all of the streets and roads in and around Borrego Springs have bike lanes, so this is a nice area for peddling off a few calories. You can get a bike route map at the chamber or the state park visitor center.

From downtown, continue toward the rocky face of the San Ysidro Mountains and you'll soon reach the **Anza-Borrego State Park Visitor Center.** En route, you'll pass **Palm Canyon Resort** that we recommend below; immediately beyond is Hoberg Road, which leads to another recommendation, **Krazy Coyote Grill.**

The park visitor center is a rather striking affair, bunkered into a slope and fronted with a fieldstone wall. Its earthen roof serves as an observation platform, where you can admire the surrounding sweep of desert. The center is open 9 to 5, daily October through May, then weekends and holidays only the rest of the year. Just north of the visitor center is **Borrego Palm Canyon Campground,** listed above.

A popular park hike, the **Borrego Palm Canyon Trail,** leads from the campground into a spectacular rocky ravine, ending at one of California's largest native fan palm groves. This three-mile round trip isn't strenuous, although it does involve a little rock-hopping. At trail's end, you'll find just what you'd expect in a desert canyon oasis—a cool, shady palm grove, but with no nubile maidens bathing in a sylvan pool. In fact, there's no sylvan pool; the hundreds of palms in this canyon get their water from underground springs. The trail goes into the grove only a few dozen yards; the palms are so thick that further progress would be difficult.

On the way back, you can fork to the right at a footbridge for an alternate return trail. However, it's useful only if you want a more challenging workout. It's longer, more rocky and it climbs higher up the canyon wall.

## DINING AND RECLINING

**Krazy Coyote Grill** ● *In the Palms at Indian Head Resort, end of Hoberg Road; (760) 767-7788. (WEB: www.thepalmsatindianhead.com) American-southwestern; full bar service. Lunch and dinner daily, plus Sunday brunch. Major credit cards; $$$.* ☐ Despite the silly name, this is a rather stylish looking café. It's done in light woods, accented by ceramic Mexican masks and—a nice touch—a row of old pots on a pony wall, each containing a sprig of desert flora. An outdoor dining area provides pleasing desert views. The menu is pleasing as well, featuring sesame-garlic pork tenderloin, seared tuna, chicken achiote and several steaks.

**La Casa del Zorro** ● *3845 Yaqui Pass Rd., Borrego Springs, CA 92004-5000; (800) 824-1884 or (760) 767-5323. Seventy-seven rooms, suites and casitas with TV/VCRS, movies, phones and honor bars; $$$$ to $$$$$. Two restaurant serve American-continental fare; breakfast through dinner; full bar service; $$$. Major credit cards.* ☐ "The House of the Fox," with a rare four-diamond AAA rating, is one of California's most elegant desert resorts. Spread over forty-two acres, this low rise Spanish-Southwest style complex has golf and tennis, three pools, spas, a fitness center, putting green, ping pong, shuffleboard and biking. Western theme oil paintings decorate the textured stucco walls of the main lodge.

**Palm Canyon Resort** • *P.O. Box 956 (221 Palm Canyon Dr., Borrego Springs, CA 92004; (800) 242-0044 or (760) 767-5341. Sixty rooms and suites with TV and phones; $$$$. Restaurant serves American fare; full bar service; lunch through dinner; $$. RV sites with full hookups; $$$$. Major credit cards.* □ This complex near the state park visitor center is almost an independent community. Facilities include lodging and dining, pool, an RV park, store and coin laundry. The resort has an "old Western desert" theme, with false front trim.

For quick bites, locals rave about **Jilberto's Taco Shop,** a simple walkup just above the traffic circle. It serves a full range of inexpensive burritos, tacos and such. Try the hefty breakfast burrito to start your day or to end your lunch. Jilberto is open daily, early morning to midnight; no alcohol or credit cards.

## Through Anza-Borrego to the Salton Sea

You have two choices for getting out of town, back into the surrounding state park and ultimately to the Salton Sea.

County Road S-22 is the most direct route. After a few miles, you'll see a dirt road on your right that leads four miles to **Fonts Point,** an overlook of the eroded **Borrego Badlands**. However, the road can be rough and sandy in spots, depending on what recent storms have done. Check at the visitor center before attempting it with an RV, or even with the family sedan. Back on S-22, now called the Borrego Salton Seaway, you'll hit a low crest offering a view of that giant pale blue oval. Just beyond, the highway passes through another badlands area before hitting State Route 86 at the edge of the Salton Sea.

The other way out is via Highway 78, reached by going southeast from Borrego Springs. At the desert hamlet of **Ocotillo Wells,** you can go south on Split Mountain Road for two natural attractions. **Elephant Tree Nature Trail** takes you past a rare collection of curiously twisted low trees with chubby, fleshy main trunks. They're common in Mexico and rare in the United States. At the end of the road you'll hit **Split Mountain,** a steep-walled ravine with a flat, sandy bottom. Unless the weather's bad, you can drive your car or rig right up to the canyon mouth, and then take a hike past its eroded formations. Back on the main highway, you'll hit the southwest corner of the Salton Sea on State Route 86.

### A salty, sad sea

Welcome to one of the most unappealing landmarks in California. The state's largest body of water, the Salton Sea is a brackish sump that was created—as we noted above—when an attempted Colorado River diversion broke through a levee in 1905. With no outlets, it has become increasingly saltier and it soon may be a dead sea. In some ways, it already is. Thousands of fish are dying from toxic water—possibly from botulism. In turn, thousands of fish-eating birds have died as well. The terrible irony is that a large section of the sea is a national wildlife sanctuary.

So why did we come here? First, the Salton Sea is fascinating in a macabre sort of way. Second, this is the most direct route between Anza-Borrego and Joshua Tree National Park. Finally, the northern shore is rimmed

*Clusters of ripening fruit hang from date palms in the Coachella Valley near the Salton Sea. Most dates ripen from early fall through early winter.*

with date palm gardens and orange groves, with several date stands along the roadways. To reach that more appealing region, head north on Highway 86, which you can do quickly because it's four-lane most of the way. It's also quite busy, as the main artery between the rich Coachella Valley above and the El Central agricultural area below. Several lakeside towns along here contribute to the traffic; most are as drab looking as the lake.

### So listen, how about a date?

The scenery improves considerably as the highway reaches the ranks of date palms and orange groves of the Coachella Valley, backdropped by the sawtoothed Santa Rosa Mountains. Date palm gardens—that's what they're called—have a regimental stateliness that has always intrigued us. And if you like this dark fruit of the desert, you're gonna love this place.

The vast majority of dates consumed in America are *deglet noors*, since they're firm and easy to pack. The more tasty and fragile varieties, such as *khawdawys, medjools* and *halaways* usually are available only at the source, since they do not travel well. Our favorite is the dry, chewy *thoory* or "bread date." This is the original from the Near East and it remains the dominant date there today. Another awesome Coachella Valley treat is the date shake, and we always have too many when we pass this way.

The first roadside date place you'll encounter is **Santa Rosa Dates** on your left. It's open daily 8 to 5 and takes MC/VISA. It offers free samples and sells a variety of dates, date products and other specialty foods. A few miles beyond is long-established **Valerie Jean's,** also on the left and recently purchased by the Santa Rosa folks. Its hours are the same and it sells the best date shakes in the Coachella Valley.

Just under five miles from Valerie Jean's, turn right at a traffic signal onto Airport Boulevard. Drive a mile and a half east to scruffy little **Thermal** on State Route 111 and turn south. You'll soon encounter **Oasis Gardens** on the right, the largest and most modern of the date places in this area, with a café and picnic area tucked among the palms. In addition to date-related goodies, it sells cookies, pies and breads. Hours are 8 to 5:30 weekdays and 9 to 5:30 weekends; MC/VISA, DISC.

Just down the road, a left turn at a traffic signal will take you through the company farm town of **Mecca** and on to Interstate 10 and the back door of Joshua Tree National Park. However, if you'd like to get closer to the Salton Sea, continue a few miles south from Mecca on Highway 111:

***Salton Sea State Recreation Area*** • *100-255 State Park Rd., North Shore, CA 92254; (760) 393-3052. Modest day use fee; campsites with water and electric $$$$; no hookups; $$; flush potties and showers.* ⬜ It seems ironic that one of the state's best equipped camping areas is on the shore of this sad sea. This place is really strange, with a gravelly alkaline shoreline littered with dead fish. It smells like a seafood market that failed health inspection; not a strong odor but a pervasive one. At a visitor center, you can learn the latest developments in efforts to keep this inland sea from dying.

---

**FUELING ADVISORY** • Once you leave State Route 111 headed eastward beyond Mecca, you'll encounter no services for about seventy miles. There is no fuel in Joshua Tree National Park.

---

Back at the Mecca turnoff, head east on an unnumbered highway that will take you to I-10, although no sign indicates this. After several miles of vineyards and citrus groves just east of Mecca, you'll enter a little known and rarely visited hilly badlands area called **Orocopia Mountains Wilderness,** administered by BLM. This is as fascinating as any landform you'll see in the desert, with tilted strata, spires, rows of fused-together cones and shapes that suggest hunched, scowling gnomes. Colors are muted, from beiges and grays to subtle pea soup greens and hints of russet. Informal camping is permitted among these strange shapes; it's a far more appealing place than Salton Sea State Recreation Area.

Cross over I-10 (there are no services at this interchange) and you'll enter the back door of one of America's newest national parks—by designation, at least:

**Joshua Tree National Park** ● *74485 National Park Dr., Twenty-nine Palms, CA 92277-3597; (760) 367-5500. (WEB: www.nps.gov/jotr) Modest day use fees are collected at visitor centers. The park has nine campgrounds with developed or primitive sites, flush or pit potties, picnic tables and barbecue grills; no hookups. Some are free because they have no piped water; there are modest fees for others. The park has no fuel or food services. Oasis Visitor Center in Twentynine Palms and Cottonwood Visitor Center near the south entrances are open daily 8 to 5.* ☐

Joshua Tree is named for one of the desert's strangest plants—a member of the yucca family with spiny bottle-brush arms that can grow as much as forty feet high. It earned its odd name from early Mormon settlers who likened these huge plants to Joshua with arms extended to heaven. However, this park's most impressive features are its awesome landforms. Millions of years ago, layers of molten lava intruded beneath an overlay of gneiss, then hardened into granite. As the softer gneiss has worn away, the granite has been sculpted into an incredible variety of shapes, from giant boulders as round as marbles to towering spires and pinnacles. Many of the park's granite upthrustings are popular with rock climbers. Intermixed with this land of sculpted granite shapes are narrow canyons, alluvial fans rich with cactus gardens and great scatterings of stone dark and sinister with desert varnish.

Although little known outside the West, Joshua Tree is certainly popular locally, drawing more than two million visitors a year. However, it's so huge, covering 800,000 acres, that it rarely seems crowded. It was established as Joshua Tree National Monument in 1936, then promoted to national park status in 1994. Prime visitor times are spring and fall, and campgrounds often can fill up on those weekends. Wintertime is less crowded since it can get cold at the park's relatively high elevations. Brief snowfalls are not uncommon.

As you enter the back gate, pause at the **Cottonwood Visitor Center** on for brochures and a preview of what lures lie ahead. Continuing into the park, you'll climb into a rich desert garden, with yellow blooming rabbit brush lining the roadside in summer and fall. You'll see some of the rugged rock formations for which the park is famous, then you'll pass through the dry, monotonous creosote bush terrain of Pinto Basin.

Climbing out of the basin, you'll complete a transition from the Colorado Desert to the higher, wetter and more lush Mojave Desert. The fantastic rock formations return, and you'll start seeing the forests of Joshua trees that populate the park. You'll also pass our favorite campground, **White Tank,** with sites tucked right among the rocks. A short hike from the campground will take you to **Arch Rock,** a granite boulder weathered into an elongated arch. Actually, it looks like an elephant's head with a large molar. There are hundreds of other granite shapes along this trail, some so massive and strange that you can imagine yourself on another planet. Say hello to Yoda. Beyond White Tank, you'll hit a T-intersection, and a left turn will take you toward Jumbo Rocks, the park's best formations. After a couple of miles, watch on your left for the **Skull Rock** trailhead. Starting at a very convincing looking granite skull, this 1.7-mile trail takes you through a splendid badlands area of rocky shapes. It passes

*Strange "trees" with grotesquely twisted arms are the trademark of Joshua Tree National Park; it's also noted for outerworldly rock formations.*

through Jumbo Rocks Campground, crosses the highway into more sculpted terrain, then returns to Skull Rock. (*NAVIGATIONAL NOTE:* To complete the trail loop, go to the right when you reach the campground.)

A few miles beyond Skull Rock, turn left at the sign indicating **Keys View.** This overlook provides a panoramic sweep of the Coachella Valley, with graphics identifying the features below. On a clear day, you can see the date gardens around Coachella and Indio, the green gems of Palm Springs' golf courses and resorts and that pale blue dead eye of the Salton Sea. Unfortunately, such clarity is rare, since winds carry smog from the Los Angeles Basin over San Gorgonio Pass and into the valley below.

One could spend days exploring this fascinating park. For the moment, retrace your route from Keys View, turn left and follow signs to State Route 62 and the hamlet of **Joshua Tree.** This drab desert town is not a pretty face. Neither is its larger and more sprawling neighbor to the east:

## TWENTYNINE PALMS

**Population: 15,000**                    **Elevation: 1,960 feet**

I first saw Twentynine Palms as a young Marine, undergoing desert survival training. I remember it as a small, dusty desert town. The base is still there—now called the Marine Corps Air Ground Combat Center—and Twentynine Palms is now a *big*, dusty desert town.

However, it does have a selection of motels, service stations and a couple of interesting places to eat. They're catty-corner, downtown at Highway 62 and Tamarisk Avenue:

**The Finicky Coyote** • *73511 Twentynine Palms Hwy.; (760) 367-2429. American; no alcohol. Morning to late afternoon; $.* ☐ This small café in a Spanish style building has a "Berkeley-comes-to-the-desert" look, with a whole-earth menu to match. It issues sandwiches, soups and salads, and specializes in fruit drinks laced with calcium, protein powder, ginseng and such. In addition to menu items, the Coyote sells a good selection of health oriented specialty foods.

**Edchada's** • *56805 Twentynine Palms Hwy.; (760) 367-2131. Mexican; full bar service. Lunch weekdays and dinner nightly. MC/VISA, DISC; $.* ☐ This inexpensive *cantina* offers tasty burritos, tacos, rellenos, tostadas, enchiladas and whatever else can be wrapped in a tortilla. Flautas are a specialty, and it also has a few "Gringo Great" sandwiches. The café is quite attractive, with Spanish arch windows, drop lamps and stylistic Mexican paintings on whitewashed walls.

☺ ☺ ☺

**Where do we go from here?** • If you head west on Highway 62 you'll hit Interstate 10, and if you go east you'll wind up in Nevada.

If you want to seguay into our next tour, it's a bit more complicated. Go east from downtown and, after about a mile, turn left at a blinking light onto Utah Trail. This takes you along the edge of the Marine base. After several blocks, turn right at a blinking amber light onto Amboy Road and just keep going. The town of Amboy is forty-seven miles away and Mojave National Preserve is another eighteen.

The highway first travels past several miles of ugly little houses on the edge of Twentynine Palms—someone's poor attempt at a desert subdivision. It then swings north through a cleft in the Sheep Hole Mountains and drops into a broad basin. The road passes over the crystalline, reticulated surface of Bristol Lake salt flat, then it bumps into Historic Route 66, here called the National Trails Highway.

Go right to tiny **Amboy**, which dates from 1858 and may not be around much longer, since it lists a population of only twenty. Don't depend on it for fuel. Seven miles from Amboy, turn left onto Kelbaker Road, which takes you eleven miles north to Interstate 10 on the southern edge of Mojave National Preserve.

---

**NAVIGATIONAL NOTE** • If you're running this route in reverse and coming south from Mojave National Preserve, continue straight across Highway 62 onto National Park Drive when you reach Twentynine Palms. You'll soon hit the Oasis Visitor Center and Joshua Tree National Park is just beyond.

---

## Tour Twenty-one

# DESERTS HIGH & LOW

## MOJAVE NATIONAL PRESERVE TO DEATH VALLEY

---

**W**e mentioned in the previous tour that high deserts tend to be more thickly vegetated while low ones are drier, with less plant variety. In our final California tour, we visit two classic examples—the high deserts of Mojave National Preserve and the *very* low deserts of Death Valley National Park. Of course, what Death Valley lacks in vegetation it more than makes up for in impressive land formations.

To begin this tour of two deserts, take Kelbaker Road or Essex Road north from I-10, depending on which region of Mojave National Preserve you want to enter. If you're arriving from the previous tour, stay on Kelbaker Road, or go east on I-10 about twenty-five miles to Essex Road. Incidentally, the visitor center is on the far side of the preserve in Baker, so you may want to write or call for information before starting this tour.

*Mojave National Preserve • 72157 Baker Rd., Baker, CA 92309; (760) 733-4040. (WEB SITE: www.nps.gov/moja) Open daily 9 to 5. There is no food or lodging within the preserve, although there are several campgrounds with tables, barbecue grills, flush or pit potties and water; $$. For tour hours at Mitchell caverns, contact Providence Mountain State Recreation Area, P.O. Box 1, Essex, CA 92332; (760) 928-2586.* ▢

# TRIP PLANNER

**WHEN TO GO** ● Death Valley is popular as a fall through spring destination; it's equally famous for its sizzling summers. Mojave National Preserve, much higher in elevation, gets chilly in winter, even with occasional snow dustings, so spring and fall are best.

**DRIVING DISTANCE** ● From the south entrance of Mojave National Preserve through Death Valley to Panamint Springs is about 340 miles. This includes a trip to Scotty's Castle and back.

**RV ADVISORY** ● Nothing on this route will seriously challenge an RV or trailer, although the climb out of Death Valley through Panamint Springs has some tight turns.

**WHAT YOU'LL SEE** ● The attractions of Mojave National Preserve, including Mitchell Caverns, Joshua tree and Kelso Dunes; and Death Valley National Park, such as Badwater, the Devil's Golf Course, Scotty's Castle and the incredible view from Father Crowley's Vista.

**WHAT TO DO** ● Take the Mitchell Caverns tour and hike to Teutonia Peak for a view of Cima Dome in Mojave National Preserve; stare up at the world's tallest thermometer in Baker; follow scenically twisting Artists Drive, explore the Devil's Golf Course and take the Scotty's Castle tour in Death Valley.

**TO BEGIN** ● Go north from Interstate 10 into Mojave National Preserve, either on Kelbaker Road or Essex Road.

## Useful contacts

**Mojave National Preserve,** P.O. Box 241 (72157 Baker Rd.), Baker, CA 92309; (760) 733-4040. (WEB SITE: www.nps.gov/moja)
**Death Valley National Park,** Death Valley, CA 92328; (760) 786-2331. (WEB SITE: www.nps.gov/deva)

## Pricing guidelines

**DINING:** Dinner entrée with soup or salad, without drinks or dessert for under $10 = **$**; $10 to $14 = **$$**; $15 to $25 = **$$$**; over $25 = **$$$$**.
**RECLINING:** A two-person room for $35 or less = **$**; $36 to $50 = **$$**; $51 to $75 = **$$$**; $76 to $100 = **$$$$**; more than $100 = **$$$$$**.
**CAMPING:** Under $10 = **$**; $10 to $14 = **$$**; $15 to $19 = **$$$**; $20 or more = **$$$$**

Although Mojave is a federal preserve, one of its more interesting areas is a California inholding—**Providence Mountain State Recreation Area**. Its primary lures are a high wilderness area of piñon and juniper forests, and limestone-decorated **Mitchell Caverns**, with guide tours. You can reach this area from the Essex Road interchange on I-10.

From the Providence Mountain region, you can continue into the federal preserve by heading north on Black Canyon Road. Two campgrounds are in the area—**Hole-In-The-Wall** below a steep, pockmarked cliff face; and **Mid Hills,** in a piñon forest at 5,600 feet. The road is paved to Hole-In-the-Wall, then you'll encounter gravel—generally well graded—if you

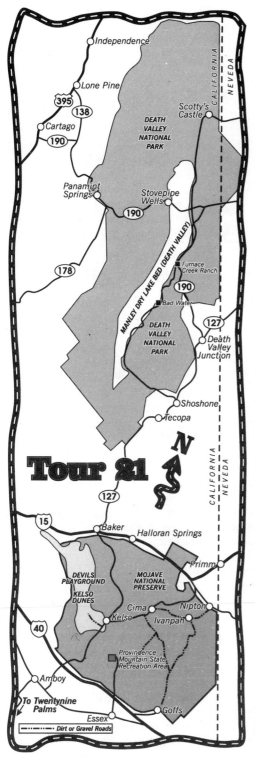

continue on to Mid Hills. Hole-In-the-Wall is better for RVs; Mid Hills is more suited to tent camping.

Having done the Providence Mountain area, you can either continue into the preserve on gravel roads, or return to I-10, go west and take Kelbaker Road north. This is all paved—the preferred route if you're in an RV or trailer rig. It slips between the Granite Mountains on your left and the western slope of the Providence Mountains to the right. After passing some interesting rock formations, you'll travel through an uninteresting creosote and mesquite desert—until you see something soft and inviting on the horizon to the northwest.

Just beyond a small complex of metal buildings and silos, turn left and follow a well-graded gravel road three miles to **Kelso Dunes.** It's one of the largest and highest sand dune complexes in the state, covering about forty-five square miles. From a parking area, you'll need to trudge for fifteen or twenty minutes through loose, sandy soil to reach the dunes themselves. It's worth the hike to explore their knife-edge ridges and subtle wind-formed rippled mounds that resemble brain coral. If possible, go early in the morning or just before sunset, when slanting rays add special drama to the formations. These dunes are so extensive and so infrequently visited that it's easy to find places with no footprints other than your own.

*Sundown adds new drama to the intriguing Joshua trees in the Cima area of Mojave National Preserve.*

Return to Kelbaker Road and drive several miles north to the almost deserted town of **Kelso,** noted for its large two-story California mission style railroad depot. Kelso was established in 1905 as a watering hole for steam locomotives on the run between Los Angeles and Salt Lake City; the depot was built in 1924. When diesel replaced steam, Kelso lost its reason for being, although the depot has survived in remarkably good shape. Officials are considering converting it into a visitor center.

Turn right in front of the depot onto Kelso-Cima Road, heading for Cima, eighteen miles away. After about fourteen miles, you'll pass Cedar Canyon Road, which will take you to Hole-in-the-Wall and the Providence Mountains Recreation Area. The campground is fifteen miles away and Providence is twenty-eight. The road is gravel or dirt and often washboarded, although a passenger car or RV—driven patiently—should have no problems in dry weather.

Continuing on toward Cima, you'll enter a huge Joshua tree forest that rivals anything in Joshua Tree National Park. In fact, it's the world's largest and most dense forest of its kind. Look to the north and you'll see—almost too subtle to notice—a large landform called **Cima Dome.** This parabolic mound rises in a low, gentle curve.

**Cima,** four miles from the Cedar Canyon Road junction, is another near ghost town, with a weather-worn building housing a post office and small store. Just beyond this sagging structure, fork left at a I-15 sign and head for the freeway, eighteen miles away.

Don't hurry, since you'll still be passing through this splendid Joshua forest. About seven miles from Cima, watch on your left for a trailhead for **Teutonia Peak.** A four-mile round trip hike passes through thick Joshua forests, then through thin stands of juniper, up through a rocky saddle of the peak. You'll encounter lush cactus gardens along the way. Part of the trail is an old ranch road and cattle may become your hiking companions. From a high ridge on the peak, you'll have a grand view of the Mojave Desert, including a good look at the subtly curved Cima Dome. Far to the northwest, you'll see tiny squares—not big enough to be Tonka toys. They're freight trucks on I-15, still many miles away.

## BAKER

You'll hit that freeway at Mountain Pass, and a twenty-eight mile drive west will take you to Baker, a popular stop on the long desert drive between Barstow and Las Vegas. It has a good selection of service stations, motels and cafés. We have a special feeling for this remote little town. Since we have a summer home in California's Sierra Nevada foothills and a winter home and office near Las Vegas, we pass this way often. On many a late-night drive, we've been sustained by a *café latté* from the Mad Greek, one of the town's more interesting restaurants.

Most travelers identify Baker as the home of the world's tallest and most famous thermometer. In fact, it's probably the world's *only* famous thermometer. Towering beside the Bun Boy Restaurant, it measures 134 feet, in honor of the highest temperature ever recorded in North America. The mercury hit 134 in nearby Death Valley in 1913. A **National Park Service Information Center** sits at the base of the thermometer. It's primarily a Mojave National Preserve facility, although it has material on Death Valley, and a good selection of nature and regional travel books. It's open daily 9 to 5; (760) 733-4040.

"The thermometer's not ours," a park ranger at the desk said defensively. "We just lease this space from the Bun Boy."

### DINING

**The Bun Boy** • *Business Route 15; (760) 733-4660. American; full bar service. Breakfast through dinner daily. Major credit cards; $$.* ☐ The Bun Boy is the oldest restaurant in town, dating from 1926 when old Route 66 carried hopeful travelers to the promise of California. However, the current look is diner-modern, with a few historic photos on the walls. It's noted for hamburgers of various definitions, all-day breakfasts and basic American dinners such as ground sirloin, liver and onions and honey dipped chicken. Incidentally, the Bun Boy's seasoned French fries are excellent; don't defile them with catsup.

**The Mad Greek** • *Business Route 15; (760) 733-4354. Greek and American; wine and beer. Breakfast through late night. Major credit cards; $$.* ☐ This cheerful blue and white bistro with Greek décor—a movie poster of Anthony Quinn as Zorba?—is the livelier and more personable of our two favorite Baker cafés. It has a large outdoor patio and a menu mix

*A lone visitor seems intrigued by Death Valley National Park's most famous feature, the brackish pool of Badwater, America's lowest point at 282 feet.*

that ranges from American fare to Greek gyros, hummus, lamb or chicken kabobs and *loucaniko*, a spicy sausage. Specialty coffees, hot or iced, will help keep you alert for long desert drives.

---

**FUEL ADVISORY** ● Gasoline is scarce on the road to from here to Death Valley and expensive in the park, so you might want to tank up in Baker.

---

## Baker to Death Valley National Park

For a pleasantly lonely drive to Death Valley, pick up State Route 127 at a four-way stop in Baker and head north. It's a fast route through relatively flat and therefore rather uninteresting desert. At a low pass called Silver Crest, you'll pop into Inyo County and catch your first glimpse of Death Valley. It appears far below as a long, slender salt flat cradled in steep and dramatically rugged mountains. The route then swings away and you won't see the valley again until your final approach.

A few miles beyond the pass, as you travel through low mesas and cliff faces the color of weak pea soup, a road to the right will take you four miles to **Tecopa.** It's a tiny, scruffy settlement with a general store, café, several empty houses and several occupied mobile homes. Turn left in front of the general store and you'll shortly arrive at **Tecopa Hot Springs,** a similarly disheveled scatter. This appears to be a resort that went broke and was taken over by the Inyo County Parks Department. You'll find two concrete bathhouses—one for gents and one for ladies; no dallying in the mineral water here, folks! Across the way is an RV park also operated by the county, with inexpensive although crowded sites with electrical hookups. Just beyond, you'll encounter two private RV parks, also crowded and with similar offerings.

Continue through Tecopa Hot Springs past an alkaline lake and you'll soon rejoin the highway. Six miles beyond, scruffy in an appealing sort of way, is the desert hamlet of **Shoshone,** sitting before a backdrop of chocolate ice cream scoop hills. It has a service station, market and **Death Valley National Park ranger station**, generally open daily 9 to 5. If it's closed, folks at the pleasingly weathered **Shoshone Museum and Gift Shop** next door can provide park information. Housed in a dead service station, the museum exhibits an old gas pump, pieces of mining equipment, a large gem and mineral collection and—quite impressive—an entire mammoth skeleton. The critter's bones were discovered nearby. The museum is open daily 9 to 4; (760) 852-4524.

About a mile beyond Shoshone, turn left (west) onto State Route 178 and climb to 3,315-foot Salsberry Pass. You'll then begin an eight-mile drop into the lowest place on the planet.

**Death Valley National Park** • *Death Valley, CA 92328; (760) 786-2331. (WEB SITE: www.nps.gov/deva) Furnace Creek Visitor Center and Museum open daily 8 to 6. The park has nine federal and two concessionaire campgrounds. Some sites are primitive and free, while others are developed with modest fees. The commercial parks have electrical hookups and their sites can be reserved. See "Dining, reclining and camping" below for details on dining and lodging concessionaires in the park. Scotty's Castle tours are conducted daily from 9 to 5; fees are moderate. Reservations aren't accepted, although the wait usually isn't much more than an hour. Call (760) 786-2392 for details.* ☐

Quick quiz: When does Death Valley receive most of its visitors—in July or December?

Wrong. It's July. And why? During summer months, about seventy-five percent of the park's visitors are from Europe and Japan and these people want to experience a hot American desert. They certainly get their wish; the average July high is 115 degrees!

For the rest of us, the best time to visit is from October through May, when temperature hover in the balmy nineties. Not all of the park is hot. Elevations range up to more than 11,000 feet and surrounding mountains are often dusted with winter snow. However, for most tourists, the reason for a Death Valley visit is to get down in the desert—to stand by that sign at Badwater marking the lowest place in America, at minus 282 feet.

The 1994 California Desert Protection Act not only upgraded Death Valley from national monument to national park status, it also added an additional 1.3 million acres. With a total of 3.3 million, it unseated Yellowstone to become the largest American national park outside of Alaska. Although it gets hundreds of thousand of annual visitors, there's plenty of acreage for everyone. The park isn't crowded even at peak season, except around the popular Furnace Creek and Stovepipe Wells areas.

Our brief tour through the park only scratches its amazing surface, although it will take you to some of its most interesting attractions. We begin by entering from a direction used by very few visitors. In doing so, you can pause at an interpretive display describing Death Valley's key feature.

As you approach from the southeast on State Route 178, watch on your left for a roadside exhibit concerning **Lake Manley.** This 90-mile-long lake filled the valley floor during the Pleistoscene Age, about 20,000 years ago. The climate changed and the lake went dry, leaving salt and alkali deposits that form the heart of Death Valley.

For the next ninety miles, you'll drive between the salt flat of old Lake Manley and the incredibly steep, fluted and craggy mountains of the Amargosa Range. Several miles above the Lake Manley exhibit, you'll encounter all that remains of that old pond—an acrid pool called **Badwater.** It's probably the most famous spot in the park.

A few miles above Badwater, turn left and follow a bumpy road to another strange feature wrought by Lake Manley. **Devil's Golf Course** is a rough and tumbled mix of salt and dirt chunks. It was created when water-bearing gravel was pushed upward by swelling salt, and then eroded by wind and rain.

Just up the road, turn right onto **Artists Drive,** a narrow lane that winds into the sculpted, multicolored foothills of the Amargosa Range. About a mile into the drive, a short, steep trail—don't try this in July—leads to an overlook above these interesting shapes. You'll also get nice look back at the salt flat which—particularly during late light—glitters like a frozen river delta. Continuing along the drive, you'll soon reach a short spur road leading to **Artists Palate,** an eroded area impressive both for its colors and its soft, rounded bakery dough shapes.

---

*RV ADVISORY* • Because of tight turns and narrow passages, trailers and large motorhomes shouldn't attempt Artists Drive.

---

Shortly after looping back to the main highway from Artists Drive, pause on your right for a brief hike into **Golden Canyon,** a serpentine, high-walled ravine. A bit beyond, turn right onto State Route 190 for **Furnace Creek Inn,** an opulent Spanish style resort bunkered into a desert slope. Stop for a visit even if you can't afford the rates, which start at more than $200 per night. Continue up Highway 190 for some nice views back at the valley floor, particularly from **Zabriskie Point.** Ten miles from Furnace Creek Inn, turn left onto a narrow, paved road that takes you thirteen miles to **Dante's View,** another noteworthy vista point.

Now, now retrace your route back to the Furnace Creek junction and continue north; Highway 190 has absorbed Route 178 to become the main park road. Immediately beyond the junction is **Furnace Creek Ranch,** an overbuilt, congested and noisy place that we prefer to avoid. Started in the 1930s when some people confused national parks with amusement parks, it has several restaurants, lodgings, a laundromat, service station and souvenir shops. **Sunset Campground,** with sites so crowded that it resembles a used rec vehicle lot, is nearby.

Don't bypass Furnace Creek completely. You'll also find the main **visitor center and museum** with fine exhibits about this amazing desert park. It's open daily 8 to 6; (760) 786-2331. Also worth a look is the **Borax Museum**, with stagecoaches, a steam train and mining gear. (The Pacific Borax Company mined borate in the valley; its famous twenty-mule teams pulled heavy borate-laden wagons to processing mills.)

About eighteen miles beyond Furnace Creek, Highway 190 swings to the southwest headed for Stovepipe Wells, while an unnumbered park road continues thirty-eight miles north to **Scotty's Castle.** The "castle" was begun in 1922 by a Chicago millionaire, who more or less adopted an old prospector, Walter Scott, known locally as "Death Valley Scotty." Although many thought this was Scotty's castle, financed by a hidden gold mine, he simply provided a bit of local color for visitors. Scott didn't have a cent in his Levi's and he lived in a simple cabin several miles away.

Like a desert version of Hearst Castle, this is an elaborate complex with a 25-room main house with eighteen fireplaces, plus courtyards, a swimming pool (unfinished, as is the castle itself) and elaborately landscaped grounds. You may have to wait an hour or so for the next tour, although there's plenty to see until your turn comes up.

Incidentally, **Mesquite Spring** on the way to Scotty's Castle is one of the park's nicer campgrounds, with well-spaced sites in a mesquite wash, tables and barbecue grills and flush potties; no hookups.

Back at the junction, head southwest on Highway 190 toward **Stovepipe Wells Village.** It's much more appealing, less expensive and less crowded than Furnace Creek Ranch. This is the area's oldest resort, started as Bungalette City in 1926, seven years before Death Valley became a national monument. Amenities included pup tents for sleeping quarters and a surplus army tent for a dining hall. Old prospectors led trail rides and sightseeing tours into the valley were conducted in Buick touring cars.

The Stovepipe Wells facilities are considerably nicer today, with a pleasantly rustic Western theme. It provides the essentials—lodging, a dining room and saloon, swimming pool, RV park and campground, service station and store. Continuing west from Stovepipe, you can take the short **Mosaic Canyon** scenic drive through a pretty area of tilted and marbled, multi-colored strata. The road is gravel and well graded, and can be negotiated by those in small RVs who don't mind a few bumps.

Immediately beyond the Mosaic Canyon turnoff, the highway begins a long, winding climb out of the valley. It tops 4,960-foot Towne Pass in the Panamint Mountains and then drops down into Panamint Valley. Climbing back out of the valley, you'll encounter the rustically attractive little **Panamint Springs Resort** with a motel, restaurant, RV park and fuel.

From here, the highway begins a steep, winding and cliff-hugging climb into the rocky, rugged and treeless Inyo Mountains. At the top of the climb, stop at **Father Crowley's Vista Point**, named for a priest who once ministered in this wild land. Pause first for a peek into deep Rainbow Canyon, with multi-colored strata in its sheer walls. From here, follow a gravel road about a quarter of a mile to a scraped-off mound, where you'll get a most impressive view of the Panamint valley and mountains.

The most interesting part of our tour ends at Father Crowley's Vista Point. Unless you plan to exit the park this way, use this as your turnaround and head back down into the desert.

### Dining, reclining and camping

In the style of older national reserves, Death Valley has elaborate visitor facilities—perhaps too elaborate. Furnace Creek Ranch has all the amenities that some folks come to remote deserts to escape, and Furnace Creek Inn is as elegant as any resort you will find in Palm Springs.

**Furnace Creek Inn** • *P.O. Box 1, Death Valley, CA 92328; (800) 236-7916 or (760) 786-2345. (WEB SITE: www.furnacecreekresort.com) Sixty-six luxury units with TV movies, phones and many amenities; $$$$$. Dining room serves American fare; breakfast through dinner; full bar service; $$$. Major credit cards.* ⊔ The high end of Death Valley lodging and dining, the inn is built into a dramatic desert niche. The décor is understated Spanish-California elegance, with flagstone tile floors, textured white walls and wrought iron chandeliers. The dining room serves upscale fare such as basil-crusted sea bass, salmon with shittake mushrooms and chicken breast with artichoke hearts. The inn was opened in 1927 by the Pacific Borax Company and it obviously has been modernized.

**Furnace Creek Ranch** • *P.O. Box 1, Death Valley, CA 92328; (800) 236-7916 or (760) 786-2345. (WEB SITE: www.furnacecreekresort.com) More than 200 units with TV movies and phones, some refrigerators; $$$$$. Food available from breakfast through dinner at the Wrangler Steakhouse, 49er café and 19th Hole; $$ to $$$. Major credit cards.* ⊔ This busy Western-theme complex includes a general store, shops, swimming pool, golf course and a pro shop, riding stables and tennis courts.

**Panamint Springs Resort** • *P.O. Box 395, Ridgecrest, CA 93556; (760) 482-7680. (WEB SITE: www.deathvalley.com) Fourteen motel units with early California décor; $$$. Restaurant serves American fare; breakfast through dinner daily; wine and beer; $$. Campground with RV and tent sites; full hookups; $$$$. MC/VISA, AMEX.* ⊔ In addition to lodging, dining and camping, this charmingly rustic resort has a small mini-mart, gift shop and gasoline. Diners can eat inside or on the lodge porch, where they can enjoy views of the surrounding Panamint Mountains.

**Stovepipe Wells Village** • *P.O. Box 187, Death Valley, CA 92328; (760) 786-2387. (WEB SITE: www.furnacecreekresort.com) Eighty-three units ranging from rustic to modern; $$$ to $$$$. Dining room serves American fare; breakfast through dinner; full bar service; $$$. RV and tent sites; full hookups; $$$. Major credit cards.* ⊔ Stovepipe is smaller, less hectic and more affordable than Furnace Creek Ranch. It has cabin type accommodations, an old fashioned saloon, service station and general store, and an attractive Western style dining room. Menu items include liver and onions, chicken stir fry and chicken Malibu.

☺   ☺   ☺

***Where do we go from here?*** • You can run Tour Thirteen in reverse by continuing past Panamint Springs to Lone Pine, about fifty miles away. If you're headed for southern California, State Route 178 just east of Panamint Springs will take you in that direction. Nevada-bound? Return to Stovepipe Wells junction and continue northeast to Beatty. That puts you in the middle of the first Nevada tour in the next chapter.

# PART IV

# NEVADA

**I**f you like uncrowded highways, you've got to love the Silver State. Except for Interstate 80 and freeways swirling around Las Vegas and the busy Reno-Tahoe-Carson City area, nearly every mile of Nevada asphalt is a road less traveled.

Eighty percent of the state is covered by the Great Basin Desert, a vast and lonely landscape of pine-thatched mountains, alkaline sinks, wandering rivers and rock-ribbed valleys. Travelers will find a remote national park, fascinating geological shapes, dinosaur digs and tough old mining towns. The "basin" is actually a rugged plateau with a bulge in the center and droopy edges. It's extremely high for a desert basin, averaging more than a mile above sea level, which tempers the summer heat and creates icy cold winters.

Despite its plateau-like topography and its lofty islands of mountain ranges, this is a true basin. Rainfall—what little there is—never reaches the sea. Many rivers flow into lakes which, with no outlets, become briny ponds. Some streams simply give up and disappear into the hot sand, creating alkaline bowls such as the Carson and Humboldt sinks. Several ancient lakes have evaporated to leave vast alkali and salt flats called *playas*.

Does all of this sound inviting? It is if you like wild landscapes and you *really* want to get far from the crowds.

We've selected four tour routes through Nevada. We'll first guide you through old silver and gold mining towns along the state's western edge, then we'll steer you across the so-called "Loneliest Road in America." Next, we'll take you down the state's eastern edge, on an even lonelier trek. Finally, we'll prove that the Las Vegas area offers more than slot machines and showgirls. Yes, there are uncrowded highways near Glitter City.

# TRIP PLANNER

**WHEN TO GO** ● This drive can be made any time of the year; fall through spring are best. Winters are nippy although snow is infrequent. And of course, summer temperatures can sizzle in Las Vegas. They'll cool as you head northward since you'll gain more than 2,000 feet in elevation. If you plan a side trip into Death Valley (Tour Twenty-one), you may not want to schedule this driving tour in summer.

**DRIVING DISTANCE** ● From Las Vegas to Virginia City, it's nearly four hundred miles. There's not much to see between towns, so you can do it easily in a day or two.

**RV ADVISORY** ● The climbs are gradual and tight turns are rare, except in the final pull to Virginia City.

**WHAT YOU'LL SEE** ● Lonely deserts corrugated with rock-tumbled mountains, the almost ghost towns of Goldfield and Rhyolite, the tough old mining town of Tonopah and its grand Mizpah Hotel, Mineral County Museum in Hawthorne, Walker Lake, the crumbling ruins of Fort Churchill, historic Dayton and touristy old Virginia City.

**WHAT TO DO** ● Catch a show at the Amargosa Opera House; prowl the ruins of old Rhyolite and the strange tailing dumps of Goldfield; peer into an open pit copper mine above Yerington; and pull some old fashioned slot machine handles in Virginia City.

**TO BEGIN** ● Get out of Las Vegas fast by heading north on U.S. 95. It begins as a busy freeway but that won't last long.

## Useful contacts

**Beatty Chamber of Commerce**, P.O. Box 956, Beatty, NV 89003; (775) 553-2225.

**Mineral County Chamber of Commerce**, P.O. Box 1277 (932 E St.), Hawthorne, NV 89415; (775) 945-5896.

**Tonopah Chamber of Commerce**, P.O. Box 869 (301 Brougher Ave.), Tonopah, NV 89049; (775) 482-3859.

**Virginia City Chamber of Commerce**, P.O. Box 464 (131 S. C St.), Virginia City, NV 89440; (775) 847-0311.

## Pricing guidelines

**DINING:** Dinner entrée with soup or salad, without drinks or dessert for under $10 = **$**; $10 to $14 = **$$**; $15 to $25 = **$$$**; over $25 = **$$$$**.

**RECLINING:** A two-person room for $35 or less = **$**; $36 to $50 = **$$**; $51 to $75 = **$$$**; $76 to $100 = **$$$$**; more than $100 = **$$$$$**.

**CAMPING:** Under $10 = **$**; $10 to $14 = **$$**; $15 to $19 = **$$$**; $20 or more = **$$$$**

**Tour Twenty-two**

# THE SILVER TRAIL

## LAS VEGAS TO VIRGINIA CITY

---

**F**olks don't seem to commute much between Las Vegas and Reno. Perhaps the people who live in Nevada's two major population centers don't have much in common, like those in the rival cities of Los Angeles and San Francisco. Whatever the reason, U.S. Highway 95—the major link between southern and northern Nevada—is very lightly traveled.

Tourism promoters, always looking for a theme, call it the Silver Trail because of several historic silver mining camps along the way. Most of our tour is on Highway 95, then it shifts to U.S. 50 and finally to State Route 341, which takes take you to the most famous silver mining camp of all—Virginia City.

### From Glitter City to dusty Beatty

Start your trip by untangling yourself from what radio and TV traffic spotters call the Spaghetti Bowl in Las Vegas. This the merge point for most if the town's freeways—I-15, I-515 and U.S. 95. With luck, you'll find yourself northbound on Highway 95. It remains a freeway for the first dozen miles, getting you quickly through Glitter City's fast-growing northern suburbs. Then it becomes a four-lane expressway for the next sixty

**283**

miles. It narrows into two lanes at Mercury, that closely-guarded entrance to the Nevada Test Site, where death angel mushroom clouds once danced in the skies.

Cruising along this expressway through a boring creosote bush desert, you'll see the lofty and inviting crests of the Spring Mountains to your left. The dominant crest, usually wearing a snowcap in winter and spring, is **Mount Charleston**, Nevada's third highest peak at 11,918 feet. We'll explore these alpine heights in Tour Twenty-five.

There's not much of interest as you continue northward on Highway 95. **Indian Springs,** an Air Force Base with a small town and casino outside its gates, comes and goes quickly. The **Mercury** turnoff is eighteen miles above.

### Side trip: Crystal and the Amargosa Opera House

Eight miles beyond Mercury, State Route 160 leads south into Pahrump Valley. There's little to see in this arid valley except a few scattered subdivisions, although you can visit **Crystal,** whose population specializes in copulation. High rollers from Las Vegas often come here to roll something besides dice, and you may see an occasional dark-windowed limo dash past. (Prostitution is illegal in Las Vegas and elsewhere in Clark County. It's legal in Crystal, in Nye County.)

Actually, this place can be innocent fun if you just want to stop by for a drink and a

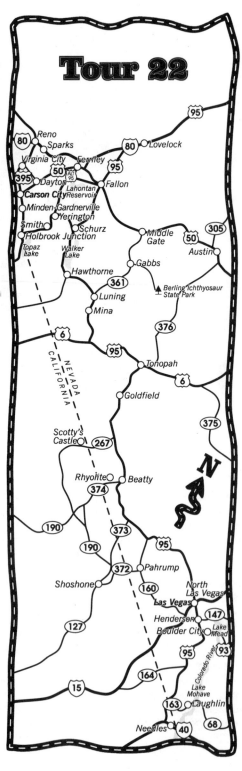

souvenir T-shirt. The girls are used to bashful tourists. Among your choices are Cherry Patch Ranch (really cute T-shirts); Madam Butterfly's, which specializes in erotic massage; and Mabel's, which specializes in—well—tension relief. To reach this den of legal iniquity, look for the Crystal turnoff to the right, a few miles down Highway 160.

A dirt road—navigable by RVs and trailers—leads fourteen miles southwest of Crystal to **Devil's Hole**. This is a detached patch of Death Valley National Park within **Ash Meadows Wildlife Management Area**. However, the hole is just that—a dark-water slot between desert rocks containing a few environmentally challenged *sytrinodon diabolis,* the desert pupfish. It's not worth the trip. However, you can explore the rest of the wildlife area, which has a couple of reservoirs and marshy areas busy with birds. A visitor center is in the middle of the reserve, southwest of the pupfish puddle; (775) 372-5435.

If you head south through the refuge, then go west, you'll hit pavement and wind up in California's **Death Valley Junction**. Once a Pacific Borax company town, it's home to a remarkable one-woman show:

*Amargosa Opera House* ● *P.O. Box 8, Death Valley Junction, CA 92328; (619) 852-4111. Performances Saturdays and Mondays at 7:45 p.m. in November, February, March and April; Saturdays only the rest of the year. Adjacent motel with modest rooms; $$.* ❑ Former Broadway dancer Marta Becket came to town in 1967 and converted an old social hall into the Amargosa Opera House. Here, she performs pantomimes and dances, playing nearly fifty different characters in a variety of shows. Her impressive show has have gained national attention.

The "opera house" is part of a well-kept Spanish style plaza built by the borax firm in 1924. It and the little town are worth a look even if you aren't here during performance times. To get back on track, head north on California Route 127. It becomes Nevada Highway 373 at the border, where you'll encounter an off-the-beaten-track casino complex:

*Longstreet Inn* ● *Stateline 373, Amargosa Valley, NV 89020; (775) 372-1777. Sixty rooms with TV and phones; $$$. Dining room serves American fare; breakfast through dinner; full bar service, $ to $$. RV park with flush potties and showers, hookups $$. Major credit cards.* ❑ Facilities at this attractive Victorian-Western style inn include a midsize casino, mini-mart, gift shop, beauty and barber salon.

---

*NAVIGATIONAL NOTE* ● If you'd like to visit the Amargosa Opera House without taking dirt roads through Ash Meadows, you can continue north on Highway 95 to Amargosa Valley, then take paved State Route 373 south.

---

Continuing north from Longstreet, you'll return to U.S. 95 at the tiny settlement of **Amargosa Valley**, then head northwest toward Beatty. An optional approach is to take California Route 190 northwest from Death Valley Junction through a slice of **Death Valley National Park** (see

Tour Twenty-one) and enter Beatty's back door. If you take this route, you'll hit the turnoff to Rhyolite ghost town before Beatty.

## BEATTY AND RHYOLITE

**Population: 3,500**                                    **Elevation: 3,300 feet**

Set among rough-hewn desert hills, dusty old Beatty got its start at the turn of the century when Montillus Beatty and his Paiute bride homesteaded ranchland along the Amargosa River. Gold was discovered nearby in 1904 and the mining town of Rhyolite quickly sprung to life. Within five years, five more mining camps emerged, then the gold gave out by 1910 and the boom went bust.

The other mining camps have faded back into the dust. However, some Rhyolite buildings were made of stone and brick and a couple of shells remain, along with a few wooden shacks losing their battles with gravity. Rhyolite is under BLM care, although it has no visitor facilities.

Beatty has managed to survive as a provisioning center and rest stop on the long stretch between Las Vegas and Reno. In addition to several motels, it has three small casino hotels.

## DINING, RECLINING AND GAMING

**Burro Inn** ● *Highway 95, south end of town (P.O. Box 7), Beatty, NV 89003; (800) 843-2073 or (775) 553-2445. Lodging, camping and dining, all in the $$ range. MC/VISA.* ☐ This Western style casino has modest-priced lodgings and 24-hour dining, plus the usual array of gaming devices and an RV park; see "Camping" below.

**Exchange Club of Beatty** ● *Highway 95/374 junction at midtown (P.O. Box 97), Beatty, NV 89003; (775) 553-2333. Lodging and dining; $$. Major credit cards.* ☐ Dating from 1906, the Exchange Club is one of the few historic structures left in town. However, it has been modernized and deprived of its early-day look. Like the Burro Inn, it offers inexpensive lodgings and around-the-clock dining and gaming.

**Stagecoach Casino & Hotel** ● *Highway 95, north end (P.O. Box 836), Beatty, NV 89003; (775) 553-2419. MC/VISA.* ☐ Largest of the town's three casinos, the Stagecoach has an Old Western façade, inexpensive rooms and meals, and the usual Nevada games.

## CAMPING

**Burro Inn** has a well-kept RV park with hookups; **$$**; (800) 843-2073 or (775) 553-2445. **Rio Rancho RV Park** adjacent to the Stagecoach has full hookups, tent sites and a mini-mart; (800) 448-4423 or (775) 553-2238; **$$**. If you'd like hot mineral water with your camping, try **Bailey's Hot Springs and RV Park**. It's four miles north of town on Highway 95, with hookups and free mineral soaks for patrons; (775) 553-2395; **$$**. The pools are available to non-campers for a modest fee.

Heading west from town toward Rhyolite, you'll see the **Beatty Museum** on your left, in a tiny cottage not much larger than a walk-in doll house. Exhibits include an old organ keyboard, a huge coffee grinder and assorted pioneer and mining artifacts. Hours are irregular, so call the

*This ruined shell once was a sturdy three-story bank building in the former mining town of Rhyolite.*

Chamber of Commerce at (775) 553-2225 to see when it's open. Nearby is a visitor information center for **Death Valley National Park**, open daily 8 to 4; (775) 553-2200.

You'll next encounter the **U.S. Department of Energy Science Center** on your right. Here, exhibits try to convince visitors that it's a wonderful idea to bury radioactive waste in the nearby Yucca Mountains. The last we heard, the Yucca Mountain Project had been given preliminary approval by federal officials. The visitor center is open Tuesday-Saturday 9 to 5; (800) 225-6972.

Continue over a rocky rise toward Rhyolite. Near the entrance to the ghost town is the large Bullfrog open pit mine, where modern science is extracting gold that those grizzled old miners missed. Just beyond, you'll find what's left of Rhyolite—the masonry and brick shells of a school and a three-story bank, a house constructed of bottles presumably emptied by thirsty miners, and a surprisingly intact Spanish colonial style railway station. Unfortunately, both the station and bottle house are fenced off to protect them from vandals.

As you wander among the ruins, your eyes will be drawn to a row of dazzling sculptures that resembles a ghostly defensive line for the NFL. They were created by Belgian artist Albert S. Zukalsk to represent The Last Supper. Rhyolite was an artists' hangout for a few years, although they've drifted away.

## Beatty to Goldfield and Tonopah

Thirty-six miles above Beatty, a left turn onto State Route 267 will take you back into Death Valley National Park, through rockribbed Grapevine Canyon to **Scotty's Castle**. We visited this remarkable desert mansion in Tour Twenty-one, page 279.

Since leaving Beatty, Highway 95 gradually has been climbing out of southern Nevada's Mojave Desert and into the much higher Great Basin Desert. You may notice the temperature change as you press northward and you'll see the flora change from boring creosote bush and bunchgrass to hairy armed Joshua trees. At 6,087-foot Goldfield Summit, you'll complete your climb over the Great Basin's lip, and then drop down into a battered old ghost town too stubborn to finish dying:

## GOLDFIELD

**Population: 400**                           **Elevation: 5,690 feet**

Goldfield seems more desolate and forlorn every time we pass through. Yet it somehow supports a small population, and it's the second smallest county seat in America, after California's Markleeville (Tour Nine, page 129). This near ghost town is the only incorporated city in sprawling Esmeralda County, which numbers 1,300 citizens.

To quote from our *Nevada Discovery Guide*:

*Sitting on a low mountain shelf, Goldfield looks more like a survivor of a blitzkrieg than a former gold rush town. The hills are pocked with tailing dumps and coyote holes; several brick and stone structures stand abandoned and neglected. Some wooden ones sag so precariously that they seem potential victims of the next good wind.*

In fact, a couple have toppled since we wrote that. One structure not abandoned is the rough cut stone 1907 **Esmeralda County Courthouse**, where business is still conducted. Most of the rest of the town consists of a scatter of modest homes, shacks and doublewides. This is quite a comedown from the boom days when Goldfield was the largest city in Nevada, with 20,000 residents. Gold was discovered here in 1904 and the county seat was shifted from Hawthorne three years later. The boom lasted about fifteen years, then a fire finished off most of the town in 1924.

If Goldfield still has a heartbeat, you'll find it by turning east onto Fifth Street and driving about four blocks:

**Santa Fe Club** ● *Fifth Street, Goldfield, NV 89103; (775) 485-3431. Rooms available in adjacent motel; restaurant serves lunch and dinner; $$. MC/VISA.* ◻ Built in 1905, this weather-battered structure is a classic Western saloon, with a "plank" polished by generations of elbows, a mirrored back bar and brass rails. Dusty antiques are scattered throughout the premises and dozens of truckers' hats decorate the ceiling. Abandoned prostitutes "cribs" out back recall the club's bawdier days. Adjacent to the saloon, looking remarkably prim, are four motel units.

To see what ruin goldseekers can bring to a landscape, drive east to the end of Columbia Street and walk among the tailing dumps of Columbia Mountain. Again to quote from the Nevada guide:

*The earth's exposed innards run the full spectrum of a perverted rainbow—curdled pea soup green, emergency room red, terminal gray and jaundice yellow. More than any other town in Nevada, Goldfield represents the mining cycle of boom, bust, rust and dust.*

Twenty miles north, you'll find another historic mining center, nestled into another moonscape ruin. However, this tough old town is downright prosperous when compared with Goldfield:

## TONOPAH

**Population: 3,600**                                    **Elevation: 6,030 feet**

It's probably just a campfire story. According to legend, a rancher and part time prospector named Jim Butler came through this area in 1900 and took shelter under a ledge when a windstorm suddenly came up. His mule wandered off, so he fetched up a rock and started to throw it when he noticed that it was laced with silver.

So goes the story of the founding of Tonopah. The town went through the same boom and bust cycle as Goldfield, although it was saved from ruin when the U.S. Army built an air base nearby during World War II. Mining has since resumed as firms dig for copper, gold, silver and molybdenum in the rough surrounding hills. That old Army air base has become the Tonopah Test Range, where the Stealth bomber and a MiG delivered to America by a defecting Soviet pilot were test flown. Like Goldfield, Tonopah is the seat of a county—in this case, the second largest one in America. Look at a map and you'll see that the town is tucked against the far western edge of 18,064-square-mile Nye County, which reaches almost to Las Vegas.

Approaching from the south, you'll note that Tonopah is rather casually scattered about the feet of several rough-hewn hills. The town is an incongruous blend of modern homes, apartment houses, thriving businesses, tired old shanties, doublewides, rusting mine machinery and tailing dumps. Two midsize casino hotels stand along Main Street—the first on the southern end and the second downtown. Both are a bit on the musty side, although the old Mizpah got new carpeting recently.

**Station House Casino** • *1100 Main St. (P.O. Box 2351), Tonopah, NV 89409; (775) 482-9777. Lodging, dining and RV park; $$. MC/VISA.* ⊡ Station House has a Western railroading theme, with a couple of restaurants, modest priced rooms and an interesting exhibit of old time slot machines. An RV park with full hookups, a coin laundry and showers is out back. A fair sized grocery store also is in this complex.

**Mizpah Hotel, Casino & Restaurant** • *100 N. Main Street at Brougher Ave., (P.O. Box 1527), Tonopah, NV 89409; (775) 482-6202. Lodging and dining; $$. MC/VISA.* ⊡ This five-story yellow brick and cut stone structure dates from Tonopah's glory days. Its fifty-six guest rooms have a Victorian look, with brass beds and print wallpaper. The **Jack Dempsey Room** downstairs is the best restaurant between Carson City and Las Vegas, with elegant Victorian décor, old boxing memorabilia and an American menu. It serves dinners only, although a casino coffee shop

keeps longer hours. The restaurant is named for the legendary heavy-
weight champ because he worked as a bartender and bouncer here. Having watched old Dempsey fight films, we assume that bar patrons didn't
give him much guff.

To check out memories of Tonopah's past, turn up Logan Field Road
(just below Station House) for the **Central Nevada Museum.** Not professionally done but nicely arranged, it has old slot machines, mining
tools, a copper still used by bootleggers and a special section on the town's
"fancy women." It's open daily 9 to 5 in summer and Monday-Saturday 11
to 5 the rest of the year; (775) 482-9676.

For some nice overviews of Tonopah, continue from the museum to Air
Force Road and follow it up to the ramparts of Mount Brougher. The upper end of the road is unpaved and twisting, so it's not recommended for
large RVs or trailer rigs. For a view from the opposite heights, return to
Main Street (Highway 95), head toward downtown and turn up McCul-
loch Avenue. Note the **Nye County Courthouse** with its silver dome
shaped like a chubby missile. Continue past the courthouse to **Butler
Park,** then turn left up Occidental, which takes you to the base of Mount
Oddie. You can hike to the top of Oddie for a view of this scattered community, its tailing dumps, abandoned headframes and surrounding hills.

The **Chamber of Commerce** is at 301 Brougher Avenue, two blocks
southwest of the highway. It's open weekdays 9 to 5; (775) 482-3859.

## Tonopah to Dayton

Fuel up in Tonopah because you'll have a long, thirsty stretch ahead.
Highway 95 merges with U.S. 6 and the two trudge across a desert waste
to **Coaldale Junction,** where you'll swing north to stay with Route 95.
The tiny towns of **Mina** and **Luning** will flash by quickly, then you'll ap-
proach a desolate region that seems to have been invaded by giant moles.
A sign on your right makes even less sense:

*Naval Undersea Warfare Center*

They've got subs that burrow underground?

Those molehills are ammo bunkers. This is part of the **U.S. Army
Ammunition Depot,** and we have no idea why there's a sub base out
here. Just beyond, you'll encounter the homeliest town in Nevada, maybe
in the entire West:

## HAWTHORNE

**Population: 4,200**                                    **Elevation: 4,375 feet**

Poor old Hawthorne! Not only is it a homely town scattered across an
ugly desert, it's surrounded by ammo dumps. This is where the U.S. Army
manufactures and stores deadly weapons of war so it can keep the peace.
Its presence does give Hawthorne a kind of nervous prosperity and a solid
employment base. That's part of the irony; it takes the threat of war to
keep the town's economy booming—no pun intended.

Even with the government providing most of the local paychecks,
Hawthorne has a tired and seedy look. A single casino, **El Capitan,** is a
bit on the tatty and smoky side. You can get a fifty-cent draft beer here, in
case that long desert drive made you thirsty. As you exit the town's north

end, look to your left—behind a pair of ack-ack guns—for the town's one reason to pause, other than fifty-cent beer:

**Mineral County Museum** • *Tenth and D streets; (775) 945-3185. Weekdays 11 to 5 in summer and noon to 4 the rest of the year; free.* ⊓ This cinderblock building once housed a supermarket and the local historical society seems intent on filling its shelves with every relic imaginable. Some of this stuff is interesting—Hawthorne's original fire truck, a pair of brass knuckles, mining gear, a mimeograph machine and bits of fossils. (Recalling that I used a mimeograph machine as editor of my high school newspaper, I began feeling like a fossil.)

Leaving town, you'll pass through the main complex of the munitions depot, marked with row upon drab row of barracks—many of them empty—and bomb assembly plants; no smoking, please.

Just beyond, your visual desert thirst will be quenched by the sight of a great pale blue pond. **Walker Lake** is one of Nevada's largest, stretching for nearly twenty miles through this treeless desert. Enjoy this cool blue vision while you can, since the Walker River that feeds it is being diverted for upstream irrigation, making this the incredible shrinking lake. Court battles are being waged and compromises are being sought to stabilize the pond, which is popular for water sports and a good source of cutthroat trout. Increasing salinity could destroy the fish crop unless the shrinking is halted.

At the lake's southern tip, **Walker Lake State Recreation Area** has sheltered picnic areas, campsites with flush potties, fishing access and a launch ramp. Just opposite is **Walker Lake Village**, a small commercial development. It's comprised of the Buffalo Stop mini-mart, Cliff House Restaurant and Motel offering moderately priced lake view dining and lodging; and a small RV park with hookups. Call (775) 945-2444 for the motel and RV park and (775) 945-5253 for the restaurant.

Cruising along the western lakeshore, you'll see signs to a couple of free primitive BLM campgrounds. And they *are* primitive—just a few treeless, scraped-away patches to pitch your tent or park your RV.

Beyond the lake's north end is the Paiute community of **Schurz** with the attractive, well-equipped **Walker River Travel Center**, a smoke shop selling provisions and fireworks.

At Schurz, fork left onto U.S. 95 Alternate and drive twenty-four miles to a town being irrigated by the Walker River—at the expense of Walker Lake. You're about to shed the desert and enter an agricultural area.

## *YERINGTON*

**Population: 2,021**                    **Elevation: 4,380 feet**

Highway 95-A skirts the northern edge of this sleepy farm town, so you'll need to turn left (south) to drag Main Street. It presents a scene right out of America's heartland, with its low rise brick and stone storefronts. Only the presence of **Dini's Lucky Club** and **Casino West** reminds you that you're in Nevada and not Nebraska. As you cruise Main, check out the Greek Federalist style **Lyon County Courthouse** with its fluted columns, classic pediment and red brick walls.

A few blocks below, you'll encounter the **Lyon County Museum** at 215 S. Main. Housed in a former church, it contains the usual pioneer relics, including a vintage pump organ, Paiute artifacts and a leather-covered money box that just may have belonged to George Washington. The museum is open Thursday-Sunday 1 to 4, with shorter hours in winter; (775) 463-6576. Next door is the **Lyon County Information Center,** open weekdays 9 to 5; (775) 463-2245.

Before we leave Yerington, it's time for another campfire story. This farming and ranching valley was settled in 1869 and the town originally was called Pizen Switch. Why? One of its first businesses was a saloon named The Switch because it was made of willows. When the barkeep's whisky barrel ran low, he'd top it off with whatever was handy—liniment, straight alcohol, a bit of turpentine. When the locals got thirsty, they'd say: "Lets go over to the Switch fer a cup o' pizen." The name later was changed to Yerington, in honor of Virginia & Truckee Railroad general manager H.M. Yerington. Citizens hoped to flatter him into routing his rails through here. He didn't, although the name stuck.

This also was a copper mining center, and you can see an impressive open pit mine on your way out of town. To find it, retrace your route on Main Street and continue north on 95-A, which makes two ninety-degree turns, first to the left and then to the right. A few blocks after the second turn, watch for a small sign on your left indicating "Weed Heights." Follow a road about a mile past a mining complex to a terraced residential area that looks like a government housing project. The Anaconda corporation mined copper here from 1951 until 1978 and this was the company town. Many of the small homes are occupied, having been sold or rented to local residents.

After hitting a stop sign at Weed Heights, turn left and then go left again into a parking area marked by three six-foot ore truck tires. Walk to an overlook and peer down into a great terraced pit, now partially filled with water. This great hole in the ground yielded millions of pounds of copper and lesser amounts of uranium, aluminum, lead and zinc.

Incidentally, the town's name isn't a commentary on its landscaping. It was named for Clyde E. Weed, then Anaconda's chairman of the board.

Continue north on the highway and, after twenty-four miles, watch for a sign to **Fort Churchill State Park.** You'll find an extensive ruin that more suggests remnants of an ancient civilization than an army fort. Only softly rounded walls of the fort remain, giving it the look of a horizontal Stonehenge. A visitor center-museum is open daily 8 to 4:30. If it's closed, you can still stroll among the ruins. This originally was Buckland Ranch, occupying a pretty little valley nurtured by the Carson River. Since it sat astride the Emigrant Trail, the Army stepped in and built Nevada's first military post in 1860. It later served as a Pony Express stop, then it began a long decline. The state stepped in to arrest its decay in 1957—although everything but the mud walls had been pilfered by this time. **Buckland Campground** is nearby. It has pit potties and no hookups, although it's in a pretty setting, shaded by ancient trees left over from the days when this was a ranch.

From here, take the dusty and bumpy Fort Churchill Road twenty miles west, following the course of the Carson River to U.S. 50. Signs along the way will remind you that you're on the old Emigrant Trail and the Pony Express route.

---

**RV ADVISORY ●** The road was very washboardy the last time we crossed. Unless it has been improved, it'll rearrange your RV's dishes and possibly its furniture. However, it is straight, wide and level so any size rig can make the crossing—with patience. If you'd rather not, return to 95-A, drive eight miles north to U.S. 50 at Silver Springs and head west. You can save a few miles by taking the Ramsey-Weeks Cutoff; watch for a small sign about six miles from the Fort Churchill turnoff.

---

If you need a place to camp or picnic, take a break at **Dayton State Park** beside the Carson River on Highway 50. It has shaded sites with no hookups, plus a picnic area and fishing access, with modest day use and camping fees.

Four miles ahead, you'll encounter one of Nevada's oldest towns, about to be enveloped by spreading Carson City:

## DAYTON

**Population: About 5,000**                    **Elevation: 4,600 feet**

A small tent community sprung up here in 1849 after gold was discovered in a nearby ravine. The settlement first was named Gold Creek, then Hall's Station for Spafford Hall's 1853 trading post. Finally, it was named after John Day, who platted a more orderly town in 1861.

Residents never did find much gold. However, Dayton became one of Nevada's most prosperous cities, processing silver ore from the Comstock Lode in the mountains above. A dozen stamp mills ran day and night, thoroughly polluting the Carson River and groundwater sources, since mercury was used to separate silver from the crushed ore. The area is now on the Environmental Protection Agency's "superlist" as one of its most toxic waste sites. The town began shrinking late in the 1800s as the Comstock mines ran dry. It had shriveled to just a few old stone buildings until Carson City developers began pushing their subdivisions out this way.

The core of old Dayton survives. You can explore it by turning right off Highway 50 at the town's only stoplight and driving up Main Street. The business district, about two blocks long, is line with old brick and stone.

Your first stop should be the **Old Corner Bar**, noted for history of a much more recent vintage. Downtown Dayton and nearby ranchlands were used for filming *The Misfits* with Clark Gable and Marilyn Monroe in 1960. Sadly, it was the last movie for both. The barroom is busy with Western regalia and movie memorabilia—mostly about Marilyn. Panties and bras—presumably not hers—hang from the antlers of game trophies. An adjacent restaurant serves hearty country cookin' for breakfast, lunch and dinner.

A block beyond, you can catch lunch or dinner at the **Wild Horse Saloon,** another Western style bar, housed in an 1887 building. It's a bit more tidy than the Old Corner Bar, with Western paintings on the walls and Naugahyde bar stools. You can lounge on a porch out front in white wicker chairs—something the old prospectors probably never did. If you continue up Main, you'll wind up at the **Dayton Cemetery,** one of the oldest in the state. It received its first patrons in 1851.

## Uphill to another "glitter city"

From Dayton, head west briefly on Highway 50, then turn right onto State Route 341 and begin climbing Sun Mountain. You're headed toward one of the world's most famous, richest and wildest mining camps.

---

*RV ADVISORY* ● Two routes snake up the south side of Sun Mountain. The main highway through Gold Canyon is very twisty, with grades as steep as fifteen percent; it's not recommended for RVs or trailer rigs. A truck route, branching off at Silver City, is a bit more gentle.

---

The Sun Mountain climb takes you up through Gold Canyon, past tailing dumps, derelict headframes and tired old shacks. You'll encounter a couple of ancient mining towns along the way. **Silver City** is a virtual ghost town, while **Gold Hill** is occupied by a handful of people. It also has the best hotel and restaurant in the region, so you might be tempted to pause for a drink or a meal, and maybe even spend the night:

*Gold Hill Hotel* ● *1540 Main St., Gold Hill; mailing address: P.O. Box 710, Virginia City, NV 89440; (775) 847-0111. Fifteen rooms with TV and phones; some private and some share baths; continental breakfast; $$ to $$$$$. Crown Point Restaurant serves American and continental fare, with full bar service; dinner Tuesday-Sunday with Sunday brunch; $$$. MC/VISA.* ☐ Dating from 1859, this is the oldest hotel in the state, now restored to its original Victorian finery. Its rooms and common areas are dressed in wainscotting, period furnishings and print wallpaper. Several have fireplaces and refrigerators. The restaurant gets good reviews from locals. Make it a point to pause at the old Western style bar downstairs with its interior stone walls, rough brick floor and cozy fireplace.

Beyond Gold Hill, the grade tilts up to fifteen percent, which is why RVs and trailers are advised to take the less severe truck route. By whichever approach, you'll soon arrive in Nevada's most visited historic site:

## VIRGINIA CITY

**Population: 1,500**                    **Elevation: 6,220 feet**

Whatever happened to historic preservation? The town that created several silver barons and helped finance the Civil War is one of the most unabashed tourist traps west of the Rockies; maybe west of the Delaware River. As you clunk along its boardwalk main street, you can buy cowboy ice cream cones, get your picture taken in Western clothing, take a trolley tour, check out John Wayne displays and browse through museums that are thinly disguised gift shops.

You also can see some splendidly restored Victorian mansions, visit several *authentic* museums and belly up to some really colorful bars. You can pull the handles of real one-armed bandits instead of feeding your lunch money into video display slot machines.

---

**RV PARKING ADVISORY** ● Once you reach Virginia City, drive south on C Street and turn downhill at the "RV parking" sign in front of the Way It Was Museum. You'll find a large gravel lot for big rigs two blocks below at E and Sutton streets. If you're spending the night, the Virginia City RV Park is a bit farther on, at F and Carson streets; see below.

---

Our *Nevada Discovery Guide* has all the details about Virginia City—both alluring and lurid. If one isn't handy, we'll suggest a few of its more interesting places:

**Bucket of Blood Saloon** ● *One South C St.; (775) 847-0322.* ☐ The name is gruesome, although it's an eye-appealing Western style saloon with Victorian trim, scores of vintage lamps hanging from the ceiling and a large, elaborately carved bar. A pianist and banjo player often entertain visitors and a picture window provides an impressive view toward the historic mining area.

**The Castle** ● *70 South B St.; (775) 847-0275. Guided tours daily 10 to 5 in summer and 11 to 5 the rest of the year; $$.* ☐ This board and batten structure is one of the most beautifully furnished mansions in town, and it's nearly all original.

**Delta Saloon** ● *18 South C St.; (775) 847-0789.* ☐ It's one of Virginia City's spiffiest saloons, with lots of Victorian trim, knotty pine walls and an ornate back bar decorated by game trophies. It also has the cleanest potties.

**Fourth Ward School** ● *South end on C Street; (775) 847-0975. Daily 10 to 5 from mid-May to mid-October; admission by donation.* ☐ This 1876 school was the fanciest in the state, with indoor plumbing and piped-in heat. It's now operated by the Nevada State Museum, featuring excellent full-dimensional models of mining equipment, material about the Comstock and the lives of those who lived here.

**Nevada Gambling Museum** ● *Palace Emporium Mall at 22 South C St.; (775) 847-9022. Daily 10 to 5; small admission fee.* ☐ Housed in a former saloon, it has a good collection of old gaming devices and interesting exhibits about card cheaters and their techniques.

**The Way It Was Museum** ● *113 North C (at Sutton); (775) 847-0766. Daily 10 to 6; moderate admission fee.* ☐ This "old" structure dates from 1958 although it is properly weathered and the exhibits, while not orderly, are entertaining. Particularly interesting are 3-D models of the incredible webwork of 700 miles of mine shafts that were burrowed into these hills.

## DINING AND RECLINING

We found no Virginia City restaurants worthy of special mention, although you won't go hungry, since C Street is lined with cafés selling fried chicken, hamburgers and such. Many are quite colorful although most menus appear to have been borrowed from fast food joints. The **Wagon Wheel** at 171 South C has a fairly broad menu, ranging from pasta to *wienerschnitzel* and its dining room provides views down into the mining area. It's open for breakfast and lunch weekdays and breakfast through dinner weekends, with wine and beer; (775) 847-0500.

As for lodging, the nicest place is a former mining supervisor's digs:

**Chollar Mansion Bed & Breakfast** ● *P.O. Box 889 (565 South D Street), Virginia City, NV 898440; (775) 847-9777. Three rooms and a cottage with TV; private and share baths; full breakfast. No credit cards; $$$$.* ☐ This elaborate 1861 mansion was the home and office of the boss of the Chollar Mine, one of the richest in the area. Furnishings are a mix of early American and Victorian antiques. Some of the original items are still intact, including a paymaster's booth and a large arched vault where silver bullion was stored.

If you plan to camp, head for the **Virginia City RV Park** on the south end of town at Carson and F streets, within walking distance of the historic district. It has RV and tent sites, with showers, a coin laundry and mini-mart; full hookups; **$$$$**. Reservations are accepted and it's probably a good idea; (800) 889-1240 or (775) 847-0999; MC/VISA.

## Reflecting on history

Virginia City can become absolutely jammed on summer weekends, although tourists crowds thin out considerably from fall through spring. Winter's not a bad time to visit, although it can get darn cold up here.

If you do arrive in summer, you can get away from the crowds by hiking up Taylor and then Howard streets, toward Mount Davidson. From the top, past the city's water tanks, you'll have an impressive view of the surrounding mountains and even distant Reno. Look down upon the tin roofs of Virginia City and try to imagine the way it was before the arrival of cowboy cones and frozen yogurt:

During its heyday, this was the richest mining camp in the world and the largest city in Nevada, with a population topping 30,000. Multi-millionaire silver barons built fabulous mansions and drank the best champagne while randy miners bent their elbows at more than a hundred saloons. Profits from its mines—along with California gold—helped finance the Union Army during Civil War. The Comstock strike was directly responsible for getting Nevada into the Union in a hurry—in 1864. Although it was sparsely settled, it was the third Western state admitted, after California (1850) and Oregon (1859).

A few prospectors sought gold here in the 1850s, but they found very little and some pesky blue mud kept clogging their sluice boxes. Then in 1857, brothers Hosea and Ethan Allen Grosch, who had come west with mineralology books and assaying tools, discovered that the blue mud was rich in silver!

However, silver is difficult to mine on a small scale. It was large corporations tearing the hills apart on a grand scale that turned this into one of history's richest mining areas. Many companies were controlled by men whose names are still familiar: George Hearst, father of newspaper baron

William Randolph Hearst; William Ralston, who founded the Bank of California, mostly by loaning small miners money and then foreclosing on them; and James Flood and William Fair, whose heirs started the Fairmont hotel chain. Many of these silver millionaires retired to San Francisco's Nob Hill, where they built some of the finest mansions in the land.

An early travel writer named Samuel Clemens helped spread Virginia City's fame. For two years, he worked as a reporter for the *Territorial Enterprise,* reeling off picturesque prose that often was as much fiction as fact. It was here that he first began using his pen name Mark Twain. He recalled in later years:

*"Mark Twain" was the* nom de plume *of one Captain Isaiah Sellers, who used to write river news for the* New Orleans Picayune. *He died in 1863 and as he could no longer need that signature, I laid violent hands upon it without asking permission of the proprietor's remains.*

☺ ☺ ☺

**Where do we go from here?** ● You have several choices as you sit atop Mount Davidson, pondering your next move. You can head back down the south side of the mountain and begin Tour Twenty-three on Highway 50, the so-called "Loneliest Road." Another option is Tour Thirteen; go west on Highway 50 to Carson City, then south to Minden-Gardnerville and follow U.S. 395 through California's Eastern Sierra.

For a scenic although very twisting drive, you can head north on State Route 341 over 6,799-foot **Geiger Summit**, which provides awesome views of the Washoe Valley. The road drops 2,000 feet into the valley and hits U.S. 395 just below Reno.

---

*RV ADVISORY* ● Although the Geiger grade is twisted and kinked like a stomped on snake, it's well engineered. Carefully driven RVs and trailer rigs should be able to handle it. Avoid it in winter, however.

---

## Tour Twenty-three

# THE LONELIEST ROAD?

## HIGHWAY 50 FROM FALLON TO GREAT BASIN

When federal officials decided to build coast-to-coast Interstate 80 several decades ago, they chose the route followed by Highway 40 across northern Nevada instead of U.S. 50 through the middle. Highway 50's scattered small towns, already suffering from dwindling mining activity, began to shrink further. In 1986, a *Life Magazine* article called Highway 50 "the loneliest road in America."

Chambers of commerce along the route feared their towns might disappear completely so they sought ways to attract visitors. Working with the Nevada Tourism Commission, they came up with a tongue-in-cheek *Highway 50 Survival Kit*. Still in use, it's available from visitor centers and merchants along the route that post a blue and white "Survival Kit" sign. It contains information about attractions, food and lodging, plus a map with a "checkoff card." Travelers who get their cards stamped in each of the remote towns along the highway receive a bumper sticker and certificate proclaiming that they've "survived" the loneliest road in America.

However, we must set the record straight. Highway 50 isn't the loneliest road in America. It isn't even the loneliest road in Nevada. For that, we'd nominate the Extraterrestrial Highway between Tonopah and Cali-

298

# TRIP PLANNER

**WHEN TO GO** • Spring through fall are the best times to travel through the Great Basin. The area is relatively high so summers aren't too hot, although winters can get cold and snow can temporarily close mountain passes. Also, most of the Great Basin National Park trails are closed in winter.

**DRIVING DISTANCE** • It's about 300 miles from Fallon to Great Basin National Park.

**RV ADVISORY** • The "loneliest road" offers no RV challenges.

**WHAT YOU'LL SEE** • The vast deserts and mountains of the Great Basin, weathered old towns of Austin, Eureka and Ely, Ward Charcoal Ovens and Cave Lake near Ely, Berlin-Ichthyosaur State Park and Great Basin National Park.

**WHAT TO DO** • Play in the dunes at Sand Mountain Recreation Area; walk the petroglyph trails at Grimes Point and Hickison Petroglyph Site; explore the moonscape tailing dumps of the Ruth mining district near Ely; tour Lehman Caves and hike the bristlecone pines and Wheeler Peak trails at Great Basin National Park.

**TO BEGIN** • Get to Fallon on U.S. 50.

## Useful contacts

**Austin Chamber of Commerce,** P.O. Box 212, Austin, NV 89310; (775) 964-2200.

**Churchill County Chamber of Commerce,** 100 Campus Way, Fallon, NV 89406; (775) 423-2455.

**Eureka County Chamber of Commerce,** P.O. Box 14, Eureka, NV 89316; (775) 237-5484.

**Great Basin National Park,** Baker, NV 89311; (775) 234-7331.

**White Pine Chamber of Commerce,** 636 Aultman St., Ely, NV 89301; (775) 289-8877.

## Pricing guidelines

**DINING:** Dinner entrée with soup or salad, without drinks or dessert for under $10 = **$**; $10 to $14 = **$$**; $15 to $25 = **$$$**; over $25 = **$$$$**.

**RECLINING:** A two-person room for $35 or less = **$**; $36 to $50 = **$$**; $51 to $75 = **$$$**; $76 to $100 = **$$$$**; more than $100 = **$$$$$**.

**CAMPING:** Under $10 = **$**; $10 to $14 = **$$**; $15 to $19 = **$$$**; $20 or more = **$$$$**

ente on routes 6, 375 and 93. The only services on this 184-mile stretch are in tiny Rachel, a town so remote that residents have posted a sign reading "Welcome, earthlings."

## Only the lonely?

Actually, Highway 50 is one of the most appealing drives in Nevada, traveling through the heart of the Great Basin Desert, with much to see and do along the way. Hardly barren, this "desert" is adorned with mountain ranges that rise from the lowlands like floating green islands. You can find ancient petroglyph sites, visit weathered old mining towns, peer into a huge open pit mine and explore one of our newest and most remote national parks. A short side trip will take you to a well-preserved ghost town and a major ichthyosaur find. The highway follows the route of the Pony Express that briefly galloped across the West in 1860-61, and you'll find several historic markers along the way.

While not all that lonely, Highway 50 fits the criteria for this book. With most traffic shifted to the north on I-80, it *is* a road less traveled. And it's quite scenic. The route bisects several of those "floating" mountain ranges, climbing over low piñon and juniper passes and then running arrow-straight through brushy desert to the next clump of hills. Although some of the passes are more than 7,000 feet above sea level, they're relatively easy to climb since the Great Basin's desert "lowlands" are often more than a mile high.

Begin your trek in **Fallon**, easily reached from Carson City on U.S. 50, from the Las Vegas area on U.S. 95 or from Reno on Interstate 80 and alternate 50. It's a good idea to fuel up in Fallon, since gasoline stations are scarce and prices increase as you continue eastward.

Are you ready for lonely? The next town beyond Fallon is Austin, 112 miles away.

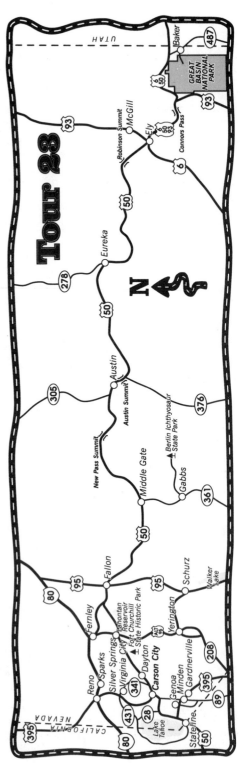

However, there are some interesting distractions along the route. And we aren't necessarily referring to Kitty's house of pleasure about twelve miles out of Fallon. The first attraction, about a mile short of Miss Kitty, is **Grimes Point,** where a path leads past dozens of pre-Colombian petroglyphs on basaltic boulders. There's a nice picnic area in the parking lot.

A few miles beyond, you'll cross the absolutely flat **Salt Wells Basin,** a *playa* or dry lake bed. At the far side is a sign marking the site of a former Pony Express station. Only remnants of stone walls remain. A short road leads from here to **Sand Mountain,** a series of dunes on the lake's eastern shore. They're busy with dune buggies on weekends, but if you arrive on a weekday, you can hike up to lonely ridges and watch the desert wind whip up plumes, like waves on a granular ocean.

## Side trip: Berlin-Ichthyosaur State Park

About twenty miles beyond Sand Mountain, turn south onto State Route 361 and drive about forty miles through *really* lonely desert to **Gabbs.** It was built in the 1940s as a company town for a magnesium mining operation and many of its prim employee houses still survive. Heading east, Highway 844 will take you over Green Springs Summit, nearly 7,000 feet high, then into pretty Ione Valley and beyond to the rugged Shoshone Mountains. Pavement ends sixteen miles from Gabbs and a well-maintained dirt road leads four more miles to your destination:

**Berlin-Ichthyosaur State Park** ● *Route 1, Box 32, Austin, NV 89310; (775) 867-3001. Modest fee for fossil shelter tours at 10, 4 and 2 daily from Memorial Day through Labor Day, then weekends at 10 and 2 from Labor Day to mid-November and mid-March to Memorial Day; by reservation only the rest of the year.* ❑ As the hyphenated name suggests, this park has two attractions—a ghost town and a ghost lizard from the past. Berlin was a turn-of-the-century gold mining center, and several wood frame houses, store buildings and a stamp mill still survive. A nearby structure shelters one of the largest *ichthyosaur* finds in America. These were sea-going reptiles (literally "fish lizards") that lived 225 million years ago and measured up to fifty feet long. Their remains were uncovered not by mining, but by erosion in 1928.

From Berlin-Ichthyosaur, you can return from whence you came, or follow a gravel road forty-four miles northeast and rejoin Highway 50 near Austin. Flanked by the Toiyabe Range and Shoshone Mountains, it travels through scenic Reese River Valley, passing the near-ghost town of **Ione.**

---

**RV ADVISORY** ● The dirt and gravel road through Ione is well graded with gentle curves, navigable by large RVs and trailer rigs in dry weather. However, you will encounter some washboards.

---

If you return the way you came, you'll pass the ruins of **Cold Springs**, a former Pony Express and stage coach stop. It's on your right about thirteen miles east of the Highway 361 junction. Continuing east-

*Leapin' water lizards! This 50-foot long prehistoric aquatic reptile is the star attraction at Berlin-Ichthyosaur State Park.*

ward, you'll top 6,348-foot New Pass Summit, drop down into a desert valley, and then begin climbing again. At mid-climb, you'll encounter a rather dramatically perched old mining town:

# AUSTIN

**Population: 450**                                                **Elevation: 6,575 feet**

Why are Austin's old brick and stone buildings cantilevered into a steep hill instead of sitting in the valley below? Because this is where the silver was. Former Pony Express rider William Talcott found a silver vein here in 1862 and Austin soon became one of the wildest towns in Nevada.

Today, it has that comfortably worn look of a former boomtown, although it is enjoying a moderate resurgence because of renewed mining in the area. In 1976, Austin lost the seat of Lander County to Battle Mountain, up on Interstate 80. However, its handsome old stone courthouse building still functions as a government annex and an informal tourist bureau. You can pick up visitor information from a brochure rack inside.

## DINING AND RECLINING

If you feel the need for a break, Austin offers a couple of interesting places to eat and some ordinary places to sleep:

**Carol's Country Kitchen** ● *631 Main St.; (775) 964-2493. American; full bar service. Breakfast through dinner daily. Major credit cards; $$.* ⊡ This remarkably cute place is a combined restaurant and Americana museum, all a-clutter with nineteenth century memorabilia. The busy menu ranges from inexpensive stews to steaks, chops and fish, plus Mexican and Chinese dishes.

**International Café** ● *801 Main St.; (775) 964-9905. American; wine and beer. Breakfast through dinner daily. MC/VISA; $$.* ◻ The café is international in name only. The menu in this Western style diner is mostly steaks, chicken and seafood. The café occupies the oldest commercial building in town, built in 1863.

If you want to sleep over, try the **Lincoln Motel**, (775) 964 2698; or the **Pony Canyon Motel**, (775) 964-2605. Both have modest rooms with TV and phones; **$$** to **$$$**.

Buckle up for another long drive; Eureka is seventy miles away. Immediately east of Austin, the highway completes its climb over 7,484-foot Austin Summit, then it spirals downhill, passing the **Bob Scott Campground** of Toiyabe National Forest. This is the steepest and most twisted section of highway on this route, although it's well engineered.

After dipping into another desert valley, you'll climb to 6,564-foot Hickison Summit and shortly encounter **Hickison Petroglyph Site.** This is an appealing place, with tree-shaded picnic and camping areas among rocks and junipers. A short path leads to a fine collection of 3,000-year-old petroglyphs. Unfortunately, some have been defaced by vandals.

## *EUREKA*

**Population: 1,000**                    **Elevation: 6,481 feet**

The next settlement is about mid-point in this drive, and a sign boasts proudly: "You are now entering the loneliest town on the loneliest road in America."

Nestled in a juniper ravine, old Eureka is experiencing a modest mining resurgence, and it shows. A brand new brick Best Western Eureka Inn sits at the town's western edge. Its owners also have restored and reopened the 1877 **Jackson House** downtown. Step inside to admire its attractive lobby, dining room and old fashioned bar.

Across the street is the 1879 **Eureka County Courthouse**, recently refurbished and thus one of the best preserved public buildings in Nevada. Nearby is the red brick 1880 **Eureka Opera House,** also renovated and serving as a meeting, convention and cultural center. If it's open, check out the stage with its old fashioned oleo curtain and the unusual horseshoe-shaped balcony. Call (775) 237-6006 for hours.

Just uphill from the courthouse is the **Eureka Sentinel Museum**, occupying an 1879 former newspaper office at Ruby Hill and Monroe streets. It features nicely arrayed pioneer artifacts and old type cases and printing presses from its publishing days. Exhibits are displayed in an interesting "read all about it" style, mounted with old clippings and photos. The museum also serves as an informal visitor center, and you can pick up a walking tour map of the town's historic buildings. Hours are 9 to 5 daily; (775) 237-5010.

Eureka was born in 1864 when prospectors from Austin found a silver vein in a shallow ravine. It became one of the first lead and silver producing districts in America, booming to a population of 10,000. However, it also was an environmental disaster, fouling the air with arsenic and lead fumes from its blast furnaces, killing wildlife, plant life and human life.

## RECLINING AND DINING

**Best Western Eureka Inn** ● *251 N. Main St., Eureka, CA 89316; (800) 528-1234 or (775) 237-5247. Forty-two rooms and suites with TV movies and phones. Major credit cards; $$$ to $$$$. Rates include continental breakfast.* ☐ This new lodge has a yesterday and today look, with old style furniture and modern amenities. Facilities include a spa and exercise room; some rooms have refrigerators and microwaves.

**Jackson House** ● *11 S. Main St. (Ruby Hill Avenue). Mailing address: 251 N. Main St., Eureka, NV 89316; (800) 528-1234 or (775) 237-5427. Nine refurbished rooms with TV movies, phones and early American décor; $$$; rates include continental breakfast. Dining room serves American fare nightly except Sunday; full bar service; $$. Major credit cards.* ☐ Built in 1887, the Jackson house was restored in 1998, with wainscotting, wooded floors and tulip chandeliers. Pause for a sip at the Western style saloon, with an imposing arched mahogany back bar. Room reservations are handled at the Best Western Eureka Inn.

**Owl Club Steakhouse** ● *10231 Main St.; (775) 237-5280. American; full bar service. Early breakfast to dinner daily. No credit cards; $$.* ☐ While not fancy like the Jackson House dining room, the Owl Club is appealing in a funky kind of way. Its kitchen issues the usual steaks, chops and chickens. The adjacent saloon is right out of a Nevada yesterday, with a 150-year-old bar, a few slot machines and a couple of blackjack tables. It's the closest thing in town to a casino.

## CAMPING

RVers can sleep for free at a rest stop just east of down, on the left. Eureka also has two small RV parks. Near the rest stop is the attractive new **Silver Sky Lodge** with pull-throughs and full hookups with cable TV; **$$$**; (775) 237-5034. Closer to town is **Eureka RV Park** with tent sites and full hookups including TV for **$$**; (775) 237-5034.

There isn't much of interest on the 77-mile run between Eureka and Ely until you reach the **Ruth Mining District**. Here, just west of town, you'll encounter a badlands of green, yellow and rust red tailing dumps, mining terraces and open pit mines. Turn right at a "Historic mining viewpoint sign" and drive to the brink of **Copper Pit,** one of the largest open mines in America.

## ELY

**Population: 6,000**                    **Elevation: 6,431**

This sturdy old blue collar town is the only serious commercial area on this long drive across Nevada. Three major highways converge here, bringing you suddenly back into civilization and possibly confusing you as to which way to turn.

As you approach from the west, Highway 50 becomes Aultman Street, which takes you into the downtown area. You'll see the brick front **Chamber of Commerce** building on the left at 636 Aultman, near Sixth. After clearing the business district, the street curves slightly and you'll note the **White Pine Public Museum** on the left near Ogden Avenue. Several rooms are busy with old saddles and other cowboy gear, native people exhibits, farm equipment, stuffed critters and other objects. It's open weekdays 9 to 4:30 and weekends 10 to 4; (775) 289-4710.

A few blocks beyond the museum, Aultman becomes Avenue F, and a turn left onto Eleventh Street carries you to the **Nevada Northern Railway Museum.** However, "museum" is a misnomer; it's an extensive early twentieth century railroading complex. Volunteer tour guides take visitors through huge maintenance sheds, past water towers, freight and passenger depots and into the roundhouse, where several trains are still parked. (If tours aren't scheduled, you can wander about on your own.) During summer months, you can take a fourteen-mile ride on a Baldwin steamer, the "Ghost Train of Old Ely," or on an old diesel ore hauler. The museum is open daily 9 to 4. Tours and train rides are available from May through September and on some holiday weekends; (775) 289-2085.

From the railway museum, backtrack to Seventh Street and turn south, following an overlap of highways 50, 6 and 93 to continue your tour across central Nevada.

## DINING, RECLINING AND GAMING

As a major commercial area, Ely is busy with cafés, motels and service stations and it has the only real casinos between here and Fallon. Three are on your tour route, and they provide the four Nevada essentials—food, booze, games and a place to sleep. They're listed as they appear:

**Hotel Nevada Gambling Hall** ● *501 Aultman St., Ely, NV 89301; (775) 289-6665. Sixty-five simply furnished rooms with TV; $$. Restaurant serves American fare twenty-four hours; $ to $$. Major credit cards.* ☐ This is Ely's only historic casino, dating from 1921. It was Nevada's first fireproof hotel and it's still the tallest building between Ely and Carson City. A back wall of the casino has a large collection of Western firearms.

**Jailhouse Casino & Motel** ● *540 Aultman St., Ely, NV 89301; (775) 289-3033. Forty-seven units with TV and phones; $$ to $$$. Cell Block dining room serves dinners only; Jailhouse Coffee Shop is open for breakfast through dinner; $ to $$$. Major credit cards.* ☐ Across the street from Hotel Nevada, Jailhouse has a Western theme. Its walls are adorned with early Nevada photos.

**Ramada Inn Copper Queen** ● *701 Avenue I (at Seventh Street), Ely, NV 89301; (800) 851-9526 or (775) 289-4884. Sixty-five rooms and suites with TV and phones; $$$ to $$$$. American fare served twenty-four hours; $ to $$$. Major credit cards.* ☐ The most attractive Ely casino, the Copper Queen has a turn-of-the-century look. The gaming area is beneath an atrium ceiling, with a pool and spa at one end and a balcony above, giving room guests and diners an aerial view of the action.

## Ely to Great Basin National Park

As you head southeast, the bundle of routes 50/6/93 becomes the Pioche Highway. Five miles from Ely, watch for a sign indicating "Cove Valley Road and Ward Mining District." A well-tended gravel road will take you eleven miles across a brushy desert basin to **Ward Charcoal Ovens State Historic Monument.**

Are these homes for coneheads? The six stone structures, thirty feet high and shaped like Utah beehives, are charcoal ovens, built in 1876 for the Ward Mining District. Charcoal, which burns hotter than wood, was needed for the blast furnaces that rendered silver, lead and copper from raw ore. Of course, wood is needed to make charcoal and this area was stripped of trees during its mining boom. The smelter operation was shut down in 1879 and the town of Ward in the nearby foothills has since vanished. There are no services at the charcoal ovens, although RVers can spend the night free. Incidentally, step inside one of the cone-shaped ovens and you'll find that they're great echo chambers.

Retrace your route from the coneheads, drive two miles south on the Pioche Highway, then turn left for **Cave Lake State Park,** tucked into the flanks of the Shell Creek Range. This is a jewel missed by most travelers but popular with locals—a pine-shrouded blue green lake sitting at 7,300 feet, at the base of a sheer mountain face. In fact, Cave Lake is so popular that its campsites may be full on summer weekends. There are two campgrounds here with modest prices, and one has hot showers. An easy combined interpretive and hiking trail leads five miles from the park through a piñon-juniper forest.

Back on the Highway 50/6/93, you'll begin a long, subtle climb into the Schell Creek Range. Notice that the roadside flora does a slow-motion transition from sagebrush and bunch grass to piñons and junipers. As you crest 7,722-foot Conners Pass, Nevada's second highest peak appears in the east, like a blunted volcano rising from a high desert basin. Wheeler Peak, often snowcapped, reaches 13,061 feet into the blue. This is the centerpiece of Great Basin National Park which, you will soon discover, is more mountain than basin.

At the Y-junction of **Majors Station**, U.S. 93 shuffles off to the south, leaving you with eastbound Highway 50/6. Majors has a saloon and café but—when we passed—no fuel. The highway swings to the northeast to tuck between Wheeler Peak and 12,067-foot Mount Moriah to the north. As you pass through Spring Valley, an historical marker points to **Oceola**, an old mining camp four miles up a dusty road. It was established in 1872 and survived well into the twentieth century, although little remains today. You'll encounter a scatter of old mining machinery and a few contemporary dwellings landscaped with junk car bodies. The road passes through Oceola and re-joins Highway 50/6 after about ten miles.

---

*RV ADVISORY* ● The Oceola road is steep and bumpy with some switchbacks for the first six miles, then it's relatively smooth before it rejoins the highway. Small to midsize RVs should be able to handle the road, although large motorhomes and trailer rigs may be challenged. If you're planning to come back this way from the park, we'd recommend doing your Oceola visit then, since it will be a downhill approach.

---

*Ruggedly handsome Wheeler Peak, shaped by ancient glaciers, is the centerpiece of Great Basin National Park. This view is from the Wheeler Peak trail.*

Back on the highway, you'll top 7,154-foot Sacramento Pass and then spiral lazily down into the Snake Valley. Fork right onto State Route 487 for **Baker**, Great Basin National Park's small, weather-worn gateway. A market, service station and a couple of motels, restaurants and saloons—not always open—constitute its commercial offerings. You can pick up park information at the **Great Basin Natural History Association** shop in town; (775) 234-7270.

If you're hungry, your first stop should be the **Outlaw Restaurant,** the favorite of locals and knowing park visitors, open from early breakfast through dinner. The Outlaw's hefty burritos provide a good carbo load for hiking in the park. You also can get a serious drink here and play a few slots and video poker machines; (775) 234-7302.

The area's largest motel is the **Border Inn** near the Highway 50 junction, with twenty-nine units with TV/VCRs and refrigerators; **$$**, plus a coin laundry and café serving breakfast through dinner; (775) 234-7300; Major credit cards. **Silver Jack Motel** has seven rooms and a gift shop with a small selection of Western and native souvenirs; **$$**; (775) 324-

7323. You can park your rig at **Mount View RV Park,** with a coin laundry and showers; (775) 234-7272. **Y Truck Stop** at the junction has a café serving breakfast through dinner, and RV hookups with showers; (775) 234-7223.

### Great Basin National Park ● *Baker, NV 89311; (775) 234-7331.*
*Visitor center daily 8 to 5. Ninety-minute Lehman Cave tours hourly from 9 to 4 in summer, then at 9, 11, 2 and 4 the rest of the year. Group sizes are limited so make your tour reservation as soon as you arrive. Lehman Caves Gifts and Café is the park's only commercial facility, open 8 to 5 in summer. (Try the great homemade ice cream sandwiches.) The park has four campgrounds—Lower Lehman Creek, Upper Lehman, Baker Creek and Wheeler Peak. All have shady sites and water with no hookups; $. Wheeler is the highest, within walking distance of several trailheads. The easiest for RVs to negotiate is Lower Lehman, the only campground open the year around.* ⊓

Great Basin is one of the hidden surprises of the national park system. It offers a striking limestone cave complex, a rare bristlecone pine forest, Nevada's only active glacial basin and the awesome beauty of Wheeler Peak's subarctic reaches. The 77,100-acre park was established in 1986, encompassing Wheeler Peak and Lehman Cave National Monument, which dates from 1922. Original plans called for 174,000 acres that would have included more Great Basin desert lands. However, local ranching and mining interests kicked up a major fuss, so a compromise was made. This is still a pretty impressive park, covering more than a vertical mile and all of the Great Basin's five climate zones.

**Lehman Cave** is a subterranean wonderland that's adorned with thousands of stalactites, stalagmites, columns, draperies, soda straws, rare shield formations and great masses of flowstone. The perfect balance of carbon dioxide, oxygen and seeping water has created one of America's finest cavern complexes. Back in 1885, local rancher Absalom Lehman was certainly impressed when he discovered the caves. A newspaper article reported:

*Abe Lehman of Snake Valley reports he and others have struck a cave of wondrous beauty. The cave was explored about 200 feet when the points of the stalactites and stalagmites came so close together as to offer a bar to their further progress. They will again explore the cave, armed with sledgehammers...*

Fortunately, today's park personnel don't carry sledgehammers. In fact, they become rather poetic about this cave of wondrous beauty. Our guide commented as we concluded a tour:

*I like to think that after we've locked the entry doors at night, the formations come alive and begin singing and dancing.*

**Wheeler Peak Scenic Drive,** the park's only paved road, climbs dramatically from the entrance up to Wheeler Peak Campground. It gains more than 3,500 feet in twelve miles, passing from piñons and sage into thick evergreen and aspen forests. These aspens put on a gorgeous color show in fall—a great time to visit the park. Two viewpoints, Mather Overlook and Wheeler Peak Overlook, provide imposing vistas of the peak and the great sprawl of the Snake Valley below. The drive climbs to 10,000 feet near the Wheeler Peak trailhead, making it one of the highest paved roads in the West.

---

*RV ADVISORY* ● Paved and gently spiraling, Wheeler Peak Scenic Drive is negotiable by small to mid-size RVs. However, the section above Upper Lehman Peak Campground is a bit steep and winding for larger rigs and trailers.

---

Other than Lehman Cave, Great Basin is primarily a hiking park. Most of its features can be reached by non-technical day hikes—even the top of Wheeler Peak. A word of caution, however: Most hikes begin above 10,000 feet and go up from there, so pace yourself. If you develop a headache, nausea or listlessness, you may be suffering altitude sickness and you should return immediately to a lower elevation.

One of the park's most popular treks is the relatively easy two-mile **Bristlecone Pine Grove trail** from Wheeler Peak Campground. Bristlecones, you may know, are the world's oldest living things—stunted and twisted pines that manage to survive for centuries in a harsh, windy subalpine environment. The world's oldest, tree-ring dated back 4,900 years, was found on Wheeler Peak. The bristlecone forest here is quite dramatic, presenting a Wagnerian scene of giant bonsai, rising from the rock scrabble below a steep, serrated cliff.

Another popular trek, considerably tougher than the bristlecone hike, is the **Wheeler Peak Trail.** This nine-mile round trip begins with deceptive ease—a gradual uphill stroll through a thick stand of aspen. (It's awesome in autumn.) After a mile, the trail zig-zags over a meadow patched with conifers. Then it begins a final, tough assault on the mountain along a rough rocky ridge. Wheeler Peak, nearly always in view, seems to retreat as you climb. You may find yourself constantly asking in this high, thin air: "How much farther?" However, you don't need to go all the way to the top to enjoy this hike. Lower sections of the trail provide fine vistas of Wheeler and the great sprawl of the Great Basin at its feet. A good surrender point is near the last clump of pines to the right of the trail, just before it climbs above the treeline.

☺  ☺  ☺

*Where do we go from here?* ● Having surrendered on Wheeler Peak, you can return to Majors Station and pick up Tour Twenty-four on Highway 93. This route along Nevada's eastern edge starts at Jackpot on the Idaho border. However, there's not much of interest up that way unless you take a detour to Wendover and the Utah salt flats, which are very interesting. If you've been there and done that, or you're just not into salt flats, you might prefer to head on south from this point.

*Tour Twenty-four*

# THE EASTERN EDGE
## HIGHWAY 93 FROM JACKPOT TO LAS VEGAS

**T**alk about lonely highways! Drive the 435 miles on U.S. 93 from Jackpot to Las Vegas and you'll really know what it's like to be solitary. Similar to U.S. 50, Highway 93 encounters occasional small towns, with nothing between them except miles and miles of miles and miles.

The eastern edge of Nevada also is the eastern edge of the Great Basin, before the terrain spills into Utah's fascinating salt flats. Highway 93 thus offers terrain similar to that along U.S. 50, although you'll go over fewer mountain passes since the mountains are oriented north to south.

The starting point for this route is **Jackpot**, a town without a town on the Idaho border. It was established in 1956 by Idaho gaming operator Don French when that state banned slot machines. He opened the Horseshu Casino and did so well that Pete Piersanti shifted his Cactus Pete's casino to the border. He'd been operating inside Nevada, twelve miles south.

Although the clubs prospered and two more casinos joined them, Jackpot still hasn't become a town. It has service stations and a market or two, but no normal city underpinnings. There are no residential areas except for a few doublewides and we wonder if most casino employees commute from Twin Falls, forty-five miles north. Or do the girlies of the girlie shows fade like shapely dust devils into the desert at dawn?

# TRIP PLANNER

**WHEN TO GO** ● Nevada's eastern edge is a spring through fall destination. As in the Great Basin's interior, elevations are high and winters are cold.

**DRIVING DISTANCE** ● Nevada is a tall state and the distance from Jackpot on the Idaho border to Las Vegas is 435 miles. If you start from Ely or Great Basin National Park, the drive is trimmed to about 230 miles.

**RV ADVISORY** ● Nothing along this route will inconvenience an RV or trailer rig.

**WHAT YOU'LL SEE** ● The surprisingly glitzy border casino centers of Jackpot and West Wendover, Bonneville International Speedway on the Utah salt flats, the old mining town of Pioche, Cathedral Gorge State Park, Rainbow Canyon, plus Caliente and its California-Spanish style railroad station.

**WHAT TO DO** ● Explore the Utah salt flats; walk the trails of Cathedral Gorge; sit and soak in mineral water at the Hot Springs Motel in Caliente; and drive past the multicolored strata of Rainbow Canyon east of Caliente.

**TO BEGIN** ● Start with U.S. 93 in Jackpot, Ely or Majors Junction, depending on how much of eastern Nevada you want to drive.

### Useful contacts

**Lincoln County Tourism,** P.O. Box 255, Caliente, NV 89008; (775) 726-3209.

**Pioche Chamber of Commerce,** P.O. Box 553, Pioche, NV 89043; (775) 962-5544.

### Pricing guidelines

**DINING:** Dinner entrée with soup or salad, without drinks or dessert for under $10 = **$**; $10 to $14 = **$$**; $15 to $25 = **$$$**; over $25 = **$$$$**.

**RECLINING:** A two-person room for $35 or less = **$**; $36 to $50 = **$$**; $51 to $75 = **$$$**; $76 to $100 = **$$$$**; more than $100 = **$$$$$**.

**CAMPING:** Under $10 = **$**; $10 to $14 = **$$**; $15 to $19 = **$$$**; $20 or more = **$$$$**

However, this isn't a dusty wide spot in the road. The casinos are relatively large, glittery and quite lively. In fact, Cactus Pete's has a rare AAA four diamond rating. The name "Jackpot," incidentally, was inspired by the public relations director for the two original casinos.

If you want to party, eat or sleep at the border, the original casinos are the largest and most attractive:

**Cactus Pete's Casino** ● *P.O. Box 508, Jackpot, NV 89825; (775) 755-2321. An elaborate resort with 293 rooms and suites with TV movies and phones; $$$. Five restaurants serve American and international fare twenty-four hours; full bar service; $ to $$. Major credit cards.* □ This surprisingly plush Southwest style gaming resort rivals many of those in Las

Vegas and Reno-Tahoe. Facilities include a show lounge that draws major stars, a large gaming area, hotel tower, pool and spa, tennis courts and an eighteen-hole golf course.

### Horseshu Hotel & Casino •
*P.O. Box 508, Jackpot, NV 89825; (775) 755-7777. A 120-room resort with TV and phones; $$$. Restaurant and coffee shop serve mostly American fare; open twenty-four hours; full bar service; $ to $$. Major credit cards.* ☐ The smaller Horseshu has a Western motif, busy with lariats, fake batwing doors, cowboy hats and other frontier regalia. Facilities include a pool and spa, and a golf course shared by Cactus Pete's. (Both casinos are now under the same ownership.)

### CAMPING
**Cactus Pete's** has an RV park with hookups and access to all the resort amenities; **$$**; (775) 755-2321. Nearby is **Spanish Gardens RV Park** with tent and RV sites, showers, coin laundry and casino shuttles; **$$**; (800) 422-8233 or (775) 755-2333.

## Jackpot to the Wendovers
Sixty-eight miles south of Jackpot, you'll hit **Wells** at the Interstate 80 junction. Once a dreary little desert town, it's now enjoying a modest mining boom, although it doesn't offer much of interest for the casual visitor. From here, take I-80 (which also is alternate 93) fifty-nine miles southeast to **Wendover** on the Utah border. You'll find another gaming center, and it's a more substantial community than Jackpot, with West Wendover in Nevada and Wendover in Utah.

An odd bit of history occurred here. It was from Wendover Army Air Force Base that B-29 crews practiced with dummy atomic bombs before dropping real ones on Hiroshima and Nagasaki to end World War II. Near

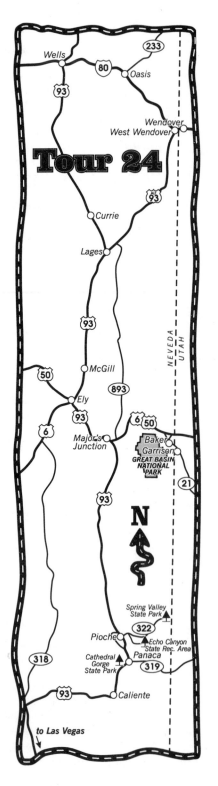

the border on Wendover Boulevard, you'll see a **Peace Memorial** dedicated to that unfortunate incident. It's in front of a joint Nevada-Utah Welcome Center. Continuing into the Beehive State on the boulevard, you'll see the **Bonneville Speedway Museum** on your right. It displays clippings, photos and artifacts relating to land speed records set at the nearby Bonneville International Speedway. The museum is open from 10 to 6, daily in summer and weekends only the rest of the year; (801) 665-7721.

If you'd like to see the speedway itself, drive into Utah on I-80, take exit 4 and go five miles north into the salt flats. It's a perfectly flat nine-mile course with a black line down the middle, especially prepared by BLM for speed tests. You'll find few other facilities here, except informational signs about the salt flats, and you may or may not see a metallic blur whizzing past. The first speed record was set here in 1914 by Teddy Tezlaff, who pushed his Blitzen Benz to 141.73 miles an hour. The current record is 622.407 mph, set by Gary Gabolich in a rocket car. In order to qualify for a record, a racer must make two runs over a flying mile, one in each direction within an hour.

Just think. At 622.407 mph, you could do this eastern Nevada tour in about forty-five minutes. Watch out for state troopers.

Like Jackpot, West Wendover has a few partying places. The two largest are jointly owned and connected by a pedestrian skybridge over Wendover Boulevard:

*Silver Smith Hotel & Resort* ● *P.O. Box 729, West Wendover, NV 89883; (800) 648-9668 or (775) 664-2231. One hundred twenty rooms with TV movies and phones; $$$ to $$$$. Several restaurants serve twenty-four hours; full bar service; $ to $$. Major credit cards.* ☐ This sleek Western-modern style casino resort has a pool and spa, large health club with a sauna and tanning beds, and tennis courts.

*State Line Hotel & Casino* ● *P.O. Box 789, West Wendover, NV 89883; (800) 648-9668 or (775) 664-2221. A 248-room resort with TV movies and phones; $$$ $$$$. Several restaurant serve twenty-four hours; full bar service. Major credit cards.* ☐ State Line has a pool and spa, gaming area, showroom, smaller show lounges and food service ranging from fine dining to snack bars.

RVers can slip into a slot at **State Line RV Park**, which has hookups, showers, coin laundry and access to the adjacent casino facilities; **$$$**; (775) 664-2221.

## West Wendover to Pioche and Caliente

Head south from West Wendover on alternate U.S. 93. You'll crest 6,045-foot White Horse Pass and eventually rejoin the main Highway 93 at **Lages Station,** which has no services. About fifteen miles down, watch on your left for a **Pony Express Station** site; it doesn't offer much more than an interpretive sign.

As you continue southward, the brushy, lumpy terrain becomes more interesting with the rise of the rugged Shell Creek Range to the east. Its 11,883-foot North Schell Peak is one of the highest mountains in eastern Nevada. After passing through small **McGill,** you'll enter **Ely**, which we visited in the previous tour. Highway 93 is stacked atop routes 50 and 6 here, and it remains that way for the next twenty-six miles to **Majors Junction.**

Below Majors, you'll travel forty miles through Lake Valley, a ranching basin rimmed by the Schell Creek Range to the west and Wheeler Peak to the east. It is of course the focal point of **Great Basin National Park** which we explored in the previous tour. At the lower end of Lake Valley, Highway 93 begins a gradual climb from bunchgrass prairie into juniper woodlands. Fork to the right at a "Scenic route" sign for a side door approach to an intriguing old frontier town.

## PIOCHE

**Population: about 400**                                   **Elevation: 6,060 feet**

Pronounced *pee-OACH*, this once thriving mining camp is tucked among tailing dumps and abandoned headframes. By taking the turnoff about three miles north, you'll pass a state prison and then enter the town's northern flank on Lacour Street. Watch on your right for the red brick **Million Dollar Courthouse**. It was named not for its value but for political boondoggling. Built in 1871, it was budgeted at $16,400 but the tab shot up to $26,000 because of overruns and skimming by crooked officials. The county floated junk bonds to make up the losses and by the time they were paid off in 1938, the debt had topped a million dollars. The former courthouse is open Sunday-Thursday 10 to 5 and Saturday 9 to 5, April through October. Docents conduct visitors through the former offices, which display some of the original furnishings.

A couple of blocks beyond the courthouse, Lacour blends into Main Street, tilted sharply uphill and lined with more historic structures. Near the intersection is the tough old **Overland Saloon**; just below and still showing movies is the 1920s style **Gem Theatre** with an old fashioned wedge marquee. A bit farther down Main is the glistening white art deco style **Lincoln County Courthouse,** completed in 1938 to replace the million dollar boondoggle.

Heading back up Main, peek into the **Lincoln County Historical Museum**, open summers only, Tuesday-Saturday 10 to 4 and Sunday 1 to 5; (775) 962-5207. While neither professionally done nor orderly, it contains a remarkable assortment of early day artifacts, from a Victrola talking machine to old mining gear. A few doors higher up Main is the cute little green **Commerce Cottage**, the local information center, open Monday-Saturday 11 to 3 in summer; (775) 962-5544.

Continue driving uphill and veer left above the business district, following a Highway 93 sign. You'll shortly encounter the weathered remnants of the **Pioche Tramway,** built in 1923 to haul ore from hillside mines to a mill in the valley below. In the sagging wooden tram house, you can see the complex gears that made the thing run. Rusting buckets still dangle from the cable above.

Pioche emerged in 1869 when silver was discovered in these rough hills. The town was a tough as the hills; fifty men supposedly died of violence before anyone got around to expiring from natural causes.

*Wind and rain sculpted these intriguing shapes at Cathedral Gorge State Park. These are small formations; note the size of the onlooker on the right.*

### DINING, RECLINING AND CAMPING

There's no gourmet excitement in Pioche, although you can find basic grub at **Pioche Café, Etc.**, a combined café and curio shop next to the Overland Saloon. It serves American fare (Mexican on Friday); lunch and dinner daily, with items such as chicken breast with pineapple, steak and shrimp; **$** to **$$**; (775) 962-5507. Across the street, the **Silver Café** dishes up American and Mexican food with wine and beer; breakfast through dinner daily; **$** to **$$**; (775) 962-5124.

You can spend the night at **Motel Pioche** on Lacour Street with phones and TV; **$$**; (775) 952-5551. **Overland Hotel** above the saloon has very basic rooms; **$$**; (775) 962-5480. RV and tent campsites are available at **Spring Valley State Park** and **Echo Canyon Recreation Area**, both east of Pioche on State Route 322.

Departing Pioche, you can continue past the tram through wooded foothills and merge with Highway 93 a bit south. You'll soon encounter one of Nevada's most remarkable little preserves:

**Cathedral Gorge State Park** • *Highway 93; (775) 728-4467. Moderate day use fee. Shaded campsites with water, barbecue grills, picnic ramadas, flush potties and showers; $$.* ☐ The name is misleading, although the park's landforms are quite dramatic. Not really a gorge, this is a shallow basin sheltered by walls only a hundred or so feet high. However, they've been eroded into thousands of spires, pinnacles, columns and fins. Serpentine ravines are cut deeply into the walls; some are so narrow that you'll have to shed your fanny pack to get through. If it's just your fanny, forget it.

Approaching on Highway 93 from Pioche, watch on your right for a small sign to **Miller's Point**, which provides a fine overview of these formations. Continue downhill and turn into the park, passing a Nevada State Parks Regional Information Center. Once inside the park, go left to the campground or right to a picnic area that's dramatically situated among the spires. From here, you can follow up a trail along the base of these serrated walls and cliffs. A fork to the right leads into a narrow ravine, where wooden steps will take you up to Miller's Point. A left fork takes you on a four-mile round trip through the main chasm, ending at the campground. You'll want to branch off frequently to explore convoluted cliff faces and slender ravines.

Half a mile below Cathedral Gorge, State Route 319 leads briefly east to **Panaca**, a quiet and ordinary farm community with a singular claim to fame. Established in 1864 by Mormons, it's the second oldest town in Nevada. It also offers a singular reason to visit—an unusual green limestone butte that rises from the back of the town's small residential area.

## CALIENTE

**Population: 400**                    **Elevation: 4,398 feet**

Fourteen miles below Panaca, quiet little Caliente has something in common with glittery Las Vegas. Both were established in 1905 by copper king William Clark as watering holes for his steam trains running between Salt Lake City and Los Angeles. Of course, Las Vegas has grown a bit faster since then.

The emergence of diesel trains ended Caliente's reason for being, although it has managed to survive as a small agricultural center. In fact, it's the most attractive little town in eastern Nevada, with the mission revival style **Caliente Railroad Station** as its handsome centerpiece. Still used as an Amtrak stop, it also houses city offices and the municipal court. The **Chamber of Commerce** operates its "RSVP" visitor center here, sharing space with an art gallery. Both the visitor center and gallery are open weekdays 9 to 5; (775) 962-5544.

As you enter Caliente from the north, note the long row of modest little matched cottages, built for railroad employees. Most are quite tidy and still occupied. Just beyond, on your left, is the railroad depot and the town's compact, well-maintained business core.

### DINING, RECLINING AND CAMPING

As with Pioche, Caliente's offerings are basic but adequate. The **Knotty Pine Café** on the south side at 690 Front Street serves ample American grub, with full bar service; breakfast through dinner daily; $ to $$; (775) 726-3194. An adjacent bar has a few slot and video poker machines. **Hot Springs Motel** on the north side has simple rooms and some kitchenettes, plus hot mineral baths, which are open to non-guests as well; MC/VISA; **$$$**; (775) 726-3777. **Young's RV Park** on the south side has full hookups with tables, barbecues, flush potties and showers; **$$**; (775) 726-3418.

## Side trip: Rainbow Canyon

Just east of Caliente, Rainbow Canyon provides an impressive gallery of geological strata. A twenty-one-mile drive on a paved road takes you past strata ranging from chalky white through the entire brown scale to yellow, pea soup green, russet and almost-orange. The most impressive feature comes near the end as the chasm narrows into the vertical chocolate brown walls of Grapevine Canyon. Clover Creek flowing through here has some inviting little willow glens—great places for picnics.

Rainbow Canyon was flooded in 1910, wrecking a million dollars worth of track and nearly bankrupting Clark's railroad. The rails were elevated as protection against future floods and they're still up there. The road travels through the canyon bottom and you'll splash through occasional seasonal creek crossings. Use caution during rainstorms. Pavement and the ravine both end half a mile beyond a ranch called Bradshaw's End of the Trail.

And we're nearing the end of our trail. Las Vegas lies 150 miles south and there's not much between here and there. Even the terrain loses much of its appeal, since the highway drops from the Great Basin into the drier and less vegetated Mojave Desert. Between Caliente and Las Vegas, you'll shed nearly 2,400 vertical feet.

South of Caliente, Highway 93 swings abruptly west, passing through an extension of Rainbow Canyon and then cresting juniper-studded 6,234-foot Oak Springs Summit. It drops down through a thin Joshua tree forest into a beige desert, then swings southward again at **Crystal Springs.** After whisking past **Ash Springs** and **Alamo**, the highway hurries through empty desert for seventy-five miles before hitting Interstate 15 northeast of Las Vegas.

☺   ☺   ☺

*Where do we go from here?* ● If you don't want to go to Las Vegas, head west toward Tonopah at the Crystal Springs junction. You'll follow America's ultimate lonely road—State Route 375, the Extraterrestrial Highway.

---

*FUEL ADVISORY* ● Fill your tank in Caliente, since fuel is expensive and scarce until you hit Glitter City. If you're going west toward Tonopah, gasoline is usually available in Rachel, seventy-eight miles from Caliente. Tank up anyway, in case the station is closed; it's nearly 200 miles from Caliente to Tonopah and there are no other services.

---

# TRIP PLANNER

**WHEN TO GO** ● Fall through spring are the most popular times to visit Las Vegas and its surrounding desert attractions. Mount Charleston is a year around destination since it's several thousand feet above sea level and it has a small ski area. Las Vegas itself is becoming more popular in summer since, at 2,050 feet above sea level, it's not *beastly* hot and everything is air conditioned. However, summer is a bit hot for hiking in Red Rock Canyon and Valley of Fire State Park, unless you get an early-morning start.

**DRIVING DISTANCE** ● If you take all three loop trips from Las Vegas, the total will be about 370 miles. **Individual distances—** MESQUITE-LAKE MEAD: Las Vegas to Mesquite and Virgin River Canyon, then south to Valley of Fire, Lake Mead and Hoover Dam and back to Las Vegas is about 225 miles. RED ROCK CANYON LOOP: Las Vegas through Red Rock Canyon and back through Blue Diamond is around sixty miles. MOUNT CHARLESTON: The loop from Las Vegas through Mount Charleston and back is approximately eighty-five miles.

**RV ADVISORY** ● The only advisory needed is to keep your air conditioner running if you attempt the Mesquite-Lake Mead and Red Rock Canyon tours in summer.

**WHAT YOU'LL SEE** ● Mesquite and Virgin River Gorge, Lost City Museum in Overton, Valley of Fire State Park, Lake Mead National Recreation Area and Hoover Dam, the art deco Boulder City historic district, Red Rock Canyon, Spring Mountain Ranch and Old Nevada, charming old Blue Diamond, and the lofty ramparts of Mount Charleston.

**WHAT TO DO** ● Explore the Virgin River Recreation Area; hike the White Domes area at Valley of Fire State Park; take a Lake Mead cruise and tour Hoover Dam; take the Ice Box Canyon trail in Red Rock Canyon; hike the Bristlecone Pines Trail and possibly even the summit trail in the Mount Charleston Recreation Area.

**TO BEGIN** ● Wake up one morning in Las Vegas with an urge get away from the glitter.

## Useful contacts

**Boulder City Chamber of Commerce**, 1497 Nevada Hwy., Boulder City, NV 89005; (702) 293-2034.

**Lake Mead National Recreation Area**, 601 Nevada Hwy., Boulder City, NV 89005-2426; (702) 293-8907.

**Las Vegas Convention and Visitors Authority**, 3150 Paradise Rd., Las Vegas, NV 89109; (702) 892-7575.

## Pricing guidelines

**DINING:** Dinner entrée with soup or salad, without drinks or dessert for under $10 = **$**; $10 to $14 = **$$**; $15 to $25 = **$$$**; over $25 = **$$$$**.

**RECLINING:** A two-person room for $35 or less = **$**; $36 to $50 = **$$**; $51 to $75 = **$$$**; $76 to $100 = **$$$$**; more than $100 = **$$$$$**.

**CAMPING:** Under $10 = **$**; $10 to $14 = **$$**; $15 to $19 = **$$$**; $20 or more = **$$$$**

## Tour Twenty-five

# LOOPING LAS VEGAS
## MESQUITE, VALLEY OF FIRE, LAKE MEAD, RED ROCK CANYON & MOUNT CHARLESTON

It's the world's greatest party town, drawing more than thirty million annual visitors. They fill a hundred thousand hotel rooms in more than sixty major casino resorts, and they leave behind twenty billion dollars and change—which probably goes into the slot machines. Las Vegas is the only city in the world devoted primarily to partying, and it's the most visited single tourist attraction in America.

If you're one of those thirty million visitors, you may wake up one morning with a smile on your lips, an ache in your head and a desire to do something besides eat, drink and be merry. The final tour in the book is designed for you.

Everyone knows that Las Vegas is surrounded by desert. However, you may not know that it's an *interesting* desert, with rugged canyons and amazing red rock formations. It even has a mountain range in the middle of that desert, topped by one of Nevada's highest peaks.

We have devised for you three loop trips that will take you to some of Glitter City's surrounding natural wonders. We know this area well, for it is our winter home.

# MESQUITE-VALLEY OF FIRE-LAKE MEAD LOOP

Are you ready to discover a "Virgin" Las Vegas? About eighty-five miles northeast of Glitter City on Interstate 15 is the small gaming center of Mesquite, on the Arizona Border. It's nestled in a pleasant little farming valley shaped by the Virgin River. Just beyond Mesquite is the Virgin River Recreation Area, where the stream has cut a dramatic steep-walled canyon.

To begin, head northeast from Las Vegas on I-15, drive about eighty miles to Mesquite and take the first exit. (If you're coming down Highway 93 from Tour Twenty-Four, head southeast on State Route 168 and pick up I-15 in Glendale.)

## MESQUITE

**Population: 3,500**                                    **Elevation: 1,597 feet**

Although most Nevada border crossings were born as casino clusters, Mesquite is a town of substance, dating from 1880 as a Mormon farming and ranching area. This rural enclave sites near the banks of the Virgin River, backdropped by the 8,000-foot Virgin Mountains. A few buttes and other eroded shapes mark this area as a gateway to the nearby Arizona-Utah canyonlands.

Mesquite has become something of a miniature Las Vegas in recent decades, with explosive growth and the arrival of four casinos. One, Si Redd's Oasis, has practically taken over the downtown area. If you take the westside freeway exit onto Mesquite Boulevard, you'll first encounter a complex that opened in 1995 as Players Island. It then changed its stripes—but not much of its décor—to **CasaBlanca** in 1997. Continuing into town, you'll hit **Si Redd's Oasis,** spreading over both sides of Mesquite Boulevard. The town's small and interestingly cluttered **Desert Valley Museum** is at 35 W. Mesquite, open Monday-Saturday 8 to 5; (702) 346-5705. Exhibits include old photos, elderly slot machines, farm machinery and—good grief!—a birthing table. The building is a museum piece as well, built in 1941 as a library and later used as a hospital. Apparently that birthing table had been left behind.

Continuing through town, you'll see a **Nevada Welcome Center** on your right near a freeway interchange, operated by the Las Vegas Convention and Visitors Authority, with some help from state tourism officials; it's open daily 9 to 5. Across the freeway is **Virgin River Casino**, with the new **Holiday Inn Rancho Mesquite** next door.

### DINING, RECLINING AND CAMPING

**CasaBlanca** ● *950 W. Mesquite Blvd., Mesquite, NV 890247; (800) 459-7529 or (702) 346-7529. (WEB SITE: www.casablancaresort.com) Seven hundred tropical theme rooms with phones and TV movies, some refrigerators; $$$ to $$$$. Two restaurants and a buffet; around the clock food service; $ to $$. RV park with full hookups, coin laundry and showers; $$. Major credit cards.* ☐ This place looks like a setting for Casablanca— both the classic movie and the Moroccan city—although it had this same palm tree look when Merv Griffin and associates opened it as Players Island. CasaBlanca has the usual amenities—lots of slots and table games, a

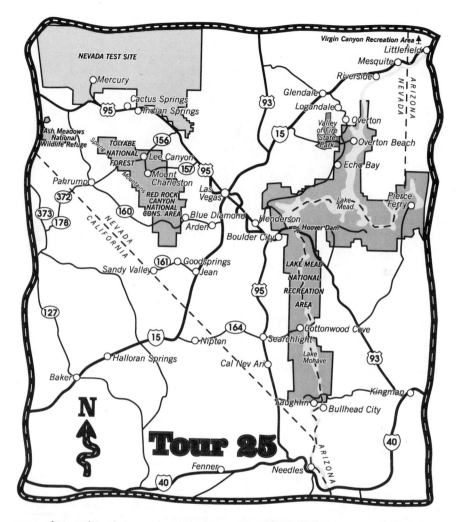

Tour 25

very nice swimming pool complex, spa and saunas and an 18-hole golf course. The restaurants have taken on Moroccan names and themes—the Purple Fez and Katherine's of CasaBlanca.

**Virgin River Hotel-Casino** ● *P.O. Box 1620 (I-15 exit 122), Mesquite, NV 89024; (800) 346-7721 or (702) 346-7777. A 723-room resort with TV movies and phones; $$ to $$$. Restaurants open twenty-four hours with full bar service; $ to $$. RV park with full hookups and showers; $$; also free RV parking. Major credit cards.* □ More folksy than CasaBlanca, the Western theme Virgin River has a pool, four-screen movie theater, large bingo parlor and the usual games of chance. It's more of a low-roller place, with some very good room rates on weekdays.

### Virgin River Gorge and Lake Mead

Although this marks the end of Mesquite and Nevada, continue northeast on I-15 through the remarkably beautiful **Virgin River Gorge** of the Virgin River Recreation Area. Under BLM supervision, this region has a

*The petrified pachyderm called Elephant Rock towers over the author near the south entrance to Valley of Fire State Park.*

couple of campgrounds, hiking trails and mostly lots of stunning canyon scenery. The borders of Nevada, Arizona and Utah converge near here, and the best scenery is in a short swatch of Arizona.

A good turnaround point—after seeing the most impressive areas of the canyon—is the Virgin River Recreation Area exit. You can park an RV or pitch a tent in a BLM campground here, with sites perched high above the stream. There's little shade other than picnic ramadas, with flush potties and no hookups; **$.**

Follow I-15 back into Nevada and, after thirty miles, take the Highway 169 exit for **Logandale** and **Overton,** two small farming communities untouched by gaming glitter. On the far side of Overton, watch on your right for a small sign to the **Lost City Museum**. It is neither lost nor a city, but a fine interpretive center on the site of an ancient Anasazi village. It was built during the Depression by the Civilian Conservation Corps and given the fanciful "Lost City" name to attract visitors. The museum has displays concerning Anazasi agriculture, weapons and social lives, plus an exhibit about those CCC boys. Outside, you can peer into a pit house and poke into a reconstructed above-ground pueblo. The Anasazi, who may have been ancestors of Arizona's Hopi tribe, roamed these parts as much as 20,000 years ago.

South of the museum, the highway passes the **Overton Wildlife Management Area** along the Virgin River. It becomes North Shore Road as it enters the upper reaches of Lake Mead National Recreation

Area. Before committing to the NRA, turn right and follow a road west to a wonderland of red rocks:

**Valley of Fire State Park** • *P.O. Box 515, Overton, NV 89040; (702) 397-2088. Modest day use fee. Visitor center open daily 8:30 to 4:30. Two-section campground, one with flush and one with pit potties. Tables and barbecue grills, no hookups; $$.* ☐ Valley of Fire encompasses a series of desert washes and ravines that have been sculpted by erosion into fantastic shapes. These sculptures—many tinged red by iron oxide—are best admired early in the morning or just before sunset, when slanting rays add additional drama to this extraordinary place.

As you enter the park, you'll see often-photographed **Elephant Rock** on your right. Pause to pay your respects to this petrified pachyderm, then continue several miles to the park visitor center, stopping to check out points of interest along the way. A winding road leads north from the center through absolutely splendid rock formations. Stop at **Mouse's Tank** for a short walk through a narrow, convoluted canyon. The "tank" is a natural water hole named for a dropout Indian who once sought sanctuary there. Just beyond at **Rainbow Vista,** follow a 1.5-mile trail along the edge of Fire Canyon to Silica Dome.

The road once ended here, and our favorite hike led through superb red rock formations to the **White Domes** area. It's marked by light beige, softly rounded monoliths. The park service recently extended a road to the domes, so drive to its end and begin your exploration from a parking area. There are few marked trails at Valley of Fire, although cross-country hiking is permitted. Choose any of a dozen dry washes and strike out—but check landmarks so you don't get lost. Take plenty of water, and good compass couldn't hurt.

Return to the main road and continue through the park, pausing at several turnouts for points of interest along the way. If you plan to camp, you'll see a road leading to the right toward campgrounds "A" (flush potties and showers) and "B" (pit potties). Both have campsites among the rock formations; those at "B" are the most impressive.

After seeing the rest of the park's attractions, do a turnabout at its west entrance, return to North Shore Road and continue south.

**Lake Mead National Recreation Area** • *601 Nevada Hwy., Boulder City, NV 89005-2426; (702) 293-8907. Information available at the Alan Bible Visitor Center; see below. Camping at several NRA campgrounds and concessionaire RV parks; $ to $$$. Lodging and restaurants at several marinas.* ☐ The completion of Hoover Dam in 1936 created the world's largest reservoir. Around it is wrapped the third largest unit of the National Park Service outside of Alaska. Lake Mead National Recreation Area covers 1.3 million acres and draws nine million visitors a year. But don't worry about crowds; most of them are out on the water. Besides, that only amounts to about fourteen people per acre.

Below the Valley of Fire, North Shore Road heads southwest through this huge recreation area. You won't see much of the lake since the road is mostly inland, passing through a rough-hewn desert. To play in the water, take any of several turnoffs to lakeside marinas, such as Overton Beach,

Callville Bay, Lake Mead Resort and Boulder Beach. Most have lodgings, restaurants and camping facilities, plus boat launches, tackle shops, boat rentals and such.

After about forty miles, you'll encounter the **Alan Bible Visitor Center,** where nicely done displays will tell you all you'll ever needed to know about the construction of Hoover Dam and the flora, fauna and geology of the area. It's open daily 8:30 to 5; (775) 293-8907.

Just beyond, you'll hit Highway 93, and a right turn will take you through Boulder City and Henderson, back to Las Vegas. Of course if you haven't done the Hoover Dam tour, turn left instead of right:

**Hoover Dam** ● *Hoover Dam Visitor Services, P.O. Box 60400, Boulder City, NV 89006; (702) 293-8321. Thirty-five minute guided tours daily from 8:30 to 6:30; moderate fees. Three-level visitor facility includes a theater, exhibits and a rooftop overlook.* ◻ Built in narrow, rock-ribbed Black Canyon, Hoover Dam is one of the world's engineering marvels. It's fun to walk across the dam and stare down this great concrete wedge to what's left of the Colorado River, more than 700 feet below. For a closer look, sign up for a tour at the new visitor facility and ride an elevator into the dam's innards. You can watch videos and study exhibits at the new center while waiting your turn.

Although visitor facilities have changed, the guides haven't. They still pummel you with statistics and facts:

*The dam's face is 726 feet high and 1,224 feet wide at the crest. Nearly four million cubic yards of concrete were poured from giant buckets into interlocking forms to create it. Despite what you've heard, no workers are buried in the dam. The buckets held tons of concrete, but each pour raised the dam's height by only six inches.*

Unfortunately, our guide concluded with:

*Now, wasn't that the best dam tour you've ever taken?*

## ACTIVITIES

**Boat and water sports rentals** ● Ski boats, fishing boats, jet skis, patio boats and other watercraft rentals are available at Lake Mead Resort, (702) 293-3484); and Echo Bay Resort, (702) 394-4000. Or contact Seven Crown Resorts, P.O. Box 16247, Irvine, CA 92713; (800) 752-9669.

**Houseboat rentals** ● They're at Echo Bay, Temple Bar and Lake Mead resorts. Contact Seven Crowns Resorts, P.O. Box 16247, Irvine, CA 92713-0068; (800) 752-9669. Houseboat rentals also are available from Forever Resorts at Callville Bay Resort and Marina; (800) 255-5561 or (702) 565-4813.

**Lake Mead cruises** ● The sternwheeler *Desert Princess* has sightseeing, breakfast buffet and dinner cruises, departing Lake Mead Resort Marina; contact Lake Mead Cruises, (702) 293-6180.

**River trips** ● Day-long float trips on the Colorado River below Hoover Dam are available from Black Canyon River Raft Tours, 1297 Nevada Hwy., Boulder City, NV 89005; (800) 696-RAFT or (702) 293-3776.

# BOULDER CITY

**Population: 2,500**                    **Elevation: 2,232 feet**

From that dam tour, head west on Highway 93 to the town that was built for the construction workers. It's now a neat and prim community and the only town in Nevada where gambling is specifically outlawed. As you climb the highway from the dam, you'll pass **Gold Strike Inn, Hotel and Casino,** where you *can* gamble because it's outside the city limits. It has inexpensive rooms and cheap, palatable grub and a midsize gaming area; (800) 245-6380 or (702) 293-5000. (It was destroyed by fire recently but should be up and running by the time you arrive.)

A few miles past the casino, fork to the left, following "Historic district" signs. This will take you through Boulder City's nicely preserved art deco section along Arizona Street. The small **Boulder City/Hoover Dam Museum** at 444 Hotel Plaza has exhibits, documents and videos concerning the dam's construction, and a small souvenir shop. A short distance away is the area's most historic structure:

**Boulder Dam Hotel** • *1305 Arizona St., Boulder City, NV 89005; (702) 293-1808. Newly renovated rooms with 1930s décor; $$$$. Tiffany's restaurant serves Italian and American fare; full bar service; $$$. Major credit cards.* ☐ Pause for a peek into the lobby of this gleaming white Dutch colonial style hotel. It features oak paneling, 1930s furnishings and a brick fireplace. Tiffany's is elegantly attired in floral wall panels, tulip chandeliers and warm woods. Meal offerings include pasta, chicken cacciatore, veal Parmesan, steaks, chops and seafood. Also in the hotel complex is the Boulder City Art Guild gallery, open daily 12 to 5. It displays and sells the works of local and regional artists.

To complete this lengthy loop, press on through downtown Boulder City, continuing west and then northwest on U.S. 93/95. You'll climb over Railroad Pass (and pass a casino by that name), and slip downhill into **Henderson**, a sprawling Las Vegas neighbor. If you take this trip at night, the combined lights of Henderson and Las Vegas are quite impressive. Just beyond Railroad Pass, the highway becomes a freeway—Interstate 515, which will whisk you quickly back to Glitter City.

If you'd like to visit one of southern Nevada's most appealing "off the Strip" casino resorts, take the Sunset Road exit in Henderson and go briefly west to **Sunset Station.** With a Spanish-Mediterranean look, this complex has several restaurants, a 448-room hotel, show lounges, large gaming area, video arcade, swimming complex and multi-screen movie theater; (888) SUNSET-9 or (702) 547-7777.

Incidentally, our winter home is in Henderson, not far from Sunset Station, so don't forget to wave.

# RED ROCK CANYON LOOP

About sixty-five million years ago, the Keystone Fault was jammed upward, then weathered into an incredibly complex series of cliff faces and canyons. To see all of this, head west on Charleston Avenue from downtown Las Vegas. After about ten miles of Southwest style suburbs, you'll finally shed civilization and see folded, russet ramparts ahead.

**Red Rock Canyon National Conservation Area** • *C/o Bureau of Land Management, HCR 33, Box 5500, Las Vegas, NV 89124; (702) 363-1921. Visitor center open daily 9 to 4; free. Conducted hikes and nature programs available. Scenic drive open 8 a.m. to dusk. Primitive camping at Oak Creek Road Campground.* ☐ More of an eroded cliff face than a canyon, Red Rock is a thirteen-mile fault extending along the base of the Spring Mountains. Begin your exploration at a sandstone-colored visitor center, on your right just after you enter the preserve. Bunkered into a desert slope, it has exhibits on the flora, fauna, geological and human history of the canyon.

From the center, a thirteen-mile scenic drive leads along the horseshoe-shaped perimeter of the Keystone Fault. Trailheads will invite you to explore further. This gently rolling route is a favorite for bicyclists.

Your first stop may be the most dramatic—a tumbled collection of red, gray and beige rocks called the **Calico Hills.** This marbled face is a striking landmark, visible for miles. Short trails lead into this twisted, multi-hued lower reaches. **Calico Canyon Trail** hugs the edge of the chasm, extending a mile to a second parking area. After a short distance, you'll come to a fork in the trail; go to the right to stay close to the canyon edge.

Continue around the drive for more views and trailheads. Our favorite hike is at **Ice Box Canyon**; it's a moderately strenuous four-mile stroll into a shallow, steep-walled chasm. The trail initially follows the canyon rim, then after a mile, it drops down to the rocky floor. Rock cairns help guide your progress through this rough-and-tumble dry wash. This isn't a loop trail and the canyon floor becomes increasingly more narrow and rocky as you press onward. Hike until you get tired of rock-scrambling, then start back. We generally go about a mile up the canyon floor.

The scenic drive blends into State Highway 159, which continues south along the weather-sculpted base of the Spring Mountains. You'll shortly see a road leading to the primitive **Spring Mountain Campground** on the right. It's not fancy, although the campsites provide nice views of the mountains. Water is available from a tanker truck, and the campground has pit potties; **$$**. Just beyond is a hideaway once owned by the reclusive Howard Hughes:

**Spring Mountain Ranch State Park** • *P.O. Box 124, Blue Diamond, NV 89004; (702) 875-4141. Grounds open daily 8 to sunset; ranch house open Friday-Monday 10 to 4, closed Tuesday-Thursday. Modest entry fee.* ☐ Spring Mountain Ranch began as a homestead in 1876, then it went through an assortment of owners—including Howard Hughes—before it was acquired by the state. Chester "Lum" Lauck of *Lum & Abner* fame owned the property in the Fifties and built the present sandstone New England style ranch house. Mr. Hughes, residing in the penthouse of the Desert Inn, bought the property in 1967, although he apparently never went there.

The ranch house is beautifully maintained, with a mix of early to mid-twentieth century furnishings reflecting the styles of its many owners. Even if it's closed, this place is worth a pause. You can stroll the landscaped grounds and stare at the craggy face of the Spring Mountains.

The next attraction, just up the highway, is of quite a different sort: **Bonnie Springs and Old Nevada** • *Old Nevada, NV 89004; (702) 875-4191. Western town open daily at 10, with various closing hours; moderate admission charge. Bonnie Springs Motel has rooms and kitchenettes with TV and phones; $$$ to $$$$$. Bonnie Springs Restaurant serves American fare; breakfast through dinner; full bar service; $$. MC/VISA, AMEX.* ☐ Like Spring Mountain Ranch, Bonnie Springs was an early homestead. It also was a way station on the Old Spanish Trail. However, almost nothing remains of the original. What has emerged in its place is a *faux* Western town with curio shops, a wax museum, shootouts, hangings and other clean fun. It was a bit scruffy when we last visited, although the restaurant is quite inviting, with its rustic look. The bar is festooned with neckties surrendered by city dudes foolish enough to arrive in city duds.

Pressing onward from Bonnie Springs, you'll soon encounter **Blue Diamond,** a former company town for a gypsum mine. It's worth a brief look, with its neat company-built cottages, shaded by giant hardwoods. At the Highway 159/160 junction, veer eastward on Route 160 and you'll soon hit Interstate 15, eight miles south of Las Vegas.

## MOUNT CHARLESTON LOOP

One of the more appealing novelties of Las Vegas is that you can lie at poolside in winter, lift your sunglasses and see snow on the Spring Mountains, thirty miles away. Within an hour, you can be playing in that snow, at the small Lee Canyon Ski Area. These mountains are even more popular in summer, as Las Vegans seek refuge from the heat. The centerpiece is Mount Charleston, Nevada's third highest peak at 11,918 feet.

Much of this area is enclosed in the Mount Charleston Recreation Area of Toiyabe National Forest. Don't expect solitude in these alpine heights; the area gets a million visitors a year. However, you can expect hiking trails, picnic sites and several campgrounds, as well as some alpine style hideaways.

The Mount Charleston region is easily navigable since three state highways—routes 156, 157 and 158—go up, cross over and descend from the heights. To get there, drive about fifteen miles north from Las Vegas on U.S. 95 and turn left onto Route 157. The climb into the Spring Mountains will take you through five life zones. In a quick botanical transition, you'll pass from creosote bush desert through a Joshua forest, into a piñon-juniper woodland and finally into ponderosa pines. All of this is accomplished within seventeen miles. Climatically, it's the equivalent of traveling at sea level from Mexico to Alaska.

As you enter the pine belt, look to your left for the impressive **Mount Charleston Hotel,** occupying a high ledge with impressive valley views. A few miles beyond, the road reaches into Kyle Canyon and ends at **Mount Charleston Village** a woodsy cluster of alpine homes, a few restaurants and a second resort, **Mount Charleston Lodge.** Just below the village, you can pick up hiking and camping information at the **Mount Charleston Ranger Station,** open daily in summer 8 to 5; shorter hours the rest of the year.

Several hiking trails begin at the end of the road above Mount Charleston Lodge, including a tough ten-mile route to the top of the peak. It's a non-technical but steep climb; start early and plan for most of a day. However, you needn't go all the way to enjoy impressive scenery and grand views down to the desert. The Mount Charleston ascent begins on the **Little Falls Trail** which takes you about half a mile to a small cataract. You can then shift to the **Cathedral Rock Trail,** with nearly a mile of moderately tough upgrade. It has some cliff-edge exposure, which—assuming you're not bothered by heights—provides fine vistas.

Back in your vehicle, retreat briefly from the village and take the Highway 158 crossover. This short link offers impressive views of the beige desert sprawl below. Park at a turnout and stroll out the short **Desert View Trail** for even better vistas. At an interpretive display, you'll learn that the desert basin below once was an inland sea and Mount Charleston was its highest island. During the Fifties, this was a popular vantage point for watching atomic blasts at the Nevada Test Site, sixty-five miles away.

At the junction of highways 158 and 156, turn left for a short drive into **Lee Canyon**, where Las Vegans and tourists come to ski in winter; see details below, under "Mountain activities." There are winter snow play areas just below the parking lots, suitable for tubing, sledding and cross-country skiing.

Our favorite Mount Charleston hike, the **Bristlecone Pines Trail,** begins below the ski area. It's a six-mile round trip and not very strenuous. To start, turn right onto an unmarked dirt road just below McWilliams Campground and follow it to a trailhead parking area.

The trail follows an old forestry road for the first three miles; it's not very interesting although views of rugged Mount Charleston's ramparts are nice. At a junction with the Bonanza Trail, the Bristlecone Trail leaves the forestry road and snakes upward into the rocky realm of bristlecone pines. The climate isn't as harsh here as it is on the heights of Wheeler Peak (Tour Twenty-three, page 309), so these pines aren't as twisted and stunted as classic bristlecones. You can identify them by their short, compacted needles that hang in clusters like green bottlebrushes. Higher up the trail, you'll find several specimens that are properly twisted and gnarled, like Japanese bonsai. After snaking through the bristlecone area, the trail winds down through a mixed woodland of white fir, ponderosa pines and quaking aspens—very pretty in the fall. It emerges onto a ridge above the upper Lee Canyon Ski Area parking lot. To complete your loop, walk down the parking area and follow the road about a mile back to McWilliams campground.

From here, Route 156 will take you quickly down the mountain, undoing all of those climate zones, and you'll soon be back at poolside in Las Vegas.

## MOUNTAIN ACTIVITIES

**Camping, hiking, picnicking and the like** • *Contact the Las Vegas Ranger District, Toiyabe National Forest, 550 E. Charleston Blvd., Las Vegas, NV 89104; (702) 388-6255; office open weekdays 8:30 to 5. Trail guides, maps and general information available.* ◻ *Mount Charleston campsites are at McWilliams, Kyle Canyon, Fletcher View and Hilltop,* with pit potties and no hookups; **$**. All except McWilliams are usually closed in winter.

**Horseback riding and sleigh rides** • *Mount Charleston Riding Stables, Highway 157 (in Kyle Canyon); (702) 872-7009. Open daily all year; major credit cards.* ☐ Depending on the season, this outfit offers horseback rides, Fletcher Canyon wilderness rides, hay wagon rides and winter sleigh rides.

**Skiing** • *Lee Canyon Ski Area, State Highway 156, Mount Charleston, Las Vegas, NV 89124; (702) 872-5462; snow and road conditions (702) 593-9500; Lee Canyon bus schedule (702) 646-0008. Open daily Thanksgiving to Easter, with snow machines to ensure good skiing.* ☐ This small complex has three lifts, a ski shop, rentals and lessons, plus a coffee shop and cocktail lounge. A dozen runs range from beginner to advanced. The facility also operates Ski Lee Rentals at 2395 N. Rancho Road in Las Vegas (646-0008), offering rental equipment, lift tickets and whatever else you might need for this desert-to-ski experience.

## DINING AND RECLINING

There are several small lodges and cafés in the Mount Charleston Village area and two resorts—one elegant and the other pleasingly rustic:

**Mount Charleston Hotel** • *Two Kyle Canyon Road, Las Vegas (Mount Charleston), NV 89124; (702) 872-5500. Rooms and suites with TV and phones; $$$ to $$$$$. Canyon Dining Room serves American and continental fare; breakfast through dinner; full bar service; $$$. Major credit cards.* ☐ This handsome structure suggests some of the grand national park chalets built during the 1930s, with its pitched log beam ceilings. Mountain and valley views are impressive from the dining room and the Cliffhanger cocktail lounge. Facilities include a spa, sauna and a small gaming area.

**Mount Charleston Lodge** • *HCR 38, Box 325, Las Vegas (Mount Charleston), NV 89124; (800) 955-1314 or (702) 872-5408. Nicely appointed log cabins; $$$$. Restaurant serves American and continental fare; breakfast through dinner; full bar service; $$. MC/VISA.* ☐ This Bavarian style hideaway at the end of the Kyle Canyon Road has been a Mount Charleston fixture for decades. Originally a restaurant-lounge only, it now has several cabins with woodsy interiors, spa tubs and oversized beds. At the main lodge, you can dine indoors or on a terrace with mountain and valley views, or sit and sip and Irish coffee beside a large circular fireplace.

☹ ☹ ☹

**Where do we go from here?** • Why go anywhere? You're in the entertainment capital of the world! However, if you've finished with your Las Vegas visit, you can continue north on U.S. 95 on Tour Twenty-two, or run Tour Twenty-four in reverse.

# INDEX

# REMARKABLY USEFUL GUIDEBOOKS
## from *Pine Cone Press*

Critics have praised the "jaunty prose" and "beautiful editing" of Pine Cone Press guidebooks by Don and Betty Martin. Their remarkably useful guides are comprehensive, accurate, witty and opinionated. Ask your book store to order them if they're not in stock. Or you can order copies directly from the publisher; see details on the next page.

### ADVENTURE CRUISING
This book focuses on small ship cruises, listing over a hundred cruise lines and hundreds of worldwide itineraries. — *340 pages; $15.95*

### ARIZONA DISCOVERY GUIDE
This detailed guidebook covers attractions, scenic drives, hikes and walks, dining, lodgings, RV parks and campgrounds. — *408 pages; $15.95*

### ARIZONA IN YOUR FUTURE
It's a comprehensive relocation guide for job-seekers, retirees, winter "Snowbirds" and others planning a move to Arizona. — *272 pages; $15.95*

### THE BEST OF THE WINE COUNTRY
Nearly 300 California winery tasting rooms are featured, plus data on restaurants, lodging, attractions & wine tasting tips. — *336 pages; $13.95*

### CALIFORNIA-NEVADA ROADS LESS TRAVELED
This is a "Discovery Guide to places less crowded," a comprehensive driving guide to fascinating yet uncrowded attractions, interesting museums, hideaway resorts, great little cafes and more! — *336 pages; $15.95*

### LAS VEGAS: THE BEST OF GLITTER CITY
It's a delightfully impertinent insiders' guide to the world's greatest party town, with detailed descriptions of the Ten Best casinos, restaurants, shows, attractions, bars, bargains, buffets and more! — *256 pages; $14.95*

### NEVADA DISCOVERY GUIDE
This guide covers all of Nevada, with a special focus on gaming centers of Las Vegas, Reno-Tahoe and Laughlin. A special section advises readers how to "Beat the odds," with casino gambling tips. — *416 pages; $15.95*

### NEW MEXICO DISCOVERY GUIDE
There's more to New Mexico than Carlsbad Caverns! This useful guide steers travelers from ancient and still-occupied native pueblos and Old West historic sites to the galleries and cafes of Santa Fe. — *386 pages; $16.95*

### OREGON DISCOVERY GUIDE
This comprehensive book guides vacationers from Oregon's wilderness coasts to snowy peaks to volcanic wonderlands. — *448 pages; $17.95*

### SAN DIEGO: THE BEST OF SUNSHINE CITY
This is a fun insiders' guide to California's second largest city, with detailed descriptions of the Ten Best beaches, resorts, restaurants, attractions, nightspots, walking and biking paths and more! — *288 pages; $15.95*

---

**More books and ordering information on the next page**

### THE TOLL-FREE TRAVELER

This handy pocket or purse sized companion lists hundreds of toll-free phone numbers for airlines, hotel and motel chains, rental car agencies and more. It's also packed with useful travelers' tips. *—162 pages; $8.95*

### THE ULTIMATE WINE BOOK

It's the complete wine guide, covering the subject in three major areas: wine & health, wine appreciation and wine with food. *— 192 pages; $10.95*

### UTAH DISCOVERY GUIDE

A busy guide to the Beehive State, it escorts travelers to Utah's canyon lands, modern Salt Lake City, Mormon historic sites, famous ski areas and the "Jurassic Parkway" of dinosaur country. *—360 pages; $13.95*

### WASHINGTON DISCOVERY GUIDE

This driving guide steers motorists and RVers from one corner of the Evergreen State to the other, from Seattle to the Inland Empire, focusing on attractions, lodging and restaurants along the way. *— 372 pages; $13.95*

---

# ORDERING FORM

Order from us and we'll charge only a nickel shipping! Add five cents to the list price and send a check or money order. (Add $3.20 for priority mail.) Use this form or jot your selections on a slip of paper.

**Name** _____ **Date** _____

**Address** _____

**City**_____ **State & ZIP** _____

| **TITLE** | Price incl. shipping |
|---|---|
| _____ | _____ |
| _____ | _____ |
| _____ | _____ |
| _____ | _____ |
| _____ | _____ |

**TOTAL** (Nevada residents add 7% sales tax) _____

**Send your order to: *Pine Cone Press*, Inc.**
**631 N. Stephanie St., #138**
**Henderson, NV 89014**